THE
PORTABLE MBA

The Portable MBA Series

THE PORTABLE MBA

Fourth Edition

Robert F. Bruner
Mark R. Eaker
R. Edward Freeman
Robert E. Spekman
Elizabeth Olmsted Teisberg
S. Venkataraman

John Wiley & Sons, Inc.

Copyright © 1998, 2003 by Robert F. Bruner, Mark R. Eaker, R. Edward Freeman, Robert E. Spekman, Elizabeth Olmsted Teisberg, S. Venkataraman. All rights reserved.

Published by John Wiley & Sons, Inc., Hoboken, New Jersey.
Published simultaneously in Canada.

For general information on our other products and services please contact our Customer Care Department within the U.S. at (800) 762-2974, outside the United States at (317) 572-3993 or fax (317) 572-4002.

Wiley also publishes its books in a variety of electronic formats. Some content that appears in print may not be available in electronic books. For more information about Wiley products, visit our web site at www.wiley.com.

Library of Congress Cataloging-in-Publication Data:
The portable MBA / Robert F. Bruner . . . [et al.].—4th ed.
    p.   cm.
    Includes bibliographical references and index.
    ISBN 0-471-22284-4 (acid-free)
    1. Industrial management.   I. Bruner, Robert F., 1949–
HD31 .C6134   2003
658—dc21   2002014907

Printed in the United States of America

10 9 8 7 6 5 4

To our children,
Who bring joy to our lives and balance to our work.

Jonathan Edward Bruner
Alexander Williamson Bruner

Noah Hamilton Eaker
Adam Samuel Eaker

Benjamin Wellen Freeman
Emma Wellen Freeman
Molly Wellen Freeman

Marit Rachael Spekman
Alyssa Haynes Spekman

Vivek Shankarram Srivatsa
Shaarada Rama Srivatsa

Thomas Olmsted Teisberg
Tyler Olmsted Teisberg

CONTENTS

PART III: NEW HORIZONS

PREFACE

We ended the preface of the third edition of *The Portable MBA* by wishing our readers, "Good luck, and may you live in interesting times." Little did we realize just how interesting and challenging those times would be and how much luck, skill, and hard work would be necessary to successfully navigate the dangerous shoals of business at the turn of the century. The major threat that business had identified was the millennium (or Y2K) problem with computers. That turned out to be a nonevent except for the almost $1 trillion spent preparing for it and the excessive liquidity the Federal Reserve added to the financial system in anticipation of a Y2K-induced credit crunch.

As it turned out, all that spending on technology and telecommunications generated a boom that dramatically altered the business and financial markets. Venture capitalists and entrepreneurs achieved celebrity status, as did the equity analysts who touted the stocks of the companies they created. Valuations reached what turned out to be absurd and unsustainable heights. Alan Greenspan coined a phrase, *irrational exuberance,* and Robert Shiller wrote a book with that title describing the mood and behavior of the financial markets. Essentially, the moral of the book was that financial markets had abandoned historic valuation techniques and historic valuation relationships. Beginning with Netscape, companies began going public before they demonstrated profitability. The dynamics of company creation changed from building successful enterprises to making a quick killing through initial public offerings and stock options.

The impact went far beyond the financial markets. Companies began to change their business models to make themselves more valuable in the eyes of the market. Rather than taking a job that put them on the first step of the corporate, investment banking, or consulting ladder, graduates of MBA programs chose to work for Internet companies flush with cash from venture capitalists who backed any concept with dot-com in its name. All of this ended and, as is almost always the case, ended badly. For many of the highest-flying start-ups, bankruptcy was the final outcome. For others, share prices fell by 99 percent. Few companies started in 1998 and 1999 were left standing, and employees and investors alike suffered.

The desire to profit from technology and the changes in the business environment went beyond the world of venture capitalists and entrepreneurs. Two companies that have become poster children for the darker side of the boom are Enron and Arthur Andersen. Enron transformed itself from a staid, regulated utility to an aggressive pioneer of power trading. As Enron's auditor and consultant, Arthur Andersen moved away from conservative accounting practices to facilitate its client's need to push the boundaries of financing operations and reporting results. As both firms continued to operate in uncharted territory, it became clear that management and boards of directors lost sight of their responsibilities to customers, employees, and shareholders. In addition, there is growing evidence that senior managers may have engaged in extensive illegal activities. Enron has already filed for bankruptcy, and Andersen's future seems headed in the same direction. It is reminiscent of a line from the movie *Wall Street:* "Greed is good." The problems evidenced here were even greater in WorldCom's fall from grace.

Those firms' actions have cast a shadow much wider than their own activities and relationships. Policymakers, academics, investors, and others have begun to question the credibility of public accounting firms, corporate management, and the wisdom of unregulated markets. The misdeeds of a few have done great damage to many.

Boom, bust, fraud, bankruptcy: It reads like a movie script, but it was the reality of business at the turn of this century. We believe that the major lessons to be learned from the period are consistent with the themes of this book. Business should be first foremost about values and value creation. Great companies are those that create and deliver value to customers, to shareholders, to employees, and to the communities in which they do business. Benefiting one group of stakeholders at the expense of others may enrich the favored group for a while, but ultimately it will weaken, not strengthen, the company. Management must look to the interests of all the stakeholders and balance the benefits that accrue to each.

Companies that succeed are those that meet the needs of the marketplace. Strategy begins with an understanding of what those needs are and how to meet them in a better or more distinctive manner than other companies do. Building an enduring business requires innovation to sustain that which makes the firm's services or goods distinctive. Executing a business model depends on the active engagement and commitment of employees at all levels of the firm, what we refer to as *leading from the middle.* Jim Collins, in his most recent book, *Good to Great,* describes this process as getting the right people on the bus and steering the bus in the right direction.

That all sounds fairly straightforward, but the lessons of the past few years are based on numerous examples of companies that lost sight of the basics. In a business environment that is turbulent, management is tempted to stray from its core values. One of our major premises is that turbulent times are exactly when firms most need to rely on core values and strengths. A company should hold fast to its guiding principles as it innovates or meets new challenges.

Much of our attention in this edition, as in previous ones, is focused on the basics. If you master the basics the rest becomes easier. There are no simple answers to tough business questions, but rather frameworks and techniques that help minimize serious mistakes. For example, in an environment where the meaning of earnings has become confusing, we stress the measurement of cash flows and their use in valuing companies. We stress the importance of discounted cash flow models to value an enterprise, not because the resulting values are precise, but because the process of that kind of valuation protects us from making gross mistakes or succumbing to irrational exuberance. We believe in the art of management, but the science of management keeps the artistry grounded in reality. At times during the past four years many people lost sight of the science. For example, the performance metrics used to evaluate Internet companies during the boom will no longer pass muster. Hits on a web site do not pay bills and certainly do not automatically lead to positive cash flows.

As you make your way through the fourth edition you will encounter more material on innovation and entrepreneurship. The excesses of the 1990s aside, we believe these two areas capture the essence of successful companies. Innovation brings new products to the market. It also represents new processes by which old products or services are delivered to customers. Wal-Mart, Home Depot, and CarMax are examples of companies in mature industries that have revolutionized how those industries operate. Their innovations have created value for customers and in turn for employees, shareholders, and their communities. Each one is also an example of successful entrepreneurship. Entrepreneurs are not all supported by venture capital and engaged in high-tech, high-risk businesses. Entrepreneurship is about building enterprises that create value. Sam Walton had little in common with the dot-com wanna-bes, but look at the enterprise he built.

You already live in interesting times. May this book and the ideas it contains help you find work that you are passionately interested in, and may you wake up every morning committed to making your firm or institution a great one. At the same time, may you seek and find balance in your life. Good luck!

PART I
What Is Business About?

In Chapter 1, "What Is Business?," we cover the basics, beginning with a brief introduction to the nature of business, its scope, and the premises upon which the remaining chapters are built. Chapter 2, "The Future," deals with planning for the future and assumes that change is constant. Scenario planning is offered as one tool for managing change, as it provides a framework for managers to plan for and anticipate the effects of future events. Chapters 3 ("Managing People") and 4 ("Business Ethics") emphasize the fact that business is truly about managing people and stress the importance of dealing with all constituents and stakeholders in an honest and fair manner. When all is said and done, a business is as successful as its people are; they are its greatest asset. Business ethics is viewed as an essential ingredient in understanding the role of business in society as well as the relationship between the firm and its employees. Changes in the "social contract" do not give managers a license to treat people in any way other than fairly and ethically. The recent events of misconduct, willful deceit, and personal greed in business, ranging from Tyco to Enron to WorldCom, stand as evidence to our position that ethics cannot be treated as an add-on to a discussion of business. It is essential to any aspect of managerial decision making and must take a front seat in the face of waning confidence in business and its leadership. Chapter 5 ("Economics") discusses the language of business, the lexicon by which we understand the costs, revenues, fund flows, external economic conditions, governmental policy, and other details of financial markets that are the vital signs used to manage a business. Taken together, this section serves as the foundation for this new edition of *The Portable MBA*.

The structure for this fourth edition has been improved and updated to provide a solid foundation for managing in this next century. Chapter 1 introduces the themes that frame the book. In addition, we begin a discussion of the Internet and the massive changes in business it has caused. Chapter 2 adds form to the book's structure by stressing the importance of planning for the future. Chapter 3 emphasizes the contributions of employees, who are an essential ingredient in the planning process. Also, the chapter talks about human resources systems and their role in development and personal growth. Chapter 4 affirms that ethical business behavior is a key principle for all business activity. This chapter adds a new discussion on how to better understand capitalism in ethical terms. The notion of "greed is good" does *not* align with our discussion of capitalism. Chapter 5 provides analytical rigor to the book's structure by exploring the economic principles that guide all business decisions.

1 WHAT IS BUSINESS?

In 1989 Peter Drucker[1] talked about sharp transformations, or divides, that signal fundamental changes in the basic structure of society. Piore and Sabel developed the same theme in their book, *The Second Industrial Divide*.[2] These authors trace the development of those processes and key transformations in business that have had profound effects on society. They begin their discussions with the creation of guilds, go on to describe the industrial revolution, and end with a delineation of business activity during the first half of the twentieth century. These authors pay homage to *The Wealth of Nations* by Adam Smith as they develop the various transformations that have led to the postmodern industrial era.

It would be easy, and almost obligatory, to proceed down the same path as these authors have described and provide a similar review of business history. Yet we need not go back that far in time, because a great deal has changed since the third edition of this book. In 1998 the Internet was beginning to blossom and dot-coms filled the landscape. Enron had burst on the scene and was changing the face of competition for public utilities. Many of the large, investor-owned utilities could not understand, even take seriously, an energy company that did not own its own generation capability. Yet within less time than it took these businesses to reach their apogee, many of them also hit their nadir. We will introduce dominant themes that are occurring in the rapidly changing business world of today. Our goal in this chapter is to briefly provide a context for the remainder of the book and to draw attention to the challenges that face managers during the new century.

These dominant themes are related, and they lay a foundation for understanding what is going on in today's business environment. By delineating these themes, we show that business as usual is a bankrupt concept. A number of fundamental changes have occurred that impact business and the larger society of which it is a part. These changes are reflected in the following themes. One theme is the new competition, in which a new business paradigm affects the very soul of the business enterprise. The second theme is based on a shift to a knowledge-based society and the rise of the intelligent enterprise.[3] The third theme refers to the rise of cooperation among firms that now compete as constellations of companies. These ecosystems[4] of firms are as strong as their weakest partner. They vie for resources and customers against other competing constellations of firms. These ecosystems redefine how managers should think about competition and competitive forces. We believe that these themes set a tone for many of the issues raised in this book. More important, these themes reflect basic changes in how business will be discussed and transacted in this new century. The fourth and final theme is the rise of the Internet and its profound effect on business through the rise of e-commerce and e-business. It can easily be argued that this innovation has been the most disruptive form of change because there were no templates available from which to learn. Management was flying blind; some firms figured it out, and others crashed.

Each of these major themes has caused management to rethink the relevance of their existing skills and capabilities. The question of core competency has become inextricably linked to the larger question of what business we are in. Referred to as the *tyranny of the served market*,[5] a firm's current business blinds management from thinking about untapped opportunities. The old adage of "if it ain't broke, don't fix it" might appear to ring true, but in reality, "when it ain't broke" might be the perfect time to challenge the status quo. Similarly, we have been taught to listen to our existing customers. *Innovator's Dilemma*[6] suggests that by listening too closely to a current customer who is steeped in a present market, new opportunities will very likely go unchallenged. Compounding the problem is that our current processes for resource allocation make it very difficult to fund projects for which the market is nascent and whose size is, at best, difficult to forecast. If the innovative project is kept within the confines of the traditional organization, it is bound to die early. The question becomes how to free the new business from the bureaucracy and shackles of the traditional business model. Partly, our goal here is to provide tools for thinking beyond the status quo and challenging current models and frameworks.

THE NEW COMPETITION

At the core of the new competition[7] is the belief that the entrepreneurial firm will drive continuous improvement. Based on the Schumpeterian notion of creative destruction, these firms offer a new approach to business production and processes. Benetton, for example, is a collection of collaboratively linked smaller firms that manufacture, design, and market a line of stylish clothing based on a model first developed centuries before by Italian lace producers. Benetton, the name most people recognize, is mainly a marketing and distribution company that relies on its alliances and cooperative relationships to design and manufacture under its label. There are many other examples of networks of companies that form virtual corporations with the sole intention of challenging the dominant paradigm by which business conducts itself. During the 1980s and the 1990s a number of industries have converged and been redefined. Recognizable names like Nike, FedEx, Nucor, Calyx & Corolla, and Dell have emerged as change agents in their respective industries. More recently, other cutting-edge companies have continued to redefine their competitive spaces. Telezoo, LendingTree, CNet, and many others have used the power of the Internet to bring buyers and sellers together and have reduced significantly the asymmetry of information between trading parties that had traditionally existed.

A number of Internet companies that thrived during the mid-1990s, fueled by venture capital dollars, came to a hard landing during the time before and after our celebration of the new millennium. Nonetheless, wealth and jobs were created, and the Internet transformed businesses because time and distance became irrelevant. The problem of information asymmetry was solved through transparency, and business as usual became the exception. The new technology that drove the Internet allowed businesses to reengineer their processes as well as to innovate new ways to deliver value across the globe. Internet sites allow shoppers to compare, via one click, dozens of competing offerings. For example, car buyers now have insight into the cost structure of a new car, and the price dance with the salesperson and the sales manager over discounts is out of step with today's music.

The new competition is based on four dimensions and is driven by a proactive approach to strategy whereby the competitive landscape is not taken as a given, but rather is subject to reinterpretation. Managers strive to invent the world in which they choose to compete, often by changing the rules of the game. These four dimensions are (1) the firm, (2) the production chain, (3) the sector, and (4) the government.

The Firm

The *firm* here is defined as an entrepreneurial company, which is in contrast to the firm as portrayed by Chandler and others[8] who view the firm through a bureaucratic hierarchy. Here, the firm strives to maintain continuous improvements in support of its strategic goals. Innovation comes as a result of marginal gains in production, processes, and organization. Innovation is seen as part of the learning process, which lies at the core of the firm's values and culture. While a centralized research and development facility can engage in sea-change levels of innovation, the entrepreneurial firm survives by its ability to induce workers at all levels to participate in small, incremental attempts at continuous improvement. There is no question that inventions derived from work at Bell Labs have changed the course of history. Yet AT&T's bureaucratic structure and regulatory environment inhibited the firm's ability to turn these innovations into competitive advantages in a number of markets. Competitors like MCI, with their relentless attempts to create innovative marketing programs, have caused AT&T to lose important and costly market share in a number of areas such as the residential long-distance market. Bell Labs was spun off with the creation of Lucent, which has fallen on hard times, partly because of the economic downturn and partly because it has fallen out of touch with its customer base. In fact, since C. Michael Armstrong has taken the helm as CEO, AT&T has shed its cable TV business that it spent billions to acquire; rumors circulated that AT&T and Bell-South were to merge and that AT&T was considering selling its long-distance business. From an apparent strategy of providing connectivity across all media, AT&T is beginning to refocus its efforts. Since the breakup of the Bell System, AT&T has struggled to redefine itself.

The Production Chain

The notion of the production chain is similar to the value chain concept in which each discrete phase of value-adding activity is traced from the acquisition of raw material to its sale and after-sale service. The traditional model presumes that these activities are all performed internally in the firm. Under the new competition, it is quite likely that firms will partner to perform value-adding activities and, through cooperation, allow one firm to better leverage the unique skills and competencies of another firm.

In an attempt to be more price competitive, firms across all sectors have searched for ways to extract more value from their total supply chain through rethinking channel flows, removing redundancies, linking value chain members through shared information systems like MRP2, ERP, and other enterprise software solutions, and/or outsourcing functions that can be done better by others. Dell and Cisco have become exemplars for others who wish to understand how to assemble virtual supply chains. Both companies have transparency throughout the supply network and use technology to effectively link all parts of the system.

The Sector

The previous discussion suggests the existence of a network of firms that transcends the single firm. Now the interfirm cooperative relationships become the appropriate level of analysis. Alliances and partnerships become key success factors in a large number of industries. The business sector becomes the focal point of discussion, and interfirm relationships driven by cooperative interests become the meaningful competitive metric. A more traditional model might view such cooperative actions as cartel-like behavior. Such an interpretation would suggest that cooperation is anticompetitive and serves to stifle innovation. Under the new competition, the opposite is true, because these new organizational linkages often give rise to heightened competition and are the result of new and innovative thinking. Milliken, for example, sits at the hub of a number of interfirm networks whose immediate goal is to improve the inventory levels of the apparel industry through economic order levels and other types of just-in-time systems. This cooperation from the mill to the fabricator, retailer, and consumer removes unnecessary costs from the entire channel of distribution. This is but one example of supply chains that have been reconfigured to adjust to changing demands, competitive pressures, or attempts to gain competitive advantage. Wal-Mart has taken the helm in the reconfiguration of its value chain. As the largest U.S. company (by revenue), it has through its information technology changed the face of retailing.

The Government

At a deeper level, the Milliken example represents a change in government policy regarding the interpretation of antitrust behavior. By focusing on a different level of analysis, concern now shifts to international trade: At stake is the survival of the U.S. textile industry as it attempts to compete against lower-cost Asian imports. There is talk of greater consolidation among the U.S. steel producers since this industry has been under siege for many years. Similar stories can be told about the horizontal alliances among global airlines, ocean shipping, and the various research consortia that exist in the semiconductor, specialized metals, and multimedia industries. In short, when the new competition is taken to a global context, firms do not have the luxury of a go-it-alone strategy and are likely to be severely disadvantaged if they try to do so.

One example of a successful consortium is Airbus, the firm created by European aerospace companies who joined forces to compete with Boeing and in recent years has proven itself to be a formidable competitor. Each of the firms would be hard-pressed to survive on its own, but their joint efforts and favorable governmental support have contributed to a rise in their market share, even in the United States. As we discuss elsewhere in the book, capital and knowledge know no company or national boundaries. Access to national resources is not sufficient to ensure success. The only sustainable means of production is knowledge. Drucker[9] suggests that the function of the business enterprise is to make knowledge productive.

THE INTELLIGENT ENTERPRISE

The notion of the intelligent enterprise has a profound impact on the definition of business. Our goal is not to argue that the U.S. economy has shifted away from its manufacturing base and has become a service economy. Rather, our intent is to show how this transition has reshaped managers' thinking.

Basic Restructuring of the Economy

Basic power relationships have shifted away from those who produce to those who control information. Whether we examine Toys "R" Us, Wal-Mart, or Boeing, it is clear that all are driven by a need to compete through reduced cycle time. For these retailers, the issue is how to reduce inventory levels so they can be responsive to changing customer tastes. To be sure, Wal-Mart tracks consumer tastes and distribution costs with equal concern. For Boeing, the question is how to develop, FAA-certify, and sell a new generation of aircraft in the fastest possible manner without sacrificing quality and safety. For all three companies, sharing information with their partners contributes to competitive success. These linking technologies permit real-time information access and sharing that have restructured the economy. It is important to recognize that the Boeing 777 went from concept to production without the different stages of development and prototypes experienced with the production of the 757 or the 767.

Different Organizational Strategies

The notion that organization follows strategy must be complemented by the second adage that structure follows technology. Organizations have become flatter as a result of technology, and the concept of mass production as the only way to achieve low costs has become passé. In later chapters we espouse the merits of mass customization. To be sure, this new paradigm has changed the face of business forever! Again, these different structures and strategies are knowledge-based and depend on information exchanges both among functional units within the firm and among different organizations. In short, command-and-control administrative systems are not effective with these new organizational forms. In addition, the strategies that emerge allow innovative relationships with customers and competitors. These new strategies are driven, in part, because of the expanding role of managers throughout the firm, as we discuss in Chapter 12, "Leading from the Middle."

Management Challenges

More and more, the distinction between manufacturing and service is fading, as the two become more intertwined. The issue becomes one of understanding the full value chain, recognizing unique competencies, and identifying the skills essential for competitive advantage. In many instances, core competencies center on an ability to use and manipulate knowledge. In addition, it is possible that this knowledge is not resident in the firm and must be leveraged from its partners. In the health care arena, for example, a number of key business strategies are involved in accessing information about patients for the purpose of improving total disease management. It was not long ago that drug companies fought for market share by drug category. Now the rules have changed, information is key, and the total cost of managing a disease is of paramount concern. The Merck-Medco merger was driven in large measure by the information Merck received from its new subsidiary about the use of drugs. Now Merck has plans to sell off Medco to fuel its new drug development efforts.

A primary challenge becomes knowing what investments need to be made in infrastructure and people to accomplish your goals. As stated earlier, both capital and information know no boundaries—if not managed wisely, these factors of production are fungible and move across both firm and national boundaries. A key goal for today's senior executives is to enable managers to encourage and develop their knowledge workers. Related to these managerial challenges are regulatory concerns affecting the nature and scope of competition, the protection of intellectual property, and global trade policies.

Knowledge Management

It is recognized that knowledge management is the key to competitive success. The key differential advantage that a firm holds rests within the heads of its employees. To tap that potential and to disseminate the collective body of knowledge throughout the firm provides limitless opportunities to both lower costs and increase revenue. Buckman Labs[10] spends close to 5 percent of its revenue on knowledge management practices to foster enterprisewide thinking. Admittedly, the return on investment (ROI) of such efforts is hard to measure. Nonetheless, the ability to transform a firm into a learning organization has significant payback. Capturing information and data that feed into both the explicit and tacit knowledge base of the firm accelerates the firm's ability to generate new knowledge. Just in the ability to share information across the firm, companies like Hewlett-Packard (HP) save millions of dollars per year. Cutting the cycle time on new product introductions that benefit from the collective wisdom of many people can have a profound effect on future profitability.

It should be noted that these knowledge systems are not about building sophisticated IT systems, although these systems and networks do enable the process. Since knowledge management feeds the innovative and creative processes of the firm, facilitating structures and systems must exist within the firm. Yet even this is not enough. The values of the firm and culture must support the idea of information/knowledge sharing. The ability to align values, strategy, and implementation to support the tenets of a learning organization is a nontrivial exercise.

UNDERSTANDING BUSINESS ECOSYSTEMS

Moore[11] uses the biological metaphor of looking at business relationships as an ecosystem to examine a new paradigm for understanding competition and the effects of competitive forces. Rather than focus on downsizing and cost reduction as the default response to a hostile business environment, managers should attempt to create market opportunities. These opportunities often come through innovation and a new way of viewing the marketplace—seeing the market from the perspective of those who can change the competitive terrain. Often, change comes by working more closely with customers and suppliers to jointly create the future. Even the term *industry* might be obsolete in that it presumes an easily delineated business area in which a fixed set of firms compete. One need only look to the convergence of voice, data, and video technologies to appreciate the difficulty in defining the scope of competition in this burgeoning industry. Partners compete with partners in one part of the market and cooperate in other parts; ventures are started and disbanded at a moment's notice; and the technology changes daily. There is an element of complexity reflected here that is unparalleled in recent business history. Survival is based on an ability to transform and adapt to new business conditions—similar to evolution in the biological arena. One consulting firm estimates that by 2004, close to $42 trillion in revenue will be generated by firms working collaboratively. However, close to 60 percent of these relationships will be plagued by underperformance. As these constellations form, much learning is needed to shed past behaviors and attitudes.

The business ecosystem evolves from conversations with suppliers and customers and is not limited to more traditional analyses that compare competitors head-to-head regarding their skills and competencies. The objective here is to cast a wide intellectual net and see where it is possible to change the rules of engagement and to develop a sustainable value proposition at the same time. If you go beyond the term as first defined by Moore and think about an ecosystem as an entire networked system that creates value, the nature of interacting with customers has changed profoundly. Companies are now symbiotically linked to provide value; information about customers is shared openly across all interfaces; customer relationships are not owned by a firm since the ecosystem is responsible for customer service/care; and all parts of the system must act in sync since the customer expects nothing less than seamless delivery.

THE INTERNET

As we reflect on the hype that accompanied the rise of the Internet, both its power and its flaws strike us. The advantages of the Internet and the ability to transcend both distance and time have proven to be effective for linking people and companies across the globe in real time. Virtual communities of interest meet to discuss topics of common interest, and companies have been built on a business model that defies traditional logic. This technology has made it possible to develop collaborative relationships and build effective cross-company teams to develop new products in record time with higher quality and lower costs than the vertically integrated model could. These Web-based technologies facilitate a firm's ability to reengineer all of its business processes, including product design, supply chain management, and sales and distribution relationships.[12] However, the Internet has, in a number of instances, not lived up to its potential. The failure of many dot-coms has focused inquiry on the causes. While there is no single explanation, it appears that failure can be attributed to execution of the business plan. It seems that there were ineffective communications—an inability to interact with customers, not fully understanding their needs and not fully meeting their expectations. The level of cash burn was not the reason for failure, but rather a measure of ineffective strategies put into place. In other instances, people began to believe their own press, and overcapacity doomed the telecom craze as markets and customers never materialized.

IMPLICATIONS

As we embark on a new century, it is clear that the criteria that defined business in the past century are less relevant. The present generation of managers has witnessed changes in how firms are managed and how they are defined. Terms like *economic value added* (EVA), *brand equity,* and *lifetime value of a customer* have changed the metric by which firms are evaluated. Exhibit 1.1 compares the market values of Bethlehem Steel and Nucor. You can infer from this exhibit that Wall Street's perception of the value inherent in integrated steel mills has decreased over time. In the early 1900s, vertical integration was a sign of market strength and dominance. Even today, some firms struggle to let go and rely on others to complete the value chain. Wal-Mart, a nonmanufacturing firm, has become the largest firm of the Fortune 500. Enron, a company that has fallen from grace, became one of the world's largest energy providers not because of the size or efficiency of its generation capacity but because of its knowledge of

EXHIBIT 1.1   Comparison of Bethlehem Steel and Nucor.

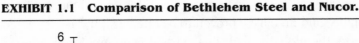
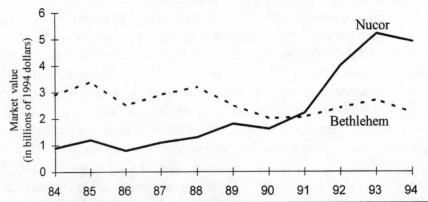

Source: Reprinted with permission of Harvard Business School Press. From CDI Value Growth Database, cited in Slywotzky, *Value Migration* (Boston: HBS Pres, 1996), p. 9. Copyright © 1996 by the Harvard Business School Publishing Corporation; all rights reserved.

energy futures. It was not the traditional electric utility concerned with balancing loads, ensuring that its distribution lines survived storms or that its customers had electricity 24/7. Instead, Enron developed its models and honed its trading acumen. Then the company began to unravel, showing its off-balance-sheet debt to be too great to sustain its growth. Enron, once a model of transformation, crashed amidst greed, questionable business practices, and ineffective governance and oversight. The list of fallen companies has multiplied as the public's confidence in business hits new lows.

The role of business has changed dramatically, and the transformations that point to fundamental changes in the basic structure of society alluded to at the beginning of this chapter are likely to occur more frequently. Andy Grove,[13] CEO of Intel, confirms this view and speaks of *inflection points* that cut to the heart of the business, threatening its existence. Inflection points reflect those moments at which changes in the nature of competition, technology, or the marketplace present profound opportunities and/or threats for a firm's future survival. The role of senior management will be to set the vision that ultimately transforms the business. However, it is often the middle manager who needs to anticipate this change, who appreciates its potential impact, and who is charged with implementing a response. Success often hinges on execution—achievement of goals is truly in the details! The chapters that follow move with facility between questions of strategy and problems of implementation. All the chapters combine to prepare the reader for the challenges that face managers in the twenty-first century. Our journey takes a number of turns and twists. Some chapters focus on the traditional functional business disciplines such as marketing and operations. Others address the details of accounting, quantitative analysis, net present value, and option pricing models.

Still other chapters soar into the stratosphere of the corporate environment by dealing with the business policy level as we address issues germane to entrepreneurship and the creation of wealth and value, to strategy and the management of alliances. These issues stand side by side with a discussion of the effects of empowerment, the stresses associated with the changing social contract, the need to incorporate business ethics as an essential part of management's thinking, and the challenges inherent in leading from the middle.

FOR FURTHER READING

Bovet, David, and Joseph Martha, *Value Nets—Breaking the Supply Chain to Unlock Profits* (New York: John Wiley & Sons, 2000).

Collins, Jim, *Good to Great* (New York: Harper Business, 2001).

Evans, Philip, and Thomas Wurster, *Blown to Bits* (Boston: Harvard Business School Press, 2000).

Hamel, Gary, *Leading the Revolution* (Boston: Harvard Business School Press, 2000).

Hammer, Michael, *The Agenda: What Every Business Must Do to Dominate* (New York: Random House, 2001).

Lewis, Michael, *Next* (New York: W.W. Norton and Company, 2000).

2 THE FUTURE

The future ain't what it used to be.
—Yogi Berra

So much of managing is about events that will occur in the future. Observers often view business success as the result of either luck or superior prediction skills. Without a doubt, luck does play a role, but few managers spend much time gazing into a crystal ball. The sense of most managers is that instead of trying to predict the future, it is more important to be prepared to respond to a variety of possible futures. In some sense, the key is to keep your options open and to know when to adjust or change course to respond to events that are different from what was anticipated. Although we might not know what the business environment and technology will be like in ten years or even five, we do know what they will be like tomorrow. In other words, the future unfolds; it does not appear out of thin air. Accordingly, we do not need to know exactly how we will manage in the year 2010, but we do need to realize that it will be different from how we manage today and that we can prepare for the uncertainty.

On the home page of the Institute for the Future, one of the many think tanks devoted exclusively to challenges and problems that corporations, societies, and nations are expected to encounter in the future, is a phrase spoken more than 2,500 years ago by Heracleitus, which never seemed more true than it does today: "Nothing endures but change." The very fact that we use the term *home page* and assume you are cognizant of its meaning demonstrates this concept of enduring change. Just a few years ago, only a minuscule percentage of the populace would have known that it refers to the World Wide Web, an entirely new medium that is revolutionizing communication.

More and more experts, many dubbed *futurists,* have been debating, presenting, and analyzing future scenarios. Conferences, publications, and organizations have sprung up with the intention of solving problems that are expected to transpire in the future. The burgeoning futurist industry would no doubt take issue with Albert Einstein's comment, "I never think about the future. It comes soon enough."[1] These organizations and experts have flourished on their perceived ability to predict the future.

In a recent survey, the American Management Association asked its members what their greatest concerns were as they looked to the twenty-first century. The most frequently expressed concern was change. (Exhibit 2.1 reports the responses.) In other words, senior managers recognize that knowledge requirements, management practices, and the markets in which they operate will be different, if not unrecognizable.

Despite the American Management Association survey results, well-known management scholars Gary Hamel and C. K. Prahalad, authors of *Competing for the Future,* believe that very little time is spent by managers in planning for the future. They ascribe to the 40-30-20 rule. According to this rule, "40 percent of senior executive time is spent looking outward, and of this time about 30 percent is spent peering three or more years into the future. And of the time spent looking forward, no more than 20 percent is spent attempting to build a collective view of the future (the other 80 percent is spent looking at the future of the

EXHIBIT 2.1 Managerial concerns of the twenty-first century.

Issue	Percent of Respondents
Change	21%
Finding and developing skilled employees	14%
Creating and managing growth	12%
Controlling costs	8%
Managing productivity	8%
Pricing pressures	7%
Dealing with regulations	6%
Keeping up with technology	4%
Other	20%

manager's particular business). Thus, on the average, senior management is devoting only *2.4 percent* of its energy to building a corporate perspective on the future."[2] Hamel and Prahalad think that senior management should in fact be allocating 20 to 50 percent of its time contemplating the future, and during this time they must be willing to develop and adapt their perspectives.

Hamel and Prahalad state that the goal for senior management is to see the future before it arrives—and to see it before anyone else does. They believe that the future can be found in the "intersection of changes in technology, lifestyles, regulation, demographics and geopolitics." CNN, with its 24-hour cable news coverage, is cited as an example of management seeing the future based on changes in lifestyle, technology, and regulation. In order to compete for the future, management needs to gain foresight based on these trends and be able to completely reconceive and revamp the structure of the corporation and the nature of the industry.

Often the future is seen by those perceived by the rest of us as contrarians, like CNN's Ted Turner. Turner has been instrumental in creating the future in much the same way as does Sony (led by visionary Akio Morita)—by telling consumers what products they want as opposed to just selling them what they ask for. The Japanese are known for planning on the horizon. Hitachi, Sony, and Fuji are developing products slated to be marketed not only 10 years hence, but 25 years in the future. Now that's future planning.

On the other hand, Ian Smith, the managing director of Monitor, a consultancy actively studying the next century, believes that companies should stop thinking in terms of strategic planning and shift to strategic thought: "Ten-year plans are not a good enough prediction of how the competitive environment works. However good your ten-year plan is, it's going to be irrelevant if the Japanese come in next week with a better product . . . CNN, Rupert Murdoch and those guys don't do ten-year plans."[3] The company of the next century is not concentrating on 10-year plans, but on 25-year plans and beyond.

The Royal Society of Arts completed a study on "tomorrow's company" and concluded, based on analyses of dozens of blue-chip companies, that there are three different types of business. "There are those which anticipate change, those which react to change, and those which ignore change. The first will flourish. The second will struggle to survive. And the third will not survive."[4] Clearly, anticipating change is one of the keys to survival, but creating change is the key to success.

As we outlined in the previous chapter, the world has become less stable and more prone to change. Organizational structures have changed, reflecting this overall instability—and have responded with a flatter, more decentralized organization capable of adapting to change more quickly than in a hierarchical, top-down control system. Tom Peters envisions a structure that he calls a "blueberry organization"—very flat, no headquarters, and all the blueberries are graded equally.[5] The blueberry organization Peters most often refers to is Veri-Fone, the booming U.S. company that makes equipment for credit-card authorization. According to Peters, this virtual company is constantly reinventing itself and could be the company of tomorrow.

It is very important to grasp that entire industries can be obliterated in a relatively short period of time. Austrian economist Joseph Schumpeter had this in mind when he described *creative destructionism,* which in simple terms postulates that it is impossible to create something completely and utterly new without significantly changing or destroying the old. Industry winners succeed at the expense of losers. An often-used example is the demise of the buggy whip due to the rise of the automobile. In the late 1800s, even the best buggy whip manufacturer was doomed by the invention of the automobile. According to Paul Saffo, a director at the Institute for the Future, "The lesson of the buggy whip is, in a period of change, everybody has to be attuned to the whispering through the trees. If you wait for the gale, it's too late. It is not what becomes obsolete, but how soon you can tell."[6]

In anticipation of change, one tool that is widely used to help firms prepare is *scenario planning,* a process whereby alternative scenarios are developed to describe the key forces or factors that will drive the industry or business environment in which the firm operates. Managers use these scenarios to prepare for or anticipate developments and to evaluate how the future is unfolding. They have a set of scripts, and by observing what actually occurs they get a measure of which script is most likely to be relevant. This process allows the managers and their firms to adjust to events.

This process was developed by Shell Oil in the 1960s. At that time there was plenty of oil, and its price was $3.00 per barrel. No one at Shell or in the industry predicted the oil crisis created by the shortage of the 1970s, but because Shell's scenarios included the possibility of a reduction in the supply of oil, the company was better prepared than other oil companies when it occurred. Although Shell did not have contingency plans, it had considered options. As the events leading up to the crisis unfolded, Shell was able to react more quickly than its competitors and, as a result, could minimize the impact on its operations.

Later in this chapter we discuss scenario planning in more detail and develop a set of scenarios. Those scenarios are based on very general macroeconomic themes as opposed to industry-specific or firm-related forces. In this way we experience with the process of scenario planning without constraining ourselves to a particular industry. Before we do this scenario planning, however, we want to look at a cautionary tale of misreading the future. Later we examine some trends that might influence the scenarios we develop.

THE MILLENNIUM PROBLEM

As the world awaited the beginning of the twenty-first century with hopes of peace, economic prosperity, and increasing freedom across much of the earth, two digits were causing a problem that knowledgeable people believed would cost the world $1 trillion. The so-called millennium problem in computers was an object lesson for all of us as we consider the future.

The problem arose in the 1960s when one of the foremost concerns of software developers was memory. To save space, programmers shortened dates by eliminating the first two digits of the year, and the 19 became implicit. Thus 1947 became 47 and 1972 became 72. This seemed innocuous enough, but as the millennium approached, those two digits became a time bomb. When the clock struck 12 on December 31, 2000, those computer programs would assign the years a prefix of 20. A 1947 date of birth would become 2047, and instead of being 53 years old, an individual born in that year would be considered nonexistent for another 47 years. Should individuals born in 1947 die in 2005, they would appear to have passed away 42 years before they were born! Pensions, interest payments on loans, insurance premiums, eligibility for federal or state benefits, and much more would be jeopardized as computers attempted to calculate starting dates, years of credit, and so forth. The solution was an end-of-century frenzy to rewrite computer codes in essentially every program at banks, insurance companies, brokerage houses, and government agencies. How could this have happened, and what does it say about how firms prepare for the future?

It happened because people overestimated the value of memory and computational time and underestimated the value and difficulty of software development. Due to technological advances, laptop computers are now more powerful than were 1960s mainframes, and saving two digits of code by ignoring the century prefix is unnecessary. At the same time, many of the programs in use today are variations of programs written 25 or 30 years ago. Embedded in these programs are the quirks and economies of software development based on old hardware. When these programs were written, it was assumed that their useful lives would not extend to the end of the century. In fact, the programs have outlived their developers, so that those attempting to correct the problem were not the original creators. This added to the difficulty. In response, consulting firms were established just to address the millennium problem and to try to develop innovative solutions. A couple of these firms went public, with market values in the hundreds of millions of dollars, reflecting the lure of capturing some of the $1 trillion to be spent on correcting the problem.

Many analysts, including Ed Yardeni, chief economist for Deutschebank, predicted that the millennium problem would push the world into recession. Yardeni maintained that forecast until the very end of 1999. However, the passage from 1999 to the new year was uneventful from an economic perspective.

There are multiple lessons from the millennium problem. First, the impact of technology and the challenges that the adoption of new technology creates are almost impossible to forecast. A single incorrect estimate about computer memory led to almost $1 trillion in expenditures. Up to the last moment, there was tremendous uncertainty about the impact of the problem; even after the fact, when the problem turned out to be a nonevent, it was still unclear whether all that money and effort had been necessary.

It is not possible to *foretell* the future. It is possible and essential to *consider* the future or, more accurately, futures. Managers need to think broadly about the forces that will influence their firms and industries. As strategies are formulated, investments made, and products designed, management must predict their appropriateness in a world that might be very different from today's. Changes in the workforce, technology, and markets will all have a significant impact on how firms are organized and on the policies and procedures they implement. Because the future cannot be predicted with certainty, management must be prepared to adapt its strategies and plans when the future unfolds differently than anticipated. Successful firms are not necessarily those that guessed right, but those that are agile enough to thrive in many different futures.

The millennium problem was unique in both the scope of its impact and the simplicity of its origin. It is a real-life example of chaos theory, where a butterfly flapping its wings in Malaysia causes an earthquake in California. Seemingly minor decisions or events can have major consequences, yet those consequences can be mitigated if we adjust as events unfold and the shape of the future becomes more apparent.

ELEMENTS OF DEVELOPING SCENARIOS

There is no precise way to develop scenarios, but a number of guidelines are helpful. Following them keeps the process from going astray. Scenario planning is neither blue-sky guesswork nor statistical forecasting. It is a process that provides structure for thinking about the future and is used by many organizations, including Global Business Network (GBN). Scenario planning entails considering different possibilities that a firm might confront in the future. Peter Schwartz of GBN has provided a list of steps to assist those who are developing scenarios.[7] Exhibit 2.2 summarizes these scenarios. GBN developed scenarios for AT&T, its first client, that predicted the possibilities of the cellular telephone boom and presented Nissan with scenarios of coping with the then-outrageous possibility of the yen falling below 100—it actually ended up falling to an all-time low of 79.

Step 1. Identifying the Focal Issue or Decision

According to Schwartz, good scenarios begin inside and then move outside toward the environment. A firm needs to identify key decisions or focal issues that will have an impact on how it does business. Schwartz gives the example of automobile companies being concerned with energy prices. Decisions such as the type of engine model design are dependent on energy prices. Should the company invest in a new engine plant to produce fuel-efficient engines or use those funds in other ways? Companies' scenarios should, therefore, contribute to their understanding of energy prices and the factors that influence them. A transportation company would also be interested in energy prices, and aspects of its scenarios might be very similar to those of the automobile firms. A financial services company, however, would be much less affected by energy prices and would benefit more from scenarios projecting different regulatory structures or alternative policies for funding pensions. Valuable information for the financial services company to know would be whether companies are offering defined benefits plans or defined contributions. The former would be serviced by institutional brokers, whereas the latter would more nearly reflect a retail

---

EXHIBIT 2.2   Steps to developing scenarios.

1. Identifying the focal issue or decision
2. Key forces in the local environment
3. Driving forces
4. Ranking by importance and uncertainty
5. Selecting scenario logic
6. Fleshing out the scenarios
7. Implications
8. Selection of leading indicators and signposts

Source: From *The Art of the Long View* by Peter Schwartz. Copyright © 1991 by Peter Schwartz. Used by permission of Doubleday, a division of Random House, Inc.

nature. The 1997 merger of Morgan Stanley and Dean Witter is consistent with Morgan believing that the retail approach will become more important in the future.

Step 2. Key Forces in the Local Environment

This step involves the major factors that will influence the success or failure of the decision. It is a list of how customers, suppliers, competitors, employees, and other stakeholders will react. Do we know that high energy prices will lead customers to want fuel-efficient cars? Does it follow that the availability of tax-deferred savings plans will lead individuals to invest in them? What alternatives might arise in the form of substitutes? Could energy prices rise so much that mass transportation would expand? These are considerations that will mean success or failure for the decision, and the scenario must include them.

Step 3. Driving Forces

These are the trends that will influence the key factors or forces in the local environment. Driving forces are big, broad, macroenvironmental trends or themes. Driving forces involve economic, political, social, and technological developments. Schwartz believes that this stage of scenario planning is the most research-intensive part of the process. It is also one of the most difficult. At this point it is necessary to stretch the analysis to consider not just the obvious or inevitable, but also the unlikely and improbable.

Demographic trends are relatively inevitable; therefore financial services companies know that the population will be graying and that individuals will live longer. This means that pensions will need to last longer. Or does it? Perhaps retirement ages, which have been declining for the past 50 years, will reverse. Health trends have not only extended life expectancy, but have kept people more active as they age. If people wait until they are 70 or 75 to retire, that will dramatically impact pension requirements, savings patterns, and investment strategies. As financial services firms think about the future, they need to consider whether the existing trend will continue or reverse. Moreover, they need to assess the various political and social forces that would lead to the reversal. For example, what legislation would be necessary to bring about the change and what social changes would have to occur to get people to extend their working lives?

Although the example is about pension funding and financial services, it is interesting to think of other businesses that would be affected by similar forces.

Retirement communities, resort and travel firms, and health maintenance organizations would all face dramatic changes if people worked until age 75.

Step 4. Ranking by Importance and Uncertainty

This is really an issue of focus. After a large number of factors have been identified, they should be ranked or sorted on the basis of importance and uncertainty. This differentiates the scenarios and makes them useful for individual firms. Using one of our examples, the aging population is inevitable and will be present in every scenario. However, changes in retirement age will have much more importance for some firms than for others. Automobile manufacturers might be affected primarily internally, whereas financial services firms will need to address changes in retirement age both internally and externally.

Step 5. Selecting Scenario Logic

With the key drivers identified and ranked, it is possible to separate out specific scenarios according to combinations of the drivers or forces. These combinations need to have a reasonable logic about them. The dimensions on which the combinations are formed mirror the key drivers. For example, the automobile company might view energy prices and the degree of trade protectionism as the drivers. We can then think of a 2×2 matrix that has high and low energy prices on one axis and high and low protectionism on the other. This gives us four scenarios: high prices and high protectionism, high prices and low protectionism, low prices and high protectionism, and low prices and low protectionism (see Exhibit 2.3).

EXHIBIT 2.3   Trade policy and energy price scenarios.

	Protectionism L	Protectionism H
Energy Prices H	High prices Low protection	High prices High protection
Energy Prices L	Low prices Low protection	Low prices High protection

The more driving forces and key trends we can identify, the more scenarios we will have. The rankings that come out of step 4 are a means of reducing the scenarios to a manageable number. In addition, we want to evaluate the combinations for consistency and eliminate any that would not make sense.

Step 6. Fleshing Out the Scenarios

The driving forces form the logic of the scenarios, but they need to be extended or embellished by understanding the trends identified in steps 2 and 3. This allows us to understand the various events that would lead a driving force to become a reality. For example, high energy prices could be the result of inflation and a general level of higher prices, or they could result from a political crisis involving oil exporting countries. We would need to understand how macroeconomic policy is made and what actions would lead to higher inflation. Also, we would have to evaluate the politics of the Middle East or the extent of transformation in Russia to be able to see how events in these countries might affect oil supplies and prices.

These causal chains need to be specific enough for us to see their impact on the driving forces. Since each scenario is the result of several different chains, we need to link them together. They compose a narrative by which the scenarios are identified and we are informed.

Step 7. Implications

With scenarios in hand it is now possible to return to the focal decision or issue and ask how that decision fares under each scenario. It is not just a matter of success or failure. The analysis of implications should reveal weaknesses in decisions or plans. These might be shored up by altering strategies. In addition, we can determine under how many scenarios a given decision is viable. If there are four scenarios and the decision is effective under each one, then the choice is easy. However, if the decision works under only one of several scenarios, then it is more problematic. Certainly in the latter case a firm might not want to make a bet-the-company type of investment.

Step 8. Selection of Leading Indicators and Signposts

We began this section by suggesting that it was not about predicting the future, but about anticipating it. The scenarios help us formulate and evaluate strategies. They prepare us in advance to react to the future that unfolds. We need to identify signposts or leading indicators to alert us to the unfolding of a particular scenario.

The earlier we become aware of events and an impending scenario, the better we can prepare and take advantage of it. When Congress starts to debate changing the retirement age to 75, then everyone is informed. We want to get information or clues earlier. It is important to be imaginative to find what some researchers have referred to as *unobtrusive measures*. With regard to changing retirement patterns, you might look at individual company policies as precursors of public policy. An analysis of temporary-work firms might be a guide. If the scenarios have been built with care and sufficient detail, then the indicators will become evident, if not obvious.

Scenarios provide a road map to the future and to the twenty-first century. Those of us who paid attention to the 1996 presidential elections heard about building the bridge to the next century. It is the managers who will have to cross that bridge. It is our road maps that will allow us to navigate through the uncharted territory. Theodore Gordon, founder of The Futures Group and a former rocket scientist, believes that there will be a new corporate focus on decision making in uncertainty. To facilitate this decision making, managers will employ new tools along with old tools. Gordon believes that successful management will become more dependent on inspired intuition than on carefully developed strategies.

MACROTRENDS

To develop a set of scenarios at this point would require us to have a specific industry and situation in mind, consistent with step 1 of the previous section. Rather than do this, we will develop three different macroenvironments that could be the foundation for many different scenarios.

These three environments begin with an extrapolation of the most important recent trends. We call this first scenario *cooperation*. The second scenario is an optimistic one in which the current trends accelerate with generally favorable outcomes, and it is marked by *coordination*. The third scenario, that of *national autarchy*, is one in which the current trends are reversed due to a negative political and social reaction to the liberalization policies of the last half of the twentieth century.

Scenario 1. Cooperation

In the current scenario, we observe a continuation of several themes dominated by moderate governments on both the right and the left in which a change of political parties in democracies and newly democratic countries would not precipitate a dramatic change in policies. In Europe that would be represented by a continuing commitment to the economic community and expansion of its membership and the transformation and enlargement of NATO to include former East Bloc countries.

European countries would eliminate many of the inefficient regulations now contributing to high unemployment and the lack of innovation among European firms. In this scenario, we would observe a slow reversal or decline in unemployment rates in Europe. Inefficient firms would be acquired by more successful companies, and there would be a consolidation within industries on a Pan-European basis.

The role of national governments on the issues of labor policy, social welfare, tax policy, and monetary policy would converge toward a European standard. A more competitive Europe would become more supportive of similar transformations elsewhere in the world.

More Latin American countries will follow the Chilean model of market liberalization, privatization, and responsible economic policy. Trade among these countries and between this region and others will become freer and more diverse. Countries that have liberalized will experience rising incomes, and their populations will enjoy improved standards of living. These countries will not only be hosts to successful foreign multinationals from the developed world, but some of their companies will emerge as transnational corporations. Their ability to compete globally will have been enhanced and tested by their need to succeed in their own markets.

In Asia, where economic development has preceded the process in Latin America, the shift will be more subtle. The quasi-capitalist systems in the Asian tiger countries will evolve into a system with less government involvement and more reliance on private markets, particularly for capital.

This scenario is one in which growth in world gross domestic products (GDPs) will be relatively evenly distributed among nations and will be in the 3 to 4 percent range. It is a world of moderate inflation, stable employment, and strong national cooperation despite the continued importance of the European Community (EC) and the regional agreements such as NAFTA, ASEAN, and MERCOSUR. The primary decision maker and engine for change will be at the national level and not multilateral.

Scenario 2. Coordination

This is in contrast to the second scenario of coordination, in which multilateral organizations come to dominate global economic policy. In this scenario, the benefits of liberalization, deregulation, and democratization are so great that governments, with the support of their populations, accelerate the pace of change. Europe moves successfully to a single currency and to a single economic policy.

This single economic policy provides for rapid economic growth, declining rates of unemployment, and near zero inflation. Europe benefits from having strong global companies that are willing and able to compete without government interference or protection. Trade barriers of all types have been eliminated. The World Trade Organization has been made superfluous because almost all countries of the world now adhere to the free trade doctrines of Adam Smith.

Although Europe has set the tone for these developments, the United States and Japan are equal participants. They have set aside any ethnocentric predispositions so that they may participate in the new global economic order.

Free trade, free movement of capital, free mobility of people, and the free exchange of ideas are the hallmarks of this economic world. In this scenario, not only have the Asian and Latin American countries participated, but in addition the nations of Africa and the Asian subcontinent have also benefited. The enthusiastic participation of so many countries has been made possible by the dramatic expansion of the world's economies, GDPs are growing in excess of 5 percent per year, inflation is close to zero, and unemployment is at record lows. This has allowed even the most impoverished and least-skilled members of society to improve their standards of living and to acquire a positive outlook.

Under either of the first two scenarios, an immediate consequence of these trends for business is that competition will grow increasingly intense, and as a result it is more important for companies to be agile and responsive to changing market conditions. Companies will need to think more globally (see Chapter 14, "International Business") and in terms of forming strategic alliances (see Chapter 13, "Strategic Alliances") in an increasingly competitive market and world. A major part of this responsiveness is for firms to develop new products and to control costs. This requires a more knowledgeable and skilled workforce (see Chapter 12, "Leading from the Middle").

The twenty-first century will not belong to a handful of countries. With the explosive emerging markets, competition will come from countries that are not yet forces in today's industries. Some countries will compete on the basis of low labor costs, but the United States and other developed countries will compete on the basis of knowledge. George Gilder, in his book *Microcosm*, talks about Silicon Valley and its development based on sand and knowledge. In the nineteenth century, the steel industry developed on the basis of availability and proximity of raw materials such as coal, iron, and water. But industries of the future can be located anywhere in the world where there exists freedom of ideas and capital.

The raw materials of the twenty-first century will be knowledge, entrepreneurship, and the freedom to act.

Scenario 3. National Autarchy

The widespread sharing in the benefits of economic growth stand in stark contrast to the uneven income distribution present in the third scenario: that of national autarchy. This scenario is characterized by a return to xenophobic policies. It is generated by the failure of the liberalization policies of the last half of the twentieth century. Growth rates slow rather than increase. Many countries experience no growth at all, or even prolonged recession. In these countries, unemployment rises significantly, especially among the young and marginally skilled. Social and political reactions to the harsh economic realities focus on foreign competition and the role of multilateral organizations. Countries retreat from their involvement in worldwide and regional economic associations. In an effort to protect jobs, governments find new ways to erect trade barriers and to restrict competition. This scenario is a return to the economic environment of the 1930s.

The political parties are extreme on both the right and left. Right-wing or extremely conservative parties continue to advocate less regulation and free markets, but only behind protective national barriers. On the left, socialist parties reemerge to reverse the market liberalization policies of the twentieth century.

Their solution to high unemployment is to embark on a new round of government regulations, subsidization, and nationalization of major industries. In their effort to address the problem of unemployment, governments resort to expansive monetary policy and large fiscal deficits. As a result, inflation rises, reaching 15 to 20 percent in many countries.

In Europe, all efforts to achieve a common currency and economic policy are abandoned. Although the EC continues to exist, it is a mere shadow of its former self. In Latin America the results are even more extreme. The discontent and malaise created by the lack of economic progress opens the door for a new generation of military dictatorships. All attempts at regional cooperation are discontinued, and national budgets are directed more toward the armed forces than to educating the workforce.

Asia continues to experience a higher than average rate of growth, but at the expense of personal liberty and consumption. Strong government and business alliances force sacrifices on the part of the working man and woman. Economic growth comes not so much from technological advances and new knowledge, but from longer hours and harder work from the population. In some countries, incipient labor strife is stopped by military action.

Globally, GDPs are barely positive and economies are beset by frequent boom and bust periods. Inflation is high, as is unemployment, and in individual countries the inequality in the distribution of income has widened, leaving a shrinking elite of haves and a growing mass of have-nots.

Although the three scenarios are sweeping and broad, they do give an indication of the thought process that is necessary to generate the macroenvironment that scenario planning requires. In full-blown, scenario-planning activities, even more extensive analysis is necessary to explore cultural, social, technological, and economic themes.

FOR FURTHER READING

Drucker, Peter F., *Managing for the Future: The 1990s and Beyond* (New York: Plume, 1993).
———, *Post-Capitalist Society* (New York: HarperCollins, 1994).
Swartz, Peter, *The Art of the Long View* (New York: Doubleday Currency, 1991).

3 MANAGING PEOPLE

James was a difficult employee for Lauren, a director of marketing at a major services company. First of all, James worked at a location 700 miles from Lauren's office at corporate headquarters. James often sent e-mail critical of her decisions to Lauren's boss and to others in his informal network. James was a longtime employee who had applied for the job opening that was given to Lauren. In addition, after the September 11 terrorist attacks, James had developed a fear of flying. Lauren found James to be moody, often depressed, cynical, and not firmly committed to the production of the world-class service that was the firm's and Lauren's main mission. Lauren knew she had to turn this relationship around, but she was uncertain how to proceed.

Lauren has to contend with at least four levels of analysis. The first is to understand James and what makes him tick. The second level is to understand the set of relationships surrounding herself and James, particularly the authority relationship. The third level is that of small-group dynamics, working together to accomplish well-defined tasks. The final level is the organization as a whole: its culture, processes, and ways of doing things that affect her and James and their relationship and the small group in which they work.

Understanding Lauren's problems on these multiple levels points us to the so-called soft side of management: people. Understanding and managing people is the most crucial task that managers face. And, given the changes that business is undergoing, its importance is increasing at a rapid pace.

As companies restructure and reorganize in the post-9/11 world, they all too often use the same old models, assumptions, and theories about what makes people tick. Without a deep and sophisticated understanding of people in organizations, all transformation paths lead to dead ends.

The purpose of this chapter is to begin the process of developing a set of concepts for understanding why people behave the way that they do in an organizational setting. Such a process is open-ended and ongoing. People are complex, and their behavior is not easily predictable. Today's managers must develop a sophisticated understanding of people, an understanding that is always open to question and revision.

We begin by reviewing business history since the industrial revolution to see how our current thinking evolved. In particular, we argue that in today's world we must broaden the concept of human beings in organizations along a number of dimensions and levels. Next we look at the individual and relationship levels and suggest that we need to understand basic human psychology to be effective managers. After that we discuss the small-group level by reviewing research on group dynamics. Then we analyze the macro-organizational level and develop some criteria for effective organizational design, paying special attention to the challenge of learning in organizations. We look briefly at human resources management (HRM) systems and their renewed importance. Finally, we suggest some practical principles for managing people.

A BRIEF TOUR THROUGH BUSINESS HISTORY

Since the start of the industrial revolution, the emergence of modern management has meant a concern with people.[1] Traditionally we have thought of the manager's job as one of planning what to do, organizing the resources to accomplish the plans, leading people in the accomplishment of the plans, and checking (or controlling) to make sure that the work was properly done. Many introductory management textbooks are organized in this manner.

To better carry out these tasks, early management theorists proposed to build a "science of management." The hallmark of the industrial revolution was the division of labor and specialization so that factories could be built on a large scale. A worker would specialize in a particular task instead of producing the entire product as in the craft approach. Henry Ford's assembly line exemplifies the benefits and difficulties of this idea.

The scientific approach to management is generally attributed to Frederick Winslow Taylor, who performed some studies at Bethlehem Steel Works in the early part of the century. Taylor believed that workers' contribution to the production process could be scientifically studied and improved. Traditionally, workers carried pig iron for eight hours straight, with production dropping off as they became tired. Taylor proved that it was possible to design the pig iron–carrying process so that workers would tire less and do more work. For example, by building rest cycles into the process, the worker would be able to sustain heavier loads over longer periods of time. Taylor studied the processes and workers and designed rules such as "Carry for 15 minutes, rest for 5."

Of course, many companies misused these time-and-motion studies to increase the productivity of workers without paying them more. The annals of business history are full of examples of exploitation of workers, and while such exploitation is often associated with scientific management and Taylorism, it is important to keep in mind that Taylor himself believed his methods would improve the lot of workers.

The underlying view of human beings that is implicit in Taylorism is that we can treat human input into the production process as just another machine.

A different way of thinking about the role of humans in business emerged from thinkers such as Mary Parker Follet, Elton Mayo, and Fritz Roethlisberger. The so-called human relations approach adopted a very different idea of people in the workplace. In a famous set of experiments known as the Hawthorne experiments, researchers began to alter a number of conditions under which workers operated. Pay concepts were changed, workers were given some choice over when they worked and when they rested, work hours were altered, and other changes were introduced. As expected, these changes had the effect of boosting productivity, but the productivity increases did not last. The researchers concluded that productivity increased simply because the workers had been singled out for special attention and because they believed that managers actually cared about them (why else would they be singled out?).

The *Hawthorne effect* says that if you pay attention to workers and show concern for their well-being, then they will respond with increased productivity. And the researchers discovered that it doesn't much matter how you show the concern.

The human relations approach says that we are complex social creatures, not machines. A complicated network of human beliefs fits into a complicated social scheme to produce behavior that has social consequences and feeds back into the social structure from whence it came.

Abraham Maslow gave us one way to understand the complexity of people by positing that we have different needs and, furthermore, that these needs could be arrayed into a hierarchy of importance. The now famous Maslow's hierarchy of needs is depicted as a pyramid, with physical needs such as food, air, water, and safety at the bottom of the pyramid and our more conceptual needs for self-esteem, respect from others, and self-actualization appearing at the top. Maslow's idea was that lower-order needs must be met before higher-order ones could be addressed. A hungry person cares about food, not self-actualization and meaningful work.

In a now famous book, *The Human Side of Enterprise,* Douglas MacGregor articulated the early views of people in the workplace as a paradox that he called *theory X and theory Y management.*[2] Theory X assumes that people basically do not want to work. To get them to work the manager has to coerce, cajole, give orders, threaten sanctions, and in general strike fear into the workers' hearts.

Theory Y assumes that people want to work, that they want to excel and do a good job, that they want to use their creative and intellectual abilities in the workplace.

MacGregor's paradox is as follows. Suppose that people are really motivated in terms of theory Y. Think of the cost of using the mistaken theory X. MacGregor believed that most companies, and certainly most ideas about management, implicitly assumed theory X, therefore incurring a tremendous opportunity cost. If companies and theories about management could be designed more in tune with theory Y, then both productivity and the happiness of workers would increase.

One theorist who did precisely this was W. Edwards Deming, the father of Total Quality Management.[3] Deming studied factories during World War II, especially those with women workers, and discovered that those people closest to the work knew the most about how that work should be organized. Furthermore, if they had some training in modern statistics they could design processes that both lowered overall costs and increased the quality of the final products. While such wisdom is standard business practice today, in the late 1940s Deming's advice was rejected everywhere he went except Japan. In Japan today, a prestigious award for quality is called the Deming Prize, and the application of Deming's principles is one reason that Japanese companies have made a substantial mark on the business world from the 1970s onward.

While Deming articulated many principles, one in particular is relevant to our present discussion. Deming believed that fear had no value in the workplace. Only by driving fear out of the workplace would workers really be free to suggest improvements that are the hallmark of Total Quality Management.

It is important to understand the evolution of management thinking from Taylor and the human relations school to Deming and MacGregor. Each theorist makes important assumptions about the nature of human beings and what we are capable of accomplishing in the workplace. So, too, does each manager in an organization make assumptions about human beings. A deeper analysis of these assumptions will help to build a more useful model of human beings in organizational settings.

THE ROLE OF INDIVIDUALS AND RELATIONSHIPS

Corporations are made up of individuals, and, as we saw in the previous section, there are many different models or ideas of individual human beings and what makes them tick.

The Problem of Motivation

The problem of understanding how to get people to act in the interest of the organization is often called the *problem of motivation*. A lot of energy is expended in most organizations trying to understand how to motivate people. Two relevant theories for understanding the problem of motivation are *needs theory* and *equity theory*.

Clay Alderfer built upon Maslow's hierarchy of needs to develop a more modern and useful version of needs theory called *ERG theory*.[4] ERG is an acronym based on the three kinds of needs in the theory. *Existence* needs are similar to Maslow's physical needs and include our desire for adequate physical comforts. *Relatedness* needs include our need to affiliate with others and to have interpersonal relationships. *Growth* needs refer to our desire to be creative, to express ourselves through our work, and to be productive. Alderfer's view is that these three sets of needs can motivate people differently from situation to situation. It is not a simple matter of moving up the hierarchy from physical needs to self-actualization. If growth-level needs are not being met, then people will revert to having relatedness needs met. Alderfer also tells us that multiple needs may operate at the same time, complicating the understanding of what individuals actually need in the workplace.

To see how ERG theory might help us to understand individuals in companies, consider a situation where an employee is having difficulty getting along with a work group. In short, that employee's relatedness needs are not being met, and he or she may well have difficulty with the interpersonal skills that are necessary to fulfill those needs.

Needs are important to understand, but *equity theory* says that there is more to motivation than just meeting needs. Equity theory postulates that how workers perceive the basic fairness of the system of rewards directly affects their own motivation. Fairness is judged either by comparisons with other people or by comparisons with some other standard (such as "more than 40 hours deserves some extra compensation"). Equity is identified as the "ratio of an individual's inputs (such as level of effort on the job) to outcomes (such as pay) as compared with a similar ratio for a relevant 'other.' "[5]

Equity theory depends on the idea that work is a social environment and that any understanding of human nature must take into account the fact that we are social creatures, always engaging in relationships with others. Reorganizing or redesigning jobs may not improve productivity if there is a perceived inequity. The managerial task is to focus on perceived fairness and to communicate how the distribution of rewards is related to efforts.

The problem of motivation is, according to equity theory, largely about reducing and eliminating perceived inequities in the workplace. Sources of inequities are diverse: from job assignments and compensation to processes like performance appraisal and promotion. Equity theory tells managers to pay attention to the underlying dynamic processes and the behavior that results from these processes in addition to the needs that employees have.

The Authority Relationship

Equity theory focuses on the relational aspects of organizations, and no relationship is more important than the authority relationship. Authority and its related concept, *power,* come in many different flavors. Some authority or power can be coercive, such as the authority that issues from the person or group with weapons trained on others. Other authority is legitimate in the sense that it is derived from consensual social processes about which there is little question. Elected officials are the paradigm case of legitimate authority, though there are many others.

Corporations work in large part because there is respect for the authority relationship. For the most part, when the boss says to do X, the subordinate actually does X. Authority is obeyed or at least accepted. In a world of stability, the dominant idea is that managers know better than workers, senior managers know better than middle managers, CEOs know better than senior managers, and a trail of legitimate authority is passed down the hierarchy. If everyone obeys authority then the organization will run smoothly. However, there is another side to this reliance on obedience to authority.

In a famous set of experiments carried out at Yale University, Professor Stanley Milgram decided to find out why people obeyed authority.[6] He devised a set of experiments designed to put subjects into a situation that had great consequences, but in which they would have to directly disobey instructions in order to prevent the consequences. The subject was introduced to another alleged subject who was in reality an actor. Both were told that the experiments were about the effect of punishment on learning. One would be the teacher and the other learner, and when the learner made mistakes in repeating work pairs, the teacher was to administer an electric shock. The subject was always the teacher and the actor/accomplice was always the learner. As the experiment proceeded, the teacher was required to deliver increasingly severe shocks. The idea was to see when the teacher would disobey and refuse to administer the shocks. The accomplice was in another room, playing a tape of standardized responses that included blood-curdling screams at certain shock levels. Steps were taken to ensure that the subject believed that the accomplice was actually in pain.

Milgram and other psychologists had predicted that few subjects would continue the experiment all the way to the end and deliver 450 volts to the victim. Yet over 50 percent of the subjects did so. Were these subjects evil? Were they sadistic? Milgram argued that the structure of the authority relationship was the issue. The experimenter was in the room with the subject and gently prodded the subject to continue, even when he or she resisted. Hence, given that the subject believed the experimenter to be a legitimate authority, there was a predisposition, built into the situation, to obey that authority.

Milgram opined that such a situational predisposition to obey is learned when we are small children obeying our parents. Such blind obedience leads to accepting authority even when it is illegitimate—such as in the case of the Nazi death camps. When questioned at his trial, Eichman responded that he was only doing his job, only doing what he was told to do.

From the Milgram studies and others like it, we can conclude that the forces surrounding authority relationships are strong indeed. Most people in most organizations do what they do most of the time because they are told to do so by those perceived to be legitimate authorities. The good news is that the authority relationship leads to the smooth working of organizations. The bad news is that in an environment where we need to try new behaviors and new ideas, where we need *innovation* and *disobedience*, we are unlikely to get either unless managers specifically encourage them.

The Gender Relationship

More than ever before, men and women are working together in today's corporations. The rise of women in managerial ranks in Western countries is rapidly being followed around the world. Yet many have argued that there is a *glass ceiling* that seems to prevent women from reaching the very top managerial levels. As of 2001, there were only six women CEOs at Fortune 500 companies.

The rise of women in business has led many people to analyze the role of gender in the structure of work and to suggest that we need to pay more attention to the way that gender influences behavior. Gender issues in the workplace include expressions of sexuality, family benefits such as child care, maternity and paternity leave, dual-career families, and sexual harassment.

Deborah Tannen has suggested that gender influences the way that we communicate with each other.[7] For instance, women often view what is said in terms of *intimacy*, because they see "a world of connection where individuals negotiate complex networks of friendship, minimize differences, try to reach consensus, and avoid the appearance of superiority, which would highlight differences.[8] Men, on the other hand, sometimes interpret conversations in terms of *independence*, because in a world concerned with status, "a primary means of establishing status is to tell others what to do, and taking orders is a marker of low status."[9] The difficulties that can arise from this difference alone are remarkable. Consider how a group of men and women working together might misunderstand each other. Requests for meetings and conversations may well be misinterpreted along the intimacy-independence dimension. Tannen goes to great lengths to say that she is not generalizing about all men and all women, but that communication is in fact gender-related and we need to be aware of it if we are to truly understand what we are saying to one another.

Judith Rossener has suggested that women lead differently from men.[10] Women are more likely to rely on charisma and personal power than on positional power conferred by title or status. Women are more likely to try to transform the interests of others into common goals than to appeal to their self-interest. Women are more participatory and go to greater lengths to include others. Rossener's conclusion is not that women's style is better than men's, but that we need to expand our definition of effective leadership to allow more people to use their strengths.

The New Psychological Contract

The changes in business—the need for a deeper analysis of human behavior as socially constructed around issues such as authority and gender—and the increased intensity and rate of change has led to a new understanding of the fundamental employment relationship. Traditionally, we could think of the employment relationship as a kind of implicit contract—a psychological contract, according to Chris Argyris—whereby the expectations of the company and the expectations of the individual were in harmony.[11] If these expectations got out of balance, then the contract would be perceived to be broken and would need renegotiation.

Traditionally the contract went as follows: Work hard, perform well, and the company will take care of you. Employee loyalty to the company will be rewarded with continued employment—virtually for a lifetime. With the advent of global competitiveness, restructuring, and reengineering, this contract has changed.[12] In a penetrating analysis, Charles Heckscher has suggested that the traditional concept of loyalty has outlived its usefulness for most employees and that it needs to be redefined.[13] Heckscher proposes that loyalty be redefined around working toward a common purpose, with both company and employee taking some responsibility for contributing to that purpose. Others have proposed a new psychological contract that focuses on employability rather than employment. Such a concept argues that the company's role is to ensure that the employee is employable (can find another job) if the work done for the company is no longer necessary. This idea has far-reaching implications, from the portability of benefits to the protection of trade secrets.

GROUPS AND TEAMS

One change that is sweeping the corporate landscape is the emergence of teams as the basic unit that produces work. Management theory has long paid attention to groups and the group process, but the basic unit of analysis has usually been thought of as the individual. That is changing rapidly as business moves to respond to the new competitive realities. However, before we examine this new emphasis on teams we need to review the basic structure of groups and group processes.

Many years ago a management thinker named B. W. Tuckman identified five separate phases of group development: *forming, storming, norming, performing,* and *adjourning.*[14] This idea has become entrenched in management literature and is an important starting point for understanding the group process.

Initially, when a group forms, members test out what kinds of behavior are acceptable and set up working rules (both formal and informal rules) as the members get to know each other's styles and expectations. As the group becomes more comfortable with one another, conflict inevitably sets in—especially with respect to individuals becoming subservient to the group. As individuals assert their personalities and styles, they often conflict with each other and the initial working rules of the group. In short, there is a battle for control of the group. This stormy period lasts until group members can agree on some norms to solve the conflicts. If the group is to function well, then all members of the group, not just the stormy personalities, must agree to the norms.

Hopefully a group can move through these first three stages quickly, and by paying deft attention to process concerns as well as task concerns a well-facilitated group can get on with the performing aspect of group work. The group can begin to work positively together as a whole, dividing tasks and sharing ideas to do the real work of the group. When its work is over, the group moves on to adjournment, but this is not as simple as it appears. Often, in adjournment, group members engage in a battle for who gets credit individually for what the group has done, especially if the group is operating in a corporate culture that rewards individual contributions and not group contributions. During this phase group members search for closure.

While every group does not go through all stages of this process, it can be a useful heuristic for understanding why many groups fail to perform. They have not gone through the initial processes necessary to create a cohesive group; thus there is little commitment to the tasks at hand.

Although the difference between groups and teams may well be semantic, the idea of "team" focuses on a common effort: namely, winning. Some companies have gone so far as to create what *Fortune* called "superteams" or "high-performance teams."[15] These teams are often cross-functional and are drawn together to solve a particular thorny problem or to reengineer a business process. For the most part, superteams are self-managing and are related to a very old idea of "autonomous work groups" that grew out of theorist Eric Trist's work with coal miners in Britain in the 1950s.[16] The idea is that if the team accepts the responsibility of leading itself, it is more likely to commit to the person or persons who are chosen or who emerge as leaders. Leadership can be shared, and the team can be more participatory.

THE ORGANIZATIONAL LEVEL

Traditionally we have thought of management as, in part, choosing the right organizational design or the right organizational structure to fit the strategic direction of a business. Given the fast-paced business environment of today, managers are better off thinking about two related issues: *managing change* and *organizational learning*. By focusing on change and learning, managers can create structures and processes, which may well be quite temporary, to match fast-shifting business conditions.

Managing Change

Professor John Kotter of Harvard Business School has suggested that we can understand how to lead and manage change through the eight-stage process depicted in Exhibit 3.1.

Of particular importance is the first stage of creating a sense of urgency.

EXHIBIT 3.1   The eight-stage process of creating major change.

---

1. Establishing a sense of urgency

- Examining the market and competitive realities
- Identifying and discussing crises, potential crises, or major opportunities

↓

2. Creating the guiding coalition

- Putting together a group with enough power to lead the change
- Getting the group to work together as a team

↓

3. Developing a vision and strategy

- Creating a vision to help direct the change effort
- Developing strategies for achieving that vision

↓

4. Communicating the change vision

- Using every vehicle possible to constantly communicate the new vision and strategies
- Having the guiding coalition role-model the behavior expected of employees

↓

5. Empowering broad-based action

- Getting rid of obstacles
- Changing systems or structures that undermine the change vision
- Encouraging risk taking and nontraditional ideas, activities, and actions

↓

6. Generating short-term wins

- Planning for visible improvements in performance, or *wins*
- Creating those wins
- Visibly recognizing and rewarding people who made the wins possible

↓

7. Consolidating gains and producing more change

- Using increased credibility to change all systems, structures, and policies that don't fit together and don't fit the transformation vision
- Hiring, promoting, and developing people who can implement the change vision
- Reinvigorating the process with new projects, themes, and change agents

↓

8. Anchoring new approaches in the culture

- Creating better performance through customer- and productivity-oriented behavior, more and better leadership, and more effective management
- Articulating the connections between new behaviors and organizational success
- Developing means to ensure leadership development and succession

---

Source: Reprinted with permission of Harvard Business Review. Copyright © 1997 by the Harvard Business School Publishing Corporation; all rights reserved. Adapted from John P Kotter, "Why Transformation Efforts Fail," *Harvard Business Review;* March–April 1995, p. 61.

General Motors has long been under attack by Toyota and other global competitors, but during the decade of the 1980s GM was posting great earnings. It was difficult to create a sense of urgency for change when profits were high. Only after a record restructuring loss of many billions of dollars did GM finally begin to feel the urgency to change.

Grand and glorious change programs have often foundered on the shoals of the everyday processes in organizations. Change requires paying attention to little details and learning to walk before running. Kotter emphasizes the importance of small, early wins that build confidence and momentum for change.

HUMAN RESOURCES MANAGEMENT (HRM) SYSTEMS

The classroom looks like any college classroom. The "professor" is talking and showing overhead slides. The "students" are taking notes and raising hands to ask questions. The subject matter "Total Quality Management" indicates a graduate course in business. The university: Motorola University. Motorola requires at least two weeks per year of training and education for all of its employees, from the chief executive officer down through the entire organization. Motorola has decided that its competitive advantage in its businesses can be maintained only through a massive investment in people.

Human resource management (HRM) is the set of philosophies, processes, and procedures that a company uses to manage (1) the entry and exit processes in the firm, (2) the growth and development of employees, (3) the reward and recognition systems, and (4) the total organizational climate for how people are treated.

A company's HRM system summarizes its approach to managing people, so it is critical that the systems built for routine issues like payroll, benefits, and performance appraisal reflect the "people philosophy" of the company.

Entry and Exit Processes

Under the set of business assumptions that produced relatively stable hierarchies as the main form of organizational design, there was an implicit (oftentimes made explicit) *psychological contract* that assured employees they would be taken care of in return for their loyalty. The paradigm case was depicted in the novel *The Man in the Gray Flannel Suit.* Employees who excelled at their jobs could expect upward promotion. Those who were average could expect continued employment and gradual increases in pay. Nonmanagement employees could expect few layoffs and a job for life through adequate performance.

In today's world that contract has changed. Almost all large firms have undergone difficult processes of restructuring. Massive layoffs at General Motors, IBM, AT&T, Xerox, Eastman Kodak, to name but a few, have affected managers and nonmanagement employees. In an attempt to make organizations more customer-market-focused, many organizations have taken out whole layers of middle managers and drastically curtailed the scope of opportunities for others.

AT&T won major praise from its employees for taking out an advertisement in newspapers offering its "good people" to other companies. Companies who set up outplacement counseling give help in finding jobs to those who are displaced, and in general create a soft landing for downsized employees have a better chance to manage the normal feelings of anger and guilt felt by both employees who stay and those who leave.

A second issue in managing the process of entry and exit of employees is related to the restructuring of firms, and this is *outsourcing:* By taking a hard look at the business processes, a corporation may contract out those processes that can be done more efficiently and effectively by a third party, replacing employees by contracts with vendors. For example, many corporations have long outsourced their cafeterias, reasoning that ARA, Marriott, and Guest Services are in the food service business and will provide the service more cost-effectively. The recent wave of outsourcing has included the management of computer and telecommunications systems, legal work, public relations, even the design and manufacture of non-core-technology components.

One standard method for outsourcing is to take workers who were employees and turn them into suppliers. The company reduces its head count and reduces its liability for medical and pension benefits, and the employee becomes a contractor rather than an employee.

One of the most talked-about issues of the 1990s was that of *diversity.* Diversity refers in part to how employees differ with regard to age, gender, race, sexual orientation, physical abilities, and ethnicity. While there are many definitions and dimensions, the basic idea is that in the United States, the workplace has traditionally been seen as the space of the white male. For the past 20-plus years, there has been a growing presence of nonwhite males in the workforce, especially in the managerial workforce.

Traditionally, work has been organized along the lines that suited the one-wage-earner (typically male) family. With the rise of different lifestyles, many companies have been forced to rethink the very definitions of work. For example, with two-career managerial couples increasingly the norm, companies have had to rethink their policies about transferring fast-track employees from assignment to assignment. Many companies have opened or begun to sponsor day-care and elder-care centers. There has been a dramatic increase in the use of technology to encourage telecommuting. All of these issues represent an incredible set of changes for managers, but diversity cuts across each of them.

A number of people have asked why the top tiers of most large corporations are heavily weighted with white males. Are the selection processes for senior managers biased? Are the entry processes for employees biased? Increasingly, managers have tried to ensure that their hiring and firing processes are free from bias. Now some have argued that this attempt to "manage diversity" is the correct thing to do from an ethical perspective and that in today's world companies must get the best people in the right positions.

The Growth and Development Process

If there are increasingly fewer middle-management positions, then the normal way of thinking about careers as a continual stream of promotions is no longer valid. There are more people and fewer managerial positions. Some companies have experimented with lateral career moves whereby an employee is "promoted" based on technical expertise but not necessarily given more managerial authority.

In addition, many organizations today are adopting team-based organization structures in which a team leader emerges or else the team is self-led, meaning there is no formal leader. Training people in effective teamwork and helping them to be good team members is an important challenge. In our individualist culture, creating an atmosphere of teamwork and effective teams is not easy.

Performance appraisal has also changed in the new business environment. A number of companies are moving from the traditional boss-subordinate models of performance appraisal to *360 feedback,* which is a process whereby employees receive input from a sample of the people with whom they work and whom they affect. Customer satisfaction data, employees in other departments, peers, teammates, and bosses all provide input into a comprehensive assessment of performance. With the new emphasis on competitiveness, many companies have tried to turn their performance appraisal processes into more effective tools for performance improvement.

To meet the challenges that we have discussed, some companies like Motorola have taken their traditional concern with training and development to a new level. Indeed, as we said at the start of this chapter. Motorola has its own "university." Motorola claims that for every dollar it spends on education, it receives a $30 return. Motorola has used education as a strategic tool to manage both the entry and exit processes as well as the growth and development processes. For example, rather than laying off an employee, Motorola offers retraining. It figures that the resulting loyalty far outweighs the cost of training, and the company retains an employee who is oriented, socialized, and knows the Motorola culture. Such a human resources policy directly supports Motorola's strategy of dominating its core markets through expertise and technology. When those markets change, the company uses the ability of its employees to learn new skills, thus entering new markets by redirecting its substantial capabilities.

While Motorola is an example of a large company that uses training and education, the much smaller Johnsonville Sausage Company in Wisconsin has a similar approach. At Johnsonville, the purpose of the company, as articulated by owner Ralph Stayer, is to serve as a means for personal growth for its members. At Johnsonville, employees are rewarded for learning, and they receive raises when they learn to do budgeting or production planning or when they serve as team leaders for a while. They learn basic economics and study competitive conditions in the industry. The atmosphere is one of constant improvement, both in the sausages that they make and in the people who make them.

By distinguishing between these kinds of rewards, managers can use the compensation system to encourage corporate or subunit goals like teamwork and customer satisfaction. All employees—not just a few top executives with large stock option packages—become engaged in the success of the organization.

In addition to meeting the demands of a changing workforce, more companies are moving to *flexible benefits,* or *cafeteria benefits.* Under these arrangements, employees can design their own package of benefits to meet individual needs. For example, one employee may well need a benefits package with child care and medical care paid for in pretax dollars, whereas another employee may prefer more catastrophic coverage or life insurance. The basic idea behind strategic pay is to design a compensation system that best meets both employees' and companies' needs for success.

At GE, senior management has used stock options as a form of variable, or incentive, pay. Managers throughout the GE hierarchy are offered options if their performance and their unit's performance warrant them.

Wal-Mart takes a different approach. After a brief initial period, all employees are encouraged to become actual owners of the company. Everyone, from managers to cashiers, is offered opportunities to buy stock. In addition, profit sharing, incentive compensation, and other techniques all link Wal-Mart "associates," as they're known, to the success of the firm. Wal-Mart executives are always available to associates. "Mr. Sam" Walton began the practice of visiting stores and listening to employees, and his successors have continued this practice. The compensation system is aligned with the other Wal-Mart values to foster the sense of ownership that makes Wal-Mart a special company with high-performance people.

Managing the Overall Organization Climate

In summary, a company's "people philosophy" in the turbulent business environment of today must foster a climate that challenges employees to better levels of performance. Of course, the organizational climate is not a variable to be managed or even designed. The key notion here is that all of the organization's processes and procedures, from its compliance with the law to its new strategic initiatives, must be aligned. Together, these processes must foster the high-performance atmosphere.

Professors James Heskett and Leonard Schlesinger have studied so-called high-performance or high-capability organizations for a number of years.[17] Leading such high-performance organizations as Wal-Mart, Taco Bell, Southwest Airlines, and ServiceMaster means that the senior managers, including the CEO, are intimately involved in the human resources management process. High-performance cultures are usually based on values and vision that are shared throughout all levels of the organization. Since the values are important in their own right, employees will go to great lengths to realize those values, especially when they are given the latitude and permission to do what it takes to get the job done. High-performance leaders are involved in the entry and exit decisions because they believe that these are some of the most crucial decisions that the organization makes. In these strong-culture companies, people almost "self-select" into and out of the organization. The growth and development of people is based in part on instilling a sense of pride in employees and pride in what they do—without the arrogance that usually accompanies it. To instill this pride, executives must constantly articulate, communicate, and embody the corporate values while setting the performance bar at a very high level.

In all of these high-performance workplaces we find that employees are not there merely to put in time and do a job. Rather, work is engaging to them; their teams and tasks matter because the organization plays an important role in their lives. Work has the connotation of joy and imagination and fun rather than drudgery and something to be sharply distinguished from play. The business challenges of the twenty-first century will involve more attention to the processes of innovation, creativity, and fun, while continuing to find creative ways to do the administrative tasks that are a vital part of a firm's success.

SOME PRACTICAL PRINCIPLES

While managing people is too complex and multilevel a process to reduce to a formula or a model, we have found the following eight principles to be a useful heuristic against which we can begin to build a more complex and individualized conception of how to manage people.

1. *Communication with employees is central to the effective manager's job.* This ought to go without saying, but some managers insist on communicating only by formal means and insist on withholding as much information as possible. We can understand needs and perceived equity only by immersing ourselves in the social life of the organization. As Tannen argued, communication is complicated and gender-based, and we need to work on hearing other voices.

2. *Effective managers also have needs and also perceive equities and inequities.* What works to motivate employees also works to motivate managers. Many successful organizations simply start with some theory Y assumptions like "People really can be great and want to win." They don't differentiate between levels of employees in terms of their motivation. They drive a sense of ownership and egalitarianism about the company throughout the organization with the result that the company can become a means to meeting the needs of all employees in a fair and evenhanded manner. At Johnsonville Sausage, CEO Ralph Stayer explicitly adopts this philosophy of the organization as a mere means.

3. *Effective managers foster an environment that celebrates need fulfillment and fairness, and one that openly addresses inequities.* Negotiations with labor unions are often an elaborate ritual. Managers need to address the perception of fairness created by issues such as opening new plants in other countries, trade agreements, and contracting out part of the production process to nonunion employees.

4. *Effective managers choose to obey authority rather than blindly follow it, and they encourage the same attitude in their subordinates, even to the point of encouraging disobedience.* At a meeting in the early 1980s to celebrate unparalleled success in Motorola's history, one sales manager stood up and amid the celebration began to complain about quality. In many companies such an act of speaking out or acting up or disloyalty would have been career suicide. At Motorola, it was the beginning of their famed quality approach called *Six Sigma quality*. Motorola encourages such acts of free speech and has benefited greatly from it.

5. *Effective managers are willing to engage in conversations about diversity. They foster an environment where everyone can fulfill their potential and seek to address issues such as gender, race, sexual orientation, ethnicity, age, and language.* At Inland Steel, a number of African-American employees were frustrated and thinking of leaving the firm. They worked

together and found someone to be a champion of starting a conversation about diversity. As a result, the company received a national award for its attention to creating a supportive and diverse workplace.

6. *Effective managers understand how groups and teams work, and they focus on creating a culture of performance through teamwork.* At Saturn, teams are the order of the day. By paying attention to cross-functional teams and giving those teams the power to lead themselves, Saturn has been able to break out of the functional silos that prevented General Motors from competing with Toyota in the small-car market.

7. *Effective managers are change leaders.* Today managers are not expected to administer—to follow bureaucratic and systematic processes that mean business as usual. Managers are expected to lead change—to propose ways to make the organization more competitive and more effective and then to marshal the resources to bring about that change.

8. *Effective managers build intellectual capital in themselves and their subordinates by focusing on learning.* Motorola, GE, and countless others have focused on learning and on learning how to learn in order to prepare their employees to act in a new business environment. Motorola found that it had to teach some employees how to read. At GE, education sessions with former CEO Jack Welch took on legendary significance, as Welch debated a number of propositions about the future of GE with employees at all levels.

Managing people is complex, and you will develop your own methods and skills. There is a story about a lion keeper in the Dublin zoo named Mr. Flood who was quite adept at breeding lions in captivity (which is difficult).[18] When asked his secret, Flood replied, "Understanding lions." When asked how he did that, he responded, "Every lion is different." So it is with managing people. In striving to develop a deep understanding of human nature and what makes people tick, we need not lose sight of the individual uniqueness that sets us apart.

FOR FURTHER READING

Belasco, James A., and Ralph C. Stayer, *Flight of the Buffalo* (New York: Warner Books, 1993) is a comprehensive guide to empowerment and treating employees with dignity and respect. This very readable book is full of lessons from life by Belasco, a world-famous consultant, and Stayer, CEO of Johnsonville Sausage, an employee-run company.

Drucker, Peter, *Management: Tasks, Responsibilities, and Practices* (New York: Harper, 1973) is a classic that keeps getting better with time. Drucker knows more about people and managing people than most of us will know in a lifetime.

Zaleznik, Abraham, *Executive's Guide to Motivating People* (Chicago: Bonus Books, 1990) is an attempt to use psychoanalytic theory to understand and analyze people in organizations. It takes as axiomatic the view that human beings are complex creatures and that simple explanations for their behavior in organizations will not work.

4 BUSINESS ETHICS

It is not unusual to open any day's edition of a major newspaper or to turn on the television news anywhere in the world and be greeted by something like one or more of the following:

- Enron and Arthur Andersen are embroiled in a major financial scandal.
- Merrill Lynch settles a conflict-of-interest case with regard to its stock analysts and its investment bankers.
- Ford and Firestone argue over who is responsible for accidents involving their products' potential failure.
- Payoffs to officials in countries around the world are alleged.
- Critics claim that executives need to deal with child labor, unsafe working conditions, and environmental degradation.

Each of these issues and countless others that bombard us on a daily basis raise questions in our minds about the relationship between business and ethics. The purpose of this chapter is to explore this connection along a number of dimensions. Here we examine some criteria for determining what makes a business issue an ethical one as well. Along the way we look at some common myths about the role of ethics in business. We examine the basic moral reasoning tools as they are applied to business, and we pay particular attention to the role of values and principles. Then we examine a way of understanding business so that ethical issues are endogenous to the way we think about our companies. We argue that this method, which we call *stakeholder capitalism,* is in keeping with Adam Smith's ideas about business several hundred years ago. Finally, we explore some difficult ethical challenges for business in today's business environment.

WHAT CONSTITUTES AN ETHICAL ISSUE?

Andrea is negotiating a difficult contract with a supplier. The supplier is responsible for a key manufacturing component for Andrea's company and has driven a hard bargain regarding terms, conditions, and price. After a tough day of negotiating in a hotel conference room, the supplier team leaves with the deal not yet consummated. After they have left, Andrea notices that a folder has fallen under the table. She picks up the folder, glances at the inside, and immediately recognizes that it contains what appears to be very important information about the supplier's cost. What should she do? Should she read the folder?[1]

Does Andrea have an ethical issue? Granted there is no large, front-page headline issue at stake, but what Andrea does could potentially have large effects on others. One could argue that Andrea needs to see this issue in ethical terms.

First, one could argue the folder is not Andrea's property, and therefore she should not read the folder or use it in any way. Suppose that Andrea had found a wallet under the table instead of the folder. Common morality requires that she should return the wallet without using the contents to her own advantage. The folder case is an ethical issue because it involves making decisions about the legitimate uses of private property. Does Andrea have the right to use other people's property without their permission?

Another argument is about fairness. According to this position, Andrea would be taking unfair advantage of her suppliers by reading this information. She would know something that they don't intend for her to know, and she would not have earned the right to that knowledge. Andrea would not be negotiating from a level playing field, and that would be unfair. An alternative to this position is to see business as a game or institution with its own set of rules: "All's fair in love and war and business" suggests that in a negotiation you can use whatever tactic is available—from bluffing to getting information nefariously. Note that even in this interpretation, Andrea still has an ethical issue about fairness. The difference in the two interpretations is not the lack of an ethical issue in one, but a disagreement about defining *fairness.*

A third argument involves the consequences of Andrea's action. Will the relationship with the supplier be sustainable? Will others think that Andrea is not a woman of good character? Will using the information lead to a better or worse outcome for Andrea's company? The supplier company? Andrea has an ethical problem because of the consequences that are possible.

Each of these arguments goes a long way in helping us to identify ethical issues. Ethical issues are usually concerned with (1) rights and duties, (2) principles such as fairness, or (3) harms and benefits. Ethics concerns how we ought to live our lives. It is about how we reason together regarding the effects of our actions on others. We always have an alternative to entering such a conversation—that alternative is violence and coercion. However, we can think of ethics as the substitution of reason for violence as we try to figure out how we can survive and flourish together in spite of our differences.

There are usually two levels of ethical issues. The first is the personal level, and our example of the folder is a good illustration. Andrea must figure out what she believes is the right thing to do, what fits with the way that she is trying to live her life and with her own principles and values. However, ethics doesn't end there. Because others are affected by Andrea's decision, their own interests, indeed the way they are trying to live their lives, are also important. Ethical issues almost always appear at the personal and interpersonal (or social) levels simultaneously.

It is a mistake to think that ethics are only personal. The standard test, "Well, I have to live with myself if I do this," is a good start, but what that test misses is that others have to live with you, too. Being true to your own beliefs—being authentic—is a good starting point for a conversation with others, but it is only a starting point.

The view that each person is the sole arbiter for right and wrong is called *ethical relativism*, and it prevents us from reasoning together. If the only criterion for the correctness of a particular action is your personal belief, then we don't need to reason about ethics. We just need to check whether a person truly acted on his or her beliefs. Furthermore, if a person or a group of people is trying to solve a difficult ethical issue, it is just a waste of time, because the real measure of correctness, according to ethical relativism, would be personal beliefs.[2]

Needless to say, ethical relativism is a thoroughly discredited view, but it does contain a grain of truth. For the most part, individuals make ethical decisions. Individuals are the locus of decision making. In an individualist culture it would be natural to give an individual a great deal of autonomy. Such individualism, the view that individuals know their interests best and should be left free to pursue them, is different from relativism. You can easily think of ethical rules agreed to by individuals in order to smooth the way for them to pursue their interests.

Almost all major issues that managers face have an ethical component. However, to read the business press or to examine business books, you would think that ethical issues are the exception rather than the rule.

Tell someone that you are worried about business ethics and you'll likely as not get a response like "I didn't know that business had any" or "Isn't that an oxymoron like jumbo shrimp?" Our common idea of business has evolved into the belief that business and ethics are somehow separate—that managers can think about business without thinking about ethics and vice versa.[3] Such a separation leads to a natural tendency for us to think of business as morally suspect and to joke about business ethics. However, if the arguments in this book are correct— that business is the dominant institution for creating value in today's world— then business must be part and parcel of the very best way that humans can live. We must intertwine business and ethics in a very fundamental way.

It is impossible to determine just how business became separated from ethics in history. If we go back to Adam Smith, we find no such separation. In addition to his famous book on business and capitalism, *The Wealth of Nations,* Adam Smith also wrote *The Theory of Moral Sentiments,* a book about our ethical obligations to one another. It is clear that Smith believed that business and commerce worked well only if people took seriously their obligations and, in particular, their sense of justice.[4]

The early capitalists in the United States, the so-called robber barons, clearly separated business from ethics, but exhibited their social responsibility through philanthropy.[5] Andrew Carnegie, in *The Gospel of Wealth,* outlined two principles for businesspeople. The *charity principle* suggested that more fortunate people in society should help those who are less fortunate by contributing to organizations designed to offer assistance. The *stewardship principle,* from the Bible, viewed the wealthy as holding their property in trust for society, with the obligation to use it for any legitimate societal purpose. Acting on these principles, Carnegie and U.S. Steel had an active program of social philanthropy. Over time, these principles became increasingly accepted, as did the idea that power implies the responsibility to use it for at least some common good.

A more modern version of these two principles could be called the *principle of social responsibility*—the view that business has an obligation to act in the interests of society. This principle has been invoked to justify many different business actions, from giving to the arts to rebuilding neighborhoods to contributions to political figures. The idea is that business must see itself as a citizen in the community and do what it can to make the community a better place.

If business did not act in a socially responsible way, many executives realize that government would regulate and force such action. Indeed, one explanation of the extensive regulatory regimes in countries around the world is that business has failed to act in a way that fulfills its social responsibility.

The chief counterview of business as a socially responsible entity was promulgated by Chicago economist Milton Friedman, who is usually identified with the view that the only ethical obligation of a business is to maximize profits. This is sometimes interpreted to mean that capitalism is an "anything goes" system without morality or humanity. What Friedman actually said is a bit different.

Friedman recognized that business creates and allocates wealth in society. He suggested that, within certain rules and constraints, the system of shareholder capitalism could efficiently create and allocate such wealth only if managers focused on managerial tasks—efficiently managing the business. Of course, Friedman knew, as did Adam Smith, that the anything-goes philosophy couldn't work, and Friedman believed that profits could be maximized within the constraints of law and ethical custom. In particular, Friedman knew that if people did not tell the truth most of the time, and if they tried to mislead others about the attributes of products and services, that business would not work very well. Capitalism as an anything-goes system is neither Friedman's idea nor a very sound one.

While there are hundreds of articles written to counter Friedman's view, the best suggestion is to think more deeply about ethics in business. What are some ways of understanding ethical rules and customs? How can we analyze ethics and business together? In short, we need to critically examine the tools that we have for ethical or moral reasoning.

THE TOOLS OF MORAL REASONING

The language of ethics is very rich. We teach our children about values, rights, duties, principles, and the like, and there is no reason to believe that these processes are not relevant to business life.

Values

Much of our thinking about ethical issues in business is based on our *values*. Values represent our desires and can be either good in themselves, *intrinsic values,* or a means to other ends, *instrumental values.* Values serve as both the reasons for and the causes of many of our actions. It is relatively important to know whether a value is intrinsic and worth pursuing for its own sake or instrumental and likely to lead to or be an indicator of something more important.

Some business thinkers (for example, Peter Drucker) have argued that a common mistake that managers make is to assume profit is an intrinsic value to be pursued in its own right. Drucker suggests that organizations are far more interesting when profit is an instrumental value, pursued for the sake of some other values.

A recent book by Jim Collins and Jerry Porras reinforces Drucker's idea. The authors found that great companies that have been built to last place achieving their core purpose above profits. Their advice is focus on the purpose, not the profits.

Merck and Company, a U.S.-based pharmaceutical company, is a good example. First of all, Merck has had a tradition of being very profitable for many years. Yet profit is an instrumental value. At Merck the intrinsic value is to help the sick. In the words of George Merck, "We try never to forget that medicine is for the people. It is not for the profits. The profits follow, and if we have remembered that they have never failed to appear. The better we have remembered it, the larger they have been." Being highly profitable allows Merck to pursue other, more important values.[6]

Obviously, individuals have values that determine in part their behavior. Not so obviously, companies also have values. On the surface, these appear to be business-related values such as "customer service," "quality," and "teamwork," but often they include more straightforwardly ethical values such as "respect" and "integrity."

Values serve as an important tool in reasoning about ethical issues in business. There is often a conflict among competing values. For instance, if a company values both customer service and respect, certain kinds of behavior are expected of its employees to meet customer service requirements. Many companies, such as Johnson & Johnson, try to capture values in a statement or code. Exhibit 4.1 is Johnson & Johnson's corporate values statement, or *credo*.

Values can help an organization and its members clarify what is important in the organization. Values serve to raise interesting and important questions and to reveal difficult trade-offs. It is a mistake to see corporate values statements as merely warm and fuzzy statements that make everyone feel good. Rather, they are statements of what an organization stands for—its main purpose for existence.

Oftentimes corporate values and individual values conflict. Even when the statements of the values don't conflict, the interpretations that bosses and employees put on the values can vary widely. If values statements are to be effective in empowering employees to work for the organizational purpose, then there must be some means to question the values and, more important, to question processes, systems, and behaviors that appear not to be aligned with the values.

Rights, Duties, and Responsibilities

Values form the background against which other moral notions can be applied. Some values are so important and pervasive that they are picked out for special

EXHIBIT 4.1   Johnson & Johnson's credo.

Our Credo

We believe our first responsibility is to the doctors, nurses and patients,
to mothers and fathers and all others who use our products and services.
In meeting their needs everything we do must be of high quality.
We must constantly strive to reduce our costs
in order to maintain reasonable prices.
Customers' orders must be serviced promptly and accurately.
Our suppliers and distributors must have an opportunity
to make a fair profit.

We are responsible to our employees,
the men and women who work with us throughout the world.
Everyone must be considered as an individual.
We must respect their dignity and recognize their merit.
They must have a sense of security in their jobs.
Compensation must be fair and adequate,
and working conditions clean, orderly and safe.
We must be mindful of ways to help our employees fulfill
their family responsibilities.
Employees must feel free to make suggestions and complaints.
There must be equal opportunity for employment, development
and advancement for those qualified.
We must provide competent management,
and their actions must be just and ethical.

We are responsible to the communities in which we live and work
and to the world community as well.
We must be good citizens — support good works and charities
and bear our fair share of taxes.
We must encourage civic improvements and better health and education.
We must maintain in good order
the property we are privileged to use,
protecting the environment and natural resources.

Our final responsibility is to our stockholders.
Business must make a sound profit.
We must experiment with new ideas.
Research must be carried on, innovative programs developed
and mistakes paid for.
New equipment must be purchased, new facilities provided
and new products launched.
Reserves must be created to provide for adverse times.
When we operate according to these principles,
the stockholders should realize a fair return.

Johnson & Johnson

Source: Courtesy of Johnson & Johnson.

acclaim in the form of rights.[7] Because we value freedom and autonomy so much, we define *rights* as a sphere of autonomy in which everyone can act equally. The right to free speech is a right that everyone has, not just a few. The rights to life, liberty, and the pursuit of happiness are broad categories of permissible actions. However, rarely are rights absolute. The scope of any individual's rights are limited by the rights of others. It is often said that my right to swing my fist ends at the beginning of your nose.

While there is much talk of rights in our society, there is little talk of a correlative concept—*duties*. Duties are obligations that we incur to take specific steps, or to refrain from taking specific steps, that are connected with the rights of others. For example, if Jack has the right not to be killed, then everyone has the correlative duty not to kill Jack. If Jill has the right to a living wage, then someone (a government, a community, a company) has the obligation/duty to provide or guarantee that wage. Rights without duties are not very useful. And duties without rights are not worth the trouble.

A third idea helps to tie together these abstract notions, and that is *responsibility*. Responsibility is a set of behaviors that we should engage in if a system of rights and duties is to be stable and useful. For instance, while Jack may have the right to free speech, it would be unwise and irresponsible to use that right in a way that constantly harmed others. Indeed, if Jack and others did such a thing, it would undermine the very nature of civil society that gives rise to the rights in the first place. In this sense, responsibility involves the judicious exercising of a set of rights.

Rights, duties, and responsibilities play an important role in analyzing ethical issues in business. What rights do customers have vis-à-vis product performance and safety? What duties do companies have regarding employees? What rights do employees have in terms of basic political freedoms? What does it mean to be a responsible company? A responsible manager? A responsible employee?

Consequences

One of the most critical concepts in ethics is quite familiar to all modes of business analysis—the idea that actions have *consequences*. Most business theories and models assume that all consequences of a business decision can be measured in economic terms and quantified, or at least specified in enough detail to allow a cost-benefit analysis. With ethical issues the consequences are not always so simple.

Consider an issue such as *insider trading*—buying and selling securities on the basis of material, nonpublic information—a practice that is illegal in the United States. The decision to trade on such information clearly allocates harms and benefits in a certain way. The insider is benefited at the expense of the person on the other side of the trade who is harmed. However, there is a more subtle consequence here. If insider trading were prevalent, then public confidence in the market could well be undermined. It is not clear how to value this consequence economically, but is must be taken into account in a thorough analysis of the ethics of insider trading.

Business ethics issues often focus on harms that have been created by business activity. Too often, benefits are ignored. We shall argue that business as an institution creates a lot of good things. Computer technology, new life-prolonging drugs, and systems for the spread of knowledge are but a few of the innovations that have made our lives better. If we blame businesses for the harm they create, then we should also give them credit for the good they create. Understanding both harms and benefits of business issues is critical to a balanced view of business ethics.

Principles and Rules

Over time, we have developed a number of generalizations from the judgments that we make about right and wrong. These generalizations are based on our values, our assignment of rights and duties, and our experience with consequences to be desired and those to be avoided. We capture these generalizations in the form of moral rules or principles.[8]

For most ethical problems we have devised a set of rules or principles on which there is widespread agreement. *Common morality* is the set of principles that determine how we live most of the time. Promise keeping, mutual aid, respect for persons, respect for property, and so forth are usually uncontroversial principles that cover a host of daily situations. We learn these principles as children, and they are reinforced in most of our social institutions.

Business is no exception here. Businesspeople keep their promises most of the time, treat others with respect and dignity, and help each other when they can do so at little additional cost. Furthermore, when we find someone not living by these common principles, we call his or her character into question. Business consultant Stephen Covey has gone so far as to suggest that we come to view the idea of leadership as living by moral principles and advocating the same in others.[9]

However, moral dilemmas arise for common morality in several instances. First, new technology makes us unsure of how a principle applies. For instance, we might agree on the right to privacy and the corresponding duty to respect the privacy of others, and we might formulate a principle such as "Unless there is an emergency, you shouldn't interfere in the private affairs of another." (The "unless" clause covers the cases where you could save someone's life by interfering, for example.) Normally, we would agree that personal mail, desk files, and so on are the private affairs of a person. However, the new computer technology may change this definition. E-mail, voice mail, electronic files, Lotus Notes, and the Web may force us to rethink the applicability of this principle. A number of meaty dilemmas are sure to be raised.

Principles can also be questioned when we encounter a society or a culture that does things differently or that applies the same principle in a different manner. For instance, in many cultures the principle of freedom of the press is not understood in as far-reaching a manner as it is in the United States. We need more conversation and more reasoning to figure out how our principles may or may not apply in those situations.

A third challenge to principles and common morality may come from new groups being empowered in society. Indeed, in today's business world, the empowerment of women and minorities in the workforce has forced a rethinking of the biases that may be present in the workplace. The very idea of respect may be interpreted differently along gender roles. We don't need a new principle, but we do need a new conversation about its interpretation and applicability.

Parallel Cases

When we are faced with a difficult ethical dilemma, one in which principles conflict, where there are uncertain consequences, and where values and rights don't clearly help us to find an answer, we need to turn to parallel cases. We need to look for cases that we are clear about and to extrapolate reasoning from those cases to ones that are similar but less clear.

Consider the case of the H.B. Fuller Company, maker of a glue called Resistol. This glue was being abused by young children in Honduras, who were called *Resistoleros.* A parallel case would be someone driving a car while intoxicated. The car is not being used in a manner for which it is intended, and if there is a crash we could hardly blame the car manufacturer. At the other end of spectrum we find Johnson & Johnson's response to the Tylenol crisis, in which deaths were caused by product tampering. Even though J&J was not to blame, the company took the product off the market until it could introduce a tamper-resistant package. H.B. Fuller weighed such parallels to find a course consistent with its corporate values and the ethical expectations in both Honduras and the United States. In fact the company undertook an extensive program of education and social service to try to help those who had been affected and to prevent others from misusing the product. Eventually this meant addressing the formulation of the product itself in an ongoing manner.[10]

A METHOD FOR UNDERSTANDING CAPITALISM IN ETHICAL TERMS

One way to connect business and ethics is to begin by understanding that businesses can affect more than just shareholders.[11] Indeed, customers, suppliers, employees, communities, and shareholders are all affected in major ways by businesses. These groups have come to be known as the *stakeholders* in the firm. The stakeholder concept tries to set forth exactly who is affected by a business and to map the set of relationships that comprises the value-creation enterprise.

The concept of stakeholders was developed in the 1960s through the work of management theorists Eric Rhenman, Igor Ansoff, Russell Ackoff, and their students. The idea is connected to a very old tradition that sees business as an integral part of society rather than as an institution that is separate and purely economic in nature. Identifying and analyzing stakeholders was originally a simple way to acknowledge the existence of multiple constituencies in the corporation. The main insight was that executives must pay some strategic attention to those groups who are important to the success of the corporation.[12]

As the pace of change accelerated in business, these thinkers and others began to advocate more interaction with stakeholders so that they would have some sense of participation in the day-to-day affairs of the corporation. We had the emergence of consumer advisory panels, quality circles, just-in-time inventory teams, community advisory groups, and so on, all designed to get the corporation more in touch with the key relationships that affected its future. During the 1980s, the idea of "stakeholder management" was articulated as a method for systematically taking into account the interests of "those groups which can affect and are affected by the corporation."

As discussed previously, we have recently seen the emergence of a strong movement concerned with business ethics. Much of the business ethics movement has been in response to perceived corporate excesses such as oil spills, financial scandals, business-government collusion, and celebrated cases of whistle-blowing. But a small number of thinkers began to ask questions about the very purpose of the corporation. Should the corporation serve those who own shares of stock, or should it serve those who are affected by its actions? The choice was laid bare: Corporations can be made to serve stockholders or they can be made to serve stakeholders.

Most thoughtful executives know that this choice between stockholders and stakeholders is not the issue. Corporations must be profitable at rates determined by global capital markets. No longer can executives ignore the fact that capital flows freely across borders and that rates of return are more complicated than indicated by internally generated financial hurdle rates and payback schemata. Business today is truly global.

Most thoughtful executives also know that great companies are not built by obsessive attention to shareholder value. <u>Great companies arise in part out of a shared sense of purpose among employees and management</u>. This sense of purpose must be important enough for individuals to expend their own human capital to create and deliver products and services that customers are willing to pay for. We need only return to the wisdom of Peter Drucker and W. Edwards Deming to see the importance of meaning and purpose and the destructiveness of fear and alienation in corporate life.

Management thinkers such as Tom Peters, Charles Handy, Jim Collins, and Jerry Poras have produced countless examples of how employees, customers, and suppliers work together to create something that none of them can create alone. And capital is necessary to sustain this process of value creation. From Cadbury to Volvo to Nordstrom to Hewlett-Packard, executives are constantly engaged in intense stakeholder relationships.

In this view, the interests of stockholders and stakeholders are very often in alignment rather than in conflict. Stockholders are a key stakeholder group whose support must be sustained in the same way that customer, supplier, and employee support must be garnered. The issue is one of balancing the interests of these groups, not favoring one at the expense of the others. Furthermore, in a relatively free political system, when executives ignore the interests of one group of stakeholders systematically over time, these stakeholders will use the political process to force regulation or legislation to protect themselves. Witness the emergence of "stakeholder rights" in the United States in the form of labor legislation, consumer protection legislation, environmental (community) protection legislation, even shareholder protection legislation.

Quite simply, there are many ways to manage a successful company. Management styles of DaimlerChrysler will be different from those of Volvo. Procter & Gamble's methods will differ from Unilever's. However, all will involve the intense interaction of employees—management and nonmanagement alike—with critical stakeholders. The more that stakeholders participate in the decisions that affect them, be they product design decisions or employment contract decisions, the greater the likelihood that they will be committed to the future of the corporate enterprise.

Contrast this commonsense view of the workings of business with the traditional business ideology that we outlined earlier: separating business from ethics, proclaiming that it is amoral, that business ethics is an oxymoron, and that business exists to do only what shareholders require. In this old philosophy, business is seen as warfare, and executives are the lonely soldiers on the battlefield of global markets, playing "shoot 'em up" with competitors. This myth of the primacy of the shareholder and its view of business as "cowboy capitalism" leads to a profound public mistrust and misunderstanding of the basic processes that make companies successful. We need a new story—one that elevates business to the higher moral ground—and one that smacks of common sense and reality in today's business world.

Stakeholder capitalism, properly formulated, is just the new story that we need. Stakeholder capitalism is based on five principles (see Exhibit 4.2), each of which is important to remember if we are to craft a capitalism that will serve us in the twenty-first century.

First of all, the *principle of stakeholder cooperation* says that value is created because stakeholders can jointly satisfy their needs and desires. Business is not a zero-sum game. Capitalism works because entrepreneurs and managers put together and sustain deals or relationships among customers, suppliers, employees, financiers, and communities. The support of each group is vital to the success of the endeavor. This is the cooperative, commonsense part of business that every executive knows, but the myth of primacy of the shareholder tells us that some stakeholders are more important than others. Try building a great company without the support of all stakeholders. It simply cannot be sustained.

This brings us to the second principle: *stakeholder responsibility.* If an entrepreneur, manager, or firm has responsibility for the effects of its actions, so, too, do customers, communities, suppliers, financiers, and employees. Firms are not the sole carriers of responsibility in today's world. Customers have a duty to use products as they were intended, or else to take reasonable care, bearing the burden of responsibility, when they do not. Employees have a responsibility to support their employers within reason. Suppliers have the duty to do their best to make the supply chain work properly and efficiently. Shareholders have a responsibility to elect responsible directors who will take seriously their duty of

---

EXHIBIT 4.2   Five principles of values-based capitalism or stakeholder capitalism.

1. **The principle of stakeholder cooperation.**   Value is created because stakeholders can jointly satisfy their needs and desires. (Capitalism works because entrepreneurs and managers put together and sustain deals with stakeholders rather than becoming agents of the owners of capital.)
2. **The principle of stakeholder responsibility.**   Parties to an agreement must accept responsibility for the consequences of their action. When third parties are harmed, they must be compensated, or a new agreement must be negotiated with all of those parties who are affected.
3. **The principle of complexity.**   Human beings are complex creatures capable of acting on multidimensional values, some of which are selfish, some of which are altruistic, and many of which are jointly created and shared with others. (Capitalism works because of this complexity rather than in spite of it.)
4. **The principle of continuous creation.**   Cooperating with stakeholders and motivated by values, people continuously create new sources of value. (Capitalism works because the creative force is primarily continuous rather than primarily destructive.)
5. **The principle of emergent competition.**   In a relatively free and democratic society, people can create alternatives for stakeholders. (Capitalism works because competition emerges out of the cooperation among stakeholders, rather than being based on some primal urge of competition.)

care to manage the affairs of the corporation. Recent attention to sweatshop working conditions in the developing world has raised questions regarding the responsibility of corporations for the actions of their subcontractors as well as those farther removed in the supply chain (sub-subcontractors) both upstream and downstream.

Third, the *principle of complexity* claims that human beings are complex creatures capable of actions based on many different values. We are not just economic maximizers. Sometimes we are selfish and sometimes we are altruistic. Many of our values are jointly determined and shared. Capitalism works because of this complexity rather than in spite of it.

Fourth, the *principle of continuous creation* says that business as an institution is a source of the creation of value. Cooperating with stakeholders and motivated by values, businesspeople continuously create new sources of value. This creative force of humans is the engine of capitalism. The beauty of the modern corporate form is that it can be made to be continuous rather than destructive. One creation doesn't have to destroy another; rather, there is a continuous cycle of value creation that raises the well-being of everyone. People come together to create something, be it a new computer program, a new level of service, a way to heal the sick, or simply greater harmony.

Finally, the *principle of emergent competition* says that competition emerges from a relatively free and democratic society and therefore stakeholders have options. Competition emerges out of the cooperation among stakeholders rather than being based on the primal urge to defeat the other person. Competition is important in stakeholder capitalism, but it is not the primary force. It is in its ability to manage the tension created by simultaneous cooperation and competition that stakeholder capitalism distinguishes itself.

Stakeholder capitalism takes a firm ethical stand: that human beings are required to be at the center of any process of value creation, that common decency and fairness are not to be set aside in the name of playing the game of business, that we should demand the best behavior of business, and that we should enact a story about business that celebrates its triumphs, admonishes its failures, and fully partakes of the moral discourse in society as a routine matter.

Stakeholder capitalism is no panacea. It simply allows the possibility that business may become a fully human institution. There will always be businesspeople who try to take advantage of others, just as there are corrupt government officials, clergy, and professors. Stakeholder capitalism bases our understanding and expectations of business, not on the worst that we can do, but on the best. It sets a high moral standard, recognizes the commonsense, practical world of global business today, and asks managers to get on with the task of creating value for all stakeholders.

ETHICAL CHALLENGES TO BUSINESS

In the global business environment of today managers must learn to deal with a host of ethical issues. *Cross-cultural issues* are the result of encountering different ways of doing business around the world—in other words, a different set of assumptions about people and their motivations. For instance, one typical cross-cultural issue is bribery. In some countries, such as the United States, bribery paid to officials is not an acceptable social practice (and is illegal); in other countries, making payments to facilitate officials' complying with a request is standard practice. Gift giving, entertainment of purchasing and marketing executives, and showing favoritism to relatives or to relatives of important clients are all issues that are dealt with differently all over the world. There are vast global differences in employment practices with respect to women and minority groups, minimum wages, and working conditions. Executives need to address these issues in sophisticated ways that can coherently justify corporate policy.

Ethics scholar Thomas Donaldson has suggested a heuristic for solving such issues.[13] Suppose that a particular practice, say petty bribery, is not permitted in the home country but is permitted in the host country. Donaldson claims that executives should ask two questions. First, is engaging in the practice a necessary condition for doing business in the host country? If it is not, then the company should not engage in the practice; since it is not ethically permitted in the home country, the company already has a good reason not to engage in it. Second, does the practice violate any important human rights as defined by international treaties that home and host country have both signed? Even in cases where a practice is necessary to do business, companies should not violate important human rights. We might argue that small payments to customs officials to expedite orders are in fact necessary in some countries and violate no important human rights. Donaldson would distinguish such a case from engaging in unsafe working practices and conditions that would indeed violate basic human rights.

Another group of ethical issues could be called *competitiveness issues.* Issues such as restructuring and reengineering, the new social contract with employees, aligning individual and corporate values, outsourcing of work, contract/ temporary employees, offshore moves of production, and many more are all ethical issues that are present in the current business environment. To address these issues with "I'm only doing what is best for the business" does not excuse the manager from making ethical justifications. We have suggested that these issues can best be addressed in a stakeholder framework, but regardless, with the information technology available today, they must be addressed in a way that passes the *publicity test:* Can our solution to this problem face the light of day? What happens when what we did is printed in the newspaper? Increasingly, competitiveness issues are public, especially for large multinational companies. Solving issues differently in different countries is a strategy that is increasingly indefensible.

Often the choice is offered between "when in Rome do as the Romans do" and "when in Rome do as we do in Charlottesville." The latter doesn't respect the Romans and leads to a moral imperialism that is increasingly irrelevant. The former doesn't respect our own values and leads to moral relativism and situational ethics that are alien to the moral point of view. Perhaps we should offer an alternative: "When in Rome do as we and the Romans can agree upon." Such a directive places a premium on learning and sharing in an open conversation about the connection between business and ethics.

A final group of ethical issues in business could be called *everyday issues.* Honest performance appraisal and objective setting, openness in communication, employee empowerment, dealing with customer complaints, treating suppliers fairly, representing corporate performance honestly, dealing with troubled employees, family and work issues, sexual harassment, the glass ceiling, racism in hiring and promotion decisions, and affirmative action are but a few of the ethical issues that companies must address on a daily basis. While there are a host of complex issues, these six questions can be used to guide an ethical analysis:

1. Who are the stakeholders? Who is affected by this issue and how? What does each party have at stake?
2. What are the most important values of each stakeholder? How is each stakeholder harmed or benefited by options that might be considered?
3. What rights and duties are at issue?
4. What principles and rules are relevant?
5. What are some relevant parallel cases?
6. What should we do?

These questions offer no more than an analytical start to asking questions about ethics in business. The role of ethics in business is likely to increase, as is the complexity of the issues involved. Today's effective executive must have a keen ability to sense and address issues in both business and ethical terms.

FOR FURTHER READING

Business Ethics Quarterly is the source for many scholarly articles, book reviews, and new ideas about business ethics.

The Dictionary of Business Ethics, edited by Patricia H. Werhane and R. Edward Freeman, Blackwell's Publishing Inc., 1997, is a comprehensive guide to topics in business ethics written by the leading thinkers in business ethics from around the
world.

The Ruffin Series in Business Ethics, published by Oxford University Press, currently
contains 16 volumes of the latest ideas, theories, and concepts about the connection of ethics to business.

5 ECONOMICS

Practical men, who believe themselves to be quite exempt from any intellectual influences, are usually the slaves of some defunct economist. Madmen in authority, who hear voices in the air, are distilling their frenzy from some academic scribbler of a few years back.
—John Maynard Keynes

Keynes himself was an economist who certainly would not have underestimated his own influence on practical men and those in authority. In fact, he probably considered all those who did not seek out and listen to his advice to be mad. And, although Keynes recognized his own importance during his lifetime, even he might be surprised by the continuing controversy and enduring influence of his ideas. It is not unreasonable to assert that, since his death in 1946, Keynes's theories about macroeconomics and the policies which have been based on them have been at the center of the debate on the role of government in the management of domestic economics and the global economic system.

To understand issues such as balanced budgets, Federal Reserve policies, and the determination of interest rates requires some knowledge of Keynesian economics and its philosophical counterpoint, monetarism. At times the theories underlying the conduct of economic policy are grounded in arcane mathematics and highly stylized assumptions, yet the essential points can be presented in an accessible manner. It is important to keep these things in mind as you proceed through the chapter. First, economics can be extremely useful in understanding what is going on in the economic financial markets, in an industry, or in the efforts of a firm trying to enhance its value to shareholders. The second point is that there remain substantial differences of opinion about many economic issues. However, while disagreements exist on precisely how policies affect outcomes, we should not dismiss the use of the frameworks of economics to refine our forecasts and improve our decision making. Think of it as a map that directs us to the correct neighborhood even if it neglects to provide the specific address. Finally, keep in mind that as Keynes pointed out in the opening quote, though we are unaware of it, many of our ideas, policies, and actions stem from the theories of economists, largely unknown and perhaps defunct.

Economics is usually divided into two areas: microeconomics and macroeconomics. *Macroeconomics* looks at the economy as a whole and provides answers (or at least insights) into how rapidly an economy grows, the rates of inflation and unemployment, and factors that determine the level of interest rates and establish the exchange rate. *Microeconomics* is more concerned with individual household, firm, or industry issues. For example, how is the price of a product determined, what influences the profit of a firm, and how do individuals allocate their limited budgets among almost unlimited wants, needs, and choices? We will not address all of these questions specifically, but we will develop a framework that relates to many of them and other important issues as well.

We begin with microeconomics because its basic framework of supply and demand is then used to introduce the macroeconomic issues. In addition, we are placing an emphasis on markets and how they function. The basic principles of markets reside on the microeconomics side of the discipline, so this is the logical place for us to start.

MICROECONOMICS

Microeconomics is frequently about choices. How much does my firm produce? At what price do we sell it? How much will we sell? These decisions are not made in a vacuum. They are affected by literally hundreds and thousands of factors, which we are going to reduce to a handful of key determinants. In addition, the determinants or factors often interact with one another. For example, the pricing decision is affected by those factors affecting the cost of production, the quantity that consumers are willing and able to buy, and the availability of alternative or substitute products. To deal with all these factors and their interactions, economists since Alfred Marshall, the nineteenth-century British economist, have used the framework or tool of supply and demand analysis.

Supply and Demand

Supply and demand graphs, tables, or equations summarize the factors or forces in a market that determine the price and quantity of a particular good, product, or service. Exhibit 5.1 is a representative graph containing a supply curve and a demand curve. Before we begin to look at factors that influence the shape and position of the curves, let's first examine the conclusions we can draw from them and by what means those conclusions are determined. This may appear a bit mechanical at first, but we will flesh out the details later.

The intersection of the two curves reflects the interaction of all the forces in the market for a particular product. In our example, make the product a six-pack of beer. The price of a six-pack of beer is $5.00, and the quantity produced and sold is 4 million units. (Remember, this is for the entire beer market, so it's probably too small a number.) That combination of price and quantity represents the market-clearing equilibrium (E_1 on Figure 5.1). Those terms are important. Equilibrium implies that there are no forces leading to a change in price or quantity. As long as all the factors stay as they are, brewers will continue to produce 4 million six-packs and consumers will buy them at $5.00 each. It is market clearing because all of the six-packs produced are sold and everyone willing and able to pay $5.00 for a six-pack gets one.

What would happen if producers attempted to set a price different from the equilibrium, say $5.50 (Exhibit 5.2)? At that price, brewers want to sell more than 4 million units. They are getting a higher price per six-pack, so they produce a higher quantity, 4.25 million. Yet at that higher price, consumers will buy less

EXHIBIT 5.1   Supply and demand for beer.

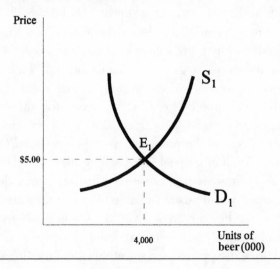

EXHIBIT 5.2   A temporary disequilibrium.

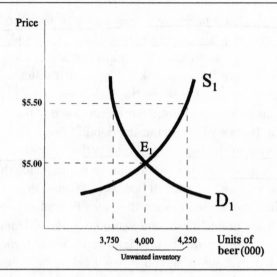

than 4 million six-packs—in fact, only 3.75 million. What happens to the difference between 4.25 million and 3.75 million? The market does not clear and brewers find themselves with unwanted inventories. As the inventories build up, brewers will cut their production and their prices. They reduce production because they have too much in stock, and they cut their prices to sell off the excess. As the price falls, the quantity bought will increase, and eventually the market will clear. At what price? We know that already: $5.00 per unit, the equilibrium price.

What happens if something occurs to disturb the equilibrium as represented by the shift in the demand curve shown in Exhibit 5.3?

The outward movement of the demand curve implies that consumers are now willing and able to buy more six-packs at any and every price that brewers might charge. A number of things could lead to the shift: higher income levels, leading consumers to buy more of everything; an increase in the price of wine and spirits, leading consumers to substitute beer for those products; or a decrease in the price of pizza, leading consumers to eat more pizza and, of course, drink more beer. At the point in time when demand changes, brewers are still producing 4 million six-packs and selling them at $5.00, but now consumers want 4.25 million six-packs. Brewers experience a decrease in their inventories, and some consumers are unable to get all they are willing and able to buy. That signals the brewers to do two things—increase prices and production. As prices rise, some of the additional demand for beer on the part of consumers at the old price disappears, and eventually the quantity of beer produced

EXHIBIT 5.3   A shift in demand.

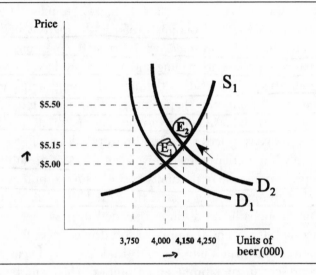

and consumed becomes equal again. That is, the market arrives at a new equilibrium, with a price of $5.15 and production of 4.15 million six-packs. Notice that this new equilibrium has a higher price and quantity than the original equilibrium because it was caused by an increase in demand. It is a change in equilibrium because demand changed, unlike the temporary changes brought about by the failed efforts of producers to raise prices and output in the face of no changes in the fundamental factors driving the market.

What determines the shape and position of the demand and supply curves? We have already alluded to several of the most important factors:

1. The level of income of consumers
2. The price of substitute goods or products
3. The price of complementary goods or products
4. Tastes, style, and fashion

In general, as income, the price of substitute goods, and tastes (preferences) increase, the demand increases and the curve will be farther to the right because there is a positive relationship between the demand for a good and those three factors. With regard to complementary goods, the relationship is reversed. As the price of a complement rises, the demand falls. In the previous example, pizza was a complement to beer, so when the price of pizza fell, the demand for beer increased. Had pizza prices risen, beer demand would have fallen.

The supply curve is equally intuitive. It is related to the cost of production. For firms in many industries (technology is changing this, as is our concept of knowledge and learning), the cost of producing an additional unit at some point increases. That is, if it costs a brewer $3.00 to make the millionth six-pack, the millionth and one costs $3.02. Economists refer to the incremental cost of producing a unit of output as its *marginal cost*. Because the marginal cost increases as output increases, suppliers are willing and able to produce more only if they can charge higher prices. That leads to the upward-sloping supply curve.

What factors determine the shape and position of the curve? Those that affect costs. The prices and availability of labor and materials are the key components. If hops and yeast prices rise, then brewers will be willing to produce a given quantity only if the prices they receive also rise. A more subtle factor that affects the supply curve is the opportunity cost of using resources to produce a particular good. The *opportunity cost* is the next best available use of those resources. What happens if the resources needed to brew beer could also be used to produce soft drinks and the price of soft drinks rises? Brewers will look at their alternatives and switch into the soft drink industry because the higher prices there represent greater profit opportunities. This would shift the beer supply curve upward to the left and reduce the quantity of beer produced. Beer prices would rise (Exhibit 5.4).

Although we have simplified enormously, the framework outlined here is a very powerful tool. It is an analytical tool that allows decision makers to quickly evaluate the impact of changes that occur in their marketplace. It can be used by policymakers to assess the effect of changes in regulation, taxes, subsidies, and tariffs. Moreover, it is an important philosophical concept. What we have

EXHIBIT 5.4   A shift in supply.

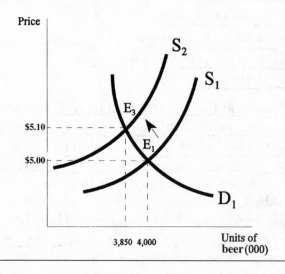

outlined in terms of the price mechanism and how it reacts to changes in supply and demand is what Adam Smith called "the invisible hand" in his classic book, *The Wealth of Nations,* published in 1776. Resource allocation is determined in a market system by reactions to and changes in prices.

An Industry Example

To be a little more concrete about demand and supply, we can examine an important policy change and see how it led to major changes in an industry. The industry or product was long-distance telephone service, and the policy change was the decision to open long-distance service to competition and to deregulate prices.

Prior to January 1, 1984, the only long-distance provider in the United States was AT&T. No other company could even offer to sell long-distance services. AT&T had a monopoly—that is, it was the sole company in the industry.

Being a monopoly and left to its own devices, AT&T would have set a very high price for long-distance service, one that maximized its profits. To determine that price, AT&T would have estimated its marginal cost and marginal revenue and delivered that quantity of service at which the two were equal. We have already defined marginal cost as the change in a firm's revenues brought about by selling one more unit. Usually, selling another unit means lowering prices, so the *marginal revenue* is the net effect of selling that last unit and getting lower prices on all the preceding ones. As long as marginal revenue is greater than marginal cost, it is worth it to the firm to produce and sell that last unit.

As a monopoly, AT&T had a lot of power in the marketplace. A company acquires or achieves that by developing products or services no one else can match. Intel is not a monopoly, but it comes close in the microprocessor market. It has achieved such a dominant position that it sets the prices for the whole industry. As a result, the firm has profit margins in excess of 60 percent. Intel reached this position by developing superior technology and by skillful marketing. So much of the software that people want to use in their PCs is based on the Intel processors that other firms have difficulty competing. Because they must compete aggressively on price, they have lower profits and therefore less ability to develop new products. Intel uses its profits to stay ahead of the competition.

Unlike Intel, however, AT&T did not win its monopoly power by superior performance. The government gave AT&T its monopoly because it viewed a single supplier as being socially efficient. Until recently, telephone service required wires or lines. It was considered wasteful to build multiple systems; moreover, once a company had a network in place, it could manipulate prices to keep out other competitors. The cost of building a system was so great that anyone attracted to the industry by the high profits would have to make a significant investment to enter the market. Since the existing provider already had made the investment, it could cut prices temporarily to discourage or damage the new competitor. Situations like long-distance service were considered natural monopolies, and the solution was to allow them to exist as *regulated* monopolies.

Regulators limited the profit that the monopoly could earn by establishing prices that were below the profit-maximizing price. In the case of long-distance service, the regulator was the Federal Communications Commission, which tried to establish a price consistent with allowing AT&T shareholders a fair return on investment—one that reflected the risk to the shareholders. Under this arrangement, long-distance prices were relatively stable. Changes needed to be approved by the regulator and were brought about either by AT&T demonstrating a change in its costs (which caused its supply curve to shift) or by a change in the fair return demanded by the shareholders.

All of this changed dramatically when long-distance service was deregulated. In a complicated settlement, the entire telecommunications industry was suddenly restructured. The major factor leading to the change was the development of new technology that allowed for alternative means of signal transmission. Satellites, microwave, and other technology meant that land-based transmission could be bypassed opening long-distance service to competition.

As companies made the investments necessary to enter the market, a number of things changed. First, prices and profits fell. The new competition forced AT&T to cut its prices as it attempted to hold onto market share. As prices fell, the amount of long-distance usage increased dramatically. As shown in supply and demand graphs, the new competition brought about an increase in supply (an outward shift of the curve). The new equilibrium was at a lower price and an increased quantity. But the changes did not stop there. The competitors, including AT&T, began to offer better and expanded services. Also, because there was competition, the firms in the industry aggressively pursued new technology and lower costs. As costs fell, the supply curves moved out even farther, and prices fell and usage increased more (Exhibit 5.5). Thus, by 1997, there were hundreds of providers of long-distance services, and the price per minute was approximately $.15. At that price, the quantity demanded was 220 million, compared to a price of $.74 and a quantity of 37.5 million prior to deregulation.

A number of lessons can be learned from the AT&T case and its related supply and demand analysis. When a firm is able to gain competitive advantages, it can increase prices and profits. In fact, a measure of its competitive advantage is the level of profit margin compared with those earned by firms in more competitive industries. When prices are held at high levels because of regulation or monopoly power, then the quantity produced is lower than in more competitive industries. The high profits attract competition. To maintain those profits, the monopoly or

EXHIBIT 5.5   The impact of deregulation.

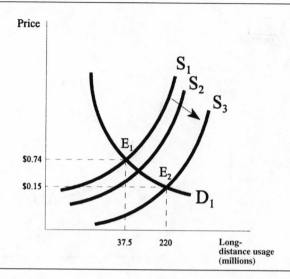

near-monopoly must have some means of keeping out competitors. The barrier to entry might be that the industry is regulated (e.g., long-distance service) or that the technological lead (e.g., microprocessors) of the dominant firm is too great to overcome. There are many other possible barriers, but the point is that firms strive to keep out competition so they can earn superior returns, and the lure of those returns makes it difficult to maintain a competitive advantage.

MACROECONOMICS

Whereas microeconomics is about individual and firm decisions, macroeconomics is about the broad state of the economy. When people ask about the state of the economy or the stock market, they generally have in mind issues that macroeconomists examine. Macroeconomics is about unemployment, inflation, growth, interest rates, and the policies that governments pursue to influence them. Because the impact of policies ultimately depends on the behavior of individuals and firms, macroeconomics cannot ignore microeconomic analysis. That is particularly true when someone is trying to develop models for the economy. We do not do that here. Instead, we focus on the key macroeconomic relationships and the two primary policy instruments: fiscal policy and monetary policy.

To begin with, we can represent what goes on in the economy with a supply and demand graph very similar to those used in the microeconomics section. Exhibit 5.6 is such a graph. Notice that we have appended an *A* to the *D* and *S*

EXHIBIT 5.6   Aggregate demand and aggregate supply.

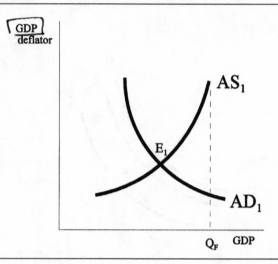

to note that we are now dealing with *aggregate* demand and supply. By aggregate, we mean all of the goods and services produced in the economy during a period of time. The more common phrase is the *gross domestic product* (GDP). The price in this case is some price index that is representative of the millions of good and services produced in the economy; the GDP deflator is the broadest. The aggregate demand and supply curves are generally determined by the same factors as individual demand and supply, although we need to interpret them in a broader way. Notice that the supply curve becomes almost vertical at some level, Q_F. That point represents the absolute highest possible level of production in the economy when all of the resources are fully employed.

Two crucial questions are implicit in the construction of the AD and AS curves in Figure 5.6. Is it possible to have an equilibrium at some level of GDP other than full employment, and is it possible to have inflation at a level of GDP below full employment? In simplistic terms, those questions characterize the debate between Keynesians and monetarists. The first question in particular is the one that Keynes addressed in his book, *The General Theory of Employment, Interest and Money,* published in 1936. Before we turn to those questions and related ideas, we first need to introduce national income accounting and examine in more detail the concept of GDP.

National Income Accounting

To understand the relationship between aggregate demand and aggregate supply and to be able to better evaluate economic policy, economists began to develop the concept of *national income accounting* in the 1920s. It attempts to measure the output or production of the economy, how that output is allocated among different uses, and what decisions are made about the income that output generates. The key to analyzing and using the national income accounts is to understand that they are based on an *identity,* a relationship that is by definition true. That identity is that the total output, what we have called GDP, is equal to the total income and that in turn is equal to the total allocation of income among the various forms of expenditure and savings:

$$\text{Output} = \text{income} = \text{expenditure} = \text{GDP}$$

This might appear to be vague at first glance, but once we have expanded the discussion it will become clearer. We have already defined *output* (or GDP) as the total value of goods and services produced in an economy during some period of time. Since the value of something equals its cost plus the profit margin, and the cost and profits represent someone's income, then GDP can be measured from an income or an output perspective. Moreover, since the recipients of the income can either spend that income, save it, or pay taxes, then the total income must equal GDP. Finally, if we look at the various types of expenditures in the economy, they must total the output, or GDP, as well. Therefore, we can work with the national income identity in the following form:

$$GDP = C + I + G + (X - M) = C + T + S$$

where

       C = household *consumption*
       I = business *investment*
       G = *government* spending
       X = *exports*
       M = *imports*
       T = *taxes*
       S = *savings*

Aside from some estimation issues, there is nothing controversial about these relationships. Every economist, regardless of his or her policy views, accepts them. Exhibit 5.7 provides the actual numbers for the United States for 2001. The controversy among economists is about defining the role of full employment and what impact, if any, government policies can have on GDP.

    The argument in support of using full employment (or nearly full employment) as an equilibrium is similar to the adjustment process described in the microeconomics section. Start by assuming that the economy is below its full-employment level. Resources are idle. Plants are running below capacity.

EXHIBIT 5.7   2001 GDP (in billions of dollars).

Consumption	$7,064.5
Business investment	$1,633.9
Government spending	$1,839.5
Exports	$1,050.4
Imports	$1,380.1
Total GDP	$10,208.1

Source: Economic Report of the President, 2002.

Workers are unemployed and raw materials are abundant. The unemployed workers begin to despair of getting a job, so they become willing to work for less. With excess capacity and raw materials available, manufacturing costs drop. As wages and other costs drop, manufacturers are willing to produce more (the supply curve shifts outward), but they need to lower prices to sell the expanded output. That is fine with them because costs have fallen. As prices fall, households, businesses, and government are all willing and able to buy more, so the quantity demanded increases. When does this stop? At full employment! At that level of output, there are no excess resources and no pressure for wages and prices to fall.

For those that believe in the power of markets, it is an elegant and convincing story. And there is no question that it has some empirical validity. When there is excess capacity, prices do fall, or at least rise at a slower rate. However, in general the evidence is overwhelming that the economy can and does operate at levels below full employment for sustained periods of time. Exhibit 5.8 shows the employment rate for the United States since the end of World War II. It is apparent that unemployment varies quite a bit and is quite high during recessions.

EXHIBIT 5.8   U.S. unemployment rates, 1947–2001.

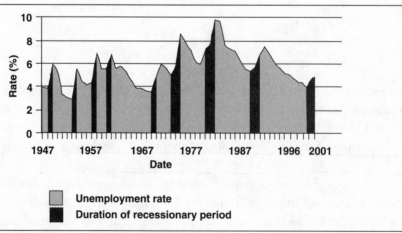

Source: Economic Report of the President, 2002.

The other side of the story begins with the view that prices and wages, although softer during weak economic periods, seldom actually fall enough to keep the economy at full employment. The reason the economy is at or below a full-employment level is that demand is insufficient to sustain the higher rate of GDP. Households have lower income because people are unemployed and spend less. Businesses that already have excess capacity reduce their investment in capital equipment. These reductions lead aggregate demand to shift to the left, or downward, and the economy stagnates. In the 1920s in Europe and 1930s in the United States, the downward spiral reached dramatic proportions as the unemployment rate exceeded 20 percent. Prices, wages, and interest rates did fall to very low levels, but there was so little demand that businesses did not invest even at a rate equal to depreciation, and they had no incentive to increase production. Many people feared for the future of democracy and capitalism because these dire economic conditions contributed to the rise of fascism and communism. Among those most concerned was John Maynard Keynes, who not only identified insufficient demand as the primary problem of the Great Depression but offered a policy to combat it.

Keynes argued that steps needed to be taken to stimulate the economy. There was a need for the government to intervene in such a way as to increase aggregate demand through expansionary fiscal and monetary policy. For reasons beyond the scope of this book, Keynes advocated fiscal policy, but the major contribution he made was that government should and could do something to keep the economy closer to full employment. After the war, that view became the dominant one among economists and policymakers, and governments have since tried to maintain stable economics by using fiscal and monetary policy to manage aggregate demand.

Fiscal Policy

Fiscal policy refers to the use of government expenditures and taxation to influence the level of aggregate demand. The government's activities have both direct and indirect effects on demand. As the government spends money on programs such as defense, education, highways, or space exploration, it is buying goods and services. This shifts aggregate demand upward and to the right, which raises prices and the level of output. In order to meet the new higher level of quantity demanded, firms need to expand production by offering more overtime or hiring new workers. Either way, wages increase and the additional income allows households to increase their spending. That represents an increase in consumption (C). At some point, firms will find themselves short on capacity, so they will buy more manufacturing equipment and build new plants. The increase in C and

I leads to an outward shift in aggregate demand that is more than the initial shift brought about by the increase in government spending (*G*). The total change in output that occurs is a multiple of the initial change in demand, and when economists speak of fiscal policy, they speak of the *multiplier effect*.

Fiscal policy is about both government expenditures and tax collections. A similar stimulus to the economy could have been brought about by the government reducing taxes instead of increasing its expenditures. As the government reduces taxes, households and businesses have more disposable income, some of which they choose to spend. That spending shifts aggregate demand outward and sets into action the round of income and spending increases described previously.

A number of programs and policies ensure that fiscal policy is countercyclical, meaning that when the economy is slowing, fiscal policy becomes more expansionary, and when the economy is growing rapidly, fiscal policy turns contractionary. These countercyclical effects are referred to as *automatic stabilizers*. What are they and how do they work? Basically, they take effect because some government expenditures and tax revenues are directly related to the level of income in the economy.

The two key places where that occurs are the entitlement programs and the progressive tax system. *Entitlements* are programs that provide some form of government payment based on an individual's income. As incomes rise, fewer people are eligible for the payments and government expenditures fall. A *progressive tax system* causes tax collections to rise as incomes rise, and as long as the tax schedule is progressive, collections rise at an increasing rate. The impact of the automatic stabilizers is to decrease government expenditures and increase tax collections when incomes rise. This puts a brake on the economy to keep it from overheating. Conversely, when the economy is slowing or enters a recession, incomes fall, government spending increases, tax collections decline, and the economy receives the necessary stimulus.

Fiscal policy, whether discretionary or automatic, cannot by itself keep the economy on an even keel. It takes time for the effects to be felt, and often other issues such as political concerns keep it from being implemented in a timely fashion. The other half of the policy toolkit is *monetary policy*, which often can be implemented more quickly and independently of the political arena.

Monetary Policy

The conduct of monetary policy is determined by the Federal Reserve System. It is the central bank of the United States and consists of two major parts, the Board of Governors and the Federal Reserve Banks, of which there are 12. The

7 + 5/12 bank presidents = FOMC

Fed Reserve System

Board of Governors
7 members

Fed reserve banks
12 banks,

determines
monetary policy

Macroeconomics   **83**

Board of Governors has seven members who are appointed by the president of the United States. Each of the banks has an administrative, policy, and research staff headed by a president who is appointed by the Board of Governors. The seven members of the board and five of the twelve presidents, serving on a rotating basis, make up something called the Federal Open Market Committee (FOMC). That group determines monetary policy.

How does monetary policy work? That is not such an easy question to answer. It is the source of considerable disagreement among economists. (You are probably getting the idea that economists are a contentious group.) To simplify, we will ignore the points of dispute and focus on the basics. Like fiscal policy, monetary policy has its impact through its ability to affect aggregate demand. It does that in two ways: by changing the interest rates and by altering the availability of credit. The former leads to more or less demand for funds and influences the amount of consumption and investment. The latter makes banks more or less willing to make loans and also influences the amount of consumption and investment. When the economy is too strong and showing signs of inflation, the Federal Reserve raises interest rates to contract credit. If the economy is below full employment, it lowers rates to expand credit.

To see how this happens, assume that the FOMC detects signs that inflation is accelerating. These signals might be that wages are increasing more rapidly than productivity, that commodity prices are rising, or that manufacturing plants are operating near capacity. The members of the committee feel that they should act, so they instruct their operating arm, the open market desk at the New York Federal Reserve Bank, to pursue contractionary policies. They might even specify quantitative targets for their policies, but basically they want the open market desk to raise interest rates and slow the growth of the money supply.

The open market desk accomplishes this by entering the securities market and selling U.S. Treasury bonds. In order to sell the securities, the open market desk will offer them at a lower price than it had previously demanded. The lower price on a bond causes its yield, or interest rate, to rise. At the same time, as banks buy the bonds from the Federal Reserve, their ability to make loans is reduced. The Federal Reserve actions drain liquidity from the banking system. Banks go along with that and buy the bonds because the interest rate on them is higher. Banks reallocate their funds from loans to government bonds. As the banks reduce their loan volume, the level of deposits decreases, and this in turn reduces the money supply.

With interest rates higher, loans less available, and the money supply smaller, aggregate demand will fall. The higher interest rates will lead consumers to put off purchases of durables like homes, automobiles, and appliances. Firms will invest less because the higher rates ensure that fewer projects pass the net-present-value test. Banks are restrictive in making loans, so credit is not available for discretionary purposes. All of these changes shift the aggregate demand curve to the left, slowing the economy and easing the inflationary pressures.

If the Federal Reserve wants to stimulate the economy by increasing aggregate demand, it lowers interest rates and increases the money supply. The appropriate open market operation would be to buy bonds, raising their price and expanding the reserves in the banking system.

Interest Rates

An important element of the macroeconomy is the level of interest rates. We have already seen that monetary policy works in part through its influence on rates. Also, because so many business and personal decisions are influenced by interest rates, they receive a great deal of attention. Interest rates are the price of credit. They are what we pay when we borrow or receive when we lend. The general level of interest rates in the economy is determined by the supply and demand for credit and the level of inflation. The specific rate an individual or firm pays depends on the general level plus a premium for creditworthiness of the borrower.

The famous economist Irving Fisher was the first to recognize the importance of inflation in the determination of interest rates. He distinguished between nominal rates and real rates, where the nominal rate includes expected inflation.

$$\text{Nominal rate} = \text{real rate} + \text{expected inflation}$$

The nominal rate is the interest rate we observe in the market or see in the press. The real rate has to be estimated or measured with hindsight, but the key is to realize that interest rates rise when inflation rises. Countries experiencing the highest rates of inflation also have the highest interest rates.

Real rates tend to be influenced by the demand for credit. During periods of economic expansion, more people want to borrow because profit opportunities are plentiful. As a consequence, we tend to see higher interest rates during periods of rapid growth and lower rates during recessions.

BALANCE OF PAYMENTS

The earlier discussions of national income accounting and economic policymaking were couched almost entirely in domestic terms. That is not as big a gap as it might at first appear. Most nations' economies are largely domestic. For the United States, only about 14 percent of the GDP consists of exports and imports. At the same time, that number has been growing, and more companies are doing business overseas, either as importers or exporters or by investing in foreign operations. As a result, it is important to understand the fundamentals of international economics.

The *balance of payments* is a statistical record of all the cross-border transactions engaged in by the residents of a country. An importer that brings wine or olive oil into the United States, an exporter that distributes movies overseas, a tourist who travels in China, and an investor who buys Brazilian equities are all engaging in cross-border transactions that show up in the balance of payments.

The range of transactions is broad, so there are a number of measures or definitions of the balance of payments. We are going to focus on one, the *current account balance,* which measures all the transactions involving goods and services and unilateral transfers or foreign aid. Using the same notation from the national income accounts, the current account balance is as follows:

$$X - M = GDP - (C + I + G)$$

Here's an intuitive way to think about the relationship:

Current account = total production − total expenditure

Countries, such as the United States, that have a current account deficit have expenditures greater than production. How does a country consume more than it produces? It borrows some of the output of other countries. That is exactly what a current account deficit represents—the borrowing of output beyond the level of a country's current production. The borrowing country gives the lending country a claim on its future output. When people describe a country as a *debtor country,* they mean that country is running a current account deficit and is issuing goods and services. Surplus countries are those that save. They consume less than they produce and acquire financial assets in exchange for their surplus production.

Numerous factors influence whether a country runs a current account deficit or surplus, many of which are related to macroeconomic policies that influence the levels of output, consumption, investment, and government spending. As an economy grows more rapidly than its trading partners, its consumption increases. Generally, that leads imports to grow more rapidly than exports and results in a deficit. A country with a higher inflation rate than its trading partners will see its goods become less desirable, and that will also result in a deficit. Policies to correct the deficit are actually policies to influence the levels of aggregate demand (expenditure) and aggregate supply (output).

To conclude this section, it is important to note that a current account deficit is not necessarily bad. At various times, it is desirable for countries to borrow in order to consume more than they produce. The key question is what type of consumption or expenditure is taking place. If the borrowing is to build infrastructure and expand manufacturing capabilities, then the deficit is positive because future output will grow, allowing the country to repay the financial claims and improve its overall standard of living. If the borrowed consumption is not invested or does not create future production, then the country will have to default on its claims and/or experience a decline in its standard of living.

PRODUCTIVITY AND THE NEW ECONOMY

One of the most puzzling and important economic phenomena of the last half of the twentieth century was the shifting productivity rate of the U.S. economy. From the end of World War II until 1973, productivity grew at a rate of about 3 percent per annum. Beginning in 1973 productivity grew at only slightly above 1 percent until 1995, when it began to grow at 2.75 percent. The causes of the slowdown in 1973 and the resurgence in 1995 are not well understood. There are a number of theories but little agreement among economists and policymakers about what caused the shifts. However, the implications for the economy of a continuation of greater productivity growth are substantial.

Productivity measures the output per hour of labor input. Productivity is calculated by dividing GDP by the total number of hours employed in the economy. Growing productivity implies that each hour of labor results in a greater amount of output. At the higher historic growth rate, output increased by 3 percent per annum without any additional input. At the lower rate, output increased by only 1 percent. That differential has a direct correlation with changes in the standard of living. The more an economy can produce from given inputs, the more there is to meet the needs of the population. Over a period of several years, the difference between 1 percent and 3 percent is substantial. For example, assume that output per hour of input begins at 20. After 10 years of 1 percent growth, output will be 22.09, whereas if growth were 3 percent, it would be 26.88. The increase in productivity from 1 percent to 3 percent leads to an increase in output that is 300 percent greater. Since the slower growth in productivity lasted for over 20 years, from 1973 to 1995, the resulting slower growth in GDP was enormous.

As significant as the impact on the level of GDP is, it is not the only important implication. Basically, it can be demonstrated that over time, real wages will grow at about the same rate as productivity. Firms can increase wages only if workers become more productive or else profits will fall. If firms expect productivity to increase by 3 percent, then they can contract with workers to pay them 3 percent a year more. However, if that expectation about productivity is not met, then profits will fall as wages rise greater than output. Firms will react by laying off workers and trying to pass the cost increases to consumers. Alan Blinder, a former Federal Reserve governor, believes that scenario fits the U.S. experience with stagflation in the 1970s.

Blinder also believes that the converse, that productivity growth exceeding expectations was a factor in the boom of the 1990s. As productivity growth accelerated, firms realized significant cost savings since wages rose less than output. Prices fell or held steady and margins expanded. Not only did GDP grow at an above-average rate, but unemployment fell, inflation was held in check, and increased profits fueled the bull market of the 1990s.

Alan Greenspan, chairman of the Board of Governors of the Federal Reserve, has spoken frequently of the impact of productivity growth on the economy and monetary policy. Greenspan indicated his view that the increase in productivity was permanent or at least part of a secular trend. As a consequence, he argued that monetary policy could be more expansive even as unemployment fell below what had previously been considered the full-employment level. The stakes are high. If Greenspan is wrong and productivity increases at a slower rate, then an aggressive monetary policy could lead to inflation. On the other hand, if productivity is increasing at the faster rate, a less expansive monetary policy will unnecessarily constrict the economy.

As indicated earlier, productivity growth is a puzzle. That is not to say that economists do not understand some of the factors that influence labor productivity. They do. Essentially, you can improve the quality of the labor force, give the labor force better equipment to work with, or improve technology. Research by Nobel Laureate, Robert Solow, in the 1950s showed that the most important factor was technological change. Three difficulties arise in using that insight to make economic policy.

The first difficulty is how to measure technological change. Some inventions or discoveries stand out, but most are evolutionary. Moreover, not all inventions are equally important. What constitutes an important innovation as opposed to one with a modest impact?

Second, it is not at all clear how to influence the pace of technological change. Patent policies, antitrust laws, and government support of R&D have an impact, but it is not well understood exactly what those impacts are. A government that wants to stimulate the development of new technology does not have a clear road map for doing so.

The third and final difficulty is the rate at which new technologies filter through the economy. Many, including Greenspan, who believe that the United States has entered a new era of productivity growth attribute the change to information technology. It's impact on the economy is pervasive at this point, but that has not always been the case. Take the Internet as an example.

What we now know as the Internet was actually invented in 1979 by the Defense Department. It is fair to say that it had almost no impact on the economy until the mid-1990s, and even today its potential is largely untapped. In other words, it took almost 20 years before an important technological change began to increase productivity, and our experience with the Internet is not atypical.

Paul David, an economist who has studied growth and the impact of technology, argues that it takes a generation after the introduction of new technology before its impact is widespread. The long delay is due to the expense of investing in the new technology, the training necessary to work with it, and the reluctance of people to abandon old ways of doing things. In other words, change takes a long time.

FOR FURTHER READING

Greider, William, *Secrets of the Temple: How the Federal Reserve Runs the Country* (New York: Simon & Schuster, 1989).

Postrel, Virginia I., *The Future and Its Enemies: The Growing Conflict Over Creativity, Enterprise, and Progress* (New York: Free Press, 1998).

Yergin, Daniel, and Joseph Stanislaw, *The Commanding Heights: The Battle Between Government and the Marketplace That Is Remaking the Modern World* (New York: Simon & Schuster, 1998).

PART II
The Functions of Business

Part I served as the foundation for this book. Part II addresses the seven functions of business, often referred to as the *core bases of knowledge* for an MBA curriculum: "Marketing Management" (Chapter 6), "Operations Management" (Chapter 7), "Entrepreneurship" (Chapter 8), "Accounting" (Chapter 9), "Finance" (Chapter 10), "Strategy" (Chapter 11). In most MBA curricula, each topic is taken in isolation and examined as though a manager can affect one business function without impacting other functions. Perhaps in theory this is true. However, we take a general management perspective that managers cannot affect policy or make decisions in one area of business without impacting other areas. It is in the spirit of business function integration that we present these seven chapters. The integration of these chapters conceptually converges on the process of value creation. Chapter 6 addresses the area of marketing and builds on the premise that marketing's goal is to create value for customers. Chapter 7 focuses on operations strategy from the perspective of the enterprise, not just from the more internally focused inventory or logistics planning process. Chapter 8 is focused on developing entrepreneurial thinking and processes within the organization. Our purpose for including this chapter is to demonstrate how important an entrepreneurial approach is to seeking business opportunities, even for the largest of organizations. Chapter 9 addresses issues germane to managerial accounting, going beyond just "debits and credits." Taken together with Chapter 10, the goal is to understand how firms create value and to better appreciate the impact of managerial decisions on the firm's financial health. Chapter 11 discusses elements of strategy and presents a framework to assist in setting the future direction of the enterprise.

MARKETING MANAGEMENT: LEVERAGING
6 CUSTOMER VALUE

Look back to 1995 and it seems almost like ancient history that we would dial an 800 number to order flowers from a catalog for a special occasion. A dozen long-stemmed roses are delivered within two days, each rose individually fed from a bulb filled with water to provide nourishment during shipment to your home or office. The concept was to provide a valuable service that allowed the customer to see the flower arrangement before ordering and to eliminate the cumbersome distribution system. Ten days often passed from the time the flowers were picked to the time they were purchased. Through a set of alliances with FedEx and independent growers, Calyx & Corolla is able to provide customer value by both eliminating the element of surprise (because the buyer knows what kind of assortment to expect) and reducing the transit time from grower to consumer (thereby increasing the freshness and life of the flowers). Through its enabling technology, Calyx adds additional value by building a database of its better customers' preferences and special dates.

The Calyx and Corolla (C&C) example is quite appropriate for the beginning of this chapter because it symbolizes a number of trends[1] that appeared on the marketing horizon in the late 1990s that still challenge managers in this new century. First, Calyx & Corolla challenged the status quo, asking why flowers have to travel through such a cumbersome distribution system. Similar to Dell Computers, Cisco, and others, C&C looked for new ways to add value and improve quality. Second, C&C is built on repeat business and works very hard to retain its base of customers. The business model is built on understanding the value of customer loyalty and can demonstrate the costs associated with customer churn and generating new business as opposed to retaining existing business. Third, the entire business proposition for C&C is built on alliances among a set of hand-picked growers, Calyx, and FedEx, providing logistical support and technical expertise. Fourth, the entire network represents a win-win value chain whereby each party works seamlessly to provide value to the customer. While functional specialization exists, the Calyx system, above all, attempts to remove those barriers and obstacles that prohibit the flow of information through the entire process. Finally, C&C illustrates the importance of services to the field of marketing. Even the giant manufacturer, GE, derives a significant percentage of its sales and profits from its nonmanufacturing businesses, in particular GE Capital.

Since C&C began its catalog operations we have witnessed a revolution in how business is conducted and what business models drive the influx of new and reborn businesses. We have seen the rise of the Internet, and a great number of dot-coms have come and gone. The movement from bricks to clicks brought venture capital rushing to the market, in many instances creating wealth on an insubstantial business model that could not be sustained. The stories of entrepreneurs and their fragile companies finally going bust filled the business press throughout the late 1990s.

To a large degree, the rise of the Internet was bolstered by the importance of customer relationship management. The argument is based on customer loyalty and the importance of understanding fully who the customer is, what problems they face, how a company can provide the solution, and building a database that tracks and stores customer information. With this knowledge marketers can better link customer preferences and desires to product development efforts, production cycles, and the formation/execution of comprehensive marketing strategy. Loyalty reduces customer churn, lowers the cost of doing business, and generates greater revenue per customer. Despite the positive press, the sad reality is that if customer relationship management is such a potent tool, why is there still a high degree of new product failures? For now, it will suffice to say that a hot product or service is not enough. The challenge for marketers goes far beyond ensuring that new product development efforts minimize time to market and maximize the fit between product attributes and customer requirements. Essential to the process is communication and those factors that enable the movement of information from the customer to the firm *and* its supply chain partners, all of whom are responsible for bringing value to the marketplace.

Throughout this text, you will hear about empowerment, business process redesign, total quality, and other remedies for business problems. It is true that all of these are key to business success; yet each taken alone is not sufficient. It is equally valid to say that each of these remedies has been billed as a business panacea and that managers sit in fear of the next big fix. Compounding the issue is the rapid changes that have come about since the Internet. The ability to share information throughout the value chain has raised customer expectations regarding a firm's ability to meet (exceed) its requirements in a timely manner. To meet these rising expectations we need a new business paradigm. The marketing concept is at the core of this new paradigm. Value creation begins with an enterprise view that holds the customer in its vortex. An enterprise view extends both across functions and among all channel partners.[2]

THE MARKETING CONCEPT

Can you think of a business that screams "commodity" more than the tire retreading business? Bandag, a major player in the tire retreading business, brings a high level of innovation to its industry. Bandag offers an added element of high technology by embedding a computer chip in the tire. The company has also trained field technicians who can monitor the tire's performance, calculate wear and tear, and determine balance, thereby providing an important set of value-added services to fleet managers. With this information, fleet managers can better gauge the total cost of tire purchases, which can run into the millions of dollars per year for large fleets of trucks. Value in use is derived through information and a tracking system that provides important savings through added tire life and reduced fuel cost.

Caterpillar, too, has installed remote sensing devices on many of its models, allowing a technician to monitor the health of the machine in the field. In this manner, a problem can be detected and corrected before the unit breaks down. A nonproductive piece of earth-moving equipment can be quite costly if the machine is expected to move dirt 24 hours a day. In both instances, the ability to provide preventive maintenance and real-time monitoring of performance is an important value-added service to customers who worry about time to first failure, downtime, and productivity. Similar sensing equipment is currently being installed on locomotives. GE and Lubrizol have formed a joint venture to monitor remotely locomotive health and also provide a new service called fluid management. The added costs of these capabilities are far less than the peace of mind that is provided in mission-critical situations.

In the 1960s, the field of marketing came to embrace the concept that its objective was to provide products and services that met the needs and wants of customers. Such a position was quite a departure from a sales or production orientation that was firm-centered, simply providing to the customer what was produced. Drucker felt that marketing was so basic to the purpose of the firm that it must permeate each functional unit and be central to the culture of the organization. He stated that "[Marketing] encompasses the entire business. It is the whole business seen from the point of view of its final result that is from the customer's point of view. . . . Because it is its purpose to create a customer, any enterprise has two—and only two—basic functions: marketing and innovation."[3]

Think for a moment about today's automobile. It has become a blend of high technology, providing the consumer with a range of features and capabilities that would have seemed within the realm of science fiction a decade ago. The e-vehicle of today allows passengers to receive and send e-mail, access the Internet, receive phone calls, call up traffic conditions and, based on accidents and slowdowns, suggest alternative routing. TRW and Michelin are developing technology that monitors tire pressure and sends a signal to the driver when inflation levels are hazardous. Johnson Controls goes beyond monitoring tire pressure and has a system that also links to home security and lighting. Radar-based sensors are on the horizon whereby obstacles on the road are detected and the driver is alerted.

This singular focus on the customer and the importance of all units to work together in support of customer value is succinctly stated at Motorola: That there are two kinds of people who work at Motorola—people who serve customers and people who serve people who serve customers. Interestingly, Motorola also invests heavily in its employees, viewing education as central to its business. The notion of value is not something produced in the factory—it is delivered in the marketplace through each customer interaction. Ian Carlsson, CEO of SAS, refers to these customer interactions as "moments of truth." Each customer interaction presents an opportunity to better meet the needs of future customers. A great deal of effort goes into training personnel to raise the probability of a positive outcome. At Nordstrom and Ritz-Carlton, the focus on customer satisfaction and the importance of creating value for the customer has created a cultlike culture. Employees are likely to self-select into the system and discover early on whether they are comfortable there.[4] Employees who do not fit into the company culture typically do not survive. A marketing culture that places customer value as the number one priority must be pervasive throughout the organization.

This priority can be translated into several simple principles.[5] First, think solutions and not products. Caterpillar sells productivity, uptime, and reliability. The OnStar system provides safety and connectivity. This knowledge can be ascertained only through an in-depth understanding of the consumer's purchase decision-making processes and by establishing formal mechanisms to listen to customers and to incorporate their voice into the firm's planning process. Second, think about the role of channel and supply chain partners and how to leverage their skills in fulfilling the customers' expectations. Your company is as strong as your entire delivery system and channel partners. A breakdown in service can result in a loss of customers. Third, walk in your customers' shoes and constantly ask what is it like for them to do business with your company. Understand the role in the value chain that each channel member plays and evaluate whether or not value is created at each stage.

The marketing concept can be expanded to encompass the objective of achieving superior customer value and to emphasize the importance of making this concern central to the processes that guide the strategy of the total enterprise. Several points implicit in our redefinition of the marketing concept are key to our understanding of marketing strategy. These points are the framework for the remainder of this chapter:

- Marketing strategy's role in corporate strategy
- The importance of customer selection
- Marketing activity pervading the organization
- Customer value creation and the role of employees
- Value creation through alliances and partnerships

MARKETING STRATEGY'S ROLE IN CORPORATE STRATEGY

If we take the view that corporate strategy must be forward thinking in order to position the firm to compete in the future, it naturally follows that strategy must search for tomorrow's markets.[6] It is not enough to excel today. Efforts must be directed to developing those core competencies that will determine success in the future. As FedEx and UPS competed for share of today's overnight delivery of packages and documents, they also addressed their Internet capabilities and the effects this phenomenon has had on the timely shipment of documents and packages. More important, it is interesting to note that both companies have reassessed their core capabilities and offer integrated logistics services. In some instances, their clients will outsource this function and focus on what they do best. Dell's logistics provider, UPS, assures the timely delivery of computers and also coordinates the box and the monitor so that the complete PC arrives when expected.

During the rush to and then away from Internet retail stocks, FedEx was viewed as a safe Internet company in that it played the critical role of fulfillment. During the late 1990s, both Amazon.com and Toys "R" Us were unable to fulfill timely delivery of gifts for the holidays. The fulfillment problem is still a major concern, as timely delivery continues to plague companies that survived the fallout. Not only has Amazon been able to successfully fix its problems, its acquired capability has allowed it to build a business that provides fulfillment capability to other firms, mostly Toys "R" Us.

The problem of fulfillment lies at the surface of managing the customer relationship and affects the flow of goods. At the core of problem, however, is trust. Trust evolves when products and services are provided in a consistent, reliable, and trustworthy manner. Enabling trust revolves around access to information, its richness and its transparency. Trust[7] can be built in a number of ways:

- Assisting customers through the buying process by simplifying the effort and providing information
- Enhancing customer service and support by making people easily reachable
- Taking the customer's perspective and supporting comparisons among competing offers

It also is built by not resting on your past reputation; a trusted company anticipates the future and plans products and services to meet these requirements in a consistent fashion. Corporate strategy must be aligned as it provides the road map by which managers plan the journey to the future and decide what mechanisms need to be in place to achieve that future state.

To some degree, this effort requires bifocal vision[8]—the ability to both serve the market today and to develop new markets. Bifocal vision allows companies to invest in current markets and customers while simultaneously developing resources to successfully face tomorrow's opportunities. For example, the face of retail banking is changing daily and the role of the branch bank is being redefined. No longer is brick and mortar essential to retail market share, as consolidation has led to a reduction in the number of branch offices nationwide. In the past several years, banks have flocked to the Internet to understand the implications for future strategy. Now the major money-center banks compete with online companies like LendingTree to provide service to consumers in search of a mortgage.

LendingTree, Inc., offers an Internet-based loan marketplace for consumers and lenders, attracting consumer demand to the marketplace through its proprietary web site, www.lendingtree.com, as well as through private-label and cobranded marketplaces enabled by its technology platform, Lend-X. In addition, through its web site, LendingTree provides access to other services related to owning, maintaining, or buying and selling a home, including a network of real estate brokers. The company also licenses and/or hosts its Lend-X technology for use by other businesses, enabling it to create its own customized cobranded or private-label lending exchanges. Through these Lend-X partnerships, the company can earn revenue from technology fees related to customization, licensing, and hosting the third-party exchange as well as fees from network sources.

To some degree, the question becomes, "What business are you in?" Marketing scholar George Day[9] sees the answer as multidimensional and central to defining your strategy. The process of reaching an answer to the question is useful to managers as they allocate resources, think about their future direction, evaluate different performance metrics, and so on. One dimension is understood by examining customer needs and how benefits are derived from competing products and services. A second dimension relates to segments and whether the firm elects to serve multiple groups of customers or a single set of customers (a niche strategy). A third dimension relates to technology and how it enables meeting the needs of customers. The fourth dimension is choosing a point along the value chain and deciding how to compete. For instance, is the firm an assembler or a producer? Does it interact directly with the end-use customer or does it go to market through independent distribution? What appear to be fairly benign questions become very complex since there are many trade-offs to consider in determining the scope of the business you serve. Note that another subtle shift occurs here as well. Rather than relying on growth rates as a key investment criteria, management now confronts issues related to value creation.

What Role Does Marketing Play in This Process?

The primary responsibility of marketing is to provide insight into the needs of current customers and competitors and to scan the relevant business environment for future opportunities. The general management role of marketing is to interpret this environment and to make decisions regarding which key customers to serve, which competitors to challenge, and what bundle of product or service attributes to assemble for the marketplace. While tensions often exist between marketing and other functional units, this information must be integrated with other functional decisions. In essence, marketing and its role as customer advocate must be core to the values of the firm and central to its strategy formulation and execution.

Recent research[10] has attempted to better understand how a marketing orientation affects a company's performance. The results seem to suggest that marketing orientation matters and that company profits are thereby improved. Equally important, however, is interpreting what a marketing orientation is, which helps us define marketing's role in the planning process. Consistent with our previous discussion, a marketing orientation consists of the following:

- *Customer focus*. Understanding customer needs, creation of value, and the importance of customer satisfaction.
- *Competitor focus*. Looking for competitive advantage, responding to competitive moves, and monitoring competitive behavior.

- *Interfunctional coordination.* Achieving functional integration, sharing information across functions, and having all functions contribute to customer value.
- *Future profit orientation.* Managing the business for future profits, not just sales.

Marketing strategy exists at three levels. At the corporate level, marketing provides invaluable input for future opportunities. Marketing provides insight to the question of what business we are in. More important, marketing addresses the question of what business we *should* be in. At the business level, marketing strategy combines with other functional strategies to bring products and services to the marketplace that, hopefully, achieve a sustainable competitive advantage. On a third level, marketing strategy includes planning marketing programs and implementing and controlling the actual marketing effort. Simply stated, segments must be chosen and targeted, offerings must be positioned, products and channels of distribution must be developed, and a consistent marketing communications plan must be executed.

THE IMPORTANCE OF CUSTOMER SELECTION

Recall a recent business trip. If you were fortunate enough to sit in the front of the plane, you were treated better than the travelers in coach by virtue of the cost of the ticket. Yet, if you watched closely, certain business-class passengers are treated even better. United calls these passengers their 1K flyers, and American and Delta have similar names for their most frequent flyers. These passengers are served first, receive upgrades, and are treated in a manner that hopefully keeps them flying on their chosen airline. The airlines are even considering special check-ins that circumvent the long security lines and provide a faster, less crowded experience for these valued customers. Not all customers are created equal, and companies are now admitting that certain customers are more valued and deserve greater attention.

One reason for this approach is the recognition that the lifetime value of a loyal customer can be very profitable. Slywotzky[11] and his colleagues argue that market share is dead, and while growth is important, it must come at a profit. Customer selection must be accompanied by value creation and capture. Value creation comes in the form of ancillary products and services that enable customers to be more successful. Central to this thinking are questions related to who the firm should serve (and not serve!) and which business model allows the firm to keep (in the form of profits) some of the value it creates for customers. It has been alleged that the airline industry collectively has not made a profit since the time of the Wright brothers. However, Southwest Airlines has consistently been profitable by not losing sight of who it serves, how it creates value for its customers, and how it has created a business model to use its assets better than anyone in the industry. Southwest Airlines is dedicated to the highest quality of customer service, delivered with a sense of warmth, friendliness, individual pride, and company spirit. This simple statement is understood by all who work there and has earned Southwest the best cumulative consumer satisfaction record, as published by the Department of Transportation. Sky Blue, a new entrant, has been trying to outdo Southwest, and recent figures suggest it is more profitable per passenger mile.

PIMS data reinforces this approach to value creation: Firms that segment their markets have higher returns than those that do not.[12] However, the evaluation of the worth of a lifetime customer is more complex and examines the future stream of profits, net of cost, discounted to its net present value. Determining the actual value is subject to probabilities and assumptions, but the point is that companies are taking segmentation to the next level and are incorporating the cost to serve and the profits earned over time. Fundamental to all marketing strategy is the recognition that often there are groups of customers who differ from other groups of customers on any one of a number of key dimensions. For the telecommunications companies, the work-at-home market has a number of identifiable segments. Given air pollution standards, the events of 9/11, and a host of other considerations, the work-at-home market is likely to get even greater attention. It is possible to isolate the self-employed and moonlighters who might be more value-driven and seek products and services that offer a strong price and performance relationship, while corporate users might be less price-sensitive because they are less likely to own their equipment and might desire better service and technical support. To the extent that marketers can understand and meet the needs of these different segments, they are able to reap higher returns, although the costs associated with segmentation exceed those of mass marketing, which does not attempt to differentiate among classes or groups of customers. Closely linked to the segmentation process are targeting and positioning, which are the sine qua non of marketing strategy.

There are two basic approaches to the marketplace, as is shown in Exhibit 6.1. Companies can approach the market as though all consumers are the same and as though differences in products, or product offerings, are not meaningful to these people. The legendary remark made by Henry Ford is an illustration of this approach: "Customers can have any color car they want as long as it is black." Interestingly, a number of health care delivery programs instituted at the federal level during the 1970s failed to acknowledge that differences exist between customer groups. Their primary desire was not to exclude anybody, so the designers

EXHIBIT 6.1   Alternative approaches to the marketplace.

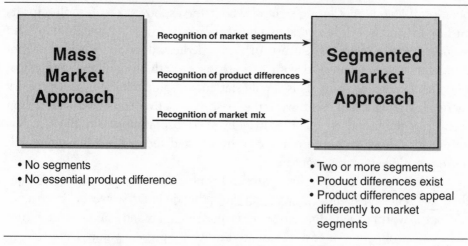

developed very general programs. The problem with this thinking is that those who were most in need of federal assistance were the most difficult to reach through traditional middle-class channels. On the other hand, customer differences occur because measurable and important differences exist between sets of customers. Both FedEx and UPS differentiate customers by their degree of time urgency—offering, at different rates, a number of options for the delivery of overnight or second-day packages and documents. Similarly, airlines price-discriminate, or segment, travelers by their sense of urgency, ability to plan ahead, and the frequency with which they fly. British Airways has recently offered its frequent travelers, who might have shunned air travel since the tragic events of September 11, 2001, reduced prices to Europe. Its $250 round-trip airfare to Paris is intended to stimulate this valued segment's return to the air.

What Is Market Segmentation?

Market segmentation is the process whereby companies recognize that differences exist between two or more customer groups and that these groups will respond differently to offerings made available in the marketplace. Differences might exist in the price-performance ratio associated with the product, as is seen in Exhibit 6.2. Or differences might exist in the channel through which the product is sold. One channel might offer superior service and technical assistance; another channel might carry the product with no service but at a more competitive price. Today's PC marketplace typifies the range of options available. A consumer can buy a PC at Sam's Club or from a value-added reseller (VAR) that supplements the basic box with customized software for specific applications, training, and on-site repair and technical assistance. The challenge exists when the same shopper frequents these two channels and begins to

EXHIBIT 6.2   Price-performance barriers.

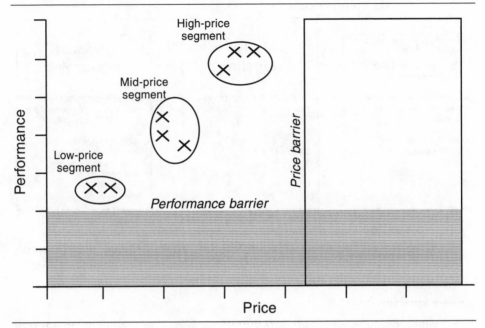

comparison-shop. To avoid channel conflict, a number of manufacturers elect to offer different products and product lines to different channels. In this manner, price comparisons are less valid, reducing the ability of a shopper to ride free on the back of the full-service retailer, whose role is to provide information and product knowledge, and then to purchase from alternative channels that offer low prices but not much service.

While it might not be obvious to the casual observer, the Weather Channel, which for 20 years has developed a brand and reputation associated with trust, reliability, and accuracy, has since the late 1990s segmented its offerings. Over the years, programming has changed to supplement the weather with content aimed at different audiences. Early morning news, directed at the executive and business traveler, contains travel-related information and stories about the effect of weather on companies. Evening programming contains stories and analysis of weather aimed at the lifetime learner, ages 25 to 54.

A customer-focused segmentation strategy involves a six-step process, as is shown in Exhibit 6.3. Firms tend to segment markets for several reasons. Among these are the following:

- Segmentation allows a firm the ability to match the product or service to the most suitable customer. Marriott, for example, has in its portfolio of hotel chains a number of choices for different customer groups. Residence Inn by Marriott is designed for the business traveler who is on an

EXHIBIT 6.3   A customer-focused segmentation strategy involves a six-step process.

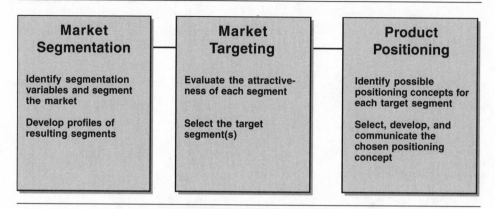

Market Segmentation	Market Targeting	Product Positioning
Identify segmentation variables and segment the market	Evaluate the attractiveness of each segment	Identify possible positioning concepts for each target segment
Develop profiles of resulting segments	Select the target segment(s)	Select, develop, and communicate the chosen positioning concept

extended stay away from home, while the Ritz-Carlton (a recent acquisition) is recognized worldwide as a fine luxury hotel. For its major clients it can offer a portfolio of hotel choices for different needs and events on a national level.

- Segmentation provides an opportunity for a company to develop alternative channels of distribution to reach different kinds of customers in a more cost-efficient manner. Motorola is experimenting with club stores as a viable outlet for its least-sophisticated mobile radios to reach the low end of the marketplace.

- Often there exists a segment of the market that is being neglected. Segmentation affords an opportunity for the firm to develop strategies to reach this part of the marketplace. For example, Charles Schwab discount brokers reached out to a segment of investors who objected to relatively high brokerage fees for transactions where no advice was given or was needed. Based on the success of this marketing strategy, a number of discount brokerage houses have sprung up; now investors can trade over the Internet. In the past two years, Ingram Micro has tried to win back the small customer that it actively neglected in the mid-1990s. Focusing on solution providers, Ingram now takes the position that it must appeal to a broader base of customers, especially since the information technology (IT) downturn. The company has invested in data-mining software to better monitor customers' buying patterns and to increase their loyalty.

- Rather than attempting to compete in a larger market, a firm might decide to select one segment on which to focus its entire marketing efforts. This narrower market might be defined as a small group of consumers within what appears to be a larger segment. For example, Paccar competes quite favorably against Ford in the long-haul truck business by concentrating its energies on the high-end, customized part of the truck-buying market. Although Ford enjoys a more favorable cost structure by virtue of its volume, Paccar's Kenworth and Peterbilt brands have a higher market share in the high end of the independent trucker market. Paccar has decided to focus its efforts on unrelentingly serving a niche part of the market, not just identifying the niche, but constantly innovating and striving to provide functionality and service that anticipates the changing needs of their customers.

Why Is Segmentation Important?

Higher returns accrue to firms that segment their markets. However, this is not reason enough to do so. From a corporate or marketing strategy perspective, the *analytical process* of segmentation is important. By *analytical*, we mean the process whereby companies attempt to define viable, sustainable, and profitable customer groups. From an analytical perspective, the process of segmentation helps define the customer universe because it provides richness to an understanding of customer groups. Industrial buyers are found not just in large and small firms or across different SIC classifications. Buyers can be adversarial in nature or collaborative; they can be risk-averse or risk seeking; they can be leaders or laggards. Such descriptions give marketing managers additional insight so they can better formulate and implement marketing programs that address the needs of these different potential market segments. The ability to thoroughly define a customer universe also provides an opportunity to track changes in buying behavior over time. For instance, to achieve differentiation in early-growth markets, buyers might require high levels of service and training as part of the product offering. It is easy to recall the days when IBM's reputation was enough to ensure serious consideration by any data processing manager because "no one was ever fired for buying IBM." Now, chief information officers debate whether it is appropriate to outsource their data processing functions. Even though IBM might still be calling on the same set of customers, over time, the decision rules have changed as they relate to information technology. Now IBM finds itself competing with the likes of EDS, PricewaterhouseCoopers, KPMG, and other consultants, not just Sun, Unisys, and others.

   Through a segmentation process, a company gains a better understanding of its own competitive position and how its products and services are perceived in the marketplace. Such an analysis provides a better understanding of areas of opportunity as well as areas of vulnerability. In the airline industry, Southwest has grown to be a significant presence in the short-haul market and has never lost sight of its target market. While American, United, and Southwest all serve the business user, each does so differently. It is important for United and American to understand where these differences lie, because neither United nor American enjoys the cost advantages of Southwest and therefore find it difficult to compete on that basis. United had to spin off a United shuttle service to handle traffic between Los Angeles and San Francisco. Although comfort and first-class service are always nice, most business travelers between the two cities were more interested in frequent flights and lower fares. Business travelers on longer flights from Los Angeles to New York or Washington are more likely to be attracted to the type of business-class comfort people have come to expect on international flights. Such an analysis helps managers to appreciate the dynamics within the industry. Therefore, it is not simply enough to describe the customer universe and devise a number of cute descriptors for different segments. A company must determine the impact on strategic decisions and on the allocation of resources.

Thus, from a *planning perspective,* segmentation provides a basis for the more precise setting of marketing objectives and strategy. Managers no longer attempt to increase their market share in the work-at-home market. They make an informed decision to focus on the corporate user rather than the moonlighter because one might be easier to reach than the other—or one manager can develop better programs to meet the needs of one versus the other. Or, by offering work-at-home products and services, the local telephone provider is able to position itself as a full-line, one-stop, telecommunications provider in the minds of its large corporate customers. In addition, companies face competition on the segment level. Battles are fought segment by segment, with market shares (and profits) going to the winner. Dell and Compaq (now part of HP) both compete in the PC market, but their strategies and success in the corporate-client server market is different from the more basic PC home-use market. For corporate clients Dell produces customized web pages that walk employees through the process of configuring and then ordering a laptop or desktop. In this fashion, the account manager for Boeing, for instance, can better attend to strategic issues. Rather than taking orders, the account manager now jointly plans Boeing's future computing requirements and how Dell fits into the plan.

It should be clear that a rigorous segmentation exercise helps guide marketing plan development, marketing mix changes, product development efforts, and the allocation of resources. For example, Exhibit 6.4 suggests that certain marketing mix elements are easier to change than others as companies attempt to meet the needs of different segments. The decision to change markets or segments can be significant and pose great risk to the firm. Management must understand that these decisions often carry longtime horizons. Again, FedEx was in the overnight package business for 10 years before UPS entered the market. Part of the slow start for UPS could be explained by its package mentality. Today,

EXHIBIT 6.4   Marketing momentum.

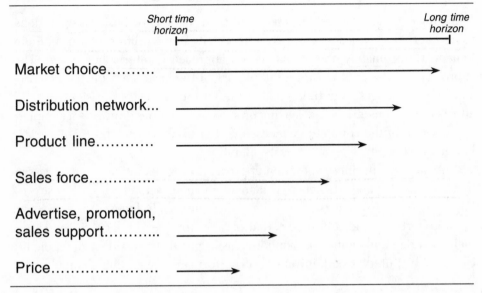

these firms don't have 10 months to react to competitive moves, because the Internet does move at the speed of light. Serving the urgent-package segment and providing complete logistics services to other key customers in high-priority markets have transformed both companies. At the other extreme, price changes can be made on the spot and, barring any antitrust considerations,[13] serve more as a tactical weapon. As would be expected, both new-product decisions and channel decisions hold reasonably longer-term consideration. New-product decisions are affected by both market and technological uncertainty.

Given the degree of clutter generated by a multitude of new products, brands, messages, and services, it is getting very difficult to differentiate offerings. If a firm fails to do its homework, it will not accurately align with its customers. There is a temptation to focus on market size rather than to target a smaller segment that better values the service offering. In Europe, smart cards have been quite successful and have replaced credit cards that do not store customer information. In an attempt to broaden its reach, Gemplus, a French manufacturer of smart cards, looked to the United States and tried to replicate its European experience. Online processing is not an issue in the United States, and the problems associated with the subsequent fraud are not as costly as to banks in Europe. The company's initial efforts failed because it did not understand the U.S. market. Gemplus then changed its focus and used its technology to develop other applications where security was important. Now the company sells phone cards to 29 percent of Americans in addition to 6 million cards to viewers who can then activate direct TV.

Segmentation in the Industrial Marketplace

Industrial companies sometimes segment their markets by business operations, using internal activities as a way to differentiate among different kinds of customers. Unfortunately, this segmentation approach is internally focused. This approach also does not permit a full picture of the customer's buying behavior and how it changes over time or how the customer makes decisions or what affects the customer decision-making processes—nor does it provide a complete appreciation of the competitive landscape. For example, Exhibit 6.5 illustrates how a business might segment by its operations.

Although a business operation approach to segmentation is not necessarily wrong, and it does depict what many companies actually do, it has several inherent weaknesses. First, this approach is internally focused and may not accurately reflect the differences that exist in the marketplace. Second, segments overlap and cannot be bounded easily, given that product functionality can be substituted at certain ranges of performance (e.g., one channel might

EXHIBIT 6.5   Segmenting by operations. (Internal=Bad)

Product segmentation	Centrex versus PBX Minicomputers versus micro versus midi Boxes versus systems (stand alone units or parts of a system)	Focuses mainly on product lines or product offerings from firm. The problem is the differences in segments might not be clean and might overlap.
Price segmentation	Sale versus lease Bundled versus unbundled	Focuses mainly on pricing options from company. Might reflect an element of buyer risk taking, but is superficial.
Distribution segmentation	OEM versus end users versus VAR	Illustrates more how the firm decides to go to market than it reflects the differences in buyer behavior and segment requirements.
Service segmentation	Service is unbundled and sold separately or is bundled as part of the total product offering.	Reflects firm's willingness to provide value-added services that capture aspects of buyer behavior or preferences.
Promotional segmentation	Deal-prone buyers Discounts, extended dating	Reflects different pricing options that firm might use. One can infer level of price sensitivity but does not easily allow trade-off analysis.

serve multiple segments). Third, such an internally focused approach oversimplifies the segmentation process and fails to fully capture the factors that drive buyer behavior and the buyer's decision-making process. We would complement the business-operations approach with a segmentation approach that is customer-based and derived from factors that more accurately describe the industrial marketplace. You will note that factors range from more macro-, industry-level variables to more micro-, individual-level characteristics. Practically speaking, as companies attempt to measure more microlevel variables, the cost of marketing research goes up significantly because it becomes impossible to rely on secondary data. Exhibit 6.6 summarizes the range of segmentation bases as well as the kinds of information gained and how a manager might use that information in the formulation of a marketing program to address the needs of a particular segment.

Exhibit 6.6 paints a different picture of the industrial buying process and provides the marketer with a much richer interpretation of the buying process from which to develop a comprehensive marketing strategy for a segment—or even an account within a segment. Macrovariables are often easy to find in trade and government publications. While the SIC code is useful, its applicability is often limited to questions of market size and market potential for a particular product by SIC segment. This SIC data is less useful in helping understand the decision-making processes of a particular segment. At the other extreme, individual and decision-making-unit characteristics bring to life the political realities of the buying process and shed light on the complex interplay between organizational members, each having a personal agenda as well as a stake in the decision outcome. While SIC code or company demographics might be adequate for certain buying decisions, it would appear that—as the decision becomes more complex and more expensive and as the selling cycle becomes longer—more information is required beyond the typical macrosegmentation variables. Bombardier, a Canadian supplier of subway and railcars, must carry its segmentation processes down to the individual level, given the complex interplay of politics involved in a local government's decision to purchase subway cars. This multiyear process entails a number of constituents and, as a result, is probably much more complex than is CSX's decision to buy a comparable number of railcars.

Final Comments on Segmentation

Once segments have been developed, they must be prioritized and resources must be allocated. Furthermore, a value proposition must be developed for each targeted segment. This value proposition addresses how the company

EXHIBIT 6.6   Different approaches to segmenting the business marketplace.

Type of business, SIC class	SIC classes 3500, 2500, manufacturing versus wholesale	Might suggest application or functionality; different industries or businesses might make different demands from the same piece of equipment.
Firm demographics (size, number of plants,sales)	Large versus small Regional versus multinational Strong corporate versus decentralized operations	Might suggest application and use of product as well as other concerns such as productivity or control. Could help understand where decision-making authority lies and the role of centralized purchasing.
Type of buying situation	New purchase Modified rebuy Straight rebuy	The type of buying situation directly affects the manner in which information is sought and how it is processed and used. It affects also the decision-making style and the decision-making participants.
Approach to decision making	Adversarial versus collaborative Decision calculus used	By understanding the approach taken to decision making, the marketer appreciates better the decision criteria that are important and how they might be weighted in the decision process.
Characteristics of the buying decision-making unit (DMU)	Composition Stage in the process Decision-making rules used	Typically, industrial buying decisions are multiperson in nature, with different degrees of influence held by different people at different stages. It is a political process.
Characteristics of the individual	Demographics Organizational role Psychographics Buying criteria used	Ultimately, people make buying decisions; organizations do not. It is useful to understand what drives people to do things.

intends to meet the needs of the targeted segment(s) and places the firm in a defensible perceptual posture vis-à-vis its competitors. The final point relates to measuring the outcome of a successful segmentation strategy. Accessing the correct segments and effectively reaching targeted customers are important. Exhibit 6.7 summarizes the steps used to develop a segmentation plan. Note that managers must determine whether these segments are profitable. At the very least, one should know what the expense-to-revenue ratio is. It would be better to know the contribution margin per segment dollar invested. The

EXHIBIT 6.7   Steps in the segmentation process.

1. Make the segmentation plan generalizable. Don't limit it to a particular product.
2. Group customers on the basis of similarities or differences.
3. Describe the groups (segments) accurately and thoroughly.
4. Use a sequential segmentation scheme so that the most important descriptors are used first and become a condition for future segmentation.
5. Develop competitive positions for each segment.
6. Make sure the development and the execution of segmentation plans are compatible.
7. Evaluate revenue-to-expense ratios for each segment to ensure profitability.

problem is that such information is difficult to capture, because most accounting systems are not market-friendly. They probably capture information at the strategic business unit (SBU), product line, or product level and cannot easily reflect the fact that products are typically sold across market segments. Movements to adopt activity based on costing are a step in the right direction. Truly market-facing companies attempt to capture such information on a segment-by-segment basis. However, such reporting systems are costly to build and difficult to implement. Thus, if a manager is going to take the time to develop a strong segmentation plan, it would be useful to know what the bottom-line implications are.

MARKETING ACTIVITY PERVADING THE ORGANIZATION

Several years ago, managers at DuPont were concerned about their perceived degree of dependence on their largest customer. During a discussion, the question was asked, "Should this customer choose not to buy from us anymore, how long would it take for our sales to disappear?" After much analysis it became clear that DuPont was less *dependent* than the two firms were *interdependent*. It also became clear that there would be six-year lag from the time the decision was made to buy from a DuPont competitor to the point where DuPont was no longer involved in any aspect of the customer's business! Some at DuPont might argue the close linkage between DuPont and its customer could be attributed, in part, to the "oval" (the DuPont logo) and its brand equity. However, a more meaningful explanation lies in the fact that customer interaction is not relegated only to the marketing department. Customer care is a concern for the total enterprise and must be the responsibility of all functions of the company that interact with the customer.

A number of barriers exist that limit a firm's ability to spread customer responsibility across the entire enterprise. The primary hurdle is that many companies are organized by independent functional silos. Each function has its own reporting hierarchy, and interaction typically occurs when task forces are assigned to solve a business problem. Frequently, when one area fails to talk to another, it establishes metrics for success that not only are internally focused, but often conflict with success criteria found in other areas. One of the most apparent areas of conflict that illustrates this point is between operations, manufacturing, and marketing. Operations would be pleased to run its factories at the lowest possible per-unit costs, which translates to few model changes, long production runs, and standard order sizes. To meet the demands of different segments and customers, marketers would prefer to have shorter production runs, many models from which to select, and very flexible order sizes and cycles. To be sure, these postures represent extreme positions; the world of mass production is less tenable in a highly competitive global economy. In other words, customers can afford to be demanding, because competitors are ready and willing to meet their varied tastes and preferences with precision and with minimal delay.

Mass customization,[14] made possible by advances in information technology, allows firms to meet customers' varied product and service requirements at low cost, in a short time, and with an ability to engage in breakthrough and continuous innovation. Panasonic, a large bicycle manufacturer, can custom-build literally thousands of varieties of bicycles to fit the buyer's size, weight, and riding style. Panasonic found that customers did not believe their bikes were custom-made because they received them from the factory too quickly! By delaying shipment and slowing down delivery to the customer, Panasonic was able to achieve the level of credibility required to compete in the customized bike business.

A shift to mass customization demands that the enterprise undergo a basic transformation in how it thinks. This transformation must be communicated throughout the company. The primary shift occurs when the primary stakeholder of the company is the customer and this person or company has unique needs and requirements that must be met. Equally as important is the tenet that such a transformation does not dismiss the need to focus on cost reduction and efficiency in meeting that customer's needs. To this end, each function of the organization must determine how its activities fit in the company's value chain. Motorola, for example, totally reengineered its pager production processes so that it is now able to produce on a single automated production line every model of its Bandit pager with zero setup time and by holding only 45 minutes' worth of inventory. Clearly, this feat could not have been accomplished if only the marketing and manufacturing areas cooperated. The need for integration among functions extended to the far corners of the firm, including R&D, procurement, and its relationship with Motorola's vendor base. This business transformation was a response to the Japanese, who have entered the U.S. market with competitively priced pagers.

Mass customization is only one example of business processes in which marketing must be integrated with other business activities to share in the responsibilities involved in meeting customer needs. A second obvious linkage is the relationship between marketing and R&D. The traditional conflict between basic and applied research is often cited as the primary source of discord between these two areas. Booz Allen and others[15] have long advocated and empirically demonstrated that higher levels of marketplace acceptance of new products can, in part, be attributed to close and formal linkages between marketing and R&D. One study shows that when functions interact in a sequential manner as the product moves through the development process, only 1 of 60 ideas results in commercial success. When functions interact in parallel, multi-functional teams, the success rate for new ideas increases to 1 in 7. By working with key customers, it is also possible to improve the hit rate, since they often have insight that the firm lacks. This insight is leveraged when the company uses a multidisciplinary team to visit customers.

Suppliers are a good source of information about both the marketplace and competitive behavior. Suppliers are also a key source of innovation and should be courted as such. Traditionally, procurement managers were not market-facing at all, viewing each purchase as an opportunity to challenge the stated price and to gain a better price. More recently, procurement has engaged in *reverse marketing*.[16] That is, by working with marketing and other areas, procurement transforms itself into a manager of external resources whose responsibility is to leverage the expertise and skills of the company's supply base. While lower costs are always a concern, the primary motivation is to work with the supply base to achieve higher levels of customer satisfaction. Recent proclamations of the value gained through either integrated supply chain management or outsourcing are extensions of this thinking. Cost reduction, therefore, becomes a benefit gained through a willful attempt to work with the supply base to improve customer value.

Does the Same Model Hold for the Internet?

Although the technology allows the marketer to track and measure customer responses to promotional campaigns, product information, and pricing, there is always the nagging question regarding the use of traditional marketing tools and techniques in e-commerce. Clearly, the weak link in the business model is fulfillment. Improvement is needed here because consumer confidence is not high. The more fundamental question is whether the standard old-economy marketing concepts and tools can be applied online. It would appear that marketers are able to take their models with them as they become more Internet-dependent. However, this movement to the Internet carries certain cautions.

Many people associate the Web with impersonal, price-driven decisions where in a nanosecond the skilled surfer can check prices on several web sites and buy the lowest-priced PC, DVD, or digital camera. Can we generate loyalty on the Internet? That's the burning question. Work done at Bain & Company, a worldwide consulting company, suggests that loyalty can be built on the Web—but it is not easy. If there is no trust, there can be no loyalty. Trust is based on more than the ability to provide a secure transaction. It means building a comfort level with the customer that entails reliable, consistent, and accurate interactions and information. Amazon.com has developed a relationship with its customers through its tailored messaging, objective reviews, and ease of shopping with its one-click option. (Having once saved your credit card information along with billing and shipping information, Amazon.com allows you to shop and then purchase with a single mouse click without having to input any billing or shipping information.)

Another benefit is the ability to attract the right customer. Vanguard's entire approach to the market and the way it defines itself is to attract the long-term investor who believes in the advantages of low-churn indexed funds. Yet in response to the growing sophistication of its clients, Vanguard has in recent years added brokerage services so it can be seen as a full-service financial institution. Careful customer selection has now been supplemented with a concern for "share of wallet."

Another strategy that lends itself to the Web is the ability to syndicate. In an Internet context, syndication means a consolidation of information content from different sources for the purpose of providing a more complete, information-rich site for customers. E*Trade brings to its web site news, quotes, research, and other information intended to help customers better decide which stocks to buy and sell. With this added information, gathered from independent third parties, E*Trade looks less like a discount broker and more like the full-service shops of Prudential and Merrill Lynch. The firm must now define its core skills and determine how it will employ those skills to bring value to customers. Does the firm create content to then be posted by its partner, or does it define its role as directly engaging the customer and managing the entire interaction. Morningstar does both. Many financial web sites rely on Morningstar to rate and review mutual funds. In addition, it has its own web site where customers can learn about stocks, bonds, and mutual funds and can also analyze their own portfolios by a number of different metrics.

MANAGING CUSTOMER RELATIONSHIPS AND THE INTERNET

While it is true that the Internet facilitates managing customer relationships, it also contributes to the complexity of integrating this new sales channel within the firm's existing marketing strategy. Companies that fail to see the Internet as a complement to traditional channels are most likely to feel the pain of integration. Simply, the Web intensifies the firm's ability to interact with and customize offerings for the customer. More important, the firm is able to accomplish this goal on a scale that had been unthinkable before.

In trying to assess the nature of your relationship with your customers it is important to first understand what the goal of the interaction is: market share, growth, share of wallet. From here it is possible to develop a strategy that fits with the level of commitment desired and the allocation of marketing tools used. A key advantage of the Internet is the ability to gain customer knowledge that is so critical to segmentation, branding, customer loyalty, and employee commitment. Through customer relationship marketing (CRM) tools it is possible to gather accurate information regarding customer acquisition and defection; customer tenure, value, and worth; percentages of inactive customers; and the effect of cross selling and other campaigns.

DoubleClick paid $1 billion in 1999 for Abacus Direct, a company that gathers information about customer buying habits. It takes catalog transactions and merges information with its own online data about consumer behavior. Armed with this data, DoubleClick can help retailers target promotions, find out what works, and modify any plans in real time. Since consumers elect to participate, there are no problems resulting from privacy issues and the use of sensitive information. With a customer base of 5,000, DoubleClick has taken the lead in this market and as a pioneer is trying to figure out where the opportunities lie.

Despite the willingness of some consumers to provide information, there are privacy concerns to consider, and these issues grow with the increasing amount of commerce over the Net. Simply, many would argue that individual privacy is a moral right. In addition, there are issues regarding security, and these concerns are often given as the primary reason for not using the Internet. In fact, the rules governing the Internet are still being written, and the full impact of the Web is not yet understood.

CUSTOMER VALUE CREATION AND THE ROLE OF EMPLOYEES

In the U.S. Navy, the Bravo Zulu flags indicate a job well done. At FedEx, the Bravo Zulu award is given for performance above and beyond in support of delivering customer value. One FedEx courier recently won the award for delivering his packages on foot after his van died.

It probably is not an overstatement to say that the word *FedEx* has entered the English language to mean guaranteed overnight delivery. In part, the FedEx success has been based on innovation and a willingness to take risks. To a larger extent, however, its success is a function of its people and their willingness to do what it takes to meet the customers' requirements. FedEx works very hard at inspiring its workers because it is aware that employees are a key resource and an essential ingredient in the company's success formula. Marketing-oriented companies are successful because they have empowered employees who can act on behalf of the company to satisfy customer requirements. The stories about Nordstrom employees are legendary. They behave professionally because they are trained to perform their jobs; the company considers continuous learning one of the obligations it has to its employees. Also, marketing-oriented companies have a supporting infrastructure that enables employees to perform their tasks in an innovative and customer-responsive manner. While L.L. Bean is widely recognized for its product quality and customer service, few people realize that its customer service representatives who answer the phone may well be working from their homes. L.L. Bean developed smart terminals, using ISDN lines to equip its home workers with state-of-the-art technology. For the customer, the interface is seamless. Customers never know that the voice at the other end of the phone is not in the large wooden facility located in downtown Freeport, Maine.

Bain & Company demonstrated that good customers are not enough and that loyal employees play heavily in gaining higher profits with a loyal customer base.[17] By investing in employees, companies enjoy less turnover, have to train fewer new employees, and can use funds to increase the efficiency of their workers. These efforts result in the desire to satisfy customers by creating increased value. This begs the question of how we can espouse loyalty in an era of downsizing and corporate restructuring. What about the new social contract? We address these questions specifically in Chapter 12, "Leading from the Middle." Nonetheless, loyalty has been redefined and no longer means lifetime employment. The more important question is how employee loyalty enhances customer value. Loyalty has been shown to directly affect customer retention and new-customer volume. Across the entire spectrum of professional services, the loss of a key employee (be it an attorney, a physician, or a haircutter) often results in the loss of existing business because people take clients with them. As word spreads of customer defection, new-customer volume falls. The cost of gaining a new customer far exceeds the cost of retaining an existing one. In financial services, higher customer retention rates correlate with greater market share. Exhibit 6.8 demonstrates the components of profits gained from retaining customers over time.

The notion of customer value being created through employees touches again on the core beliefs of the organization and is related to the notion of managing

EXHIBIT 6.8   Costs associated with customer loyalty.

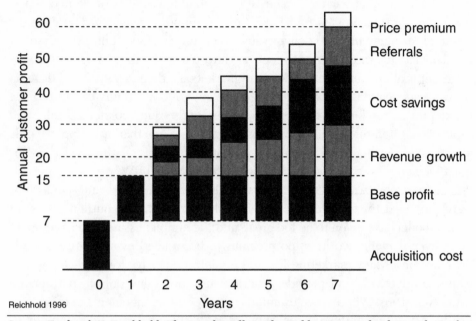

Reichhold 1996

through values. In everything management does, it must convey the message that the customer is key and that all systems and structures exist to support the idea of creating customer value. All sights must be focused outward on customers and competitors to create internally an innovative and responsive organization. This culture of customer orientation cannot exist in a highly structured organization where functional roles are narrowly defined and limited in scope. Employees must understand the role they play in bringing value to customers and must bring their hearts and minds to the job each and every day.

VALUE CREATION THROUGH ALLIANCES AND PARTNERSHIPS

At the start of the chapter we spoke about Calyx & Corolla and how, through a network of partnerships, C&C provides the seamless delivery of flowers from grower to final customer in one-fourth the time of traditional channels. This symbolizes the new competition, in which firms realize that they do not have or cannot develop internally the competencies needed to compete in world markets. Market access may be unattainable, technology unaffordable, resources unavailable, or other barriers may exist that prohibit a single firm from competing alone. Partnerships and alliances become important and, in fact, become essential for many firms to deliver value to customers. Both Sun Microsystems and Hewlett-Packard are dependent on third-party distributors to provide tailored applications for certain key niche markets. Certainly, both could develop software applications. However, limited windows of opportunity do not provide the requisite time for this to occur. Dell rewrote the rule book for PC sales and service and often refers to FedEx as its warehouse—one that just happens to fly at 550 miles per hour. And the repair person who makes on-site service calls is not a Dell employee; he or she might work for IBM or TRW.

The corporate model of the 1970s and 1980s, when growth and acquisitions were the ticket to corporate success, is no longer valid. The burden of cost of such a model has proven to be too great, and the nimbleness needed to compete in an ever-changing world is too precious to be saddled by slow, bureaucratic organizations. Many marketing-focused organizations have found that they can compete effectively and provide superior customer value only in partnership with other firms. Whether we examine comarketing arrangements in the airline or pharmaceutical industries or value-added distribution in the computer or manufacturing sector, it is clear that networks of firms are competing with other networks of firms for global markets. Interestingly, these networks are quite fragile, and the global telecom partners (e.g., Concert and Global One) have all disbanded.

As the marketing concept must pervade the firm, it must also pervade the partnership or the alliance and all its members. It should be apparent that an interdependent network of cooperating firms is only as strong as its weakest member. The challenge becomes one of developing a marketing orientation among a loosely aligned group of firms so that no one firm has direct control and upon whom all depend. While it might be difficult to develop a customer-focused orientation within a single firm, it is even more so across firms. Corporate cultures often are not the same, company objectives might not always coincide, and a number of other factors might inhibit such a culture change. Despite these challenges, many firms do not have a choice, and they must partner if they are to deliver value to the customer. Webster[18] suggests that the alliance leader, the firm at the core of the network, must make the marketing concept a core value of the alliance. Not only do functional and organizational barriers have to fall, but also alliance leaders must educate their partners to appreciate that mutual gain results only when all members of the alliance embrace the marketing concept and come to recognize the importance of creating superior customer value.

For firms that relied on internal processes to order, manufacture and assemble, and then sell and distribute its goods, the Web can enable outsourcing each of those functions and activities to experts who join forces and become a virtual company. *Business Week*[19] reported that 80 people from different consulting companies wrote a report about the economic impact of September 11 on the City of New York in six weeks. Such a project would normally take six months. Other collaborations are not so lucky and fail to materialize for a number of reasons such as technology glitches, a concern for competitive issues, old habits that lead to a lack of trust. Despite the mixed results, collaboration is on the rise, and with more experience problems are worked through and past mistakes are corrected. One key point is that reliance on just the technology is a grave mistake; alliances are about people, and the need to manage and create face-to-face time is essential. Such a caution is applicable to any form of alliance. Exhibit 6.9 illustrates the range of possible alliance activities.

EXHIBIT 6.9   Different forms of business alliances.

Type of Business Alliance	Explanation	Illustration
Product development	Firms use the Web to orchestrate product development and gain early development time supplier involvement	The auto and aerospace industries are able to decrease and increase quality by sharing digital information.
Supply chain	To reduce inventory, outsource manufacturing, and improve in-stock positions	Across most industries managers realize that it is possible to trade information for inventory and to reduce redundant costs systemwide.
Sales channels	The power of the Web is its ability to track, monitor, and deliver leads to resellers and sales forces	Toshiba Canada has reduced order processing by 50%. Telezoo serves the telecom equipment market by providing hot leads to its subscribers (Cisco, Nortel, Lucent).
Logistics	The power of the Internet takes waste out of the system by consolidating shipments, managing the flow of goods, and enabling instant price quotes	Georgia Pacific and General Mills share a cross-country route that has resulted in a $600,000 price savings.

SUMMARY

The lifetime value of a customer, segments of one, customer relationship management, and the like have come to the fore in the past few years and have changed the revenue model that many firms employ for assessing business decisions. The marketing function and the different activities performed therein have taken on new meaning with the advent of the Internet. The asymmetry of information that previously existed between buyers and sellers placed buyers in a fairly dependent posture. That has now changed a great deal. For example, before you shop for a car, you can find out the price levels from neighboring dealers, evaluate the costs for different options packages, and have enough information to place yourself on an equal footing with the dealer. Beyond negotiating a very favorable price, buyers are forcing the automakers to offer other value-added services that can close the deal. Clearly, manufacturers and their distribution channels must be intimate with the needs of their customers and then be able to bring together the array of tailored service offerings to the marketplace. In other instances, the Internet serves to bring buyer and seller together for mutual gain. Telezoo, an Internet company in the business-to-business (B2B) space, allows potential purchasers of telecom equipment to compare competing offerings on an apples-to-apples basis. In addition, it provides a service that allows serious buyers to construct request for proposal (RFP) based on the results of their search. The manufacturers who list with Telezoo now receive hot leads, because Telezoo can prequalify serious buyers from window-shoppers.

Our point is that the face of marketing has changed in a very short period of time and has been influenced greatly by the power of information. Now, because of technological advances, information becomes a source of differential advantage. Information and knowledge become part of the product/service offering. Now marketers work hard to build relationships that afford them share of wallet for the long term. Customer loyalty is the illusory part of the equation. There is too much clutter, too many options, and too little time for the customer to select among the various product offerings. Think of the twenty-first century as providing both challenges and opportunities to marketers. The objective is to harness the technology without losing sight of fundamental questions such as "what is it like to do business with my company?" Building trust becomes a key activity, and that is what, in the long term, will separate winners from losers.

FOR FURTHER READING

Charan, Ram, and Noel Tichy, *Every Business Is a Growth Business* (New York: Times Business, 1998).

Kotler, Philip, Dipak Jain, and Suvit Maesincee, *Marketing Moves: A New Approach to Profits, Growth and Renewal* (Boston: Harvard Business School Press, 2002).

Reichheld, Frederick, *Loyalty Rules* (Boston: Harvard Business School Press, 2001).

Rust, Roland, Valerie Zeithaml, and Katherine Lemon, *Driving Customer Equity* (New York: Free Press, 2000).

Trout, Jack, and Steve Rivkin, *Differentiate or Die* (New York: John Wiley & Sons, 2000).

Wind, Yoram, Vijay Mahajan, and Robert Gunther, *Convergence Marketing* (Upper Saddle River, NJ: Financial Times/Prentice Hall, 2002).

7 OPERATIONS MANAGEMENT: IMPLEMENTING AND ENABLING STRATEGY

Firms exist to create and deliver value to customers, shareholders, employees, and society. Operations are the processes by which the firm creates and delivers value. These processes embody the firm's capabilities, which determine its future options. Key capabilities—that is, the activities and processes the firm does better than its competitors—critically affect how successfully the firm competes and how effectively it improves and renews itself. Excellence in operations creates strategic opportunities by freeing resources for new uses.

WHAT IS AN OPERATIONS MANAGER?

An operations manager oversees the organization's processes that transform inputs into outputs of greater value. This includes service operations as well as manufacturing, and it includes processes such as project management, improvement programs, and training. An operations manager may be concerned with manufacturing, new products, research, technology, procurement, distribution, and customer service. (See Exhibits 7.1 and 7.2.)

Operations implement the firm's business strategy. It is the job of the operations manager to ensure that the firm achieves and maintains a position on the frontier of best practices and to push the frontier forward by continuous improvement or by developing and implementing new approaches to the firm's

EXHIBIT 7.1   New strategic choices: The winner's dilemma.

In 1993, Raychem Corporation's Interconnection Systems Division faced the winner's dilemma of how to grow.[1] Only three years earlier, Raychem had considered selling or closing the division. Given the division's dramatic turnaround, however, the corporation was ready to expand its investment in the business. Operating income had rebounded from −$3.5 million in 1990 to $6 million in 1993, despite a $2 million decrease in revenue. Revenue per employee had increased 44 percent, and inventory turns had more than doubled.

In 1990, the situation seemed almost hopeless. "[Because] we were always running around trying to find orders and get them finished and shipped, we never had time to think about the future," commented one manager. Of the 285 employees, half were directly involved in assembly and parts manufacturing, while the other half performed supervisory, support, and development roles.

A new operations manager initiated a change to a cellular manufacturing process based on work teams. The new system enabled a 33 percent reduction in employees serving overhead functions. Replacing the old batch-based operation, a just-in-time (JIT) flow process was established within the firm and then with vendors. Inventory at the division dropped by $7 million over the next several years. With the new cost structure, Raychem could consider entering markets in which it could not previously compete profitably. By focusing on process improvement and operational excellence, the division was not only able to regain its profitability, but to create significant strategic opportunities for the future.

processes. (See Exhibit 7.3.) Improving operational effectiveness may take many forms, such as enhancing quality in products or processes, reducing defects, developing better products faster, implementing improved production processes, employing new capital equipment, expanding capacity, improving testing, increasing on-time delivery, streamlining purchasing, outsourcing nonstrategic activities, eliminating waste, employing more advanced technology, motivating employees better, reducing absenteeism, improving workplace health and safety, increasing efficiency, improving customer satisfaction, and/or empowering organizational learning. Achieving and sustaining operational excellence requires vigilant analysis and willingness to change in a continual and relentless effort to improve the firm's processes. It also requires integration with marketing the

EXHIBIT 7.2   Investing to build future capabilities: Hitachi-Seiki.

In 1952, Hitachi-Seiki, a small Japanese manufacturer of machine tools, set the ambitious goal of developing the capabilities to become a world leader in computerized automation.[2] To build its knowledge base, the company performed basic research about automated production, hired electrical engineers, and set up a new engineering discipline, "mechatronics." The first two projects, although financial failures, taught the company critical lessons about taking a systems approach to develop a flexible manufacturing process. By the mid-1980s the company had become one of the world's leading suppliers of computer-controlled equipment that could perform variable sequencing of machine tasks. By setting long-term goals to build future capabilities, the company was able to leverage the lessons and skills developed over time to design a world-class flexible manufacturing system.

EXHIBIT 7.3   **The productivity frontier defines the state of best practices. Firms operating below the frontier (B) have higher costs than competitors, or deliver less value to customers, or both. Firms operating on the frontier (A) offer value to customers that competitors cannot match at a lower cost. The challenge is to improve operational effectiveness and move the frontier outward, enabling even more value to be delivered at the same (or lower) costs.**

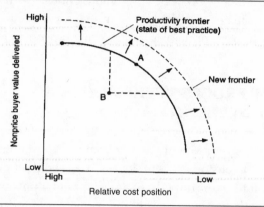

Source: Michael E. Porter, "What is Strategy?" *Harvard Business Review,* November–December 1996, p. 62. Copyright © 1996 by the Harvard Business School Publishing Corporation; all rights reserved.

other functions of the firm so that improvement efforts throughout the firm reinforce each other and so that the functions work together to create and enhance value for customers.

Operational Excellence Is Necessary for Sustained Profitability

Operational effectiveness is critical to a firm's competitiveness; it enables a firm to get more from its inputs or to use less of them to produce high-quality output (or to provide better service). A firm that lags behind its competitors' operational effectiveness will face higher costs, offer fewer features or lower-quality output (at a given level of costs), or both. For example, in the 1980s many Japanese companies achieved operational effectiveness so far above their Western rivals that the Japanese firms were able to offer customers both lower cost and superior quality. When a firm is on the frontier of best practices, however, competitors will not be able to outperform it on both cost and noncost features simultaneously unless they are able to redefine best practices and push out the entire frontier.

As firms improve their operational effectiveness, they move toward the frontier of best practices or redefine the frontier and push it out ahead of other firms. Indeed, the frontier of productivity continues to shift outward as new technologies, processes, and management methods are developed. During the 1980s and 1990s, concern with improving operations led to programs in Total Quality Management, continuous improvement, time-based competition, empowering the learning organization, change management, benchmarking, reengineering, and outsourcing. All of this attention has made the development, operation, and improvement of productive processes even more critical for the survival and success of a business. This chapter looks first at measures of process performance and then presents 12 basic principles for achieving process improvement.

MEASURES OF PROCESS PERFORMANCE: WHAT IS IMPROVEMENT?

The goals of process improvement are increasing and sustaining profits and creating more value for customers, employees, shareholders, and communities. This can be difficult to assess directly, so, for a particular process, managers often use other measures that influence profitability, such as efficiency, quality, capacity, delivery time, and flexibility. These secondary measures can provide important insights about the firm's processes and its opportunities to increase profitability. The trap that often confounds managers is focusing on secondary measures for their own sake and losing sight of the goals of increasing long-term profits and creating of value for people.

The secondary measures of profitability are also useful for diagnosing problems and identifying opportunities for improvement. If revenues are rising but profits are falling, measures of process performance can shed critical light on where and why costs are increasing. Thus, even if direct data on profits is available, other measures of operational effectiveness should be monitored and analyzed. (See, for example, Exhibit 7.4.)

The measures that a firm manager uses are critical. What is measured and how it is measured set very strong incentives for the firm's employees. The old adage that "what you measure will improve" is true. Indeed, many argue that the adage is understated because it may be extremely difficult to affect change on aspects of a process that have not been measured and so are not worked into the practices and culture of the workplace. It is therefore important to understand commonly used indicators of operational effectiveness.

Efficiency

Efficiency is sometimes used to mean cost reduction, but it is important to look at costs of a process relative to the value it creates. Efficiency of an *economic*

EXHIBIT 7.4   Understanding profits by analyzing operational effectiveness.

Profits fell 83 percent in 1992 for a U.S. producer of plastic pellets.[3] Managers were baffled, because other measures of performance that year were positive. A new marketing strategy aimed at broadening the company's product line and increasing the number of customers had produced record sales for the year. Revenues had increased 20 percent, production rates had increased 7.4 percent, and average setup times had decreased 5 percent. It seemed that the year should have been a success.

The key to understanding the plunge in profits was analyzing operational effectiveness and the fit between operations and marketing efforts. The broader product line had required 10,000 hours of additional setup time for 2,000 additional hours of production. Small batch sizes and large numbers of setups had escalated production costs, causing the drop in profits. Marketing efforts had not taken into account the cost structure of the firm. For the broader-line marketing strategy to be profitable, the firm needed an even more flexible production process. Given the process in place, marketing would add more to profitability by increasing the volume of orders on a smaller number of products.

---

system relates the value of the output to the value of the input. Thus, efficiency should exceed 100 percent in a very efficient process, the value of the output (product or service) is much higher than the costs of all inputs used. When value added or profitability is used to indicate efficiency, however, it is important to note that all of the costs or benefits of a process may not be realized in one time period. Benefits may accrue in the future, or if cost reductions are made in ways that hurt quality and reputation over time, then the apparent efficiency, indicated by short-term profits, may be false. Thus, long-run profitability is a better measure.

Efficiency or utilization of a *physical system* relates the amount of the output created to the amount of the input used or the percentage of the available (input) resource that is actually used. It cannot exceed 100 percent. For example, firms measure the percent of time that a machine is actively producing product rather than sitting idle or being serviced. Energy efficiency is another frequently used measure; even the most efficient plant or engine will not deliver more energy than it consumes, so, again, efficiency cannot exceed 100 percent. For example, firms measure direct labor utilization to determine how many of the hours of paid work were actually used in the manufacture of the product or delivery of the service.

While more efficient physical systems are generally assumed to be better, this is not always the case. For example, a given machine may operate most efficiently with a large batch size, but if the flow of the plant is not balanced, the resulting inventory costs may outweigh the apparent economics on the single machine. When measures other than profitability are used as surrogates, it is important to keep in mind how these measures affect the profitability of the entire operation.

Quality

Quality can be defined on many dimensions, but it boils down to the following: *Quality* is meeting the customers' requirements. It is what the customer values and pays for. Quality can affect both the cost and the revenue sides of long-run profitability. Poor-quality output will immediately or eventually reduce the market value of products or services as well as increase costs of repair, customer service, and handling complaints. These costs may be magnified by reputational spillovers affecting the value of the firm's other products or brands. In addition, poor process quality can increase costs by increasing scrap and rework, reducing utilization and efficiency, increasing downtime, or decreasing customer satisfaction with service processes. The point is that poor quality can create other problems that require time, resources, and managerial effort to resolve. In general, prevention of quality problems costs less than inspection and correction.

Output quality can be assessed with internal or external measures. Internal measures generally show how well products or services meet specifications or report the percentage of output that is defective. External measures may compare the product or service to competitive offerings or may assess actual or potential customer satisfaction. In product development, techniques such as quality function deployment or quality architecture focus on identifying customer desires and translating them into engineering specifications for product design to enhance the customer value of the new product.

Process quality affects output quality, and it can be controlled to ensure higher-quality output. Firms may measure such things as missed promises, customer complaints, or on-time deliveries. Service processes and customer interactions may be monitored. Firms may also monitor the settings, temperatures, or force used by machines to ensure proper and consistent operation. Statistical process control measures tend to look at two dimensions of quality: (1) whether the process is *in control,* thus stable and predictable, and (2) whether the process is *in compliance,* or within the specifications required for the product or by the customer.

Capacity

Capacity is the maximum rate of output generated by a process. It affects the revenue side of long-run profitability by determining how many customers can be served or how many products can be produced. It affects costs in that people must be hired and plant and equipment purchased or rented. These costs may include large capital investments in plants, machines, buildings, or new technologies.

Capacity is measured in units of output (or customers served) per unit of time. In practice, capacity is difficult to measure because it shifts over time with changes in the inputs, the mix of outputs, labor, and managerial decisions about the process. In addition, few processes can produce at capacity for long periods or without defects. Effective capacity for the production of nondefective output is much more relevant, but it is also more difficult to measure.

The capacity of an integrated or multistep process is determined by the portion of the process with the least capacity, or the bottleneck of the system. Thus, identification and relief of bottlenecks are important issues in process management.

only as strong as the weakest link

Delivery Time

Speed of delivery may affect the revenue contribution to long-run profitability. The ability of a firm to provide dependable (i.e., on-time) or fast delivery of a product or service may allow it to command a premium price or to sell more units at the standard price. Speed of delivery may also occur in the development cycle, enabling a firm to benefit by offering the first product or the best revision of a product or to spend less on the upstream product development activities.

Delivery of existing products and services can be measured as the lead time from order to market. Shorter is generally better, but shortening process lead times can adversely affect input costs, quality, or capacity, and thus benefits can be outweighed by new costs. Sometimes, meeting the schedule (providing on-time delivery) is more important than the lead time itself.

Speed of delivery in research and development of new products is trickier to measure because the process involves many contingencies and because the output may not be defined when the research begins. Recent attention focuses on methods for speeding product development, such as concurrent design and engineering.

In service businesses, waiting lines, or queues, may form when customers arrive faster than service is delivered. The length of the queue and the speed at which customers move through it are important measures of the process performance. Long waits may result in lost or disgruntled customers, affecting profitability by reducing the number of current customers, decreasing the rate of repeat customers, and undermining the firm's reputation for quality service.

Flexibility

Flexibility affects profitability through both costs and revenues. A flexible process has a relatively low cost (or short time) for changing inputs used or outputs produced. On the revenue side, the ability to adjust output cheaply or quickly may enable a firm to increase customer satisfaction or to serve additional customers. There is a trade-off, however, because flexible systems may cost more in terms of initial capital investments, operating costs, or both. Managers are keenly aware that flexibility adds value to operations, but they must balance that value with its costs to determine how it affects profitability.

Although the value of flexibility is widely recognized, it is difficult to measure. The value of flexibility is usually discussed in qualitative terms or roughly measured with option value models or decision analysis.

In the context of operations strategy, flexibility refers to opportunities available in the future because of the firm's current capabilities. With superior capabilities, a firm may have opportunities that are not available to competitors or that are available at lower costs than competitors face. Thus, as managers choose among investments or among process improvements, they must highlight in their considerations the capabilities, future flexibility, and options the investments will create. While the value of future options is difficult to measure, it is clear that such options may have significant value and significant effects on long-term profits.

ACHIEVING PROCESS IMPROVEMENT: PRINCIPLES OF OPERATIONS MANAGEMENT

The improvement of processes is a very broad mandate. Much insight can be gained by attacking the issues from a variety of perspectives that offer different principles for process management. Cumulatively, the following perspectives are extremely powerful in identifying problems, suggesting improvements, and building capabilities:

- Process capacity management
- Inventory management
- Quality improvement
- Supply chain management
- Development of capabilities

Process Capacity Management

Principle 1: Capacity is determined by the limiting resource or bottleneck. To increase capacity, increase the limiting resource.

The tendency of managers to be concerned with the efficiency of every machine or person involved in a process is misguided. The capacity of a system is not determined by the number of idle resource hours. It depends directly on the capacity of the weakest (or least-productive) link in the chain. Once this is recognized, a number of managerial insights follow.

First, since bottlenecks determine capacity, identification and alleviation of bottlenecks is the top priority for increasing capacity. Exhibit 7.5 shows five ways to identify bottlenecks. To alleviate bottlenecks, resource allocations should be ranked by the project's contribution to the scarce or limiting resource.

Second, balancing the flow of work through a process will maximize capacity. Maximizing the capacity of individual machines or processes is ineffective, because the bottleneck will constrain the system.

Third, downtime is very expensive because an hour lost on a bottleneck is lost on the entire system. Idle machines or workers in nonbottleneck activities may not have any adverse effect on capacity. Thus, idle time per se need not be viewed as a problem, but idle time *at the bottleneck* reduces the capacity of the entire process.

[handwritten margin note: beware of idle time @ the bottleneck!]

Fourth, aggregate measures of capacity, utilization, or throughput provide little actionable information. Problem diagnosis and prescriptions for improvement require that analysis be broken down for individual resources. For example, one way to increase capacity is to reduce the time spent on setup of the processes or machines, but this is effective only when setup is reduced on the bottleneck. Reducing setup in other parts of the system will increase the capacity of individual pieces of the system, but not of the process as a whole. Moreover, the bottleneck may be the capacity of machines or of labor, so the analysis should be separated on that dimension as well. For example, a hospital may have plenty of operating rooms for its surgeries, but if there are not enough nurses to staff them, the number of surgeries will be limited by the nursing capacity, not by the physical facilities.

Finally, if there is variability, excess capacity is needed at the bottleneck to keep the flow balanced. If the system has barely adequate capacity on average, then variations above the average will result in shortfalls, creating long waits for

---

EXHIBIT 7.5   How do you identify a bottleneck?

- *Least capacity:* Output of a process is limited by the capacity of the bottleneck.
- *Most utilization:* Activities with the highest rates of use are prime bottleneck suspects. If there is variability in the flow, these areas will sometimes have insufficient capacity.
- *No slack:* Bottlenecks tend to be busy all of the available time.
- *Worker complaints:* There tend to be large numbers of worker complaints about a bottleneck operation.
- *Piled-up inventory:* Inventories (or waiting lines) accumulate upstream of a bottleneck.

output or expensive work-in-process inventory or both. This raises the question of how much excess capacity is reasonable. The answer varies, but in a number of industries, utilization rates much over 80 percent deserve an extra check to confirm that the capacity is truly adequate.

Principle 2: Capacity also depends on the configuration of processes. Product structure and process structure should be matched appropriately.

Different types of processes are appropriate for different types of services or products, for different types of customer requirements, and for achieving different bases of competitive advantage. Hayes and Wheelwright (1984) identified five process types with corresponding appropriate product types:

1. Management of unique projects is generally appropriate for one-of-a-kind products such as a communications satellite or custom-made houses.
2. Job shops that produce small batches of a number of different products are appropriate for product lines with high variety and relatively low volume.
3. Disconnected line-flow (or batch) processes produce moderate volumes of several products requiring somewhat similar tasks.
4. Assembly line (or connected line-flow) processes may be machine-paced or operator-paced, using uniform production paths to produce relatively large volumes of products, usually to inventory.
5. Continuous-flow processes involve high-volume, automated, capital-intensive production, usually of commodity-type products.

The basic intuition is that a firm usually will want to operate according to this fit, which is described by the diagonal of the product-process matrix shown in Exhibit 7.6. Conversely, a firm would not want to be off the diagonal *unintentionally*. Unintentional moves off the diagonal occur, for example, when managers bow to competitive pressures by increasing product variety without adjusting operations to the expanding product line.

There are, however, several good reasons for *intentionally* choosing to be off the diagonal. First, flexible automation techniques enable firms to use connected line-flow processes to produce low-volume products economically, as do cellular manufacturing processes, putting the firm below the diagonal on the matrix. Second, a firm may choose to differentiate its product by handcrafting when competitors use automated processes. Steuben glass is a good example of differentiation by handcrafting. Third, a firm may move to automation in anticipation of growth before there is really enough volume to justify the automation.

EXHIBIT 7.6   Product process matrix.

PROCESS STRUCTURE	PRODUCT STRUCTURE			
	I Low volume, low standardization, one of a kind	II Multiple products, low volume	III Few major products, higher volume	IV High volume, high standardization, commodity products
I Jumbled flow (job stop)	Commercial printer			
II Disconnected line flow (batch)		Heavy equipment		
III Connected line flow (assembly line)		Flexible manufacturing Cellular manufacturing	Auto assembly	
IV Continuous flow				Sugar refinery

Source: Robert H. Hayes and Steven C. Wheelwright, *Restoring Our Competitive Edge: Competing Through Manufacturing* (New York: John Wiley & Sons, 1984). (Flexible and cellular manufacturing added.)

Inventory Management

In accounting and finance, inventory is often described as raw materials, work in process, or finished goods. That categorization tells *what* is in inventory, but not *why*. For operational decisions about how much inventory to hold or how to reduce the amount of inventory, it is more useful to classify inventory by the reasons for which it is held. Cycle stock is inventory held to supply the normal production process, to take advantage of economies of scale, and to avoid changing setups too often. Safety stock is inventory held in case of a disruption in supply or an unanticipated surge in demand. It is intended to cover variability in supply or demand without stock-outs or service disruptions. Buffer stock is held between workstations if the production process is not perfectly balanced. In addition, firms may have pipeline stock of goods in transit, anticipatory or seasonal stock of raw materials or finished goods held in anticipation of changes in availability, or *speculative stock* of goods held in anticipation of price changes.

All inventory has costs. The costs to firms of holding inventory include

costs of inventory
warehousing
insurance
interest (haven't sold the product yet)
currency risk

132   Operations Management: Implementing and Enabling Strategy

warehousing and insurance costs as well as the interest cost of paying for the inputs before they are used. The opportunity cost of capital tied up in inventory is often large. In addition, for firms with global operations, the cost and risk of holding inventory may depend on where the inventory is held. For example, inventory held in Brazil faces greater risk of currency fluctuation than stock held in Canada. On the other hand, if the firm experiences a shortfall, it faces the cost of a shortage or service problem as well as the setup costs or ordering costs for resupply. In addition, inventory enables a firm to fill customer orders faster than the actual production lead time.

Exhibit 7.7 gives some powerful examples of firms increasing profits by improving inventory management.

EXHIBIT 7.7   The profit impact of inventory reduction.

- Inventory management is a critical key to Wal-Mart's success.[4] The centerpiece of its operational excellence is a logistics technique known as *cross-docking*. Goods are delivered to Wal-Mart warehouses, where they are redispatched to stores, often without ever sitting in inventory. Passing products from one loading dock to another in 48 hours or less has enabled Wal-Mart to avoid inventory and handling costs associated with large orders, and 85 percent of its goods are handled through this warehouse system, which reduces its costs of sales by 2 to 3 percent compared with the industry average.

- In 1991, Campbell Soup attempted to change traditional industry dependence on promotional pricing schemes.[5] During promotions, retailers would stock up, purchasing up to three months' inventory to take advantage of the cheap unit prices, which caused huge upswings in volume at manufacturing sites. In an attempt to reform the system to even out inventory fluctuations, Campbell created the Continuous Product Replenishment program, an everyday-low-price strategy, in which Campbell would manage inventories for retail and wholesale customers through a 3090-computer mainframe. Every morning, retailers transmit inventory data electronically to Campbell, which then transmits an electronic purchase order by 2 P.M. each afternoon. Orders are shipped the following day. Inventory analysis and order placement is handled automatically by the computer. As a result, Campbell has been able to ship smaller, more frequent orders, which reduces warehouse space for both Campbell and its retailers and reduces paper-order errors and handling costs. By 1996, the program managed 30 percent of Campbell's inventory and reduced annual inventory costs by $60 million.

- High inventory levels are a costly way to disguise problems.[6] Hewlett-Packard faced the inventory dilemma of high holding costs versus late delivery costs when it realized that only 21 percent of deliveries to its 50 manufacturing divisions were on time. Early deliveries were expensive to store and hold, but late deliveries wreaked havoc on production lines.

  Defining *on-time delivery* to be anywhere from three days early to zero days late, Hewlett-Packard began to assess reasons for the breakdown in the delivery process. It found that in 60 percent of the cases, a lack of clear communication contributed to the delivery problems. Working with suppliers, Hewlett-Packard rewrote its purchase order to diminish misunderstandings and devised an electronic purchase order that flowed directly from its own computers to its suppliers' open-order management systems. The result: On-time deliveries to manufacturing divisions increased by 30 percent, decreasing bottlenecks and reducing inventory expenses by $9 million.

Principle 3: Inventory decisions hinge on the trade-off between the cost of holding more inventory and the cost of holding less (frequent setups and the risk of shortfalls). Both sides of the trade-off can be managed to reduce inventory costs relative to customer service.

The choice of *how much* cycle stock to hold depends on the trade-off between holding costs and setup or ordering costs. Larger batches require more inventory to be held, but may enable the firm to take advantage of economies of scale in purchasing and to reduce setup costs by setting up less often. Shorter setup times enable a firm to produce smaller lots more economically and thus hold less inventory. Indeed, the same basic insight underlies efforts to reduce setup times, size batches economically, and achieve just-in-time production. Decreased batch sizes allow lower inventory, reduced waste, shorter lead time, and faster recognition of quality problems.

Choices about how much safety stock to hold (or when to order cycle stock, which is another way to decide on safety stock) depend on the trade-off between the cost of holding inventory and the cost of a shortage or of service problems (as well as economies of scale in purchasing). Pipeline inventory decisions hinge on the cost of holding the inventory compared to the costs of longer lead times or shortages. Anticipatory inventory choices must balance the holding costs with the costs of shortages, substitutions, or subcontracting arrangements. Inventory held for speculation reasons will depend on the holding costs compared to the cost of price fluctuations or shortfalls.

The management of these trade-offs is often thought of in terms of order quantities, but actually also involves a much richer array of decisions, as shown in Exhibit 7.8. For example, management of safety stock is not just a matter of deciding how much inventory to carry. The need for safety stock can be managed by improving quality so that fewer replacement parts are necessary, by reducing variability with long-term contracts, by reducing lead times so that products are made to order (or more nearly made to order), or by improving forecasts so that production can track demand better.

Inventory can also be reduced by holding fewer types of products or parts in reserve. This may be done by reducing product variety, by designing products to share component parts, or by delaying the customization of different products as long as possible and holding inventory only of parts that different products have in common. (See Exhibit 7.9 for a good example of delayed customization.) These reductions in product variety, component variety, or inventory variety essentially pool the risks and require less inventory in total than if individual products or parts were held separately. Centralization of production can facilitate this type of inventory reduction effort.

EXHIBIT 7.8   Inventory flow.

Reasons for Inventory	Trade-offs	Decisions
Pipeline (distance)	Cost of inventory versus cost of reducing lead times	Change lead times Change mode of transit Invest in materials-handling equipment Backward-integrate Improve scheduling and loading practices
Cycle (lot size)	Setup cost versus holding cost	Change lot size Change warehouse procedures Change setup time Invest in technology Affect demand
Safety	Cost of inventory versus cost of downtime or cost of shortfall	Reduce variability Increase quality Change customer service requirements Reduce lead time Reduce forecast errors
Anticipation (seasonal)	Holding cost versus cost of overtime or subcontracting *or* cost of shortage	Change amount of inventory Implement quick-response manufacturing Decrease forecast error Smooth out changes in demand
Speculation (changing prices)	Holding cost versus price fluctuations, shortages	Change vendors Hedge

Source: Adapted from James Freeland, "Managing Inventories," Darden Graduate Business School Case #UVA-OM-0623. Copyright © 1987, 2000, Darden Graduate School of Business Administration.

Principle 4: Don't use inventory to mask production problems. The more production processes and quality are improved, the more inventory can be reduced without increasing the risk of shortfalls.

Inventory provides protection that is needed less and less as processes are streamlined and quality is improved. A useful analogy is to think of inventory as the water in a river and process problems as rocks. As rocks are removed, the water runs more freely, but when the water level is lowered, more rocks become apparent. When the process is repeated enough times, the river flows freely with a much lower level of water—that is, much less inventory. The message delivered by this analogy is that the cycle of improving the process and reducing inventory must be *repeated* for continuous improvement and the full benefit of skillful inventory management.

EXHIBIT 7.9   Delayed customization: Hewlett-Packard.

Hewlett-Packard (HP), in an effort to redesign its products for mass customization, has developed many different solutions to reducing production costs.[7] Because retailers needed desktop printers to be delivered on demand, HP produced to stock and faced high inventory costs. To address the problem, the company decided to redesign the product and delay the customization step. For example, instead of customizing the DeskJets for the European market at its factory in Singapore, generic printers (made in Singapore) are sent to its European distribution center in Germany. The distribution center purchases the materials to differentiate the printers (power supplies, packaging, and manuals) and customizes them for appropriate European market. While manufacturing costs are higher than if the Singapore factory customized the printers, HP is able to hold far less inventory because it now pools risk and holds stock of the generic printer rather than holding stock of each type of customized printer. Total manufacturing, shipping, and inventory costs have decreased by 25 percent.

Principle 5: Customer waiting lines (queues) may reduce the value of a product or service. Queues need to be managed to balance the (direct and indirect) costs of making customers wait versus idle server time.

In service businesses, "inventory" sometimes takes the form of queues (or waiting lines) of customers waiting to be served or, worse yet, deciding not to wait and going elsewhere for service. Queues involve servers providing a service, which normally varies in time or complexity, to customers who arrive at random (unscheduled) times. Managing the length of waiting lines is important because waiting is often costly to customers, reducing the value of the product or service for them and thus reducing the revenues that the firm can earn. The idle time of the server is also costly to the firm since the worker is being paid while idle. Given the uncertainty in both service times and arrival times, waiting time and idle server time cannot be entirely eliminated; the objective is to adjust the wasted time to minimize the sum of the costs of poor service and idle servers. (Exhibit 7.10 shows the inverse relationship of service costs and waiting costs.)

Waiting time and idle server time can be managed in a number of ways. The number of servers can be adjusted, using more servers at peak times and fewer at slower times. The rate at which service is provided can be speeded up with training, process analysis and redesign, or investment in technology. The pattern of customer arrivals can sometimes be altered with incentives for customers to arrive at nonpeak times or by extending available service hours to weekends and evenings or with 24-hour telephone services. Arrival rates can also be managed by moving to appointments rather than a first-come, first-served queue. Combining multiple waiting lines helps to ensure that one server is not idle while another has customers waiting. Sometimes this is as simple as forming

EXHIBIT 7.10 **Management of waiting times involves balancing the trade-off between making customers wait and employing more servers. Waiting cost goes down and service cost goes up as more servers are employed.**

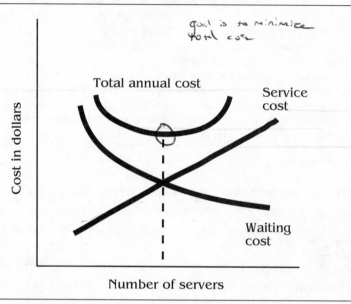

a snake line at the airport ticket counter. In other situations, cross-training servers and combining service locations may be necessary to combine queues.

As these choices are considered, it is important to keep in mind the relative costs. Idle time is not necessarily bad. It may be preferable to have a clerk idle in the stockroom part of the day than to have a queue of highly paid engineers or mechanics regularly standing idle while they wait for parts at the stockroom window.

Quality Improvement

The management of product and process quality is critical to meeting customer needs, adding value for customers, and reducing costs. Quality is a multidimensional concept encompassing product quality (e.g., performance, reliability, conformance, features, durability, value, and serviceability), service quality (e.g., atmosphere, comfort, waiting time, value, reliability, and convenience), and process quality (e.g., low cost, low variance, low defects, low waste, control, and predictability). For example, BMW and Toyota both make high-quality cars, but the dimensions of quality that they emphasize are different.

Quality management programs span departmental and even organizational boundaries. Quality programs may include measuring product defects or service problems, establishing systems to prevent quality problems, redefining supplier relationships as partnerships, improving the customer interface to better understand and deliver what the customer values, developing new products to better meet customer needs, changing employee incentives and compensation schemes, and changing business paradigms when necessary to improve processes.

Principle 6: Poor quality is costly. High quality is not free, but it can be a very good investment.

Successful quality management programs pursue quality, not for its own sake, but to enhance the net value delivered to customers by improving efficiency and by improving product or service value. Sometimes efforts to improve quality directly reduce costs by lowering the number of defects or by reducing scrap or rework. In these cases, productivity is improved by doing things right the first time around. Sometimes when quality management raises costs, the resulting products or services are differentiated in such a way that customers will pay a premium above the costs of quality management. TQM advocates point out that in both of these instances, quality is free.

Other times, quality management increases costs without an accompanying current price premium. Although quality is not free in that situation, it is a good investment if managers anticipate *future* payoffs in the form of more loyal customers, higher demand, or a future price premium based on the record of high quality. As with other investments, quality process improvement investments may not pay off instantly, but should be undertaken if they provide positive net present value to the firm. The point is not that managers should try to quantify precisely all of the benefits (which may be difficult to measure), but that the value of pursuing quality should be considered relative to its costs, especially since a poorly implemented quality program can add unnecessary costs to the business.

Principle 7: Prevention is less expensive than inspection and correction.

> *I worry that whoever thought up the term* quality control *believed that if we didn't control it, quality would get out of hand.*
>
> —Lily Tomlin

Total Quality Management, or TQM, means different things to different people, but the essence of TQM is using analysis and management of quality to improve profitability. The analysis is critical because it provides the understanding that is the basis of prevention and improvement. The alternative to prevention is inspection followed by correction of problems or selection of which goods to sell and which to scrap. Generally, it is less costly to get it right the first time than to attempt to catch problems and fix or scrap them.

There are two basic sources of problems: (1) *common causes* of quality problems due to management or process design and (2) *special causes* of quality problems due to individual workers or machines. Common causes are *systemic* and due to deficiencies or oversights in process design or management such as poor product design, machines out of order or in poor repair, inadequate training programs, poor quality or scheduling of incoming materials, improper bills of materials, inappropriate incentives for workers, poor working conditions, or other problems shared by numerous operators, service providers, or machines. Special causes are attributable to particular workers or equipment, such as lack of skill, inattention, one machine operating outside of specification, or one bad lot of incoming material. Statistical process control can be used to distinguish between the two types of problems, followed by action to redesign the system to address common causes and attention to specific workers or activities to correct special causes. Often this action takes the form of continual incremental improvement; however, it may require more radical redesign, or reengineering, of systems.

Many companies define *quality* as conformance to requirements. Service or production processes are then considered *capable* if the output meets specifications or customer requirements. If output does not meet specifications, common causes need to be addressed. Service or production processes are considered *in control* if the output is stable and predictable, although it is possible that this output could be outside of acceptable specification limits (and thus need attention to common causes to achieve capability). If a process is capable but not in control (and thus unpredictable or drifting away from acceptable output), attention to special causes is warranted. Clearly, the preferred situation is to have capable processes that are also in control.

Principle 8: Quality requires clear communication and commitment throughout the organization. What you measure and reward will improve.

In contrast to the narrow definition of quality as conformance to specifications, quality is sometimes said to be meeting customer expectations, or *what you would want if you were the customer.* From this perspective, continuous improvement requires effective systems and incentives to enhance customer value. This requires managers to identify indicators of customer value that can be measured and effectively tied to compensation. Good indicators of quality are closely tied to attributes of products or services that will command a premium price or will lower the price of a product that is as good as competitors' products.

A relatively short and stable list of clear and timely indicators is most effective. While it is easy to make long lists of possible indicators, it is better to identify a few clear measures that keep the focus on the primary goals of improving customer value. Long, detailed lists of metrics blur the focus. Similarly, focus is blurred by changing the measures too often. The program will be most successful if rewards are tied to measures that employees can improve with effort, not just by chance. Moreover, it is critical that efforts to continually improve these measures not be allowed to block potential big leaps.

The most dramatic improvements tend to come from redesigning or engineering the process to improve value delivered to customers. (Exhibit 7.11 offers an example of dramatic profit improvements from reengineering that could not have been achieved through continuous improvement.)

Quality programs have the additional benefit of being positively focused. Executives explain that after years of programs to improve productivity, they finally achieved their goals by implementing quality programs. While productivity

---

EXHIBIT 7.11   National Bicycle Industrial: Reengineering for mass customization.

In the mid-1980s, the Japanese bicycle industry hit a plateau, threatened by inexpensive imports from Taiwan and Korea and a declining U.S. export industry.[8] National Bicycle Industrial Co., one of the three largest bicycle manufacturers in Japan, needed to rethink how it would be able to compete with these low-cost producers without having to relocate offshore. Bicycle parts were purchased from large component manufacturers and assembled by a labor-intensive assembly production process. National Bicycle had also developed a competitive advantage in the development of a 3-D measurement computer system that measured the dimensional accuracy of each bike frame. The company wanted to position itself for an anticipated boom in sport bicycles, which sold for more than three times the price of transport bicycles. Expensive component parts and the inability to predict demand due to fast-changing trends in sport bicycle fashion, however, made the product extremely risky—a single instance of overproduction could strike a critical blow to the company.

Believing that customization might solve the product differentiation and inventory risk problems, the company set out to reengineer its marketing and production processes in order to produce customized bicycles on demand. Like tailored suits, each bicycle would be specially made to fit the exact size, weight, color, and accessory preferences of each customer by using the computerized measurement already developed by the company. To achieve this, a totally new process for ordering would be required. The Panasonic Order System included a list of specifications to be supplied by the customer and an adjustable "fitting scale" in each retail store, as well as a fax machine at each store to send orders immediately to National Bicycle. Guaranteed delivery within two weeks was made possible by enabling mass customization through the use of computer technology and a completely redesigned production process.

Over the next four years, unit sales for the customized sport bicycle increased by 73 percent, with over 1,500 international retailers adopting the customized system. While revenues for the Japanese industry decreased 12.1 percent from 1985 to 1991, revenues for National Bicycle increased 28.5 percent over the same time period.

programs sometimes appear technically daunting or threatening to jobs, well-executed quality programs may provide better motivation to achieve the desired results.

Supply Chain Management

Operations management considerations extend beyond the boundaries of the firm to the coordination and configuration of supplier and distributor relationships. As competitive advantage is increasingly achieved by networks of firms, each firm in the network can benefit when the preceding principles of *process capacity management, inventory management,* and *quality improvement* are applied by others in the network. This is why there is such a strong current trend toward cooperation among firms and their suppliers or distributors.

Examples abound. Firms such as Toyota invest substantial time and effort in helping suppliers to improve operations. The Gap works with its suppliers to ensure identical products from multiple sources. Raychem helped suppliers to convert to cellular manufacturing so that its own efforts in cellular manufacturing would not be constrained by suppliers' batch process delivery schedules. Laura Ashley overhauled its information systems and consolidated warehouses, achieving a fivefold increase in inventory turns over three years. National Semiconductor increased sales by over $500 million in two years while reducing distribution costs by moving products from the factory to the customer in four days or less. On the flip side, Compaq Computer estimated that it lost more than $500 million in sales in 1994 because its computers were not available when and where the customers were ready to buy.

Principle 9: Network management requires a mind-set of cooperation among partners rather than competition with suppliers.

Increasingly, it is networks of firms that determine competitive advantage; therefore, counter to the traditional view, suppliers must be thought of as partners, not as adversaries, along the value chain. In this new context, the development of trust is critical. This can be tricky, especially when firms are competing in some contexts but cooperating in others.

Network relationships should be structured to give each player incentives to make improvements that benefit the whole chain. For example, a network will not lower costs if one firm attempts to lower inventory simply by requiring a supplier to hold the inventory. Overall inventory costs, however, can be reduced by sharing information among firms so that uncertainty is reduced and less safety stock is needed, or by moving to a just-in-time system throughout the network with smaller production batches and shorter lead times. The point is that the potential gains are greater if the costs are removed from the network rather than just shifted within it. (Exhibit 7.12 defines kanban implementation of JIT.)

Principle 10: Improving information flows among network partners reduces costs by reducing variability and uncertainty and improving planning and forecasting.

The old mind-set of competition with suppliers led to practices of rarely, if ever, sharing information. Lower prices from suppliers, however, can be achieved by sharing information that enables suppliers to plan more accurately, lower inventories, and make more accurate delivery decisions.

Toyota, for example, shares its materials requirements planning (MRP) forecasts with suppliers. MRP is a widely used computerized tool that develops schedules for placing orders and performing production tasks based on data about the structure of a manufactured product, its required parts and subassemblies, and the lead times for ordering parts and making subassemblies. This tool was originally developed for firms to improve their own ordering and scheduling decisions. Toyota, however, takes a broader view. It uses MRP to give suppliers forecasts for the schedules of needed parts. This improves suppliers' information and enables reliable deliveries within lower levels of safety stock inventory. Toyota, however, does not place its orders for parts based on the MRP forecasts. Orders are based on Toyota's actual demand; the forecasts just prevent the supplier from experiencing uncertainty that is greater than Toyota's.

MRP has also been extended to enterprise requirements planning. This extends the concept of anticipating requirements beyond manufacturing to include human resources and other functions. Enterprise requirements planning methods can be used within the firm or applied to the anticipation of needs among firms in a network.

Better information flows among networks are also often achieved with information technology links such as electronic data interchanges (EDI), which enable suppliers to be notified automatically of product replenishment needs. Campbell Soup uses this approach to increase accuracy and reduce costs of keeping grocery store shelves stocked with its soups and other products.

EXHIBIT 7.12   Kanban: JIT system.

Kanban (a Japanese word meaning "card") is a way of implementing just-in-time (JIT) inventory. It is a simple system that enables suppliers to deliver JIT by signaling with a card, fax, or empty basket when supplies are needed. Thus, demand dictates the flow of inventory, in contrast to a system based on schedule or anticipation.

Principle 11: Lead-time reduction throughout the supply chain is a powerful way for the network to reduce costs and improve customer service.

Long lead times increase uncertainty, increase inventory costs, and decrease responsiveness to customer needs. Reduction in lead times throughout a network enables a just-in-time system that addresses each of these costly problems to some extent. Just-in-time systems operate on the principles of smaller batches, shorter lead times, reduced waste, and faster recognition of quality problems. These systems emphasize the critical nature of supplier relationships, because a firm may not be able to achieve the full benefits of just-in-time production unless its suppliers also operate in a just-in-time delivery (or production and delivery) mode.

Another approach to reducing network lead time is to manage capacity efficiently across product lines so that products with more certain demand are made ahead of time and items with more variable demand are made as close to the purchase date as possible. This improves the market forecasts for the harder-to predict products. Sport-Obermeyer uses this type of planning logic to work within the capacity constraints of its suppliers and reduce the peak supplier capacity that it needs to meet seasonal demands for its skiing apparel.

Development of Capabilities

A firm's processes of production and service delivery embody its capabilities. For better or worse, these capabilities position the firm for the future. It is therefore critical that decisions about current operations are made with a view to the potential future benefits of the knowledge, experience, and processes that the company develops. The development of key capabilities enables a firm to succeed in its strategy in spite of the uncertainties and changes of a dynamic marketplace.

Principle 12: The development of proprietary capabilities that enable future flexibility requires commitment and investment.

There is much misplaced debate about whether the essence of strategy is making commitments of invested capital or maintaining flexibility. Strategy critically involves both commitment of resources that build capabilities and flexibility. While some future opportunities are equally available to any fast-acting firm, many future opportunities are available only to the firms that have developed capabilities or complementary assets. The irony is that in order to have that privileged future flexibility, firms must make prior commitments. These commitments often take the form of investments in research and development, in plants or capital equipment, or in the development of capabilities. The resulting proprietary knowledge or firm-specific capabilities create an advantaged position for the firm in some possible future conditions. It is not the flexibility per se, but the advantaged position relative to firms without the prior commitment that offers significant value for the firm. The point is that the prior investment enables the firm to react more effectively, more quickly, or at lower cost than those that have to build the capabilities after the need is more certain and apparent.

Managers wanting to create strategic flexibility, therefore, cannot simply wait for opportunities to come along. Investments in flexibility must be carefully chosen to fit within the firm's strategy and values, not to reverse direction and become what the firm has chosen not to be. For example, Corning Incorporated invests in many technologies not needed for its current products, but its investments are linked to its vision of being the world leader in glass and ceramics. Corning's strategy determines appropriate investments in flexibility, and the firm devotes very substantial resources to developing capabilities in those areas.

By investing in capabilities that enable future flexibility, the firm positions itself to prosper *because* of uncertainty, not in spite of it. As the uncertain future unfolds, firms that have developed the necessary capabilities will be in advantaged positions relative to those firms that have not made the prior commitments, and thus the forward-looking firms will have benefited from the uncertainty that disadvantaged others.

OPERATIONS STRATEGY IS THE SELECTION AND BUILDING OF CAPABILITIES

Beginning in the 1980s the critical role of operations in achieving competitive advantage led firms to think strategically about operations management; they began developing and assessing operations strategies. These operations strategies, or patterns of decisions over time, should consistently support and enhance the competitive advantage sought by the firm's business strategy. Indeed, each of the firm's functional strategies (operations, finance, marketing, R&D, etc.) must be aligned with the purpose, intent, and values of the business unit strategy for the firm to achieve the full potential of that strategic vision.

Operations strategy must go beyond the pursuit of best practices and meeting the competition in implementation of the latest and greatest improvement programs. Operations give strategic leverage to a firm when efforts are focused on building capabilities in specific processes or activities that the firm does better than competitors. Thus the selection and building of capabilities is the core of operations strategy. These capabilities create opportunities for the firm to succeed in a dynamic, changing, competitive environment.

FOR FURTHER READING

Burt, David N., "Managing Suppliers Up to Speed," *Harvard Business Review,* July–August 1989.

Colley, John Jr., "Instructional Note—Planning Labor Requirements in Service Operations," Darden Graduate Business School Note #UVA-OM-0528, 1984.

Feitzinger, Edward, and Hau L. Lee, "Mass Customization at Hewlett-Packard: The Power of Postponement," *Harvard Business Review,* January–February 1997.

Fisher, Marshall L., "What Is the Right Supply Chain for Your Product?" *Harvard Business Review,* March–April 1997.

Freeland, James, "Managing Inventories," Darden Graduation Business School Case #UVA-OM-0623, 1987.

Garvin, G. A. "Competing on the Eight Dimensions of Quality," *Harvard Business Review,* November 1987.

Goldratt, Eliyahu M., and Jeff Cox, *The Goal* (Great Barrington, MA: North River Press, Inc., 1992).

Gray, Ann E., "Process Fundamentals," Harvard Business School Case #N9-696-023, 1995.

Hayes, Robert H., and Gary P. Pisano, "Beyond World-Class; The New Manufacturing Strategy," *Harvard Business Review,* January–February 1994, pp. 77–86.

Hayes, Robert H., and Steven C. Wheelright, Restoring *Our Competitive Edge: Competing Through Manufacturing* (New York: John Wiley & Sons, 1984), p. 209.

Heskett, J. L., et al., "Putting the Service-Profit Chain to work, *Harvard Business Review,* March 1994.

Maister, David H., "Note on the Management of Queues," Harvard Business School Note #9-680-053, 1979.

McClain, John O., L. Joseph Thomas, and Joseph B. Mazzola, *Operations Management: Production of Goods and Services* (Englewood Cliffs, NJ: Prentice Hall, Inc., 1992).

Morris, Peter A., Elizabeth O. Teisberg, and A. Lawrence Kolbe, "When Choosing R&D Projects, Go with the Long Shots," *Research-Tech Management,* January–February 1991.

Porter, Michael E., "What Is Strategy?" *Harvard Business Review,* November–December 1996, p. 62.

George Stalk, Philip Evans, and Lawrence E. Shulman, "Competing on Capabilities: The New Rules of Corporate Strategy," *Harvard Business Review,* March–April 1992.

ENTREPRENEURSHIP: CREATING SOMETHING NEW AND ENDURING WITH VERY LIMITED 8 RESOURCES

Entrepreneurship is about creating a successful new business starting off with resources that you already have. Successful entrepreneurs, through their imagination, energy, talent, knowledge, contacts, and activities, create new wealth in societies. They do this in two ways: by reducing or eliminating existing inefficiencies in markets and firms or by bringing new products and services to people. When people create new businesses or firms to exploit inefficiencies or create and sell new and innovative products we call them *entrepreneurs* and their activities *entrepreneurial*.[1]

Inefficiencies arise (1) when it is difficult to remove poorly used resources from where they are currently employed and reapply them in ways that are more useful and (2) when different people have different information, conjectures, or ideas about the future prospects of resources, products, customer needs and preferences, the value chains of industries, and the broad social, economic, political, and technological trends. These inefficiencies offer enterprising people a rich pool of opportunities for the creation of successful new businesses. Practically every industry has pockets of such inefficiencies, although the scale and scope of such inefficiencies are likely to be much higher in newer industries, where the technologies or customer tastes and habits have had less time to form and mature, than in older ones.

Opportunities to create new products arise because of limits to our current knowledge and also because we humans are creative and are constantly looking at the world around us in new ways. An example of limits to our knowledge would be the limitations in technology needed to satisfy certain known but unfulfilled market needs. For example, we know that the disease of cancer exists and that the market for a cure is both huge and worthwhile, but we have limited knowledge and means with which to develop a cure that would solve the problem. This known inefficiency is obviously a target for aspiring entrepreneurs (in universities, in biotechnology firms, and in large pharmaceutical companies). Every industry faces such technological frontiers (in design, manufacturing, distribution, sales, marketing, logistics, quality, etc.) and is therefore a source of both *known* and sometimes *unanticipated* opportunities.

It is from these major sources—namely, stickiness of resources, information asymmetries, limited knowledge, and creativity—that new wealth is often created for the enterprising entrepreneur and for society. Many of the great success stories of our times are ones in which ordinary individuals overcame significant odds to create something new and exciting with commonly available resources. Think of companies like Apple, Netscape, Wal-Mart, and Cisco, to name a few. How did successful entrepreneurs create such important institutions from so little? What can we learn from them? Is it possible to reduce their experiences to a set of principles that we can use? Let us now turn to these questions.

Entrepreneurial Creation

Entrepreneurial creation is the process of carving out a specific new business idea from the raw material of broad social, economic, technological, and political trends with the help of our commonly held resources, namely, talent, imagination, energy, education, time, and contacts.

Entrepreneurial Leader

An entrepreneurial leader is one who imagines a future business possibility within a framework of macroforces and trends, acts to bring the future into existence with a sense of urgency, unconstrained by the limited set of means at his or her disposal, with commitment and flexibility during the creation process, in order to profit from the journey.

WHAT IS AN ENTREPRENEURIAL OPPORTUNITY AND WHERE DOES IT COME FROM?

The first principle of entrepreneurship is that opportunities are rarely found; they have to be created and earned.

Principle 1: Entrepreneurial opportunities are rarely *found;* they have to be *created and earned.*

We have all heard the apocryphal story of the economics professor walking down the street with a student when the student exclaims, "Look, Professor, a hundred-dollar bill," and we have a good laugh when the professor says, "Don't bother picking it up—it must be a fake—if it were real, someone would have picked it up by now."

The economics textbook notion that it is impossible to anticipate and profit from "easily discovered money" appears to run counter to the many examples we find around us. We think of giant corporations, such as Microsoft and Cisco, built from modest beginnings, with many lucky breaks along the way. We also think of the many successful restaurants, retail stores, and manufacturing companies that were built and run by ordinary individuals, some less talented than us. While we certainly appreciate their hard work and sacrifice, we realize that given the right breaks and circumstances, we could be in their positions.

In one sense, the professor in our story is indeed correct. Really, how many of us have found hundred-dollar bills lying around—even once? How many people do we know who have found hundred-dollar bills twice or thrice? Opportunities rarely lie around—they have to be created and earned through imagination, hard work, and, certainly, a little bit of good luck. What we loosely call *entrepreneurial opportunities* are really broad macroforces, such as social trends, demographic shifts, technological breakthroughs and inventions, and political revolutions from which we as individuals have to carve out a specific piece that eventually becomes an opportunity for creating something new.

Entrepreneurial opportunities rarely come in prepackaged forms (like our hundred-dollar bill lying around). They usually have to be created from trends and forces much larger than the ones we directly control. To understand entrepreneurship, then, we have to understand the raw materials of entrepreneurial opportunities (the macroforces), how entrepreneurs imagine and crystallize specific new business ideas, the way in which the imagined future is created by embodying human aspirations in concrete products and markets, and the actions and forces that dictate which futures are worthwhile and which are not.

A major source of entrepreneurial opportunities is the emergence of significant changes in social, political, demographic, and economic forces that are largely outside the control of individuals. Economists call these kinds of macroforces *exogenous* changes because they often occur outside the boundaries of the business environment and are rarely influenced by them. On the contrary, these changes have a profound impact on the business world. Of course, sometimes social and political changes are a result of business practices or cultures (such as globalization),[2] but in most cases, individual firms can rarely influence such forces.

These large-scale macroforces give rise to fundamental changes in how we live, where we live, and what we prefer, thus providing numerous opportunities for entrepreneurs to create and market new products and services. Indeed, these changes also provide opportunities to renew and reinvent existing products and services. When existing firms cannot or will not adapt to these changes, opportunities are created for entrepreneurs in new firms. Demographic changes alter the size, average age, structure, composition, employment, educational status, income, and health of the population.

Social, political, and economic changes have the effect of altering the mind-sets and preferences of people. Feminism, environmentalism, globalism, health and fitness, urbanization, suburbanization, democratization, affluence, poverty, decreasing crime, and a variety of other social, economic, and political movements have fundamentally changed the attitudes of people about what is important and urgent in life. Whether or not facts change, their meaning and implications do change for us. Sometimes successful products themselves have the effect of ushering in profound changes—some claim that the birth control pill ushered in feminism and all the changes associated with this movement in society. In rare instances, the offerings of an entrepreneur unleash a profound social or political change,[3] but more often than not, social and political changes serve as the necessary ingredients from which lucrative business ideas can be hatched.

Because of these demographic, social, political, and economic changes, new needs emerge, or can be induced, in a wide variety of areas, including health, education, entertainment, financial security, housing, and travel. These changes also alter the relative size of segments and markets for existing products and services, as once dominant or popular brands and products go out of fashion and others emerge to take their place. Thus, demographic, social, political, and economic changes provide the aspiring entrepreneur with the ideal conditions for creating solutions to new, and sometimes even old, problems.

A second source of opportunity occurs through inventions and discoveries that produce new knowledge. Technological developments and breakthroughs in university laboratories and other research institutions, corporate or otherwise, offer excellent prospects for commercial opportunities. Of course, we need not interpret technology narrowly in scientific terms. The latest advances in science, arts, crafts, and music all present conditions for fashioning entrepreneurial opportunities. These developments may occur not only in scientific labs, but also in craft shops, garages, studios, and basements.

Almost all technological breakthroughs first begin as scientific or artistic discoveries or inventions. To be useful to society these discoveries and inventions have to be converted to products and processes of everyday use. It is when knowledge is embodied in products of everyday use that the intellectual property of the artist, scientist, or the lab becomes a tradable item and can be produced and exchanged for profit. Whenever and wherever artistic and scientific breakthroughs occur, conditions are created for converting the new knowledge into products and processes to solve existing problems or to create new needs and markets for these needs. One needs only to think of the recent developments in genetic and computing technologies to appreciate the possibilities of converting the science of these technologies to products and services to satisfy the everyday needs of people. This process of converting artistic and scientific knowledge into products and processes that satisfy specific needs and problems is another major source of entrepreneurial opportunity.

A third source of entrepreneurial opportunities may be found in the inefficiencies embedded in a society's existing economic structure. Inefficiencies often manifest themselves in the form of incongruities. An *incongruity* is a "discrepancy, a dissonance, between what *is* and what *ought* to be."[4] Incongruities exist when there are contradictions within the economic realities of an industry (for example, high growth accompanied by low profitability); when the reality of an industry clashes with the assumptions about it (when the things people within the industry know and think about themselves are different from the things people outside know and think about them); when there is a gap between perceived and actual customer needs and expectations; and when there is a gulf between the pace of change in the business processes within an industry and the world around it. Whenever and wherever these incongruities are large, we are faced with forces to carve out profitable new entrepreneurial opportunities. Thus, *incongruities* present conditions that are favorable for the creation of something new.

INDIVIDUALS AND MACROFORCES AND TRENDS: THE NEXUS OF OPPORTUNITY AND THE INDIVIDUAL

It is one thing to observe and appreciate the unfolding forces and trends, but an entirely different matter to be able to fashion an opportunity out of these trends and forces. How does one fashion a specific opportunity from such macroforces and trends? Norbert Wiener, an eminent scientist, commented that at the beginning stages of a new idea, the effectiveness of the individual is enormous: "Before any new idea can arise in theory and practice, some person or persons must have introduced it in their own minds. . . . The absence of original mind, even though it might not have excluded a certain element of progress in the distant future, may well delay it for fifty years or a century."[5]

The *Oxford English Dictionary* defines *opportunity* as "a time, juncture, or condition of things favorable to an end or purpose, or admitting of something being done or effected." Thus, at the minimum, an opportunity involves an end or purpose and things favorable to the achievement of it. Therefore, for something to be an opportunity there must be an "original mind," as Weiner put it. Further, in the case of an entrepreneurial opportunity, the "things favorable" consist of two categories: (1) beliefs about the future and (2) actions based on those beliefs. Thus, "before there are products and firms, there is human imagination; and before there are markets, there are human aspirations."[6] To form beliefs and to act on them requires information and a predilection to act on this information.

Where is the inspiration and information that allows one to endow and enrich the abstract and impersonal forces and trends with specific meaning so that the individual is able to imagine a product, a market, and the means to bring them together? It is partly within us and partly outside. Austrian economist Friedrich von Hayek postulated the concept of dispersed knowledge, where no two individuals share the same knowledge or information about the environment. We can distinguish between two types of knowledge: first, the body of scientific knowledge, which is stable and can be best known by suitably chosen experts in their respective fields; second, the dispersed information of a particular time and place, whose importance only the individual possessing it can judge.[7] This dispersion has an extremely important implication as far as entrepreneurial opportunities are concerned. Dispersed information explains how an enterprising individual and unfolding forces and trends combine to crystallize into an opportunity to create and exploit new products in existing or new markets.

The key is that this information is diffused in the economy; it is not a given and not equally at everyone's disposal. Thus, only a few people know about a particular scarcity, or a new invention, or a particular resource lying fallow. This knowledge is typically idiosyncratic *because it is acquired through each individual's own circumstances, including occupation, on-the-job routines, social relationships, and daily life.* It is this specific information, obtained in a particular information corridor, that leads to someone seeing opportunities for profit making.

Each and every one of us experiences the grand and impersonal forces and trends, both differentially and through our everyday activities and experiences. It is useful to separate two main categories of information sources: primary and secondary. *Primary sources* are those that exist within us: experiences, knowledge, and information that are personal. *Secondary sources* are experiences of other people and institutions, and these often involve deliberate search among sources outside of ourself and experience. Exhibit 8.1 shows some primary and secondary sources from which we can make sense of macroforces and trends to carve out a specific entrepreneurial opportunity.

EXHIBIT 8.1   Forces that create an entrepreneurial opportunity.

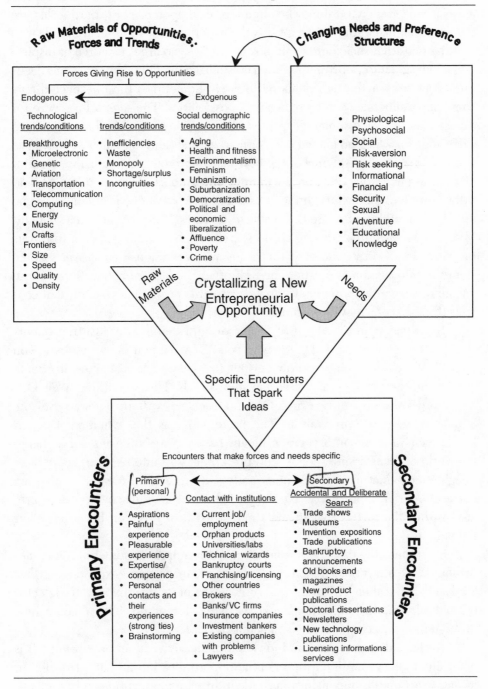

We may look within ourselves and use our painful and pleasurable experiences for inspiration. Or it may be our areas of competence or expertise that are the source of inspiration. Perhaps it is the experience of those near and dear to us—the ones that sociologists call "strong ties"—who are the source of inspiration about specific opportunities. Such crystallization of opportunities may occur serendipitously or through deliberate search. Sometimes the unexpected outcome of a deliberate search creates new possibilities. The search for a cure for cancer may well yield some unexpected new solution to an old problem, or even a new idea for which no known need or market exists and for which we may have to create a new market. Some of the best-known products are actually the result of such serendipitous creation, including Post-it notes, developed by 3M, and nylon from DuPont, where the scientists set out to solve one problem but came up with something unrelated. The biggest success story of our time, namely, Microsoft, got its break during IBM's search for an operating system to run its proposed PC. Correspondingly, the necessary inspiration for ideas may come from the information and experiences of other people or organizations. These encounters have the potential to provide us with specific information that contains the seeds of a new opportunity.

In summary, in the words of Professor Saras Sarasvathy, "Entrepreneurship is a function of individuality: who you are, what you know, and who you know."[8] We cannot imagine how certain firms could have come into being aside from the particularity of certain individuals: Disney without Walt Disney, Ford without Henry Ford, General Electric without Thomas Edison, Wal-Mart without Sam Walton. The bottom line is that when we use our individuality and our idiosyncratic means to make specific sense of a changing world of ideas, issues, needs, and preferences around us, then act on it to imagine a product-market combination, we are indeed in the presence of an entrepreneurial opportunity. We can say that we have discovered it or created it, but the fact is that it exists and it exists very much because of our individuality.

Sometimes the discovery or creation is serendipitous; sometimes it comes without much effort or search. At other times, we may have to expend much creative and physical energy to crystallize it. Some of us may be able to detect it through sheer imagination and analysis, while for others it may come only through the very act of creating a new business.

We have discussed how an individual might arrive at an opportunity. It is one thing to arrive at an entrepreneurial opportunity, but an entirely different matter to act on this opportunity and ride it through to execution and profitability. Let us now turn our attention to the predilection to act on an entrepreneurial opportunity.

PROBLEMS IN PURSUING AN OPPORTUNITY WITH LIMITED RESOURCES

Entrepreneurial opportunities present us with possibilities for both a gain and a loss. By definition, entrepreneurship requires making investments (time, effort, and money) today without knowing what the returns will be tomorrow. Economist Frank Knight pointed out an important quality about entrepreneurial opportunities—namely, that there is a fundamental uncertainty about them. He observed that one cannot collect more information or perform more analysis to reduce uncertainty. Rather, only the collective actions of competing entrepreneurs, resource suppliers, and customers can reduce uncertainties. There is no meaningful way in which to predict the future prospects of an entrepreneurial opportunity and then act on it. Knight pointed out this important distinction between *uncertainty* (outcomes that cannot be imagined and are unknowable) and *risk* (both outcomes and their probabilities can be subjectively assigned). You can insure against or diversify away risk, but you cannot insure against or diversify away an uncertainty.

Bringing new products and markets into existence usually involves an element of downside (partly influenced by risk and partly by uncertainty). Indeed, risk and uncertainty provide the opportunity for profit in the first place. This opportunity for profit attracts many people to entrepreneurship. Individuals vary in their perception of downside risks, profit opportunities, and in their aptitudes and capacities to deal with and manage them. From past research we know that people have systematic biases and heuristics for dealing with risk and uncertainty. Two biases are relevant for us. These are a *bias toward analysis* and a *bias toward action*.

Sometimes people focus on the risk and uncertainty involved in an entrepreneurial opportunity. Fear of realizing the downside often prevents individuals from acting on such opportunities. Instead, individuals have a great need to search for information in an attempt to reduce the risk and clear the uncertainties. The natural reaction is to analyze the information in order to improve one's chance of success. While such analysis can certainly improve one's chance of success, too much information gathering and analysis can lead to paralysis. More information often has the effect of raising even more questions and doubts about the entrepreneurial opportunity. Recall that such opportunities involve uncertainties that cannot be reduced by more information gathering or analysis. The only way to deal with such uncertainties is to act on them. Thus, we have a conundrum. While more information gathering and analysis may improve our chances of success, analysis begets more analysis, and the individual may never act on the opportunity. This leads to our second principle of entrepreneurship. A fear of realizing the downside increases the bias for analysis. A bias for analysis decreases the probability of acting on an entrepreneurial opportunity, even as it improves the odds of success if you act.

Principle 2: A fear of realizing the downside of creating a new business biases one toward analysis. A bias for analysis significantly decreases the probability of business entry, but increases the probability of success.

Sometimes people focus on the profit potential of an entrepreneurial opportunity. Fear of missing the upside propels individuals to act and act quickly on an entrepreneurial opportunity. In a desire to be first to market or preempt potential competitors, individuals may enter a market with poorly thought out strategies, faulty products, ill-conceived ideas, and insufficient resources. While the opportunity may be an attractive one, the urgency to act creates many loose ends and increases the number of things that can go wrong with the new venture. While a certain amount of reflection, analysis, and planning might allow the individual to improve the quality of execution, the fear of losing the upside to real or imagined competitors biases the entrepreneur toward action. Again, we have a conundrum. While the urgency to act certainly increases the probability of entering a market with a new product or service, the same urgency increases the probability of failure due to an ill-conceived idea and poor execution. This gives us the third principle of entrepreneurship. A fear of missing the upside of a good opportunity biases you toward action, which significantly increases the probability of business entry, but often decreases the probability of success.

Principle 3: A fear of missing the upside of a good opportunity biases one toward action. A bias for action significantly increases the probability of business entry, but often decreases the probability of success.

How do successful entrepreneurs deal with the tension between a bias for analysis and a bias for action, between the fear of realizing the downside and the fear of losing the upside? Through her research on successful entrepreneurs, Saras Sarasvathy found that such entrepreneurs use what she calls the *affordable loss* principle. Affordable loss is the amount of personal resources that an entrepreneur feels psychologically comfortable committing to an idea, and, at the extreme, this means committing zero resources to market. The entrepreneurs that Sarasvathy studied chose strategies and methods that involved generating early revenues with minimum expenditure of resources such as time, effort, and money. The affordable loss principle allows entrepreneurs to act without being paralyzed by fear of the downside because they do not stand to lose much if the venture fails. This leads us to the fourth principle of entrepreneurship: By adopting the affordable loss principle, enterprising individuals are able to resolve the tension between a bias for analysis and a bias for action.

Principle 4: By adopting the affordable loss principle, enterprising individuals are able to resolve the tension between a bias for analysis and a bias for action.

While idiosyncratic insight and the propensity to act on an idea are necessary for successful creation, these same qualities also present entrepreneurs with other problems. In a typical scenario, the enterprising individual does not own or control all the resources required to create the product, develop the market, establish the value-chain infrastructure, and eventually profit from his or her particular knowledge. Most of these resources have to come from other people and institutions. Thus the entrepreneur has to assemble the resources and the value-chain infrastructure before potential profits can be realized. The process of creating products and markets implies that much of the information required by potential resource suppliers—for example technology, price, quantity, tastes, supplier networks, distributor networks, and strategy—is not reliably available. Relevant information will become available only when the market has been successfully created.[9] Potential stakeholders thus have to rely on the entrepreneur for information, but without the benefit of the entrepreneur's special insight. In almost every project, entrepreneurs have more information about the true qualities of the project and themselves than do any of the other parties. Because of this information asymmetry, buyers and suppliers may be unwilling to commit the necessary investments in the specialized assets required by the entrepreneur or enter into formal contracts to develop the business. As a result, resources are difficult to assemble at the early phase of a new venture.[10]

Even if suppliers and other resource controllers were willing to overlook the uncertainty or were willing to make specialized investments by charging a risk premium, there remains the ever-present danger of opportunism,[11] in which the entrepreneur or the resource supplier may willfully fail to comply with contracts and agreements. Once specialized investments have been committed, the entrepreneur can hold the other party hostage in order to drive bargains that are more favorable.[12] Of course, once an investment has been made, it is not possible to ensure that the entrepreneur's every action (or inaction—also called the problem of *shirking*) is in the best interests of the resource suppliers.[13] In this situation, establishing cooperative relationships is difficult unless the entrepreneur is willing to make significant and irreversible commitments to the business in order to establish his or her credibility. This drives up sunk costs and therefore exposes the entrepreneur to a potential loss.

We thus have a vicious cycle. No product implies no customers; no customers implies no revenues; no revenues implies no cash for investment; no investment implies no legitimacy or credibility; no legitimacy implies no resources; no resources implies no product. This brings us to the fifth principle of entrepreneurship. All creative endeavors involve a vicious cycle: no product . . . no market . . . no revenues . . . no capital . . . no resources . . . no product.

Principle 5: All creative endeavors involve a vicious cycle: no product implies no customers; no customers implies no revenue; no revenue implies no cash for investment; no investment implies no legitimacy or credibility; no legitimacy implies no resources; no resources implies no product.

While the affordable loss principle allows the entrepreneur to keep the loss exposure low, a strategy of starting with what you already have to build the business rapidly is important for breaking out of the vicious cycle. By using their human capital (talent, education, and knowledge), special abilities (creativity, resourcefulness, enthusiasm, and optimism), and social capital (contacts with people and their contacts), entrepreneurs are able to *leverage* the necessary resources required to break out of the vicious cycle without increasing their overall exposure to loss from a failed venture. In the entrepreneurship literature, we call the strategy of using commonly available resources to break out of the vicious cycle *bootstrapping*. Bootstrapping starts with the resources that the entrepreneurs already have (rather than the idea or product) and allows them to build up the business gradually, customer by customer, product by product, employee by employee (i.e., pulling themselves up by their bootstraps).[14]

Sarasvathy extends the bootstrapping idea one step further by suggesting that many good entrepreneurs do not even start with a specific idea but develop the business idea during the process of creation. She calls this a strategy of *effectuation*. In the effectuation process, rather than starting out with a specific business idea, the entrepreneur tries to figure out what businesses can feasibly be created with the resources he or she controls. The question she asks herself is: Given *means*, what *ends* can I create? Successful entrepreneurs do not necessarily cling to a specific product or company idea but are willing to let these ideas emerge and evolve as they use the resources at their command to create a successful business enterprise. This leads us to the sixth principle of entrepreneurial creation: It is out of commonly available resources (intelligence, energy, enthusiasm, education, and contacts) that you have to break the vicious cycle.

Principle 6: It is out of commonly available resources (one's own human capital, special abilities, and social capital) that you have to break the vicious cycle.

Bootstrapping involves at least three components. These are using assets parsimoniously, leveraging social assets, and employing resourcefulness. By studying habitual entrepreneurs (people who have started several new businesses), Ian MacMillan and his colleagues highlighted the fact that these entrepreneurs used resources very sparingly.[15] They call the systematic approach to operating with sparse resources *asset parsimony strategy*. Asset parsimony strategy keeps the loss exposure of the entrepreneurs very low and at the same time allows one to create something with little. As habitual entrepreneur Zenas Block says, the basic tenet of asset parsimony strategy is to *invest your imagination before you spend your money*. The logic of asset parsimony rests on employing underused resources and thus keeping costs low. With a frugal investment strategy, the entrepreneur can pursue or create opportunities and, if necessary, abandon them with limited exposure. We can illustrate how the logic works with the following rule of thumb.[16]

- Do not buy new what you can buy used.
- Do not buy used what you can lease.
- Do not lease what you can borrow.
- Do not borrow when you can barter.
- Do not barter what you can beg (moral obligation is incurred).
- Do not beg what you can scavenge.
- Do not scavenge what you can get for free.
- Do not take for free what someone will pay you for taking.
- Do not take payment for something that people will bid for (create an auction).

While one may not be able to practice all of this successfully in an endeavor, the discipline provided by this way of thinking forces the entrepreneur, as Professors McGrath and MacMillan point out, "to find ways of avoiding costly investments and commitments until there are revenue streams to justify them. The philosophy is that assets and fixed costs are earned by the evidence of income."[17]

Where does an entrepreneur pursuing an idea obtain underused resources? One major source is the entrepreneur's social network. The currency of one's social network is friendship and goodwill rather than dollars. Since entrepreneurs have limited resources to invest, they must creatively exchange the goods and services they need for noncash assets at their disposal, such as information, friendship, charm, enthusiasm, obligations, time, and imagination. The basis of these exchanges are emotions and values rather than logic and reason. In exchanges based on social relationships, entrepreneurs use their social skills and accumulated social capital to obtain the resources necessary to build on their initial ideas much more cost-effectively than by purchasing these resources at open-market prices.

Professors Starr and MacMillan have identified five categories of *social capital* that are relevant for entrepreneurship. They are obligation, gratitude, trust, liking, and friendship.[18] Think of these as debts that people owe you because of many favors you have done for them or happy moments you have shared with them over the years. In the course of our lives, we have all accumulated an inventory of social capital and are in a position to deploy these assets at the time and place of our choosing. Building a new business offers aspiring entrepreneurs an opportunity to exchange these social assets for resources of value to the business.

Obligation is a mutually perceived understanding of a debt incurred sometime in the past and a mutual expectation that this debt will be released under suitable circumstances. Thus, obligation is earned and discharged like any other commodity. However, it remains an unstated expectation. The other person may or may not return the favor. *Gratitude* is a more valuable asset than obligation because the emotional ties are stronger. This is a case where there is clear recognition, not just an expectation, that a favor must be repaid in the future and that the account will be discharged by the return of the favor. *Trust* is even stronger than gratitude because there is a more formal recognition that favors will be returned, as opposed to mutual but unspoken expectation or perception. In contrast to obligation and gratitude, where there is always an uncertainty that an emotional debt will be repaid, trust reduces the uncertainty that an appropriate repayment will take place in the future. *Liking* takes us further in this spectrum of emotional debt. The feeling for the other individual is more intense, and there is a genuine desire to help the person we like. Our happiness and well-being are enhanced when the person we like does well, especially when we play a part in their achievements.

Finally, *friendship* evokes the strongest emotional reaction. Friendship's distinctive quality is that it can be used repeatedly without being exhausted, unlike gratitude and obligation, which may be exhausted after past favors or debts are fulfilled. Indeed, the act of helping a friend in need may actually reinforce the friendship. However, friendships are fragile, take a long time to initiate, nurture, and deepen, and are relatively rare. There are very limited opportunities to deliberately construct and use such social assets.

It is by *resourcefully* finding and employing underused assets that an entrepreneur can work his or her way out of the vicious cycle. Using social capital resourcefully to *purchase* valuable assets is not only less costly but also less risky than acquiring these assets through regular markets. This leads us to the seventh principle of entrepreneurship: Bootstrapping is an ideal way to break the vicious cycle at start-up.

Principle 7: Bootstrapping is an ideal way to break the vicious cycle at start-up.

A central tenet of entrepreneurship is the refusal to accept a lack of resources as an insurmountable constraint. Indeed, many entrepreneurs claim that you are better off having sparse resources because it lowers risk, forces you to be more creative, and focuses your attention on generating revenues to build the business—the cheapest form of capital available. Having sparse resources may have its advantages, but it also presents problems. It is well known that failure rates of new business are high. While exact statistics are not available, it is fair to say that more than two-thirds of all business start-ups do not make compensatory returns for their founders. The most common reason cited for failure is undercapitalization. That is another way of saying the new firm ran out of cash.

Cash is the most important asset for any start-up because it is the ultimate store of value that can be traded for other valuable assets. While social capital certainly helps, it is not as liquid or as tradable as cash. Further, social capital is most effective at the earliest stages of a creative process. Growth demands a more fungible asset, such as cash. The ability to *sustain* the creation process therefore hinges on the availability of cash. As soon as cash dries up in a business, it is susceptible to failure. It is important to appreciate that a business can be profitable and yet go out of business if it runs out of cash. For example, you could be very successful in selling large volumes of your product, but your customers may not pay you when you make the sale. Instead, the sale may remain locked up in *accounts receivable*. Thus, even though you have accounting profits, you have not yet collected the cash. If you have to pay your employees or if a loan outstanding comes due, you do not have the necessary cash to make these payments. While you could certainly sell your accounts receivable at a discount to institutions willing to purchase them, not all such assets are as liquid as cash, nor are the markets for these assets as predictable and reliable. If cash inflows and cash outflows in a business do not match each other, then the probability of running out of cash is quite high. This imbalance can be caused by many factors: lags between sales and collections, seasonality of business, inability to reliably predict inflows and outflows because the business is too new to be able to do so, and so on. The literature on entrepreneurship calls these problems *liabilities of newness* and *liabilities of smallness*.[19] Because your firm is new and small, you face systematic challenges in management, especially cash management.

The worst possible time to raise cash (through debt, fresh equity infusion, speeding up inflows and drying up outflows with more effective management or through sale of assets such as accounts receivables) is when you need it most. It is then that you have the least bargaining power. The need is greatest in the early stages of a new venture and when you face a crisis. Not only is your bargaining power weak, but the uncertainty surrounding your business is at its highest and your personal credibility is at its lowest when you start out and when you face a crisis. As a result, the cost of capital could become prohibitive. This leads us to the eighth principle of entrepreneurship: Cash is king/queen. Cash is most expensive when you need it most.

Principle 8: Cash is king/queen. Cash is most expensive when you need it most.

In addition to the liabilities of newness and smallness, entrepreneurial ventures face what may be called the *liabilities of complexity*. One need not emphasize the point that managing a business venture is a highly complex process. Three specific complexities need special mention. They are management of ideas, management of attention, and management of logistics.

For an entrepreneur the biggest challenge is to pursue an idea to its conclusion. Indeed, experienced entrepreneurs often claim that there is no such thing as a bad idea, only poor execution. It is generally accepted that entrepreneurs are action-oriented and need to occupy themselves with new problems and challenges. This often tends to promote short-term problem orientation and a need to demonstrate progress. This has the effect of inducing premature abandonment of ideas because even if problems are not being solved, the appearance of progress requires moving on to the next batch of problems. Thus, because of their inherent impatience, many entrepreneurs often leave behind half-solved problems or premature ideas. Related to this is also the problem of management of attention.

It is well established empirically that most individuals lack the capability to deal with complexity. People have short attention spans. The average person can retain raw data in short-term memory for only few a seconds. Because of this inherent limitation of the human mind, people are most efficient at repetitive tasks—you do not need to concentrate on repetitive tasks once they are mastered. But new business creation is hardly repetitive. There are many details to think about and execute. Each task and each new problem looks different from the earlier ones. The entrepreneur has to take on all roles, from janitor to strategist. An average person can hold or deal with only seven (plus or minus two) bits of information or issues at any given time. The moment the number of issues exceeds this, people become more subjective, solutions become increasingly error-prone, and rationalization replaces rationality. New business creation often entails dealing with more than seven or so issues at a time.

Finally, new entrepreneurs have to learn a host of new roles and functions and create new structures and systems for everything—accounting, sales, purchasing, information systems, payroll, and so on. Due to the variety and the number of tasks involved, entrepreneurs have to learn as they go. Thus errors are common as they learn the new business. These added costs from learning on the job systematically lower the probability of survival of new ventures. This leads us to the ninth principle of entrepreneurship: If cash does not kill you, logistics will!

Principle 9: If cash does not kill you, logistics will!

With so many challenges and so many things that can go wrong, why bother with entrepreneurship? How is it ever possible, especially for first-time entrepreneurs, to be successful? Is luck the only solution to success? In answering these kinds of questions, it is always good to get back to the basics and to keep things simple. As we have emphasized throughout this book, the main business of business is to create value. Entrepreneurship is about discovering or creating a new formula or yet another way to create value. By combining resources in a new and better way or by purchasing resources more cheaply and applying them to more profitable uses, entrepreneurs can create value and keep some of that added value as a reward for the creation. Indeed, "an entrepreneurial discovery (or creation) occurs when someone makes the conjecture that a set of resources is not put to its 'best use' [i.e., the resources are priced too low given a belief about the price at which the output from their combination could be sold in another location, at another time, or in another form]. If the conjecture is acted upon and is correct, the individual will earn an entrepreneurial profit. If the conjecture is acted upon and is incorrect, the individual will incur an entrepreneurial loss."[20] This is a roundabout way of saying that the essence of entrepreneurship is finding ways to buy low and sell high!

The point of this chapter is to make clear that each one of us already possesses the fundamental resources required to create value in the economy. We possess differential information. We have valuable contacts and a social network. We possess human capital: our education and knowledge. We possess intellectual resources: our talent, imagination, and emotional energy. If success in business is all about buying low and selling high, we already start with the cheapest resources at our disposal. The task of entrepreneurship is to creatively endow these resources with value that society will appreciate and for which it will pay dearly. At the end of the day, there are only a few ways to combine resources in order to create value. These few actions either influence the costs of doing business or the sales accruing from them. At the early stages, every business has three to five variables that have the most impact on costs and revenues. The trick is to find these critical factors and focus on them. By focusing the limited time, attention, and intellectual energies on the three to five critical factors that can make or break the creation process, entrepreneurs can have more control over the process. It keeps the complex, uncertain, and risky task of business creation simple and manageable. This leads us to the final principle of entrepreneurship: Every new business has three to five fundamental drivers. Find them and focus on them. The task of creation becomes easy.

Principle 10: Every new business has three to five fundamental drivers. Find them and focus on them. The task of creation becomes easy.

Entrepreneurship is about finding new formulas or ways to create value. You profit if you can find ways to use resources more cheaply and creatively to offer products and services that customers value. In this chapter we have discussed some simple rules you can follow to ensure that that the probability of success during this discovery and creation process remains high while the potential exposure to loss due to failure is kept at affordable levels.

FOR FURTHER READING

Bhide, Amar, *The Origin and Evolution of New Businesses* (New York: Oxford University Press, 2000).

Drucker, Peter, *Innovation and Entrepreneurship* (New York: Harper & Row, 1985).

McGrath, Rita, and Ian MacMillan, *The Entrepreneurial Mindset* (Boston: HBS Press, 2000).

Sahlman, William, Howard Stevenson, Michael Roberts, and Amar Bhide, *The Entrepreneurial Venture,* 2d ed. (Boston: HBS Press, 1999).

9 ACCOUNTING

Accounting is simultaneously a language, a technique, a profession, and an intellectual discipline. Often called "the language of business," accounting provides the structural framework and the quantitative vocabulary with which problems and solutions in all the disciplines of business may be expressed. Fischer Black, a partner at Goldman Sachs and academician said,

> Accounting is a language that people within a firm can use to discuss its projects and progress with one another, and that they can use to tell outsiders what's happening in the firm without giving too many of its secrets to competitors.[1]

The process by which this quantitative vocabulary is expressed is the technique of double-entry bookkeeping. Accounting is one of the oldest disciplines, tracing its roots to the invention of double-entry bookkeeping by Venetian merchants in the fifteenth century. Today, the profession is highly developed, with codes, rules, self-governing bodies, and a certification process for its practitioners. Governing bodies, courts of law, and the general public give great credence to the representations of performance given by CPAs.[2] Finally, accounting reports help decision makers target problem areas of the business, thereby beginning the process of implementing change.

This chapter has five objectives:

1. Introduce double-entry bookkeeping, and suggest that it embodies the *systemic* nature of the firm.

2. Emphasize that accounting reports are at best *approximations* of reality.
3. Offer a step-by-step guide to reading financial statements.
4. Illustrate the analysis of financial statements for the purpose of deciding on the financial health of a company.
5. Explore how variance analysis of a project or business unit can yield valuable insights for the operating manager.

DOUBLE-ENTRY BOOKKEEPING CAPTURES THE SYSTEMIC NATURE OF THE FIRM

In studying the financial statements of a firm, the novice often digs no deeper than the results that appear on paper. But the seasoned businessperson sees through these statements to the considerable richness of activity represented by them. Financial statements model the fact that the firm is a *system,* an entity with linkages among its internal parts. To attune your thinking about how financial statements may be used to see into the rich activity of the firm, consider two ideas about how systems behave:

- *Systems resonate under turbulence.* Turbulence doesn't stay contained. Changes in one part of the firm ripple elsewhere in the firm. The marketing department is affected by what happens in the manufacturing department. A difficult customer can delay payments, return goods to your warehouse, cancel orders, or demand superpremium service—any one of these actions affects two or more areas of your company. A decision to spend cash to buy a machine will result in an increase in the assets found on the plant floor and a decrease in the cash balance of the firm's checking account. Subsequently, the periodic recognition of depreciation expense related to the machine will affect the firm's profits and assets. Accounting provides a means of documenting the resonance within the firm under turbulence.
- *Systems can amplify or dampen turbulence.* A growing firm is a classic example of how turbulence can become *amplified* within the firm. Anticipating that next year's sales will be greater than this year's, managers might invest in more inventory (to prevent stock-outs), beef up the marketing staff, invest in more productive capacity, and expand bank lines of credit. But good management practices might also *dampen* turbulence: tightening inventory controls, asking staff to work longer hours rather than hiring more people, adding a third shift in the plant rather than buying more machinery, and so on. Accounting can't change the turbulence, but it can

help document how the internal workings of the firm manage turbulence and thus prepare managers to make better decisions.

"Systems thinking" is a management approach oriented to dealing with the unusual turbulence of recent years arising from forces such as deregulation, globalization, rapid technological change, and demographic change. To think systemically is to take into account all direct and indirect effects of a managerial decision—anywhere those effects might hit the firm. In representing the "system" of the firm, accounting facilitates systems thinking.

The fundamental concept of the accounting model of the firm is that the resources of the firm and the claims upon those resources *balance*. This mirrors economic common sense: Claims on the firm should equal the assets standing behind those claims:

$$\text{Assets} = \text{liabilities} + \text{owners' equity}$$

The notion of balance is reflected in the equal sign in this equation. Increases in assets must be financed by increases in liabilities (e.g., a bank loan) or in equity (e.g., a sale of stock). Decreases in assets (such as a debt payment or dividend payment) must be offset with decreases in the corresponding type of capital. Stated in terms of this equation, changes (Δ) must balance out somewhere in the closed system of the firm:

$$\Delta\text{Assets} = \Delta\text{liabilities} + \Delta\text{owners' equity}$$

The simplest event in the firm must have at least *two* entries in the firm's accounting books, because this is necessary to capture the nature of balancing, and thus arises the term *double-entry bookkeeping*.

Typically, one encounters three financial statements in an annual report:

1. *Income statement.* This is a measure of the *flows* of business over a period of time expressed in terms of profit and loss. Some of these flows will have been adjusted or matched in time to occur with other flows that are economically related. For instance, a unit of goods might have been shipped in 2000, but the cash from this sale not received until early 2001. Accounting policies might recognize the sales revenues in the 2000 fiscal year since that is when the sale occurred in economic terms. This represents the *accrual basis* of revenue recognition.

2. *Balance sheet.* This presents a snapshot of the assets of the firm and the claims on those assets at a particular point in time (i.e., the end of the fiscal year). In other words, the balance sheet measures the amount of assets, liabilities, and owners' equity.

3. *Statement of cash flows* Since the income statement and balance sheet result from accruals and allocations made by accountants, it can be difficult to tell what actually happened to the firm in terms of the flows of cash: Did it generate more cash this year than last? The statement of cash flows recasts the performance of the firm into cash-based accounting and helps the reader understand the changes in cash and their causes.

The raw material for developing these statements is a series of *accounts* or "bins" into which the transactions within the firm are recorded. At least one account exists for each line item in a financial statement. For a large corporation, each line item would have many supporting accounts; these accounts run into the thousands. Keeping the books in balance is accomplished by a simple notion of debits and credits and by envisioning an account as two columns framed by a *T* (see Exhibit 9.1).

- *Debit* refers to the left side of a T-account and is used to record an increase (if it is an assets T-account) or a decrease (if it is a T-account in liabilities or owners' equity). Because the results of the income statement flow into the owners' equity account, debits record expenses of the business.
- *Credit* refers to the right side of a T-account and is used to record a decrease in assets or an increase in liabilities or owners' equity. Credits record revenues of the business.

These definitions guide the bookkeeper in deciding how to record a transaction in a firm's system of accounts. Also, at the end of an accounting period, the increases and decreases in an account are summed to get the closing balance for the period. Much of the artistry in bookkeeping is in correctly judging through which accounts in the closed system of the firm a transaction should ripple.

To illustrate double-entry bookkeeping, consider these examples. First suppose that The Walt Disney Company sold $100 million *Pocahontas* videotapes. Suppose the cost of these goods was $25 million.

- To reflect the receipt of the sale proceeds, the bookkeeper would debit (increase) cash $100 million, and credit (increase) sales revenues $100

EXHIBIT 9.1   T-Account.

	T-Account	
Debits		**Credits**

million; the sales revenue causes an increase in owners' equity of an equal amount.

- To reflect the shipment to customers of goods with a cost of $25 million, the bookkeeper would credit (decrease) inventories $25 million and debit (increase) cost of goods $25 million; the cost of goods sold is an expense that causes a decrease in owners' equity of an equal amount.

Consider another example. In 2001, Disney paid its shareholders a dividend of $438 million. To reflect this transaction, the bookkeeper would credit (decrease) cash and debit (decrease) shareholders' equity. Unlike the recognition of cost of goods, however, a dividend represents a distribution of earnings and is not considered to be an expense of the business.

As a final example, Disney borrowed $3.1 billion in debt in 2001 and used part of it to repay debt of $2.8 billion. To reflect the borrowing, the bookkeeper would debit cash $3.1 billion and credit debt $3.1 billion. To reflect the debt repayment, the bookkeeper would credit cash $2.8 billion, and debit debt $2.8 billion.

Common to every one of these transactions is this simple but important feature: Every debit (credit) has a balancing credit (debit) somewhere in the system of accounts. At the end of the year, the summation of the credits and debits in each account expresses the *flow* of transactions through that account and the *stock* or standing of that account at the end of the period. The total of the debit account balances must equal the total of the credit account balances.

THE TRUTH ABOUT ACCOUNTING: IT PRECISELY GIVES AN "APPROXIMATE" VIEW

Outsiders view accounting as a highly precise, careful specialty, guided by hard rules and professional certification. To novice decision makers, the figures presented in a financial statement carry the aura of certainty. But the truth is that *financial statements are only estimates of reality,* not quantities known with certainty.[3] E. Richard Brownlee II, CPA, has written the following:

> Accounting is a necessary and useful, but not sufficient, language. Here are some reasons why. Our traditional accounting system was primarily designed for merchandising and manufacturing companies engaged in domestic business activities in an environment characterized by gradual, not rapid, change, and whose *assets* were largely tangible and whose *liabilities* were largely known both in terms of type and amount. Timely financial reporting typically requires extensive estimates and judgments by management. *Two* overriding concepts prevail—*matching* and *conservatism,* yet these can conflict. The financial reporting model attempts to

achieve *two* primary qualities—*relevance* and *reliability,* yet these can conflict. The underlying accounting standards are influenced by politics and personalities, special interests, and compromise. The financial reporting model is intended to present a fair representation of the past, yet also meet the needs of users whose primary interest is in forecasting the future.[4]

In trying to represent the economic reality within a firm, accounting recognizes revenues and expenses not when cash changes hands, but when the goods are delivered (in the case of revenues) or the goods are used (in the case of expenses). This reflects the belief that performance is best reflected when related revenues and expenses are *matched* in the same period. Because of the time lags between the start and completion of an economic event, it may be necessary to *accrue* financial results so that they can be matched. Accrual accounting is the dominant practice in business. But accrual accounting requires many judgments, as Brownlee acknowledges. The "precisely estimated approximation" nature of financial statements is well illustrated by a careful reading of the financial statements of the firm.

HOW TO READ AN ANNUAL REPORT

Reading financial statements is one of the best ways to gain an understanding of accounting and its significance to business. The Walt Disney Company's *2001 Annual Report* covers the activities of the firm in fiscal year 2001 and its condition at September 30, 2001. Annual reports of public companies are public documents that can be downloaded as Form 10-K from www.sec.gov. The following guided tour illustrates the nature of Disney's financial statements, how to read them, and how to read the rest of the report. Let's enter Disney's financial "Magic Kingdom."

Step 1: Read the letter from the chair of the board.
This is usually the first item in the annual report and is valuable mainly for understanding at the start the *strategic intent* of the managers of the firm. The letter usually sums up performance during the past year and expresses elements of the CEO's goals, values, and vision for the future. The letter in the 2001 annual report from Michael D. Eisner, chairman and CEO of Disney, suggests a troubled 2001, but exhorts shareholders to be optimistic that the company will ". . . ride out the current turbulence . . . ultimately moving on to new levels of success." Here are more excerpts from Eisner's letter:

> . . . I want to make clear my disappointment with the fact that the overall equity value of the company as I am writing this has not risen as it has in the past. . . . We

are a public company, and we want you to own a growth company. At the same time, I don't think about The Walt Disney company quarter to quarter. I think about The Walt Disney Company quarter to quarter to quarter to quarter to quarter; in other words, over the long term. It is important for this great institution to always be positioned for the future, to spend the needed capital, to steer the prudent and moral course, to make sure we are here to entertain another day. I think therefore we are poised for another growth spurt as investors around the world recognize what we've done and where we are headed creatively and how strong our brand and balance sheet are.

Through these words, a careful reader would get a hint of the issues to look for in the firm's results for 2001, along with insights about the next year. For instance, consider the following possible issues and insights:

- *Shareholder wealth is important.* How profitable has the firm been in the past year? How has shareholders' equity changed? Did the firm share much of its profits with the shareholders in the form of dividends? Were the firm's actions and performance consistent with trying to increase the firm's stock price?

- *Growth is a key objective.* Eisner thinks Disney is "poised for another growth spurt." What growth initiatives has the company implemented? Has Eisner managed costs and investments carefully while pursuing his strategy? Are his expectations for growth realistic?

- *The Disney brand is a huge asset.* Unfortunately, according to historical-cost and conservatism principles of Generally Accepted Accounting Principles, internally developed intangible assets such as patents, brands, and R&D are accorded no value on the balance sheet. Are there other places in the firm's financial performance where the valuable brand might be reflected?

Critical thinking prompted by a close reading of the Chair's letter can lead to better analysis of a firm's financial statements.

Step 2. Look at the auditor's letter.

Investors in companies ordinarily require an annual audit of those companies' financial statements—this is one of the most basic protections intended to ensure compliance with generally accepted accounting and reporting standards. At the end of the financial report, one usually finds a letter from the firm's independent auditors explaining what they did and what they concluded. Following the Disney 2001 financial statements, PricewaterhouseCoopers wrote the following:

In our opinion, the accompanying consolidated balance sheets and the related consolidated statements of income, stockholders' equity, and cash flows present fairly, in all material respects, the financial position . . . in conformity with accounting principles generally accepted in the United States of America.[5]

This is a positive report. A negative opinion by an auditor might cite unfair or unacceptable presentation, nonconformance with Generally Accepted Accounting Principles (GAAP), and material misstatement. In some cases, auditors must explain any material uncertainties affecting the financial statements—these uncertainties depend on the probability of loss due to uncertainty of such things as the "going concern"[6] assumption that underlies the preparation of most financial statements, uncertainty regarding the valuation or realization of assets, or uncertainty due to litigation. *Anything but a positive report (such as Disney's) should, like a flashing red light, signal a major concern to the reader of the report.*

Step 3. Review the income statement.

The income statement is prepared using accrual accounting and is the primary measure of operating performance of the firm. It is organized on the following simple notion:

$$\text{Revenues} - \text{expenses} = \text{profits}$$

This model can help the reader sort out three concerns in looking at the income statement:

1. *The degree of profitability, and why.* Is the firm making or losing money?
2. *The trend of profitability, and why.* Are profits increasing or declining over time? Are these due to changes in revenues, expenses, or both?
3. *The composition of profits.* Are the size and trend of profits due to ordinary operations or to odd events that might distort the true profitability of the firm?

To illustrate, consider Disney's 2001 income statement, shown in Exhibit 9.2. The company went from a $920 million profit in 2000 to a loss of $158 million for 2001. Profits for 2000 likewise receded from 1999 by $380 million. Earnings per share went from $0.57 in 2000 to −$0.02 in 2001. This is bad news for investors. To what can we attribute this?

- *Revenues were down.* A 0.5 percent decrease in 2001, attributable to the Media Networks and Consumer Products[7] businesses.
- *Operating margins decreased slightly.* Segment operating costs as a percent of sales increased to 84.2 percent in 2001 from 83.8 percent in 2000, mostly due to the Media Networks business.

EXHIBIT 9.2   Income statement, The Walt Disney Company.
(values are in millions of U.S. dollars except for per-share figures)

Year Ended September 30	2001	2000	1999
Revenues			
Media networks	$9,569	$9,836	$8,012
Parks and resorts	7,004	6,809	6,141
Studio entertainment	6,106	6,011	6,176
Consumer products	2,590	2,762	3,126
Total	25,269	25,418	23,455
Costs and expenses			
Media networks	7,811	7,851	6,500
Parks and resorts	5,418	5,194	4,647
Studio entertainment	5,846	5,885	6,014
Consumer products	2,189	2,376	2,534
Total	21,264	21,306	19,695
Operating income			
Media networks	1,758	1,985	1,512
Parks and resorts	1,586	1,615	1,494
Studio entertainment	260	126	162
Consumer products	401	386	592
Total	4,005	4,112	3,760
Other Income/(expenses)			
Corporate and unallocated shared expenses	(406)	(354)	(335)
Amortization of intangible assets	(767)	(1,233)	(456)
Gain on sale of businesses	22	489	345
Net interest expense and other	(417)	(497)	(612)
Equity in the income of investees	300	208	(127)
Restructuring and impairment charges	(1,454)	(92)	(172)
Total	(2,722)	(1,479)	(1,357)
Income before income taxes, minority interests, and the cumulative effect of accounting changes	1,283	2,633	2,403
Income taxes	1,059	1,606	1,014
Minority interests	104	107	89
Income before cumulative effect of accounting changes	120	920	1,300
Cumulative effect of accounting changes			
Film accounting	(228)	—	—
Derivative accounting	(50)	—	—
Net (loss) income	($158)	$920	$1,300
Earnings/(loss) per common share			
Diluted	($0.02)	$0.57	$0.62
Basic	($0.02)	$0.58	$0.63
Average number of common and common equivalent shares outstanding			
Diluted	2,100	2,103	2,083
Basic	2,085	2,074	2,056

Source: 2001 Form 10-K, The Walt Disney Company, filed with the U.S. Securities and Exchange Commission.

- *Unfortunately, the cost of corporate activities ballooned.* But this is due mostly to restructuring and impairment charges. In fact, Disney launched cost-cutting measures in 2001, including trimming its workforce by around 4,000 and streamlining certain operations. Hopefully, these measures will improve profitability in the coming years.

- *Income before taxes and accounting changes was down by 87 percent.* This is an important line to inspect, because taxes and accounting changes can obscure operating profitability.

- *Accounting changes took a large bite out of earnings in 2001.* Almost $278 million. Nevertheless, these accounting changes are odd events that try to bring the statements in line with new policies rather than reflecting fundamental changes in profitability. Moreover, these accounting changes are probably not *cash events,* so from an investor's standpoint they may not be material to the recent year's results.

Overall, this is a very disappointing income statement for investors. Disney's profitability suffered a blow in 2001.

Step 4. Review the balance sheet.

The major categories of assets are classified and ranked on the balance sheet according to their liquidity, with cash and other current assets (those that should be converted to cash within one year) at the top and fixed or intangible assets at the bottom.[8] On the other side of the sheet, current liabilities (those due within one year) are listed at the top. Next is debt and other liabilities. At the bottom is shareholders' equity, the residual claim on the firm. Most components of the balance sheet are reported at the lower of *historical cost* or *market value.* The balance sheet does not report all assets and liabilities of the firm, only those that are *measurable, reasonably certain,* and *relatively easy to value*—this is just another manifestation of the conservatism principle in accounting. Contingencies (potential assets or liabilities arising from past events such as a lawsuit) can be difficult to measure and uncertain. The values of brand names, trademarks, and, in Disney's case, proprietary animated characters are difficult to measure and uncertain and thus are not reported. In reading the balance sheet, one should aim to satisfy four questions:

1. *Is the firm solvent?* Solvency is the ability to pay liabilities as they come due. The primary test of this is to see whether the value of assets exceeds the value of liabilities.

2. *Are the firm's assets sufficiently liquid?* Liquidity measures the ability to meet near-term cash obligations—these might be liabilities that need to

be repaid, a forthcoming payroll, or the need to purchase raw materials in advance of a sudden surge in demand. One test of liquidity is whether current assets exceed current liabilities (whether the *current ratio* is greater than 1.0.) Another test focuses on "quick" current assets such as cash and receivables and asks whether these are greater than current liabilities (the *quick ratio* is another way to gauge the relative size of these balances.)

3. *What is the mix of assets?* The reader should look for unusual concentrations or categories of assets. Concentration of the firm's resources into a speculative venture would be a cause for concern. Concentration in cash might suggest undue risk aversion or the lack of investment opportunities with attractive return potential. Also, asset categories that seem to have no relevance to the firm's business purpose should raise a red flag.

4. *What is the mix of financing?* Most mature firms finance their businesses with *some* debt. The absence of debt, or a very high proportion of debt, should raise questions about the outlook of senior management, and/or the bets they are making. Again, odd categories of capital (e.g., exchangeable subordinated bonds[9]) may indicate managerial creativity, or it may indicate desperation on the part of management—either way, it should invite the thoughtful investor to dig deeper.

The balance sheet of Walt Disney Company as of September 30, 2001, is shown in Exhibit 9.3. The firm appears to be *solvent* in general terms, since the assets ($43.7 billion) handily exceed liabilities of about $21 billion. The firm appears to be *liquid,* too: Current assets (totaling $7.0 billion) exceed current liabilities (accounts payable, accruals, taxes payable totaling about $6.2 billion). The decline in total assets from the previous year is not necessarily cause for alarm; it might have been brought about by good reasons (e.g., more prudent capital spending) and/or bad reasons (e.g., write-off of assets). Further investigation would be warranted. Disney's mix of assets doesn't seem unusual—certainly the concentration in theme parks is understandable because of the capital intensity of that business. Finally, the financing mix of the firm shows no sharp departures in 2001 from 2000—bank debt has increased only slightly. Overall, the balance sheet raises no red flags.

Step 5. Read the statement of cash flows.

This statement reports the cash receipts and outflows classified as operating, investing, and financing activities—a breakdown that helps the reader determine where changes in cash emerge. The key questions a reader should ask include the following:

EXHIBIT 9.3   Balance sheet, The Walt Disney Company.
(values are in millions of U.S. dollars except for per-share figures)

Year Ended September 30	2001	2000
Assets		
Cash and cash equivalents	$618	$842
Receivables	3,343	3,599
Inventories	671	702
Television costs	1,175	1,162
Deferred income taxes	622	623
Other assets	600	635
Total current assets	7,029	7,563
Film and television costs	5,235	5,339
Investments	2,061	2,270
Parks, resorts, and other property, at cost		
Attractions, buildings, and equipment	19,089	16,610
Accumulated depreciation	(7,728)	(6,892)
Subtotal	11,361	9,718
Projects in progress	911	1,995
Land	635	597
Subtotal	12,907	12,310
Intangible assets, net	14,540	16,117
Other assets	1,927	1,428
Total	$43,699	$45,027
Liabilities and shareholders' equity		
Current liabilities		
Accounts payable and other accrued liabilities	$4,603	$5,161
Current portion of borrowings	829	2,502
Unearned royalty and other advances	787	739
Total current liabilities	6,219	8,402
Borrowings	8,940	6,959
Deferred income taxes	2,730	2,833
Other long-term liabilities, unearned royalties, and other advances	2,756	2,377
Minority interests	382	356
Stockholders' equity		
Preferred stock, $.01 par value		
Authorized—100.0 million shares; issued—none		
Common stock		
Common stock—Disney, $.01 par value		
Authorized—3.6 billion shares; issued—2.1 billion shares	12,096	9,920
Common stock—Internet Group, $.01 par value		
Authorized—1.0 billion shares; issued—45.3 million shares as of September 30, 2000	—	2,181
Retained earnings	12,171	12,767
Accumulated other comprehensive income	10	(28)
Subtotal: common equity	24,277	24,840
Treasury stock, at cost—81.4 million and 31 million Disney shares	(1,395)	(689)
Shares held by TWDC Stock Compensation Fund II, at cost		
Disney—8.6 million and 1.1 million shares	(210)	(40)
Internet Group—0.9 million shares as of September 30, 2000	—	(11)
Subtotal: shareholders' equity	22,672	24,100
Total liabilities and shareholders' equity	$43,699	$45,027

Source: 2001 Form 10-K, The Walt Disney Company.

- Was the firm a net user or a net generator of cash that year?
- What operational, investing, or financing elements proved to be major drivers of cash flow?
- Are there any major departures in the trends of the cash flow items?

Exhibit 9.4 gives Disney's statement of cash flows. This shows that the firm was a net user of cash in 2001 ($224 million), which was a significant change from 2000 and 1999 when Disney was a net generator of cash. This swing can be attributed to a decline in cash from operations after taxes (about $700 million) and an increase in cash used in investing activities of about $900 million. The line items suggest a couple of interesting occurrences: (1) Investments in parks, resorts, and other property slowed down (perhaps Disney is winding down on an expansion phase and getting ready to harvest the fruits of its spending), and (2) repurchases of common stock increased from $166 million in 2000 to $1.1 *billion* in 2001. At the same time, new borrowing nearly offset Disney's repayment of debt. The reader can conclude that at least part of Disney's borrowings were used to repurchase stock. After all, as Michael Eisner hinted in his letter to shareholders, Disney's stock did not perform too well during the year, thus providing a buying opportunity. Overall, the statement of cash flows does not cause any reason for concern.

Step 6. Read the footnotes to the financial statements.

These can be very technical and difficult for the novice to understand. But aficionados of annual reports say that the footnotes often contain juicy insights. For instance, the footnotes to Disney's report offer, among other things, the following important information:

- A breakdown of revenue, operating income, capital expenditures, and depreciation expenses by business segment
- A breakdown of restructuring charges (interestingly enough, the bulk of which came from the impairment of an Internet-related intangible asset)
- An update on the turnaround at Euro Disney (which, after a five-year restructuring period, is finally paying royalties and management fees to Disney!)
- Details of acquisitions and dispositions by Disney during the year
- Disney's borrowings, pension liabilities, off-balance-sheet financing activities, stock incentive plan, and tons of other good stuff!

Individually, such tidbits may not be terribly significant at present, but they can offer insights into the future of the company and can signal management's outlook.

EXHIBIT 9.4 Statement of cash flows, The Walt Disney Company.
(values are in millions of U.S. dollars)

Year Ended September 30	2001	2000	1999
Net income (loss)	($158)	$920	$1,300
Operating items not requiring cash			
Depreciation	987	962	851
Amortization of intangible assets	767	1,233	456
Cumulative effect of accounting changes	278	—	—
Restructuring and impairment charges	1,247	92	70
Gain on sale of businesses	(22)	(489)	(345)
Equity in the income of investees	(300)	(208)	127
Minority interests	104	107	89
Other	187	303	205
Changes in			
Receivables	279	205	376
Inventories	54	65	103
Other assets	33	183	(165)
Accounts and taxes payable and other accrued liabilities	(283)	(41)	388
Film and television costs	(183)	192	(867)
Deferred income taxes	58	231	(20)
Cash provided by operations	3,048	3,755	2,568
Investing activities			
Investments in theme parks, resorts and other property	(1,795)	(2,013)	(2,134)
Acquisitions (net of cash acquired)	(480)	(34)	(319)
Dispositions	137	913	—
Proceeds from sale of investments	235	207	202
Purchases of investments	(88)	(82)	(39)
Investments in Euro Disney	—	(91)	—
Other	(24)	9	—
Cash used by investing activities	(2,015)	(1,091)	(2,290)
Financing activities			
Borrowings	3,070	1,117	2,306
Reduction of borrowings	(2,807)	(2,494)	(2,031)
Repurchases of common stock	(1,073)	(166)	(19)
Commercial paper borrowings, net	(186)	(741)	(451)
Exercise of stock options and other	177	482	204
Dividends	(438)	(434)	—
Cash (used) provided by investing activities	(1,257)	(2,236)	9
Increase (decrease) in cash and cash equivalents	(224)	428	287
Cash and cash equivalents, beginning of year	842	414	127
Cash and cash equivalents, end of year	$618	$842	$414
Supplemental disclosure of cash flow information:			
Interest paid	$625	$583	$659
Income taxes paid	$881	$1,170	$721

Source: 2001 Form 10-K, The Walt Disney Company.

Step 7. Read management's discussion of the year's performance.
An annual report typically contains a detailed discussion of the year just past. The management discussion usually reflects management's efforts to influence the reader's assessment of the company (accounting rules and government regulations limit management's leeway in other areas of the annual report). Disney's annual report is no exception—it is filled with pages of photographs and an upbeat review of the year. It helps for one to cultivate a critical frame of mind before reading the management's discussion.

ASSESSING THE FINANCIAL HEALTH OF A FIRM

Unfortunately, simply reading the annual report of a firm may not give you the basis to conclude whether the firm is healthy. Further, independent analysis almost always rewards the investor with fresh insights. The key to this added work is *ratio analysis*. Financial ratios show the performance of the firm in four important areas:

1. *Profitability* is measured both in terms of *profit or expense margins* and as *investment return*. Investors focus on the latter measures of profitability.

2. *Leverage ratios* measure the use of short-term and long-term debt financing by the firm. In general, higher use of debt increases the risk of the firm. Higher ratios of debt to equity and to capital suggest higher financial risk. The ratio of *earnings before interest and taxes* (EBIT) to *interest expense* measures the ability of the firm to cover its interest payments; lower levels of this ratio (such as two times or less) suggest high risk.

3. *Asset-utilization ratios* measure the efficiency of asset use. For instance, the sales-to-assets ratio shows how many dollars of sales are generated per dollar of assets; a higher figure suggests more efficiency, and a lower figure suggests less efficiency. Over the long term, differences in the growth rates of sales and assets can lead to production problems of over- or undercapacity. Days in receivables[10] shows how many days it takes to collect the average credit sale; the longer it takes, the greater the investment in receivables.

4. *Liquidity ratios* measure the resources available to meet short-term financial commitments. The *current ratio* is the ratio of all current assets to all current liabilities. The *quick ratio* is the ratio of only cash and receivables (i.e., assets that can be liquidated quickly) to all current liabilities.

The careful analyst should examine both the *size* and *trend* of these ratios, and, if possible, compare them to the ratios for peer firms (i.e., firms in the same industry).
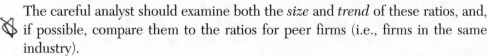

It can be difficult to assemble a unified view of the firm from these ratios. Fortunately, the *DuPont System of Ratios* can help the analyst integrate his or her insights. The DuPont System was developed during World War I when the financial officers of E.I. du Pont de Nemours and Company sought a system to assess the health of their firm and of the segments within the firm. This system decomposes *return on equity* into several constituent pieces: *return on sales*, which measures the profitability of each dollar of revenue; *sales turnover*, which measures the dollars of sales produced by each dollar of assets; the ratio of *assets to equity*, which measures the *financial leverage* of the company (i.e., dollars of assets carried by each dollar of equity). Algebraically, the product of these three components is the return on equity:

Return on equity = Return on Sales × Sales Turnover × Financial Leverage[11]

$$\frac{\text{Profit}}{\text{Equity}} = \frac{\text{profit}}{\text{sales}} \times \frac{\text{sales}}{\text{assets}} \times \frac{\text{assets}}{\text{equity}}$$

By examining the DuPont System for comparative years, it is possible to determine the sources of changes in return on equity.

Exhibit 9.5 presents selected ratios calculated from Disney's 2001 Form 10-K. The profitability ratios show Disney's profitability decline in 2001, both at the operating and net income levels. It is worth noting, however, that profitability at the net income level dropped off much more sharply than at the operating level. The leverage ratios indicate a slight increase in debt financing—however, the interest coverage ratios show that Disney still has plenty of room for leverage. The asset utilization ratios show improvement in 2001 over 2000—the firm is using its assets more carefully. Finally, the liquidity ratios of the firm have improved in 2001 from 2000, suggesting an improved ability of the firm to meet its cash demands as they appear. In conclusion, a financial ratio analysis of Disney's statements reveals that the company had a difficult 2001 but that it remains a very healthy firm.

ASSESSING PERFORMANCE AGAINST A PLAN: MANAGERIAL ACCOUNTING

Financial statements present the performance of the firm to outsiders such as investors, creditors, government regulators, and concerned citizens. However, these statements are too aggregative and backward-looking to help operating managers in their day-to-day work in pushing the firm toward annual performance goals.

Managerial accounting uses many of the tools and concepts of financial accounting to help the operating manager understand his or her unit's performance

EXHIBIT 9.5   Ratio analysis of financial statements, The Walt Disney Company.

Year Ended September 30	2001	2000	1999
Profitability			
Operating Margin (%) (Operating Income/Sales)	15.8%	16.2%	16.0%
Pretax Profit Margin (%) (Income Before			
Taxes & Accounting Changes/Sales)	5.1%	10.4%	10.2%
Return on Sales (%) (Net Income/Sales)	−0.6%	3.6%	5.5%
Return on Equity (%) (Net Income/			
Shareholders' Equity)	−0.7%	3.8%	—
Return on Net Assets (%) (Net Income/(Assets-			
Payables and Accruals))	−0.4%	2.4%	—
Return on Assets (%) (Net Income/Assets)	−0.4%	2.0%	—
Leverage			
Debt/Equity Ratio (%)	43.1%	39.3%	—
Debt/Total Capital (%)	30.1%	28.2%	—
EBIT/Interest (×)°	5.0	5.5	4.8
Asset utilization			
Sales/assets	0.58	0.56	—
Sales growth rate (%)	−0.6%	8.4%	—
Assets growth rate (%)	−2.9%	—	—
Cash and invest. to sales (%)	2.4%	3.3%	—
Days in receivables	48.3	51.7	—
Payables to sales	18.2%	20.3%	—
Inventories to sales	2.7%	2.8%	—
Annual depreciation/gross P&E	5.2%	5.9%	—
Liquidity			
Current ratio	1.13	0.90	—
Quick ratio	0.64	0.53	—

°EBIT does not include restructuring and impairment charges.

Source of data underlying the ratios: 2001 10-K Statement, The Walt Disney Company.
Source of ratios: Author's analysis.

against a plan, budget, or standard. A *plan* or *budget* is a target or forecast of performance, expected but uncertain. A *standard,* such as a standard cost, suggests a norm against which actual cost may be compared. One can assess performance of a project or business in terms of *variance* from the benchmark. A *favorable variance* is either actual revenues higher than expected or actual costs lower than expected. An *unfavorable variance* is the reverse.

Variances in revenues and costs can be decomposed into variances due to price or cost changes and variances due to volume changes. Whether a variance arises because of variances in volumes or variances in prices (or costs) is extremely valuable information for the manager. It points the way toward remedying problems and/or rewarding outstanding performance. Consider this simple hypothetical case study regarding the videocassette release of a new movie by Gotham Cinema Company.

Gotham Cinema Company: Videocassette Release

At the beginning of 2001, annual videocassette sales for Gotham's year 2000 hit movie were expected to realize revenues of $50 million. This was based on an assumed sale of 5 million units, yielding revenues of $10.00 per unit to Gotham. At the core of the marketing strategy for this video release was a plan to aggressively promote the release through high-volume, mass-market discount retailers. The budgeted $10.00 unit revenue was a best guess about how substantial would be the concessions demanded by the discount retailers. The cassettes were to be manufactured on contract by a Taiwanese firm for a unit cost of $3.00. The production contract specified a production volume of 5 million units for 2002. Changes in the production volume or product would entail price increases to Gotham because of substantial job-change and setup costs.

At the end of the year, Gotham's marketing manager beamed with delight as she reported that revenues on the videocassette release would be $54 million, resulting from 6 million units sold at an average price of $9.00. She pointed out that the submission of cash rebate coupons had been higher than expected, as had the concessions to mass-market discount retailers. Gotham's purchasing manager was not as happy. She reported that the increased volume had prompted the supplier to impose surcharges on the price to Gotham: The average unit cost of the videocassettes was $4.00. Gotham's CEO grumbled that the project had earned only $30 million instead of the budgeted $35 million. What had gone wrong? Who was to blame? Why?

- *Revenue variance: price or quantity?* The price and volume variances were as follows:

Sales price variance = (actual price − standard price) × (actual units sold)
$$-\$6,000,000 = (\$9.00 - \$10.00) \times (6,000,000)$$

The sales price variance was unfavorable to Gotham.

Sales volume variance = (standard price) × (actual volume − expected volume)
$$+\$10,000,000 = \$10.00 \times (6,000,000 - 5,000,000)$$

The sales volume variance was favorable to Gotham.

Overall, the special price discounts and promotions produced an increase in volume that more than compensated for the lower average price realized. The revenue variance analysis shows that the promotional effort paid off:

$$\text{Total revenue variance} = \text{volume variance} + \text{price variance}$$
$$+\$4,000,000 = +\$10,000,000 - \$6,000,000$$

The pickup in volume had been more than enough to compensate for the decline in price.

- *Cost variance: price or quantity?* Regarding the cost to Gotham of buying the cassettes from the manufacturer, we can analyze variances from budget using similar formulas:

$$\text{Unit cost variance} = (\text{actual unit cost} - \text{budgeted unit cost})$$
$$\times (\text{actual unit volume})$$
$$+\$6,000,000 = (\$4.00 - \$3.00) \times 6,000,000$$

The unit cost variance was unfavorable to Gotham; it cost Gotham more to have the cassettes made than the company had budgeted. The increase in cost was due to the clause in the supply contract that permitted the supplier to hike the price to Gotham if the production run was higher than expected.

$$\text{Volume cost variance} = (\text{budgeted unit cost})$$
$$\times (\text{actual volume} - \text{budgeted volume})$$
$$+\$3,000,000 = \$3.00 \times (6,000,000 - 5,000,000)$$

The cost volume variance was also unfavorable to Gotham—this stands to reason since it had to buy more units than it expected. Overall, the total cost variance was unfavorable:

$$\text{Total cost variance} = \text{unit cost variance} + \text{volume cost variance}$$
$$+\$9,000,000 = +\$6,000,000 + \$3,000,000$$

The videocassette release project turned out worse for Gotham than expected. Instead of earning $35 million on the release, it earned $30 million. (Under the budget for the videocassette release, sales were to be $50 million, and costs $15 million; The actual results for the project were sales of $54 million and costs of $24 million.) Putting the variance analysis of sales and costs together helps show the sources of Gotham's disappointments. Exhibit 9.6 shows that price decreases and cost increases are unhappy outcomes, that sales volume decreases and cost volume increases are unhappy outcomes, and that profits equal sales less costs. Row totals show that the shortfall in budgeted profits was due to the fact that costs rose faster than revenues. But before we criticize the purchasing manager, consider that part of the rise in costs is due to the fact that Gotham simply ordered more units than it had budgeted. Also, look at the column totals, which show that the unhappy news originates in the unit price or cost area and that culpability is *shared equally* between the purchasing manager

EXHIBIT 9.6   Gotham Cinema Company videocassette release: Analysis of variance against plan.

	Price or Cost Variance	Volume Variance	Total Variance
Sales	$6,000,000 ☹	$10,000,000 ☺	$4,000,000 ☺
Costs	$6,000,000 ☹	3,000,000 ☹	$9,000,000 ☹
Total	$12,000,000 ☹	$7,000,000 ☺	$5,000,000 ☹

Note: ☺ = favorable variance. ☹ = unfavorable variance.

(who negotiates the supply contracts) and the marketing manager (who handles sales policy): Half of the unfavorable price/cost variance of $12 million originates in sales and half in costs.

A general manager can use analysis such as this to take thoughtful action. One possibility is that Gotham should stiffen its spine in negotiations with suppliers and customers. Perhaps the managers of purchasing and marketing should be sent to a negotiation skills workshop. Maybe the purchasing manager should be assisted by a skillful lawyer who could draft an agreement limiting the supplier's ability to hike the unit price. Gotham might consider searching for suppliers with more flexible production operations for whom a change order is not an expensive proposition. Finally, Gotham should reconsider the strategy of selling through mass-market discounters—they imposed internal turbulence (in the form of higher-than-expected volume) that rippled backward through the supply chain and left Gotham earning $5 million less than it had budgeted.

CONCLUSION

A basic mastery of accounting is absolutely essential for the success of the modern manager. Such mastery should include an ability to read financial statements and derive basic insights about the health of the enterprise from them and to assess the performance of a business or project relative to a budget or standard using *variance analysis* of prices, costs, and volume.

Perhaps more important, a basic mastery of accounting will instill in the manager a general sense of irony about performance measurement. On close examination, one sees that the process of preparing a presentation about the condition of the firm is heavily laden with judgment. Financial accounting is a "precisely approximate" art. Managers need to recognize the many alternatives they face in presenting financial results and make faithful, ethical choices. Investors and creditors need to read financial statements with thoughtful caution, recognizing that accounting reality is an abstraction from true economic reality.

Finally, accounting presents an extremely important framework for thinking about the internal workings of the firm. Assets must equal liabilities and owners' equity; transactions must *balance,* which is preserved through double-entry accounting. This represents the firm as a system through which turbulence resonates and in which the turbulence can be amplified or dampened. The challenge for executives is not to eliminate turbulence, but rather to manage it. To achieve this, one needs to view the firm as a system and to consider the sources of turbulence and its direct and indirect effects throughout the system. This is the thrust of the "systems thinking" approach as developed by Peter Senge and others. Viewed from this standpoint, accounting is not a narrow and technical specialty, but rather an essential tool for corporate renewal and transformation.

Professionalism in business and accounting goes well beyond the mastery of vocabulary, tools, and quantitative analysis. As suggested in the bursting of the Internet bubble and the business collapses during 2001 and 2002 (e.g., Enron, WorldCom, Global Crossing, and Qwest), accounting skills can be abused and can harm stakeholders of the firm in at least four ways:

1. *Amplifying earnings* by accelerating the recognition of revenues or deferring costs or converting them into investments.

2. *Evading taxes* by overstating costs or understanding revenues. Yes, most corporations keep two sets to books, one to report to investors and the other to report to the government for tax purposes. It is possible for a firm to do these first two things simultaneously.

3. *Hiding liabilities* through the use of special purpose entities (SPEs). By stretching complex rules, it is possible for a firm to force its debt onto an SPE, thereby making the firm look less indebted than is economically realistic.

4. *Amplifying assets* by delaying writeoffs of obsolete equipment or attributing glowing prospects to an economically unattractive business.

GAAP gives managers enormous discretion with which to report the operating results of a business—such flexibility is not only good, but necessary. Nevertheless, such flexibility easily morphs into fraud. Against this background, business professionals must not only master the technical knowledge of their field, but must bring a clearer orientation to right and wrong to their daily work. Referring to the criteria on which he judged people with whom he might do business, J. P. Morgan said, "The first thing is character."

FOR FURTHER READING

Haskins, Mark E. *Financial Accounting and Reporting* (Homewood, IL: Irwin, 1993).

Senge, Peter, *The Fifth Discipline* (New York: Doubleday, 1990).

Weil, Roman L., Clyde P. Stickney, and Sidney Davidson, *Accounting: The Language of Business,* 8th ed. (Sun Lakes, AZ: Horton, 1990).

White, Gerald I., Ashwinpaul C. Sondhi, and Dov Fried, *The Analysis and Use of Financial Statements* (New York: John Wiley & Sons, 1994).

10 FINANCE

Finance is concerned with *raising* and *investing* money. The underlying goal of decision makers in finance should be to *create value*. How one creates value (or inadvertently destroys it) through raising and investing money is the gist of all MBA training in finance. The field has an elaborate underpinning of economic theory and empirical research, all of which boils down to this piece of advice: *Buy low, sell high*. Seemingly stupid in its simplicity, this aphorism has two profound implications for managers. First, it directs them to think about value (what *low* and *high* mean). Second, it directs their gaze outside the firm, to the capital markets, to test their thinking (i.e., in order to buy or sell).

The field of finance is devoted to estimating *intrinsic values* as a foundation for action taking. Hence, *valuation analysis* is the core skill used in this field. How you buy low and sell high is guided by the following principles:

1. Think like an investor.
2. Invest when the intrinsic value of an asset equals or exceeds the outlay.
3. Sell securities (raise funds) when the cash received equals or exceeds the value of securities sold.
4. Ignore options at your peril: They are pervasive, tricky to value, and can strongly influence a decision.
5. If you become confused, see principle 1.

PRINCIPLE 1. THINK LIKE AN INVESTOR

A classic education in finance covers the thinking of three sets of decision makers: investors, intermediaries, and sellers of securities (typically corporations). These players are linked inextricably through the *capital markets,* the markets where such financial instruments as stocks, bonds, options, currencies, and futures are traded. Exhibit 10.1 shows that intermediaries stand between issuers and investors in the capital markets. The figure also suggests that capital markets not only embody the flows of cash and securities, but, in effect, they convey *information.* For example, a stock price will reflect information obtained from annual reports and press releases from issuers, recommendations and hot tips from brokers, and in-depth securities analyses from both issuers and investors.

Corporations: Issuers of Securities

Most MBAs choose to concentrate on corporations because that is where most jobs are and where most interesting dilemmas for intermediaries and investors originate. Corporations are huge investors and raisers of capital, accounting for around $1 trillion in new investment each year.

Even inside a corporation, it is necessary to think like an investor (see Exhibit 10.2). Corporations are investors themselves—finance argues that corporate managers are *agents* of the owners of the firm. In making investment decisions, managers should take into account the wishes of the owners. Similarly, one can argue that as issuers of securities, corporations need to anticipate the wishes of investors as they design and price those securities.

EXHIBIT 10.1   Major players in capital markets.

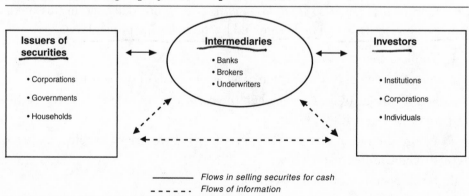

EXHIBIT 10.2   Examples of areas in which firms should think like an investor.

Investing	Raising capital
Capital budgeting	Bank borrowing
New products	Selling bonds
Cash management	Selling equity
Market expansion	Leasing
New technology	ESOPs
Plant closing	LBOs
Merger/acquisition	Bankruptcy
Divestiture	

Intermediaries

As the word, *intermediary*, suggests, these players stand between issuers and investors and help make the market in securities. To *make the market* means simply to help connect buyers with sellers. Intermediaries earn a fee with the completion of each transaction. Examples of intermediaries are banks, which link depositors (sources of lendable funds) with borrowers (users of lendable funds). Another example would be investment banks, which link issuers of long-term securities (such as corporations) with investors. A final example would be insurance companies, which pool or combine the exposures of many risk-averse persons so that risk bearing may be spread.

Intermediaries are large in absolute terms and in their significance to the national and global economy. For instance, Merrill Lynch, a leading American investment bank, has an asset base of over $400 billion. Fidelity Management and Research, a mutual fund management company, manages funds totaling almost $900 billion. In addition to their size, these firms are *opinion leaders*, or "lead steers," in the valuation of investments—they help frame standards for investment in America and worldwide.

Because intermediaries earn their fees from deals that others make, they have an interest in growth, in the smooth functioning of capital markets, and in liquidity. Most important, intermediaries must act in their clients' interests: Issuers need to obtain capital at fair prices, and investors need to earn fair rates of return. For this reason, students of finance tend to proceed directly to an understanding of issuers and investors rather than to dwell very long on intermediaries.

Investors

Even though all eyes are (or should be) turned toward investors, it is stunning to find the conventional thinking that investors are sleepy, ignorant, and indifferent to corporations' performance. In fact, the reality is quite the opposite. It is true that individual investors are major holders of securities—around half of American households today own equities. But individuals tend to buy and hold their securities and to look toward professional analysts and advisors for recommendations. Around 20 years ago, only 5.7 percent of households owned mutual funds; today, around 45 percent own mutual funds. The *thought leaders* in the pricing of securities are sophisticated institutional investors who today account for over 90 percent of the trading volume on major securities exchanges. These large players spend a great deal of money obtaining the best analysis and obtaining it sooner than others.

How Do Investors Think?

Principle 1 tells us to think like an investor. A considerable amount of academic theory and research is devoted to modeling how investors think. Here are some attributes of the investor mind-set:

1. Focuses on economic reality, not accounting reality
2. Accounts for the cost of the lost opportunity
3. Knows that required return follows risk
4. Looks forward and accounts for the time value of money
5. Understands that diversification of portfolios is good
6. Focuses on wealth creation
7. Invests on the basis of information and analysis, assuming that the market is generally efficient
8. Knows that the alignment of management and owners is beneficial to firm value

Fortunately, the behavior of the most successful investors (such as Warren Buffett and Peter Lynch[1]) convey many of the same attributes:

1. Focus on economic reality, not accounting reality.

Financial statements prepared by accountants might not adequately represent the *economic* reality of a business. Accounting reality is conservative, backward-looking, and governed by Generally Accepted Accounting Principles (GAAP). Investment decisions, on the other hand, should be based on the economic reality of a business. In economic reality, intangible assets such as patents, trademarks, special managerial know-how, and reputation might be very valuable, yet under GAAP, they would carry little or no value. GAAP measures results in terms of net profit; in economic reality, the results of a business are its *flows of cash*. Warren Buffett has written,

... Because of the limitations of conventional accounting, consolidated reported earnings may reveal relatively little about our true economic performance.... [We] both as owners and managers, virtually ignore such consolidated numbers.... Accounting consequences do not influence our operating or capital-allocation process.[2]

2. Account for the cost of the lost opportunity.

The concept of the *opportunity cost* is one of the most important in finance and marks finance as a sibling of economics: Economics encourages decision makers to think not in terms of simple yes/no decisions, but rather in terms of either/or decisions. In almost all business decisions there is an explicit or implicit *alternative opportunity*—in the case of investing, it is to buy another asset with attributes similar to the one you are considering. In investment decisions, for instance, one should compare the attractiveness of a contemplated asset against an alternative investment that would be forgone (lost) if you proceeded to invest in the first asset. This is nothing more than common sense: *Test any course of action against your next best alternative.* The concept of the opportunity cost implements that wisdom in finance. Warren Buffett demonstrated that he accounts for opportunity costs by stating that an important standard of comparison in testing the attractiveness of an acquisition is the potential rate of return from investing in common stocks of similar companies.

3. Look forward and account for the time value of money.

To look forward means that one should not take into account *sunk costs*, expenses already incurred or events that happened in the past. Buffett holds that intrinsic value is the *present value* of future expected performance:

> [All other methods fall short in determining whether] an investor is indeed buying something for what it is worth and is therefore truly operating on the principle of obtaining value for his investments. . . . Irrespective of whether a business grows or doesn't, displays volatility or smoothness in earnings, or carries a high price or low in relation to its current earnings and book value, the investment shown by the discounted-flows-of-cash calculation to be the cheapest is the one that the investor should purchase.[3]

Enlarging on his discussion of intrinsic value, Buffett said,

> We define intrinsic value as the discounted value of the cash that can be taken out of a business during its remaining life. Anyone calculating intrinsic value necessarily comes up with a highly subjective figure that will change both as estimates of future cash flows are revised and as interest rates move. Despite its fuzziness, however, intrinsic value is all-important and is the only logical way to evaluate the relative attractiveness of investments and businesses.[4]

4. Diversification of investments is good.

As the old wisdom says, "Don't put all your eggs in one basket." Peter Lynch wrote, "It isn't safe to own just one stock, because in spite of your best efforts, the one you choose might be the victim of unforeseen circumstances."[5] Also, as Buffett said, "Diversification is protection against ignorance."[6] This idea, one of the most important in finance, was recognized by the Nobel Prize in 1990. Diversification is good because it spreads (and thus reduces) the risk of loss. This principle is widely illustrated by banks that seek to minimize the impact of credit loss by diversifying their portfolios of loans and by insurance companies that seek to reduce the impact of insurance loss by diversifying their portfolios of insured exposures.

5. Required return follows risk.

Common sense tells us that the more risk one takes, the more one should be paid. Thus, the required returns (or discount rates) used in determining intrinsic values should be determined by the risk of the cash flows being valued. This is an extremely important idea in finance and is illustrated daily in the behavior of traders and investors in the capital markets. Consider, for instance, the rates of return available on bonds of different *credit risk* (risk of default by the borrower).

Exhibit 10.3 shows that the riskier the bond, the higher the rate of return demanded by investors. Indeed, the logic used by many investors in determining required rates of return on assets was to add a risk premium to the long-term risk-free rate of return (such as the U.S. Treasury bond yield).

This intuitive relation between risk and return offers another profound concept to managers: *Risk is in everything—the point should not be to eliminate it, but rather to price it properly and to manage it carefully.* Walter Wriston has written,

> Our American Economic system, like our political system, is untidy—it offends those people who love tidy, predictable societies. We make a lot of mistakes in this country, we have a lot of failures. Some people see only the failures; they cannot seem to grasp the fact that the failures are the price we pay for the successes. It's as though they wanted to have "up" without "down," or "hot" without "cold." We read in our newspapers, and even in our business magazines, solemn words about "risky investments" and "risky loans" from writers who do not seem to realize that these phrases are as redundant as talking about a one-story bungalow. All investments and all loans are risky because they are based on educated guesses about the future, rather than certain knowledge of what will happen.[7]

EXHIBIT 10.3   Yields by bond ratings (December, 2001).

Bond Quality Grade	Annual Yield to Maturity
U.S. Treasuries (commonly regarded as the least-risky bond investment).	5.85%
AAA "Capacity to pay interest and repay principal is extremely strong."	7.02%
AA ". . . very strong capacity . . ."	7.32%
A ". . . strong capacity . . . somewhat more susceptible to the adverse effects of changes in circumstances and economic conditions."	7.62%
BBB ". . . adequate capacity . . . adverse economic conditions or changing circumstances are more likely to lead to a weakened capacity . . ."	8.47%
BB+	9.94%
BB/BB–	10.47%
B ". . . regarded as predominantly speculative with respect to capacity to pay . . . outweighed by large uncertainties or major risk exposures to adverse conditions."	11.53%

Source: Standard & Poor's Bond Guide, December 2001; *Bloomberg Financial Services.* Rating definitions are quoted from Standard & Poor's *Ratings Guide* (New York: McGraw-Hill, 1979), pp. 327–28.

6. Measure wealth creation by the gain in intrinsic value, not accounting profit.

Buffett had this to say:

> Our long-term economic goal . . . is to maximize the average annual rate of gain in intrinsic business value on a per share basis. We do not measure the economic significance or performance of Berkshire by its size; we measure by per-share progress.[8]

The gain in intrinsic value could be modeled as the value added by a business above and beyond a charge for the use of capital in that business. One way to measure this gain is with *economic value added* (EVA™), also called *economic profit.*

Economic profit = NOPAT – charge for capital used

[handwritten annotations: "Net operating profits after tax" pointing to NOPAT; "WACC × capital base" and "required rate of return if investors" pointing to charge for capital used]

NOPAT is *net operating profits after tax.* From this is deducted a charge for capital estimated by multiplying the firm's weighted average cost of capital times its capital base. The *cost of capital* is the blended rate of return required by all investors (creditors and stockholders) in the firm. When economic profit is positive, value has been created. When economic profit is negative, value has been destroyed. Analysts in leading corporations use this yardstick to assess financial performance of corporations and of units within corporations. The appeal of economic profit is that it gives simple and clear guidelines to operating managers about how to create or avoid destroying value:

- *Increase sales.* Holding other factors constant (e.g., costs and capital), an increase in sales will increase NOPAT, which will increase economic profit.
- *Cut costs.* Holding other factors constant (e.g., sales and capital), a decrease in costs will increase NOPAT and economic profit.
- *Reduce capital employed.* Holding other factors constant (e.g., sales and costs), reducing the capital employed in a business will increase economic profit.
- *Minimize the weighted average cost of capital (WACC).* It may be possible to lower WACC through sensible management of the firm's capital structure (more is said about this under principle 3). But be careful in the way you think about WACC: The cost of capital is determined by investors, not managers. In competitive markets there is only one reliable way to reduce the cost of capital: Take less risk. But investors want managers to take sensible risks in pursuit of premium rates of return. For a manager to try to cut the cost of capital beyond sensibly trying to mix debt and equity capital would be wrongheaded.

7. Invest on the basis of information and analysis, supposing that the market is generally efficient.

Experience shows that it is extremely difficult to beat the market consistently over time. One explanation for this is that the market is very efficient in incorporating news and analysis into current stock prices. If the capital market is efficient in absorbing news into security prices, then securities will be fairly priced on average and over time. Clearly, there are exceptions to market efficiency, and it is to these exceptions that the great investors flock. Buffett repeatedly emphasized awareness and information as the foundations for investing and was fond of repeating a parable told to him by Benjamin Graham:

There was a small private business and one of the owners was a man named Market. Every day Mr. Market had a new opinion of what the business was worth, and at that price stood ready to buy your interest or sell you his. As excitable as he was opinionated, Mr. Market presented a constant distraction to his fellow owners. "What does he know?" they would wonder, as he bid them an extraordinarily high price or a depressingly low one. Actually, the gentleman knew little or nothing. You may be happy to sell out to him when he quotes you a ridiculously high price, and equally happy to buy from him when his price is low. But the rest of the time you will be wiser to form your own ideas of the value of your holdings, based on full reports from the company about its operations and financial position.[9]

Graham believed that an investor's worst enemy was not the stock market, but oneself. Superior training could not compensate for the absence of the requisite temperament for investing. Over the long term, stock prices should have a strong relationship with the economic progress of the business. Indeed, a reasonably large mass of research suggests that stock prices impound economic news rapidly and without bias—this is the phenomenon of *capital market efficiency*. Efficiency does not suggest that stock prices are the "real" or "correct" intrinsic values but rather that they impound what is known about the company: Investors could still overvalue or undervalue the share of stock, as Graham recognized, but it would be difficult to rush in and out of stocks with every new tidbit of news and consistently earn a profitable rate of return.

8. Alignment of agents and owners.

When managers think like investors, the goals of managers and investors are said to be *aligned*. Usually, the point of agreement is on creating value. Explaining his significant ownership interest in Berkshire Hathaway, Buffett said, "I am a better businessman because I am an investor. And I am a better investor because I am a businessman."[10]

As if to illustrate this sentiment, he said,

> A managerial "wish list" will not be filled at shareholder expense. We will not diversify by purchasing entire businesses at control prices that ignore long-term economic consequences to our shareholders. We will only do with your money what we would do with our own, weighing fully the values you can obtain by diversifying your own portfolios through direct purchases in the stock market.[11]

Managers are aligned with the interests of owners through the creation of effective corporate governance systems (beginning with the board of directors) and with the implementation of good incentives. For four of Berkshire's six directors, over 50 percent of their family net worth was represented by shares in Berkshire Hathaway. The senior managers of Berkshire Hathaway subsidiaries held shares in the company and/or were compensated under incentive plans that imitated the potential returns from an equity interest in their business unit.

PRINCIPLE 2. INVEST WHEN THE INTRINSIC VALUE OF AN ASSET EQUALS OR EXCEEDS THE OUTLAY

Thinking like an investor when you work inside a corporation can be a challenge, because you aren't necessarily managing your own money and because the investment decisions you face generally don't involve stocks and bonds, but physical assets instead. Principle 2 can help you think like an investor when you face corporate investment decisions.

Time Value of Money

"Time is money," said Benjamin Franklin. Our intuition tells us this is true because a dollar we receive today could be invested for the next year to return the dollar plus some added value. Thus, receiving a dollar today is worth more than receiving a dollar one year from now.

Compounding Estimates Future Values

To find out what a dollar invested today would be worth one year from now (i.e., to find the future value or FV), consider that at the end of the year we will receive the dollar back, plus a profit or return—this return can be calculated by multiplying r, the interest rate if we invest in bonds or a dividend rate if we invest in stocks, times our invested amount. At the end of the year, we will receive back $(1 + r)$ times our initial investment.

This logic can be extended to more than one year. Over two years, we receive $(1 + r)$ times the investment at the end of the first year—*and then turn right around and reinvest it at the same rate for the second year.* This means that at the end of two years, we have a future value worth our investment times $(1 + r)(1 + r)$. The pattern continues for three years and longer. Fortunately, the use of exponents simplifies what could otherwise become a lengthy equation—the following equations show the future value of one dollar invested today at the rate of return r.

assuming ~ is think $\}$ constant

$$\begin{cases} \text{FV, year } 1 = \$1.00 \times (1 + r) = \$1(1 + r) \\ \text{FV, year } 2 = \$1.00 \times (1 + r)(1 + r) = \$1(1 + r)^2 \\ \text{FV, year } 3 = \$1.00 \times (1 + r)(1 + r)(1 + r) = \$1(1 + r)^3 \end{cases}$$

Discounting Estimates Present Values

Of more interest to most decision makers is today's value of some future value. Because of the hidden opportunity cost in virtually all investments one makes, it is necessary to recognize the time value of money. Instead of just waiting for the future value to arrive, perhaps there is an alternative course of action that would give us some *present value,* which, if invested, would yield a future value larger than the one we foresee. Only by discounting all future values to the present can we compare them on an apples-to-apples time basis.

Arithmetically, the process of discounting is just the reverse of compounding—we divide the future value by the compound interest factor:

$$\text{PV of year 1 FV} = \frac{\$1.00}{(1+r)} = \frac{\$1.00}{(1+r)}$$

$$\text{PV of year 2 FV} = \frac{\$1.00}{(1+r)(1+r)} = \frac{\$1.00}{(1+r)^2}$$

$$\text{PV of year 3 FV} = \frac{\$1.00}{(1+r)(1+r)(1+r)} = \frac{\$1.00}{(1+r)^3}$$

Here's an example of the kind of investment decisions faced by operating managers. Suppose that you manage a manufacturing plant. An important machine in your plant has reached the end of its useful life and must be replaced. One of your analysts suggests two alternatives. The first alternative is to put in a new machine costing $1 million, which is just like the old one. The second alternative is to put in a new machine that costs $200,000 more to buy but that saves $50,000 per year in labor costs, frees up $25,000 in work-in-process inventory on the plant floor, and can be sold at the end of its life for $30,000. The required rate of return for an investment in either machine is 10 percent. (In other words, the investors expect you, the manager, to earn per year an annual profit of 10 cents on every dollar invested in the machine.) This is a classic choice between saving on an investment outlay today versus saving on operating expenses in the future. Which should you choose?

First, to think like an investor means to focus on *relevant cash flows,* not on profit or loss. The relevant flows of cash in this decision are the additional investment outlay, the after-tax labor savings each year, the additional depreciation tax shield, the release of inventory, and the salvage cash flow. These are presented in Exhibit 10.4. The discounted cash flow value of the second alternative over the first is $17,626. This figure is called the *net present value* (NPV) because the outlay is netted against the present value of future cash flows. NPV has a very important interpretation: It is the amount by which the value of the firm will increase (or decrease if negative) if the second alternative is chosen over the first. Thinking like an investor, we would choose the second alternative because it creates value: As a rule of thumb, when the NPV is positive, make the investment.

EXHIBIT 10.4 **Estimate of the value added from the new machine compared to the old.**

	Now	Year 1	Year 2	Year 3	Year 4	Year 5
New machine						
Labor		−$150,000	−$150,000	−$150,000	−$150,000	−$150,000
Depreciation on machine (over 5 years)		−240,000	−240,000	−240,000	−240,000	−240,000
Reduction in tax expense (35% of labor and depreciation)		136,500	136,500	136,500	136,500	136,500
Impact on after-tax profit		−253,500	−253,500	−253,500	−253,500	−253,500
Add back depreciation		240,000	240,000	240,000	240,000	240,000
Reduction in inventory		25,000	—	—	—	—
Salvage value		—	—	—	—	30,000
Investment outlay	−$1,200,000	—	—	—	—	—
Free cash flow	−1,200,000	11,500	−13,500	−13,500	−13,500	16,500
Old machine						
Labor		−200,000	−200,000	−200,000	−200,000	−200,000
Depreciation on machine (over 5 years)		−200,000	−200,000	−200,000	−200,000	−200,000
Reduction in tax expense (35% of labor and depreciation)		140,000	140,000	140,000	140,000	140,000
Impact on after-tax profit		−260,000	−260,000	−260,000	−260,000	−260,000
Add back depreciation		200,000	200,000	200,000	200,000	200,000
Reduction in inventory		—	—	—	—	—
Salvage value		—	—	—	—	—
Investment outlay	−1,000,000	—	—	—	—	—
Free cash flow	−1,000,000	−60,000	−60,000	−60,000	−60,000	−60,000
New machine free cash flow	−1,200,000	11,500	−13,500	−13,500	−13,500	16,500
Old machine free cash flow	−1,000,000	−60,000	−60,000	−60,000	−60,000	−60,000
Incremental free cash flow	−$200,000	$71,500	$46,500	$46,500	$46,500	$76,500
Discounted cash flow value of free cash flows, at 10% discount rate	$17,626					

Source: Author's analysis.

The Drivers of Value Creation

The positive NPV in the machine-investment example is a happy surprise and perhaps a mystery. But the source of the value creation need not remain an enigma. Four factors determine the extent to which an investment creates or destroys value:

1. The internal rate of return on investment
2. The investors' required rate of return (also called the *cost of capital*)

3. The rate of reinvestment in the project (the percent of the cash thrown off that you plow back into the project each year)

4. The length of the project's life

To illustrate how these factors interact to create or destroy value, consider the hypothetical case presented in Exhibit 10.5. Suppose a company has the opportunity to invest $100 million in a business. This is its cost, or *book value*. This business will throw off cash at the rate of 20 percent of its investment base each year. Suppose that instead of receiving any dividends, the buyer decides to reinvest all cash flow back into the business. At this rate the book value, or investment value, of the business will grow at 20 percent per year. Suppose that the investor plans to sell the business for its accumulated investment value at the end of the fifth year. Does this investment create value for the individual? One determines this by discounting the future cash flows to the present at the investment's *opportunity cost*, the required return that could have been earned elsewhere at comparable risk. Suppose that the opportunity cost in this case is 15 percent. Dividing the present value of future cash flows (i.e., Buffett's "intrinsic

EXHIBIT 10.5   Hypothetical example of value creation.

Assumptions:
1. Five-year term of investment, at the end of which you liquidate at accumulated investment value.
2. Initial investment is $100 million.
3. No dividends are paid. All cash flows are reinvested. Plowback is 100%.
4. Return on equity = 20%.
5. Required return on equity (discount rate) = 15%.

Year	Now	1	2	3	4	5
Memo: accumulated investment value	$100	$120	$144	$173	$207	$249
Investment	−100	—	—	—	—	—
Returns		20	24	29	35	41
Reinvestment		−20	−24	−29	−35	−41
Liquidation proceeds		—	—	—	—	249
Total cash flow	−$100	$0	$0	$0	$0	$249

Net present value = (estimated at required return on equity) (15%)	$23.7
Market or intrinsic value =	$123.7
Book value =	100.0
Market/book ratio	1.237

Value created: $1.00 invested becomes $1.23 in market value.

Source: Author's analysis.

value") by the cost of the investment (i.e., Buffett's "book value") indicates that every dollar invested buys securities worth $1.237. Value is created.

Consider an opposing case, summarized in Exhibit 10.6. The example is similar in all respects except for one key difference: The annual return on the investment is 10 percent. The result is that every dollar invested buys securities worth $0.801. Value is destroyed.

Comparing the two cases in Exhibits 10.5 and 10.6, the difference in value creation and destruction is driven entirely by the relationship between the expected returns and the discount rate (or required return). In the first case, the spread is positive and value is created. In the second case, the spread is negative and value is destroyed. Only in the instance where expected returns equal the discount rate will value be neither created nor destroyed. The capital markets demonstrate this relationship between spreads and value creation each day. Exhibit 10.7 presents the distribution of the 30 companies in the Dow Jones Industrial Index by the spread between their cost of equity and their expected return on equity on the vertical axis and the market-to-book-value ratio (which measures value creation). Immediately, one is struck by the positive slope of the cloud of companies: Positive spreads are generally associated with value creation;

EXHIBIT 10.6 Hypothetical example of value destruction.

Assumptions:
1. Five-year term of investment, at the end of which you liquidate at accumulated investment value.
2. Initial investment is $100 million.
3. No dividends are paid. All cash flows are reinvested. Plowback is 100%.
4. Return on equity = 10%.
5. Required return on equity (discount rate) = 15%.

Year	Now	1	2	3	4	5
Memo: accumulated investment value	$100	$110	$121	$133	$146	$161
Investment	−100	—	—	—	—	—
Returns		10	11	12	13	15
Reinvestment		−10	−11	−12	−13	−15
Liquidation proceeds		—	—	—	—	161
Total cash flow	−$100	$0	$0	$0	$0	$161
Net present value = (estimated at required return on equity) (10%)	($19.9)					
Market or intrinsic value =	$80.1					
Book value =	100.0					
Market/book ratio	0.801					

Value destroyed: $1.00 invested becomes $0.801 in market value.

Source: Author's analysis.

EXHIBIT 10.7   Market-to-book values versus returns on equity.

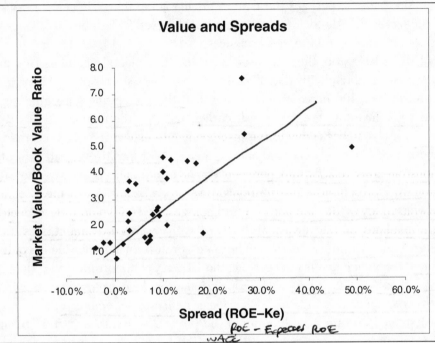

Ticker Symbol	Company Name	ROE-K_e	Price/ Book	Ticker Symbol	Company Name	ROE-K_e	Price/ Book
AA	Alcoa	6.8%	1.39	HON	Honeywell	7.3%	1.47
AXP	American Express	8.6%	2.57	INTC	Intel	10.0%	4.59
T	AT&T	−4.1%	1.18	IBM	International Business Machines	15.0%	4.47
BA	Boeing	18.2%	1.73	IP	International Paper	−1.0%	1.40
CAT	Caterpillar	7.4%	1.62	JNJ	Johnson & Johnson	11.4%	4.53
C	Citigroup	3.0%	1.80	JPM	J.P. Morgan Chase	1.8%	1.30
KO	Coca-Cola	26.3%	7.60	MCD	McDonald's	7.9%	2.44
DIS	Disney	−2.5%	1.38	MRK	Merck	26.8%	5.48
DD	DuPont	2.8%	2.15	MSFT	Microsoft	3.1%	3.73
EK	Eastman Kodak	10.6%	2.02	MMM	Minnesota Mining and Manufacturing	10.6%	3.78
XOM	Exxon Mobil	8.9%	2.67	MO	Philip Morris	48.8%	5.01
GE	General Electric	10.0%	4.08	PG	Procter & Gamble	17.0%	4.37
GM	General Motors	0.2%	0.74	SBC	SBC Communications	9.2%	2.40
HWP	Hewlett-Packard	3.1%	2.47	UTX	United Technologies	6.2%	1.59
HD	Home Depot	2.6%	3.33	WMT	Wal-Mart	4.4%	3.60

negative spreads are generally associated with value destruction. (Perfectionists may wonder why the figure does not show a straight line of dots to indicate a perfect correlation. The expected returns and capital costs may be estimated imperfectly. Alternatively, perhaps the market pricing is inefficient in certain stocks. But the fact is that the degree of association observed in Exhibit 10.3 is pretty good for economics and the social sciences.)

Exhibit 10.7 varies the *reinvestment rate* in the project. In Exhibits 10.4 and 10.5, we assumed implicitly that all cash generated was simply plowed back into the project (i.e., 100 percent reinvestment). If the reinvestment assumption is scaled back, investors get some cash earlier, but the lump sum at the end is smaller. Exhibit 10.8 shows what happens to the NPV and market-to-book ratio if reinvestment varies between 100 and 0 percent. With positive spread projects, the investor is worse off with lower reinvestment rates. This is because the cash coming out of the project is implicitly assumed to be reinvested at the discount rate, which is lower than the rate of return being earned on the project. With negative-spread projects, the investor is *better off* with lower reinvestment rates. This is because the investor can earn a higher rate of return by redeploying his or her cash in the capital markets (and earning the 10 percent opportunity rate) than by plowing it back into the project. The conclusion is that *higher reinvestment amplifies the creation or destruction of value; lower reinvestment dampens it*.

Exhibit 10.9 varies the lifetime of the project. In Exhibits 10.5, 10.6, and 10.8 we assumed a five-year life of the project. But what if managers can take

EXHIBIT 10.8   Illustration of value creation and destruction as reinvestment in the project varies.

	1	Reinvestment Rate				
		0%	25%	50%	75%	100%
Return on equity	20% ↑	1.168	1.183	1.199	1.217	1.237
	15% —	1.000	1.000	1.000	1.000	1.000
	10% ↓	0.832	0.825	0.817	0.809	0.801

Note: This table presents the market/book ratios associated with projects offering three different returns and five different reinvestment rates. The cost of equity is constant across all cases, 15 percent. Therefore, where return on equity is 20 percent, the project offers a *positive spread* over the required rate of return. Note that all of these positive spread projects create value (i.e., their market/book value ratios are greater than 1.000). Where the return is only 10 percent, the spread over the required return is negative—these projects destroy value (i.e., their market/book value ratios are less than 1.000). Where the return is 15 percent, the spread is zero, and the project neither creates nor destroys value (the ratios are equal to 1.000).

The table shows that as the reinvestment rate increases, the creation or destruction of value is amplified; as the reinvestment rate decreases, the creation or destruction of value is dampened.

Source: Author's analysis.

EXHIBIT 10.9   Illustration of value creation and destruction as the lifetime of the project varies.

			Lifetime in Years		
			5	10	15
Return	20%	↑	1.237	1.531	1.893
on equity	15%	–	1.000	1.000	1.000
	10%	↓	0.801	0.641	0.513

Note: This table presents the market/book ratios associated with projects offering three different returns and three different lives. The cost of equity is constant across all cases, 15 percent. Therefore, where return on equity is 20 percent, the project offers a *positive spread* over the required rate of return. Note that all of these positive spread projects create value (i.e., their market/book value ratios are greater than 1.000). Where the return is only 10 percent, the spread over the required return is negative—these projects destroy value (i.e., their market/book value ratios are less than 1.000). Where the return is 15 percent, the spread is zero, and the project neither creates nor destroys value (the ratios are equal to 1.000).

The table shows that as the lifetime lengthens, the creation or destruction of value is amplified; as it is shortened, the creation or destruction of value is dampened.

Source: Author's analysis.

actions to extend or shorten the life of the project? The life of machinery can be extended by quality maintenance, careful use, and tinkering. The life of profitable consumer products can be extended by reformulations, repackagings, and repositionings in the markets. Alternatively, money-losing plants can be shut down. Value-destroying product lines can be discontinued. Exhibit 10.9 shows that *longer life amplifies the creation or destruction of value; shorter life dampens it.*

In summary, value is created by positive spreads and destroyed by negative spreads. Lengthening the project life and increasing the reinvestment in the project amplifies the creation or destruction of value. Shortening the life and disinvesting dampens the value effect. Understanding the value drivers of an investment and their managerial implications is an enormously important contribution of finance to the work of general managers. Using this framework enables one to not only think but also to act like an investor.

PRINCIPLE 3. SELL SECURITIES (RAISE FUNDS) WHEN THE CASH RECEIVED EQUALS OR EXCEEDS THE VALUE OF SECURITIES SOLD

The field of finance also sheds light on how the firm should raise its capital. The orientation to thinking like an investor and to the value creation framework is relevant here, too. The main difference one encounters is that the firm *takes the perspective of a seller* rather than of a buyer, because in financing itself the firm is selling securities and receiving cash.[12] Principle 3 invites us to compare the "gives" and "gets" (similar to principle 2) and proceed with the financing if the "gets" are greater than or equal to the "gives." This decision can be reduced to a problem of valuation.

An Example: Valuing an Issue of Debt

Suppose that you manage a hospital that needs $1 million with which to build a new wing. You hire a financial advisor and underwriter who recommend that your hospital issue bonds with repayment in a lump sum at the end of five years. The bond rating agencies give this issue a single-A rating.[13] Your financial advisor tells you that an 8 percent coupon should be offered.[14] But your underwriter thinks she can place the bond issue with some investors who believe that the bond and your hospital are really worth a double-A rating. The yield on other single-A-rated hospital issues is currently 8.5 percent; on other double-A issues it is 7.75 percent. Should you proceed to issue this debt?

Exhibit 10.10 gives the net present value calculation of this bond. The proceeds of the issue are $1 million, which represents a positive inflow. Outflows are the annual interest payments and the principal payment at the end. Because you agree with the single-A rating, you discount these cash flows at 8.5 percent and estimate the net present value to be $19,703. This financing creates value for the hospital because the proceeds (+$1 million) exceed the present value of the liability incurred ($980,297). In this example, the source of value is the underwriter's ability to place the securities with investors who disagree with you about the risk (and required return) of the issue.

EXHIBIT 10.10   Simple NPV calculation of a bond's cash flows from the standpoint of the issuer.

Assumptions
1. Coupon rate = 8%
2. Term = 5 years
3. Principal repaid at maturity

	Now	Year 1	Year 2	Year 3	Year 4	Year 5
Principal	$1,000,000					$(1,000,000)
Interest	—	$(80,000)	$(80,000)	$(80,000)	$(80,000)	(80,000)
Cash flow	1,000,000	(80,000)	(80,000)	(80,000)	(80,000)	(1,080,000)
NPV @ 8.5%	$19,703					

Source: Author's analysis.

But the net present value calculation ignores one other potential effect: tax savings on interest payments. As a for-profit hospital, your interest payments are a deductible expense in the calculation of tax payments. By permitting this deduction, the government in effect subsidizes the bond issue's cost to your hospital. The benefit of this subsidy should also be reflected in your decision.

Exhibit 10.11 recomputes the NPV of the bond issue, reflecting the *tax shield* of the interest expense. This reduces the cost of the issue dramatically. The NPV now is $130,041.

Finding the Optimal Mix of Debt and Equity

As the bond valuation example shows, the tax deductibility of interest payments creates an enormous incentive to borrow. Shareholders reap the gain of the government subsidy of debt costs. The naive conclusion under the "think like an investor" principle would be that the firm should borrow to the hilt, since more borrowing means more positive NPV.

The problem with this naive conclusion is that more borrowing increases the risk that the firm will default on its debt payments (to *default* means to be unable to pay interest or principal on schedule). The operating earnings of almost all firms are uncertain. They expand and contract with the regular cycle of the national economy, with changes in technology, with the entrance or exit of competitors in the industry, with changes in consumer sentiment, and so on. Unfortunately, debt payments are fixed by legal contract; they do not increase or decrease as the firm's capacity to pay increases or decreases. Lenders and

EXHIBIT 10.11   Simple NPV valuation of a bond's cash flows, reflecting corporate tax deduction of interest expense from the standpoint of the issuer.

Assumptions
1. Coupon rate = 8%
2. Term = 5 years
3. Principal repaid at maturity
4. Corporate tax rate = 35%

	Now	Year 1	Year 2	Year 3	Year 4	Year 5
Principal	$1,000,000					$(1,000,000)
Interest	—	$(80,000)	$(80,000)	$(80,000)	$(80,000)	(80,000)
Tax shield	—	28000	28000	28000	28000	28000
Cash flow	1,000,000	(52,000)	(52,000)	(52,000)	(52,000)	(1,052,000)
NPV @ 8.5%	$130,041					

Source: Author's analysis.

investors in firms are quite conscious of this risk of default and set their required returns in reference to that risk. Beyond some reasonable level of indebtedness, lenders and investors will sense that the firm is assuming more and more default risk, and will raise the required returns (the interest rate) on their loans and on their equity investments.

For instance, bond investors make an assessment of the firm's creditworthiness through a process of credit analysis. Credit analysis could be as simple as making qualitative judgments on a set of standard criteria such as the "five Cs of credit" or as complicated as a highly technical computer simulation of the probability of default. The five Cs of credit are as follows:

1. *Cash flow.* Is the firm's expected cash flow large enough to meet the debt payments?

2. *Collateral.* If we have to foreclose on the loan, are there sufficient assets in the firm that we could sell to repay the loan?

3. *Conditions.* Do the current economic conditions favor timely debt payments?

4. *Course.* Is the use to which these funds will be put appropriate? Is the general strategy of this firm on course?

5. *Character.* Are the people involved not only sufficiently intelligent and skilled, but also *morally inclined* to honor the repayment commitment?

For many long-term bonds, creditworthiness is summarized in a bond rating. As the firm borrows more, the rating will decline. As the rating declines, the return that investors require will rise.

As required returns are increased, the NPVs of the bonds will fall. This is the simple result of time value of money: The higher the discount rate, the lower the present value. As the borrowing of the firm increases, the effect of default risk will *reduce* the value created by borrowing. At some point in the range between all equity and all debt financing of the firm, the impact of default risk will begin to more than offset the benefits of debt tax shields. That point is the optimum mix of debt and equity financing for the firm. Cast in graphical terms, Exhibit 10.12 illustrates this effect. The value of the firm rises as the firm goes from no debt to a moderate amount. This is because of the beneficial effects of the debt tax shields. Then the effect of default risk begins to be felt: As leverage increases beyond the optimum, the value of the firm begins to decline. Increasing the mix of debt beyond the optimum destroys value—it is equivalent to accepting financing whose cash received is less than the present value of future debt payments. Destroying value is the opposite of principle 3. To think like an investor in financing the firm is to choose the mix of debt and equity that maximizes the value of the firm.

EXHIBIT 10.12   Finding the optimal mix of debt and equity.

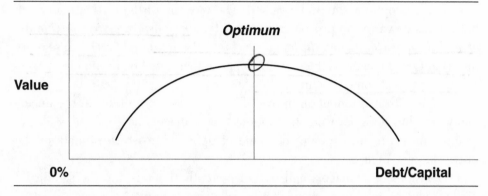

PRINCIPLE 4. IGNORE OPTIONS AT YOUR PERIL: THEY ARE PERVASIVE, TRICKY TO VALUE, AND CAN STRONGLY INFLUENCE A DECISION

Principles 2 and 3 are presented in terms of discounted cash flow valuation, but DCF does not tell the whole story of finance. DCF is based on fixed, point-estimate forecasts, possibly ignoring contingent choices that the firm may have today or in the future. Contingent choices are rights to take actions that are sensible only if other things happen. Here are some examples:

- The right to abandon a nuclear power plant *if* it loses money
- The right to hand over the reconstruction cost of a burned-out plant *if* you have a fire
- The right to exploit a mineral deposit *if* exploration proves the existence of the deposit
- The right to call a loan (demand immediate repayment) *if* the borrower defaults

Options are rights (not obligations) to take action. Options permeate the business economy. For instance, all insurance policies are options. Any time a manager says "I have the flexibility to . . ." he or she is expressing a right or an option.

All options are valuable, even if it seems unlikely that they would ever be exercised. In the financial pages of the newspaper you can find traded options that are deeply *out of the money* (i.e., to exercise the option would not be profitable)—yet these options trade at a positive price. The reason all options are valuable is that there is some chance (however small) that the option would be *in the money* (i.e., profitable to exercise) at some future point.

A great deal of research in universities and in the financial community has modeled how options should be valued. The modeling is highly mathematical, but it boils down to the provocative insight that *options are more valuable the greater the uncertainty and the longer the life of the option*. This is because more uncertainty and longer life increase the chance that it will be profitable to exercise the option at some time in the future.

DCF, with its foundation in fixed forecasts, does not embrace the uncertainty and thus does not value the options that managers have. To think like an investor means to incorporate the value of options into your estimate of the instrinsic value of an asset.

Decisions by managers and firms frequently demonstrate the significant hidden value of options, as shown by the following examples.

- A manager approves an investment proposal in R&D to reengineer an aging product. The proposal has a negative NPV, but the manager believes the R&D may lead to profitable product extensions or entirely new products. This investment consists of an unattractive fixed portion and a valuable call option on new discoveries.

- XYZ Company must choose between two communities, Sparta and Corinth, in locating a new plant. The communities are equally attractive on all counts, except that Sparta has higher taxes but grants companies more flexibility to trade pollution liabilities than Corinth. XYZ chooses Sparta: Even though the DCF value is worse, the option value there is sufficiently greater to overcome the comparatively negative DCF.

In summary, options are pervasive and potentially highly valuable. The standard valuation approach (DCF) ignores option value. Wise investors do not ignore potentially valuable options. To think like an investor one must incorporate options into one's assessment of business opportunities and problems.

PRINCIPLE 5. IF YOU BECOME CONFUSED, RETURN TO PRINCIPLE 1

Mother never said finance was easy. Business problems are rich and complex. The use of economic models and advanced quantitative methods appears to deepen the complexity. It is easy to become confused. Finance argues that thinking like an investor is an excellent point of departure for sorting out financial problems. Of course, investors themselves rarely agree precisely. (If they did, there would be no trading of stocks and bonds and no market. On every trade there is a pessimistic seller and an optimistic buyer.) But no fields in business offer strictly "right" answers—they merely help us avoid the wrong ones. Making financial decisions when you are ignorant of the demands and perspective of investors is a formula for calamity. By thinking like an investor one increases the likelihood of success.

FOR FURTHER READING

Bernstein, Peter L., *Capital Ideas: The Improbable Origins of Modern Wall Street* (New York: Macmillan, 1992).

———, *Against the Gods* (New York: John Wiley & Sons, 1996).

Bierman, Harold, and Seymour Smidt, *The Capital Budgeting Decision,* 8th ed. (New York: Macmillan, 1993).

Copeland, Thomas, Michael Koller, and Timothy Murrin, *Valuation* (New York: John Wiley & Sons, 2000).

Homer, Sidney, and Martin L. Liebowitz, *Inside the Yield Book* (Englewood Cliffs: Prentice Hall, 1972).

Lewis, Michael, *Liar's Poker* (New York: Penguin Books, 1989).

Lynch, Peter, *One Up on Wall Street* (New York: Simon & Schuster, 1989).

Malkiel, Burton G., *A Random Walk Down Wall Street,* 4th ed. (New York: Norton, 1996).

Stewart, G. Bennett, *The Quest for Value* (New York: HarperCollins Publishers, 1991).

11 STRATEGY: DEFINING AND DEVELOPING COMPETITIVE ADVANTAGE

The purpose of business is to create value for people, including shareholders, employees, customers, and communities. Strategy defines the purpose, intent, and mission of the firm—how it aims to create value. Sustained superior returns require a clear and well-communicated vision of how the firm creates value. Leaders have a critical role in defining and clearly communicating these goals and in demonstrating commitment, courage, and resolve.

Jim Collin's recent study of firms with extraordinary performance over a sustained period of time found that leadership is critical, but not as usually assumed. Superb leadership is characterized not by power and charisma, but by humility and firm resolve. Consistent with this finding, strategy development requires the firm's leaders, at all levels, to understand the firm's core values, continually looking hard at how to be ever more unique and valuable, and how to stay true not only to the firm's mission, but to what the firm does *not* do.

This chapter looks at the strategy development process, which provides frameworks and questions that leaders throughout the firm can use to design and improve strategy and performance.

WHAT IS STRATEGY?

Firms strive for sustained, superior return on investment. *Superior returns*, relative to other competitors in the industry, require a sustainable competitive

---

EXHIBIT 11.1   What is strategy?

In "What is Strategy?" Michael E. Porter defines strategy as creating a company's position, making trade-offs, and forging fit among activities:

"Strategy is the creation of a unique and valuable position, involving a different set of activities."
"Strategy is making trade-offs in competing. The essence of strategy is deciding what not to do."
"Strategy is creating fit among a company's activities."

Source: Michael E. Porter, "What is Strategy?" *Harvard Business Review,* November–December 1996, pp. 68, 70, 75.

advantage (i.e., a way of providing value to customers that is unmatched by competitors). *Sustained profits* require investment in capabilities that enable the advantage to improve, renew, and change. *Strategy,* therefore, is concerned with the definition of competitive advantage and the development of activities, resources, and capabilities that enable the firm to sustain advantage in a changing world.[1]

Essentially, strategy is the definition of how a firm competes: its values, its commitments, and the opportunities it creates. Strategy defines the firm's competitive position in an industry and develops consistency of purpose among the firm's activities to achieve that position. Strategy is not a detailed plan describing what the firm will do; instead, it provides direction for making significant choices

---

EXHIBIT 11.2   Three levels of strategy: Corporate, competitive, functional.

A firm's strategy is often discussed at three levels: *corporate,* or multibusiness strategy, *competitive,* or business unit strategy, and *functional* strategy within a business. This chapter focuses on competitive strategy. Functional strategies are discussed in Chapter 6.

1. *Corporate strategy* is the definition of the firm's values, financial, and nonfinancial goals. It centers on the identification and building or acquisition of key resources and capabilities and entails the decisions in which industries the firm will compete and how the businesses will be linked. Corporate strategy determines how resources will be allocated among the businesses of the firm, and thus the constraints on what the firm will do and will not do.

2. *Competitive strategy* defines how a firm competes in a given industry. A firm's competitive strategy is how the firm creates a valuable position in the industry. This involves a vision (explicit or implicit) of what customers the firm serves and how it delivers value for them. But competitive strategy is more than vision; it is the combination of specific activities and processes throughout the firm's operations that enable a firm to create unique value for customers. Thus, strategy also entails the fit among the firm's activities so that efforts throughout the firm consistently reinforce the potential advantage in the firm's competitive positioning.

3. *Functional strategies,* such as marketing strategy, financial strategy, research strategy, and operations strategy, reinforce the firm's competitive strategy and define activities and processes to enable the firm to achieve the benefit of its competitive position. Articulating and analyzing functional strategies clarify whether and how the firm's functions each fit with the competitive strategy and focus explicit attention on coordination among functions.

Supports competitive strategy

and strong guidance about what the firm will *not* do. Strategy is most powerful when at its core are clearly understood values that guide and motivate choices and actions. In highly successful firms, strategy often has the feel of a shared cause. (See Exhibits 11.1 and 11.2.)

The strategy development process creates insight about how to create and enhance uniqueness and sustainable competitive advantage. The challenge of strategic thinking is to open the minds of managers, provide new perspectives on threats and opportunities, challenge conventional wisdom, and develop a vision of the firm's uniqueness.

THE STRATEGY DEVELOPMENT PROCESS

> *Plans are worthless; planning is priceless*
> —Dwight David Eisenhower

Strategy Is *Not* "Making Plans"

A variety of strategy development approaches are used in practice, such as frameworks for analyzing industry profitability, competitive positioning, core competencies, capabilities, resources, strategic intent, and future scenarios. Each of these frameworks provides a guide for thinking through critical questions; none provide answers. The "answers" come in the form of the insights generated by the process. Using any of the frameworks well is an art, so different managers may find they are more effective in developing insights with different frameworks.[2]

Think of a framework as a box. The box limits vision if you step into it and close the lid and think "in the box." But throwing the frameworks away can be just as limiting; without any frameworks, managers tend to overlook critical considerations or put great effort into reinventing well-understood ideas. So getting "out of the box" is only part of the challenge. The trick is to use the box without getting trapped in it! Instead, use the framework (or box) as a foundation for developing insight, then stand on top of the box to expand your view of the horizons ahead.

The value of a strategy framework can be seriously limited by the person using it. Be skeptical when someone says that a given framework is useless; the statement may simply mean that the person has other frameworks in mind for the same purpose, or it may mean that person does not know how to use the framework to develop insight. Frameworks used only to validate old views are useless. Frameworks must be used to gain insight and inspire vision, to see new perspectives and develop new ideas.

**EXHIBIT 11.3   The seven steps of the strategy
development process.**

1. Industry analysis—industry profitability today and tomorrow
2. Positioning—sources of competitive advantage
3. Competitor analysis—past and predicted
4. Current strategy assessment—relative position and sustainability
5. Option generation—a creative look at new customers and position
6. Assessment of capabilities—positioning for future opportunities
7. Choosing or improving a strategy—position, trade-offs, fit

Also be alert to the allure of the latest and greatest frameworks and buzz-words. Although new approaches for thinking about strategy can help managers to perceive new opportunities, the danger is that popular strategy fads encourage rivals to compete in similar ways and thus undermine the firm's attention to competing differently than other firms. Competing *differently*—with unique positioning, specially targeted customers, or innovative ways of performing combinations of activities—is the essence of competitive advantage.

A complete strategy development process usually includes using several frameworks and doing a lot of creative thinking about the implications of the analysis. The seven-step process outlined in this chapter covers the critical strategy questions from a variety of perspectives. (See Exhibit 11.3.)

Step 1. Industry Analysis: Industry Profitability Today and Tomorrow

One of the fundamental insights of competitive strategy is that average profitability varies among industries. Average return on investment in the pharmaceutical industry in the late 1980s and early 1990s was about 25 percent, whereas the trucking industry averaged only about 5 percent. Those differences in averages are due to structural differences in the industries; the key for a firm in either industry is to outperform the average and achieve superior return relative to its competitors.

Industry analysis is critical for several reasons:

- First, the success of the firm is indicated by its *return relative to other firms in the industry*. A 15 percent rate of return in trucking in the early 1990s was impressive, but a 15 percent rate of return in pharmaceuticals indicated serious underperformance.

- Second, industry analysis allows managers to *understand the drivers of industry profitability* and thus how profitability may change in the future.

A common mistake is to analyze only the current profitability, but much of the power of the analysis is in using it to consider potential future changes and their implications for the firm's strategy.

- Third, different segments of the industry may have different profit potential. Industry analysis can help to identify the *attractive and unattractive segments*.

- Fourth, the current level of industry average profitability should not be taken for granted. Firms may have significant opportunities to *improve industry structure* or to prevent its deterioration. These opportunities may apply throughout the industry or in a specific industry segment.

- Fifth, industry analysis provides a good first *test on the rigor of new strategy frameworks and approaches*. Frequently, the examples claimed to prove the validity of the latest strategy fad can be entirely explained by differences in industry average profitability, leaving the additional insight of the current fad in question.

Determinants of Industry Profitability

Industry profitability (or *attractiveness*) can be analyzed by considering five forces: buyer power, supplier power, rivalry, the threat of substitutes, and the threat of new entry.[3]

Exhibit 11.4 displays the five forces and the drivers of their power. By assessing the strength of each of these forces, one can understand and predict industry average profitability. So, for example, the high average profitability of the pharmaceutical industry in the 1980s and early 1990s was explained by industry structure. Buyer power was low because patients did not shop based on price. Doctors chose products with little reason to consider price; patients (or insurance companies) simply paid. The threat of substitution was low because substitutes of other types of therapy or going without treatment usually offered little value compared to effective pharmaceuticals. Supplier power was low because the inputs tended to be available from multiple sources. Rivalry was limited by firms competing in different niches with patent protection. The threat of new entry was blocked not only by patents, but also by the complicated regulatory process for new drug approval and the difficulty of establishing sales forces and distribution systems. Even a firm with a new biotech drug might need to ally with a major drug company to produce, market, and distribute its product.

Conversely, the trucking industry faced large, powerful, price-sensitive buyers that could easily switch to other truckers. Suppliers included large

EXHIBIT 11.4 **The five competitive forces that determine industry profitability.**

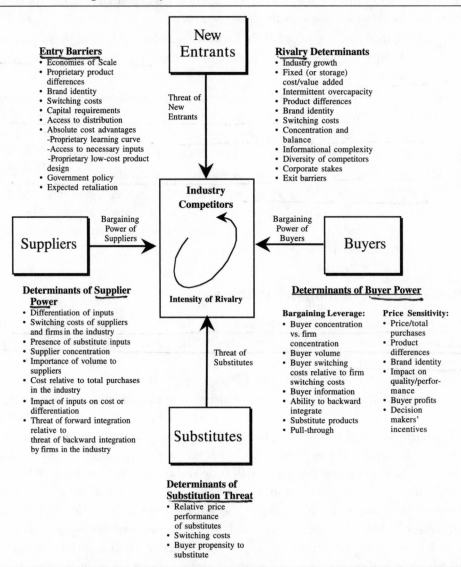

automakers as well as powerful unionized labor. Substitutes such as rail and air-freight provided real alternatives. Rivalry was intense because many competitors were vying for the same business without distinct strategic positions. Entry was as easy as leasing a truck, although given the other industry forces, one would not expect to make much money doing that.

In general, to do an industry analysis one must gather data and make observations about the considerations listed in Figure 11.1. Although the examples of pharmaceuticals and trucking are unambiguous, the picture is often less clear. Frequently, some forces are positive and others negative, so one must assess the strength of the forces and qualitatively weigh the overall picture to make a judgment about industry average profitability. Often, one can gather profitability data about some firms in the industry and use that to help calibrate current profitability.

It is critical, however, not to stop the analysis with a judgment about current industry average profitability. Much of the power of the analysis is in the view of the future that it can provide. The next step is to consider trends and drivers of possible changes in the industry and then analyze how these changes would affect profitability. For example, if current buyer power is moderate and supplier power is low, but both are increasing, the industry can be expected to be less profitable in the future. As a result, rivalry is likely to become more intense unless the firm can alter the drivers of change or position itself to compete in an industry segment where competitors are unlikely to venture or succeed.

The pharmaceutical industry provides an example of industry structural change under way. Buyer power is increasing as buyers consolidate. Large government payers and HMOs are covering drugs and becoming price-sensitive to a degree that individual patients never were. Rivalry is becoming more intense as generics become increasingly common and as price pressure fuels competition. The threat of substitute products is rising in markets where over-the-counter alternatives are available. And the threat of new entry by biotech companies is increasing. A few biotech firms have even managed to develop their own marketing and distribution channels.

Industry analysis of separate industry segments can be used to consider which segments are most profitable or are likely to be more profitable in the future. For example, proprietary drugs have a much more profitable industry structure than generics. Similarly, future industry analysis can sound a critical warning about industry segments that are likely to experience serious decline in profits and can provide critical insight about how to provide unique value in a changing world.

Analysis of future industry structure is tough to perform because change is difficult to predict. Established firms often get trapped in conventional wisdom and lulled by widely shared forecasts, making them less able to see the problems and opportunities presented by possible future changes. Thus, free-ranging brainstorming about the future and challenges to conventional wisdom about the industry should be encouraged in this process. It is often useful to ask what the competitors might predict, what technologies might leapfrog those currently used, and how a seemingly unlikely future might be explained if it came to pass. It is also important to ask how a better future can be created. Used in this manner, industry analysis is a powerful tool for developing insights about strategy for future success.

Step 2. Positioning: Sources of Competitve Advantage

Positioning analysis is about uniqueness. It addresses the question of why some firms outperform industry average profitability and others fail to achieve it. Superior performance demands that a firm has a sustainable competitive advantage and invests in the development of capabilities that will enable it to renew that advantage as the future unfolds.

Fundamentally, competitive advantage stems from superior value creation for customers. *Value* in this context is the way a consumer thinks when shopping; it is enhanced either by a lower price for the same product or service or by qualities or features that are superior for a given customer. An inferior product may not be a good value, even at a low price. Conversely, a superior product at too high a price is not a good value.

Conceptually, the two sources of superior value creation for customers are *lower cost* and *differentiation*. (See Exhibit 11.5.) In both cases, competitive advantage stems from offering more value to customers than competitors offer.

EXHIBIT 11.5   Types of Competitive Advantage

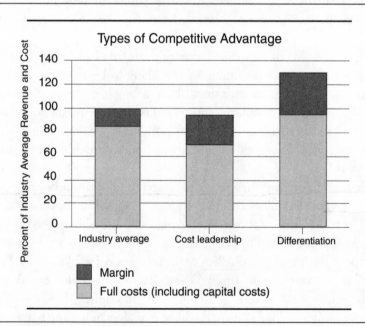

This additional value is delivered by performing activities and processes differently from competitors in ways that reinforce or accentuate the value.

Analysis of positioning is often facilitated with a diagram such as a *value chain* (see Exhibit 11.6) or *business system map.* These diagrams show all of the firm's activities and processes from procurement to after-sales service, including also research and development and overhead activities. They are used to enable or encourage a thorough analysis of how each activity throughout the firm affects costs and differentiation. They may also be used to identify important processes or linkages among activities that span several functions or are performed through alliances or by suppliers.

Increasingly, competition takes the form of a network (a loose alliance of a firm with its suppliers and distributors) competing with other firms or other networks.[4] A firm may perform activities differently and increase value for its customers by the way it manages the linkages among its own activities or by the way it manages the linkages with other firms in its network. This underscores the potential benefit of coordination among firms in a network to lower the overall cost for customers or enhance the noncost elements of value delivered, such as shorter lead times or better service. Rather than focus on appropriating value

EXHIBIT 11.6 The value chain.

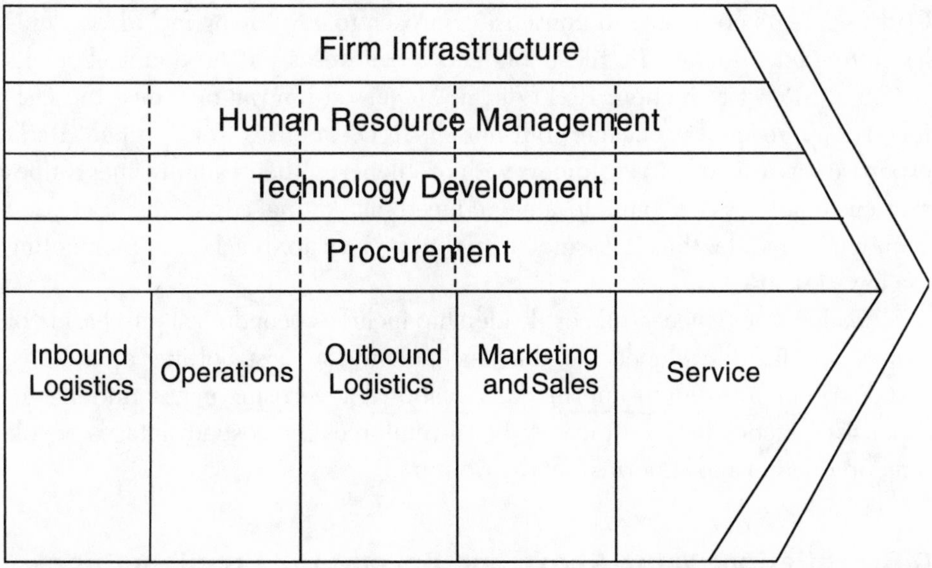

Source: Reprinted with the permission of The Free Press, a Division of Simon & Schuster Adult Publishing Group, from *Competetive Advantage: Creating and Sustaining Superior Performance* by Michael E. Porter. Copyright © 1985, 1998 by Michael E. Porter.

from buyers and suppliers in the firm's network, the cooperative mind-set of network management needs to consider how the network as a whole can create the most value. Relationships need to be built and managed so that each player in the network profits by advancing the network's strategic position.

Cost Leadership: Equal Quality at Lower Costs

Cost leadership stems from performing activities and processes (or groups of activities) in less expensive ways than competitors. It is not a matter of providing inferior products or services; indeed, matching (or exceeding) the quality of competing products or services is critical for providing greater value to customers. Above-average returns result from being able to charge a higher margin than competitors for equal-quality products without charging a higher price (as pictured in Figure 11.2) or from selling an equal-quality product with the same margins as competitors, but at a lower price, thus commanding a bigger market share. Sometimes the firm can achieve cost advantage by offering a lower price to a focused group of customers that is happy to forgo certain product features or service attributes. Because this group of customers does not care about the additional features, they view an inherently less costly product as having equal quality, and they benefit from its lower price.

Brilliant examples of cost leadership, such as Crown Cork and Seal in tin cans, have strong consistency of purpose throughout the firm's functions. Crown Cork and Seal's no-waste, no-nonsense approach to cost saving included relentless attention to detail. Its tile floors and metal desks left no doubt about its attention to cost reduction. R&D did not focus on innovation, since the fast-follower approach was cheaper. But not all R&D expenses were pruned. R&D expertise was available to customers with problems on their canning lines. Superior customer service built loyalty, reduced marketing costs, and increased economies of scale; thus it was not a frill but a savvy approach to implementing the low-cost strategy.

Gallo Wines' successful cost leadership includes economical purchasing of grapes, specially developed blending technology, low-cost bottling operations, and distribution through supermarkets. National advertising may sound like an expensive practice for a cost leader, but it reinforces the cost advantages of volume production and supermarket distribution.

Differentiation: Value Above and Beyond the Premium Price

Differentiation is a matter of delivering nonprice value for which customers are willing to pay. Thus, differentiation is much more than simply offering a different or better product. The key to success is making additional (costly) expenditures only on activities or features that cost the firm less than the value they add for customers. Diligent cost cutting remains important in all areas that do not affect the differentiation for which customers will pay a premium price. The result is usually a premium-priced product or service, but it is still a good value (or even a bargain) to customers who desire the additional benefit of convenience, customization, special service, durability, or some other dimension of nonprice value. As this suggests, differentiation often involves choosing a defined customer base and not trying to serve other customers who value different attributes than the company's target market.

As in a well-executed low-cost strategy, well-executed differentiation shows up in many processes or activities performed differently from competitors. For example, Sony achieves differentiation in high-quality consumer electronics with extensive R&D into new consumer applications, minimal defects in manufacturing, an authorized sales and service network, and responsive after-sales service. Many of these activities entail extra expense to achieve the quality that differentiates Sony. On the other hand, Sony reduces costs with efficient-scale facilities and tight cost control.

Drivers of Competitive Advantage

While discussions of competitive advantage often focus on the value perceived by customers, the firm must understand the sources of advantage in terms of specific activities or processes that it performs throughout the firm to reduce costs or increase nonprice value. This is where the functional strategies within the firm come into play. Excellence in the implementation of each function is critical to achieving advantage, but the functions must be well coordinated or they may undermine each other's efforts. One role of strategy is to guide the fit among the various functions and coordinate efforts toward a common, clearly communicated vision. Clear goals and values enable managers, and indeed all employees in a firm, to enhance the firm's success consistently.

Failure to understand actual costs is a common pitfall for both low-cost and differentiation strategies. It helps to consider each function of the firm (including support activities as well as line operations) and to attempt to compare costs of that function with competitors' costs. This analysis should then be followed by a hard look at possible ways to reduce costs further or enhance the nonprice value added for customers. Careful thinking through how, why, and when the product or service is used often adds ideas for ways to accentuate value that were not initially obvious. In addition, the drivers of low cost and differentiation listed in Exhibit 11.7 may spark other ideas for sources of improvement.

EXHIBIT 11.7   Cost drivers and differentiation drivers.

Cost Drivers	Differentiation Drivers
Scale	*Intrinsic*
Learning	Product quality
Capacity utilization	Product variety
Linkages within the value chain	Bundled services
Interrelationships across business	Timing and delivery
Levels of integration	*Signals of value*
Timing	Reputation or image
Location	Cumulative advertising
Institutional factors	Product appearance
	Installed base
	Price

Source: Reprinted with the permission of The Free Press, a Division of Simon & Schuster Adult Publishing Group, from *Competetive Advantage: Creating and Sustaining Superior Performance* by Michael E. Porter. Copyright © 1985, 1998 by Michael E. Porter.

Step 3. Competitor Analysis: Past and Predicted

Although common sense points to the importance of analyzing competitors before deciding how to compete, ignoring competitors is a frequent mistake.

- Clorox should have predicted that a new product offering combining bleach and detergent would be swiftly matched by Procter & Gamble, but it did not anticipate that response when it entered the detergent market in 1988. Clorox might even have predicted that the marketing muscle of P&G and the strength of the Tide brand would have the net effect of reducing the bleach market, yet Clorox faced that outcome as an unpleasant surprise.

- Epson may have predicted that offering a low-priced laser printer in 1989 would hasten the decline of the dot-matrix printer market. But, it appears to have assumed that the decline would not matter because loyal Epson customers would buy Epson laser printers. Epson failed to foresee that Hewlett-Packard, the leader in laser printers, would notice the competitive entry and could match the entry product's lower prices. The unfortunate result for Epson was the accelerated decline of its dot-matrix market combined with rapid growth in HP's laser printer sales.

The moral of these all-too-common stories is that a vital step in strategy development is viewing the issues and opportunities from the perspective of specific competitors. One should consider not only how competitors may react, but also what strategic initiatives competitors may pursue. Although managers often mistakenly assume that competitors are caught in a state of inertia, one should instead assume that competitors are pushing ahead at full speed. Ongoing analysis of the competitors' perspective is important for avoiding unpleasant surprises that should have been predictable.

Beyond improving prediction of competitors' moves, competitor analysis may enable a firm to influence those moves. Again, rather than stopping with an improved understanding of the situation a firm faces, managers can use strategic analysis to spur thinking about ways to reshape the future. In addition, competitor analysis provides a new perspective on one's own business and on relative sources of competitive advantage.

Considerations for Competitor Analysis

Competitors' moves and reactions are often consistent with their stated goals, their past assumptions, their known strengths and weaknesses, and their leaders' public statements. Thus, a competitor analysis should assess the following for each competitor:

- Current strategy (uniqueness and source of advantage)
- Leadership (recent or anticipated changes)
- Capabilities (cost position, value provided to customers, exclusive relationships, proprietary skills or processes, intangible assets, etc.)
- Future goals (what, when, and why)
- Assumptions (that firm's view of the future market and of other competitors)
- Stakes (economic, strategic, and emotional)
- Signals they have sent to other firms

A surprisingly clear picture of competitors' future intents can be developed from public sources and customer and supplier comments. The goal is to develop the competitor's profile rather than to get caught in the trap of simply collecting data that validates current assumptions about the competitor. (See Exhibit 11.8.)

EXHIBIT 11.8   Competitive dynamics: Good moves and poor tactics.

Good Moves . . .	Poor Tactics . . .

• Are hard for your competitor to match
  —Would cost their firm more
• Have commitment value
  —Are costly to reverse
  —Intentions will be believed
• Fit with the firm's capabilities
	• Simply increase advertising
	  —Easy to match
	  —Little commitment value
	• Price cuts by a higher-cost firm cost
	  —Give lower-lost competitor an advantage
	  —Intensify rivalry; provoke price wars
	• Provoke competitors

Step 4. Current Strategy Assessment:
Relative Position and Sustainability

Assessment of the firm's competitive position in the industry integrates the insights from analysis of the industry, the firm's position, and the competitors. At this point it is critical to clearly identify the firm's current position in the industry, both in terms of its financial results and in terms of its strategy. The insights from the previous stages of the strategy process may provide a new perspective on the firm's strengths and weaknesses relative to others in the industry.

The trend toward networks of alliances among firms means that a firm may need to assess the position of its network relative to other networks. A cooperative mind-set is then required to consider how the weaknesses in a network can be corrected by combined efforts, such as working more closely together, sharing information, or changing processes to improve coordination or reduce costs.

It is also critical at this stage to go beyond the analysis of the present to consider the sustainability of the firm's (or network's) competitive advantage in the future. Even stunning current success does not guarantee the future. Examples abound of leaders assailed, such as Fairchild in semiconductors, Kodak in film, or Caterpillar in earth-moving equipment. Over time, new products and services become more commonplace, easier to copy, or less valuable relative to more recent innovations. Without investment and improvement, a firm's profitability will fall as other firms invest and improve.

Generally, threats to sustainability fall into four categories: imitation; substitution; appropriation of value by firms upstream or downstream; and shrinkage in profits due to rising costs of salaries, discretionary expenditures, or changes in the division of revenues among partners.[5]

Step 5. Option Generation:
A Creative Look at New Customers and Positions

Change, often viewed as a threat to profitability, is the most powerful source of new opportunities. The insights from strategic analysis can help firms to identify new needs, new customers, new distribution channels, promising new technologies, and new sources of uniqueness.

To generate options, one wants to think in an entrepreneurial mind-set, adopt the perspective of industry outsiders, and challenge conventional wisdom about how to compete. The goal is to generate a broad, creative list of truly different strategies. New strategic positions are not obvious; they rely on inspiration, vision, and insight. On the other hand, the quality of the brainstorming of future strategic possibilities can be greatly enhanced by a solid understanding of the industry, customers, competitors, and firm's own strengths. The trick is to avoid narrow thinking about traditional ways of competing.

Remember that a strategic position defines how a firm creates value for its customers. New strategies stem from new ways to create value, serving new sets of customers, or finding better ways to provide the real value the customer seeks. Unserved customer groups and empty or previously unimagined strategic positions can present important opportunities. Thus significant insight is uncovered by a focus on the customers' goals and values. When the customer is a business, insight is gained by looking for ways to improve how that business serves its customers.

One of the most common strategic errors is to match competitors or copy their positions. Copying, however, only increases competition without adding new value. Many hospitals in the United States in the 1990s and early 2000s have illustrated this mistake by frantic efforts to match their rivals and become increasingly alike and increasingly broad rather than focusing on becoming uniquely excellent. Conventional wisdom often supports the mentality that rivals must be matched, but, in truth, that mentality undermines uniqueness and success.

Step 6. Development of Capabilities: Positioning for Future Opportunities

Future success of the firm depends critically on the capabilities the firm develops. New strategic positions usually require additional capabilities that cannot be acquired or built overnight. Thus, the options under consideration must be analyzed from the perspective of required future capabilities. Developing those capabilities will involve a series of investments and changes in activities or processes. The direction and vision can be specified, but the precise steps cannot. The point is that each of the strategic options under consideration may have different implications for development of capabilities, because different capabilities support different sources of competitive advantage. The difficulty of developing the required capabilities and the potential payoffs from the capabilities should be explored, and goals that cause the firm to stretch and learn need to be encouraged.

Komatsu's strategy in earth-moving equipment shows a progression of capability development. Threatened by Caterpillar in Japan in the 1960s, Komatsu first developed improved quality, then undertook serious cost reductions. Critical capabilities were product and process excellence to defend its home market. Komatsu next developed export markets, and in the 1970s it launched significant efforts in new product development. Future success required more; it required innovation to shape the new product offerings and lead the market.

Although some argue that developing capabilities is an implementation issue, it is important to consider future capabilities and the investments they require in the strategy development process for three reasons. First, a strategic position is a path, not a point. The dynamic development of the path should not be taken for granted. Analyzing required capabilities focuses the decision makers on the future, on the creation of opportunity, and on learning. Second, the development of future capabilities may require significant current investments. Analysis of these investments is an important aspect of choosing a strategy. Third, some capabilities can be gained effectively through network relationships among firms, but others will be less expensive or more effective if the firm develops them itself.

Investing in development capabilities is risky in the usual (financial) sense of investing capital for uncertain returns. *Not* investing, however, is at least as risky, but in the strategic sense of falling behind or failing to sustain profits. Compromised capabilities lead to lost opportunities. Lost opportunities, however, lead to failing to improve capabilities. A vicious cycle of failure may result.

Step 7. Choose or Improve Strategy: Uniqueness, Trade-offs, Fit

Competitive advantage stems from difference: serving different needs, different customers, or different geographic locations, or providing different access, different products, or different dimensions of value. The objective is to find a way of creating value that customers will not get from other sources. The most common error in choosing strategy is *imitation*. Successful strategy requires choices *not* to follow competitors.

Another common error is to try to eliminate the trade-offs between firms' different competitive positions. Superficially, it may seem advantageous to be able to match the competitor, but one must remember that eliminating trade-offs also makes it easier for someone to challenge your position. Strategy should aim to sharpen the trade-offs between positions, not to eliminate the trade-offs. In addition to making competitive advantage more sustainable, very distinctive positions can improve industry structure.

Strong leadership is necessary to define the firm's different, unique position and delineate directions in which the firm will *not* go. Strong leadership is also necessary to communicate the firm's values and strategy clearly so that choices made by managers throughout the firm will be consistent with the firm's intent. That consistency is critical to the successful implementation of strategy;

without it, decisions made at the functional level (i.e., in marketing, operations, or finance) may work against each other or against the source of competitive advantage that the firm seeks. (See Chapter 7 for examples.)

With increasingly global competition, part of the challenge of creating fit among activities and consistency with strategic goals is deciding where to configure activities around the globe and how to coordinate dispersed activities.[6] Generally, large economies of scale, steep learning curves, and tough coordination issues push toward the decision to concentrate activities rather than disperse them around the globe. Dispersion is increasingly attractive when local market needs or governments require local presence, transportation costs are high, learning is country-specific, or a single site has significant risks that can be hedged with multiple locations.

When activities are dispersed, the challenge of creating fit and consistency among activities is accentuated. Information, knowledge, and technology from diverse locations must be effectively integrated; strategic goals and choices must be clearly communicated throughout the worldwide functions of the firm. Because these challenges make an effective global configuration difficult to copy, well-executed coordination can make appropriately dispersed activities a significant source of competitive advantage.

CHARACTERISTICS OF GOOD STRATEGY

Evaluating a strategy is not simply a matter of looking at results. Because the goal is sustained, superior return on investment, short-term profits are not a sufficient indicator of success. Indeed, some firms that achieve brilliant success begin with five or more years of negative cash flows. How does one know if a strategy is good?

- A good strategy is built on values and purpose.
- A good strategy has at its center a specific understanding of competitive advantage. This understanding should be clear enough to state its essence in a single sentence.
- A good strategy is consistent. It is pursued consistently through combinations of activities that create a whole that is strongly reinforced and much more than the sum of its parts.
- A good strategy does not flip-flop over time. It defines a dynamic path that clearly bounds the firm's choices but does not constrain the firm from adjusting to the uncertain future.

STRATEGY: COMMITMENT OR FLEXIBILITY?

There is a long-standing debate about whether the essence of strategy is commitment or flexibility. One side argues that strategy requires commitment (in the economic sense, meaning fixed investments), so place your bets wisely. Strategy does require commitment, but this advice is about as useful as "buy low, sell high." It doesn't tell one how to choose wise bets. The other side argues that in a changing world, strategy requires flexibility, so keep your options open. Strategy does require flexibility given the world's uncertainty, but this advice is about as useful as "do nothing risky." One cannot keep all options open, and this advice does not tell which options to foreclose.

Strategy actually requires *both* commitment and flexibility. The two are not in conflict when one recognizes that a firm must make investments now (commitments) in order to develop the capabilities (flexibility) that will enable it to succeed in the changing and uncertain future. Strategy defines the types of capabilities to invest in and the types of investments to forgo. Commitment to core values and to a vision of the essence of the firm's competitive advantage is critical. Those values and vision point to a strategic path that is not fully defined or planned in advance. Choices along the way are guided by consistency with the values and vision. This means that the vision has to be explicit about how the firm differs from competitors rather than simply stressing high quality, leadership, or other laudable but vague goals.

Flexibility does not mean simple opportunism. Flexibility is developed through investments in building capabilities that other firms will not have without similar advance investments (known in economics as *real options*). For example, prior investments in a product line create the option to expand the line. Prior investments in new technologies enable the firm to use these technologies or to apply them better (or less expensively) than competitors as the future unfolds. Prior investments in processes and organizational knowledge enable the firm to perform its activities in ways that competitors cannot easily match.

Flexibility is not a strategic position but an outcome of strategic thinking. Investments in developing capabilities provide flexibility to implement a strategy successfully in a changing world. These investments define the firm's future opportunities that sustain competitive advantage. Thus, while it is not reasonable or even desirable to keep *all* options open, successful strategy must develop the capabilities required to create value for future customers. The choices of which capabilities to develop and which types of future opportunity to create must be driven by the core values and future vision at the heart of the firm's strategy. Thus *commitment*, in the sense of purpose, values, and mission, *is* critical because commitment is this sense is the compass that guides the firm's future direction.

FOR FURTHER READING

Collins, James C., *Good to Great: Why Some Companies Make the Leap . . . And Others Don't* (New York: Harper Business, 2001).

Ghemawat, Pankaj, *Commitment: The Dynamic of Strategy* (New York: The Free Press, 1991).

Ghemawat, Pankaj, "Sustainable Advantage," *Harvard Business Review,* September–October 1986.

Hamel, G., and C. K. Prahalad, "Strategic Intent," *Harvard Business Review,* May 1989.

Ohmae, Kenichi, "Getting Back to Strategy," *Harvard Business Review,* November–December 1988.

Mintzberg, Henry, "Crafting Strategy," *Harvard Business Review,* July–August 1987.

Porter, Michael E., *Competitive Advantage* (New York: The Free Press, 1985).

————, "The Competitive Advantage of Nations," *Harvard Business Review,* March–April 1990.

————, *Competitive Strategy* (New York: The Free Press, 1980).

————, "What is Strategy?" *Harvard Business Review,* November–December 1996.

Prahalad C. K., and G. Hamel, "The Core Competence of the Corporation," *Harvard Business Review,* May–June 1990.

Stalk, George, Philip Evans, and Lawrence E. Shulman, "Competing on Capabilities: The New Rules of Corporate Strategy," *Harvard Business Review,* March–April 1992.

Teisberg, Elizabeth, "Strategic Response to Uncertainty," Harvard Business School Note # 9-391-192, 1991.

————, "Methods for Evaluating Capital Investment Decisions under Uncertainty," in Lenos Trigeorgis, ed., *Real Options in Capital Investment: Models, Strategies, and Applications* (Westport, CT: Praeger, 1995).

PART III
New Horizons

Part III addresses topics that raise challenges for businesses entering the new century. Chapter 12, "Leading from the Middle," captures the essence of this new edition of The Portable MBA. We reinforce the position that the barriers that inhibit empowerment must be lifted for firms to succeed in the twenty-first century. Enterprisewide thinking, open and honest communications, shared information and decision making, the value of learning, and a deliberate sense of action must prevail and become embedded in companies if they wish to survive. Chapter 13, "Strategic Alliances," further extends the leading-from-the-middle metaphor and posits that firms no longer can afford to act in isolation. Constellations of firms, in cooperation with each other, determine ultimate competitive success. These constellations, or alliances, compete on a global basis for market share, low-cost supply, and access to resources. Chapter 14, "International Business," places the entire book in perspective and emphasizes the truly global nature of business. Capital knows no boundaries; the Internet makes information available to millions with a keystroke; and human assets are not restricted to a single location based on the availability of natural resources. Simply put, businesses compete locally but must think globally. And Chapter 15, "Some Final Thoughts," brings the book to a close with some brief reflections about value creation.

12 LEADING FROM THE MIDDLE: A NEW LEADERSHIP PARADIGM

In 2000, the Great Harvest Bread Company threw out the rule book and decided not to dictate to its franchisees how to run their businesses. They abandoned the command-and-control mentality that most franchise operators impose to ensure uniformity. Great Harvest defined its value proposition as the freedom for the local operator to run the business as he or she sees fit. To ensure that all 120 units share best practices, technology, case studies, conferences, and other venues are used to enhance systemwide learning. Good ideas are used and bad ones fall by the wayside. Taking a lesson from nature, Great Harvest and many other firms have come to realize that it is not the strongest one who survives, it is the one who adapts, is connected, communicates, and cooperates. Most other franchise operations take a very proactive role in the governance of their franchisees and believe that uniformity and centralized control are essential.

Fundamental changes have occurred in the business environment during the past 20 years, yet our understanding and response to these changes have been at best partial and at worst woefully inadequate and harmful. We must rethink the very idea of management as a hierarchical and directive activity concerned primarily with efficiency. Middle management as we know it and as we teach it in MBA programs and executive development seminars around the world is bankrupt. We begin this rethinking by examining the most important management role of all: leadership. We need to replace our idea of leadership as a top management task that is directed downward toward middle managers and workers with the idea that managers lead from the middle. Although the phrase "leading from the middle" at first blush may appear to be ambiguous, it is the core concept necessary for reinventing corporate life.

INTRODUCTION

Leading from the middle has three different yet connected meanings, each of which is relevant to understanding business today. First, managers must lead from the middle of the hierarchy. The traditional role of having middle managers carry out the directives of senior managers and then supervise the implementation of these orders by lower managers and workers is irrelevant. Second, managers must lead from the middle of an organization's core competencies, values, and purpose. In short, leading from the middle in this sense is about leading from commitment. Third, managers must lead from the middle of a network of relationships, some of which include organizational members, but also customers, suppliers, and others. Exhibit 12.1 is a depiction of these three modes of leading from the middle. The rest of this chapter sets the stage for understanding these three meanings.

The idea that the CEO is the smartest person and has all the answers does not track with reality. Organizations are not built on the shoulders of one person; teams are key and employees are proactive contributors as team members. Command-and-control systems, in which decision making is centralized at the top, needs to be changed. The task of management is not to dictate; rather, it is to coach and collaborate. The symbolism of leading from the middle supports this idea and brings focus to the notion of empowerment and the importance of giving employees voice to share their views. The second part of the equation is to bestow the authority to take action and shoulder the responsibility to be accountable for the actions taken.

First we discuss two basic changes that have profoundly affected the management of today's corporation: (1) the liberalization of markets, particularly the freeing of capital markets from geopolitical constraints, and (2) liberalization of the political institutions in society, from the Helsinki Agreement on Human Rights to the more recent fall of totalitarian regimes. We speculate about the role of technology as the underlying cause of these two changes, and we postulate that the effects of technology on managerial and corporate behavior have been and will continue to be profound. In essence, these changes require a new framework and a rethinking of the entire process of management.

EXHIBIT 12.1   Leading from the middle: Three views.

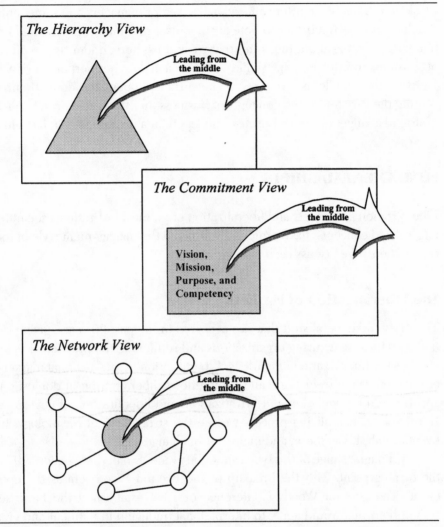

After that we examine some partial solutions to the managerial problems raised by the shifts in the economic and political institutions in the world. In particular, we focus on Total Quality Management, reengineering, mass customization, and strategic alliances. We outline how such solutions have achieved mixed results at best, allowing a managerial practice that ignores the fundamental shifts that have occurred.

Next we explore the three meanings of *leading from the middle*. We explain the new mind-set that is needed to lead from the middle, and we propose some of the activities and skills that are necessary to achieve this goal. We begin such a task here. Finally, we offer some advice to senior managers and some tentative conclusions. It is important to note at the outset that many scholars and practitioners are writing about the issues that we address here, under the broad rubric of "business transformation." While our approach does not purport to view leading from the middle as a panacea, it nevertheless opens the door to our reinventing the very terms and concepts of business life. If we are correct about the profound changes affecting business, no less than a revolution is in fact afoot.[1]

FUNDAMENTAL SHIFTS

Liberalization of markets and liberalization of political institutions, separate but interrelated concepts, have profoundly affected the management style of today's corporations. We discuss each in turn.

The Liberalization of Markets

The first fundamental shift that has occurred in the past 20 years, giving rise to the need for restructuring organizations and rethinking the practice of management, is the liberalization of markets. Liberalization of international markets has occurred through freer trade and capital flows, liberalization of domestic markets through deregulation and privatization, and liberalization of governments. In this broad liberalizing process we see the strong arm of technology. It has been a catalyst, facilitator, and motivator of change.

Although change of this type cannot be precisely dated, we believe 1973 was the turning point, with the breakup of the Bretton Woods era as the epochal event. The Bretton Woods Conference of 1944 established the basic set of assumptions that would apply to international trade and investment and created the institutions that would govern these activities. Coming after the Great Depression and World War II, the design of the system that Bretton Woods established was largely directed at providing stability for international commerce.

It is not our purpose to debate the success or failure of Bretton Woods, but we believe that the environment it created was a major factor contributing to the dominance of American industry in the postwar era, giving rise of the hierarchical, command-and-control corporation that characterized it. The successful, prototypical corporations of this era were U.S. Steel, General Motors, and IBM. The model of corporate governance and control was described by Alfred Sloan in *My Life at General Motors* and generalized by business historian Alfred Chandler in *Strategy and Structure*. This success, however, was not without its systemic problems.

While Sloan wrote of GM as an enormous and efficiently running machine, others (e.g., Peter Drucker) believed it was a machine without a heart or a soul.

Economist Joseph Schumpeter predicted the problem long before the current wave of restructuring, rightsizing, and other ways of revitalizing large corporations were ever conceived. In *Capitalism, Socialism and Democracy*, published in 1942, he stated that large, rigid organizational forms would eventually dominate industry and government. Corporations would become hierarchical and bureaucratic, with rules and strategies that deterred innovation. These nonentrepreneurial firms would seek to maximize the return on investment by prolonging product lives rather than introducing new products. They would extend the lives of capital equipment rather than develop new processes. Management in these firms would emphasize cost containment and predictable efficiencies related to growth rather than entrepreneurial reinvention. There was no place in this corporate world for what Schumpeter called "creative destruction," which was the essence of entrepreneurial spirit and activity that he felt contributed to innovation and dynamic, rather than static, economies. The entrepreneur discovered a better product or process, which was the creative side of the equation. The entrepreneur could then put together a deal that brought suppliers of material, labor, and capital together with customer needs and desires. The creation of new products and processes would naturally lead to the destruction of the old way. Capitalism, in Schumpeter's view, contained its own seeds of reinvention through the process of creative destruction. The early 1970s began to look like an inflection point when the policies of governments and the structural imperatives for corporations began to change. It is difficult to pinpoint a single cause for this phenomenon, although George Gilder's view of technology in his book, *The Microcosm*, offers an intriguing premise. Gilder argues that the application of quantum physics to the development and production of electronics altered the forces that determine economic success. The silicon revolution has disengaged corporate institutions from specific physical locations. Economic success in the Industrial Age depended on access to physical or material resources. The great steel industry of the United States, for example, developed in Pennsylvania, where there was a confluence of water for transportation and power, iron ore, and coal. But Silicon Valley, with its vast electronics industry, could be located anywhere. It was far less dependent on physical resources than on human resources.

The microcosmic pursuit has been global. According to Gilder,

> The United States has led only because the United States has been most open to global forces, immigrants and ideas. There are no separate destinies in the microcosm. There is just the difference between being free and in tune with the deeper disciplines and possibilities of the time, and being entangled and stultified by the materialist superstitions of a grim past of nationalist bondage and poverty.

The liberalization of capital markets caused enormous upheavals in the way today's corporations are run, but few have understood that these changes are fundamental, as Schumpeter, Gilder, and others have pointed out. During times of relative stability, hierarchical organizations with command-and-control systems can thrive. Today, with capital and resources flowing more freely than ever across geopolitical boundaries, hierarchies simply cannot anticipate change fast enough. In addition, the pace of change is accelerated because these very geopolitical boundaries that serve as forces of stability are themselves under siege.

The Liberalization of Political Institutions

Once physical resources became less important, the regulatory systems and organizational structures put in place to protect them could no longer ensure commercial success for the enterprises that owned these resources. In the United States and other Western countries, we began to see a large-scale decline in the trust citizens afforded to their governments. Some of the factors that contributed to this lack or trust were the social and political crusades that started in the turbulent 1960s, the emergence of worldwide agendas regarding the rights of women and minorities, the environmental crisis, and the so-called human rights movements in repressive regimes from China to South Africa. In short, government was identified as part of the problem.

The development of information technology, from Minicams to satellites to fax machines to personal computers to the Internet, put the human rights issues into the living room of millions of people around the world via CNN. Like it or not, human rights and economic activity are now inextricably tied together. (It is, of course, ironic to come to such a realization almost 200 years after Adam Smith told us the very same thing.[2]) In many ways, technology itself contains the elements of this linkage, since it is increasingly difficult for political regimes to hide their repression. There are too many ways to be found out. Second, the information technology that processes information at the local level (at the nodes rather than at the central network processor) encourages a kind of local control of information. Again, the emergence of the Internet is but one dramatic example of global reach in real time. The connection between the liberalization of markets and the liberalization of political regimes is easy to see. Success for the firm depends on how well it can harness its human resources and its mental capacity. In the old structure, a CEO or strategic planner set the direction for the firm. In the new model, however, direction must come from throughout the organization. Hamel and Prahalad claim, "It is an amalgamation of the collective intelligence and imagination of managers and employees throughout the company who must possess an enlarged view of what it means to be 'strategic.' "[3] At the center of any new mind-set must be the creative potential of the human beings who make up the corporation.

For the CEO in this new century, basic skills are essentially the same. The importance of functional expertise and business acumen has not changed. The areas of difference, however, are much more profound and lie in the difference between managing and leading. If a CEO/manager is a supporter of command and control, the capabilities of one's workers are never harnessed. The firm suffers, and its competitive position is jeopardized. Instead, if CEOs and managers see their role as nurturing the creativity and intellect of those around them, the results are quite amazing. Listening becomes an important attribute, as does the ability to help foster a relationship and sense of commitment between the employee and the company. Successful managers are thinking today about the skill sets needed tomorrow, and they develop a path to get people there. It is important to challenge people, to provide learning opportunities, and to give them the freedom to act.

The Implications for the Practice of Management

Corporations and their managers face a fundamental revolution in structure, conduct, and performance. This revolution has been brought on by a gale of creative destruction induced by the inadequacies of large corporations to respond with agility to changes in demographics, technology, regulation, and lifestyles— forces that have liberated capital markets, political regimes, and the people who make up these institutions. The agents of these simultaneously creative and destructive processes are invariably outsiders: foreigners, entrepreneurs, inventors, managerial iconoclasts, visionaries, and academicians.[4]

The response of corporations has been dramatic: extensive downsizing (the loss of 1.4 million managers, executives, and administrative professionals between 1987 and 1993, double the rate of the previous five years), process reengineering, building alliances, and so on. In the next section, we observe that each of these efforts represents at best a partial solution to an underlying need created by this wave of creative destruction. Before exploring this topic, let us briefly investigate the current managerial mind-set that is in need of change. Exhibit 12.2 shows some characteristics of the dominant mental model.[5]

Obsession with Command and Control

The largest component of the old mind-set is the obsession with command and control. From human resource systems to production planning, the old mind-set makes the avoidance of surprise a number one priority. And small wonder, if Schumpeter is correct. As institutions emerged to make the world more stable,

---

EXHIBIT 12.2 The dominant model of managerial practice in the old mind-set.

Obsession with command and control
Vision of a stable or predictable future
Competitive advantage through economies of scale and/or expertise
Specialization of labor
Hierarchical structure: centralization of power
Control by technical rationality
Separation of personal and professional life

---

organizations that thrived on that stability invented systems to take advantage of it. Firms are slow to give up control, which often leads to an inability to respond to changing environmental conditions. If there is little trust, there is need for command and control.

Vision of a Stable Future

A second attribute of the old corporate mind-set lies in the expectations of senior management about the future: predictability, steady growth, and the absence of discontinuous changes due to technology, regulation, demographics, or lifestyle attitudes. The planning activities of the old corporate mind-set are oriented toward extrapolating the past and present into the future rather than toward questioning fundamental assumptions or exploring radically different scenarios.

Competitive Advantage Based on Economies of Scale and Expertise

The old corporate mind-set seeks profitability and competitive security through sheer size and domination of markets and through the commitment of massive investments in relatively fixed and inflexible plants, equipment, information systems, and organizations. Commitment to a strategy of scale and inflexibility is a tangible manifestation of a relatively certain future, a future that looks not unlike the present or the past. Scale and scope might still matter; however, core competence lies in the capabilities of your employees.

Specialization of Labor: The Emergence of Narrow and Repetitive Work

The push for scale economies transforms factory and service work by focusing on specific tasks that the worker could learn to do quickly. The worker *becomes* part of the machinery or service process as employee discretion declines. Work protocols are designed to maximize the throughput of materials and the output of standardized products.

Hierarchical Structure: The Centralization of Power

The structure of these organizations is a high and steeply sloped pyramid. Reporting relationships and career progression are *vertical and typically tracked along functional lines.* Power in the form of information, money, expertise, and decision authority are concentrated at the apex of the pyramid. Executives manage by *command,* from the top down. Silo mentality breeds turfism.

Control by Technical Rationality: The Rule by Rules

Upward-oriented planning and reporting are major administrative activities for middle and senior managers. Corporate policies and procedures manuals blossomed in the post–World War II world as a way to institutionalize rational decision processes (e.g., discounted cash flow investment decisions). This has had the effect of homogenizing and slowing the evaluation of business opportunities and the flow of innovation. Somewhat analogous to factory workers, managers and administrative professionals have become part of the administrative machinery.

Separation of Personal and Professional Life

An individual's contribution to the success of the enterprise is on the corporation's terms. Employees conform in order to advance in the hierarchy. Chester Barnard believed that the executive who functioned well in the bureaucracy might well have a public persona different from that of his or her private life. The past 40 years is replete with stories from literature such as *The Man in the Gray Flannel Suit* and *Something Happened,* which explore the psychic pain of this separation.

So What?

The advent of information technology, distributed computing, and network communications release information and expertise quickly and widely. Intensifying competition in product markets demands a sense of urgency, which is inconsistent with the sedateness of the command-and-control decision-making processes. The same competition demands higher performance in quality and lower cost, both which are achieved through cross-functional teamwork. The more extensive freedom of people requires a relaxation in the process rules that dictate who may be heard, how, and when. Experimentation with teamwork clashes with functional turfism, suggesting sideways reporting relationships and career progression. Finally, the fuller engagement of people challenges the separation of personal and professional life.

Given the rise of the Internet, the more traditional mental models of the past have to adapt. In the world of financial services, trading has become a seamless, automated, end-to-end process linking key players globally who must operate against the backdrop of national and international rules and codes of practice that have not kept pace with the technology. Manufacturing companies also face the challenge of operating globally, as suppliers and customer are spread across the globe. Both product and service companies have become virtual businesses in which the integrity of information is paramount. Trust is the glue that links these global firms. On one level, trust connotes that the data has integrity and is reliable. On another level, trust is embedded in the definition of a true partner. Trust ensures that one partner in these virtual corporations will not act opportunistically to the detriment of the other members. Simply, these virtual businesses are held together by trust, a common vision, acknowledged synergies, and information technology.

PARTIAL SOLUTIONS

Unfortunately, the responses of many who are concerned with the changes that are affecting the practice of management miss the fundamental nature of the transformations that have occurred. Many corporations have resorted to a modest amount of strategic and operational introspection, oriented around competitive advantage rather than addressing the fundamental shifts described in the previous section. The question for many companies has been how to adjust and refine ongoing activity to respond to these changes in the surrounding environment. In short, corporations have responded by trying to adapt to these shifts under the old mindset. Not surprisingly, the vehicles companies have chosen to accommodate the new and more turbulent competitive conditions are rolled out with much celebration, only to founder on the shoals of time in two to three years. We are treated monthly to the popular press accounts of how the latest fads repeatedly fail.

We know the litany of familiar terms: Total Quality Management (TQM), reengineering, mass customization, and strategic partnering. Corporations have heartily embraced these programs to enhance innovation and quality, streamline operations, and forge partnerships to match or exceed similar initiatives by competitors. Undeniably, each of these programs has promised benefits, and many have delivered on some of these benefits. However, these efforts often have proven to be time- and resource-intensive, with few clear deliverables. These programs have been implemented in a workforce that has a considerable skepticism generated from weariness of this month's new transformative program.

Strategic reasoning regarding the selection and cultivation of alliances or committed reengineering efforts is inappropriate or a waste of corporate resources. There will always be a cutting-edge-like mass customization or TQM, as groups of very bright people craft improvements in ongoing operations. These initiatives, in combination, have indeed defined the new competitive status quo. To play the game in international markets today, companies must restructure and be more innovative. Through the implementation of such programs, companies have attempted to reach a best-practices standard, thereby improving quality, building in new product and process efficiencies, and becoming more flexible and innovative through mass customization and alliance building. Today, all tough competitors are asking how to become more market- and customer-driven. Companies are examining and changing their internal systems whereby product and service quality is maintained at the highest level. They are searching kindred industries for strategic partners that can significantly leverage their firm's resources. These efforts are to be commended. However, these efforts should be seen as the minimum requirements to compete at the top of an industry. These programs are the new basic standard to which anyone wishing to remain competitive must aspire. They are the new entry hurdles.

Total Quality Management (TQM)

Total Quality Management certainly is an important process. We do not deny that such programs have become essential for competition in today's market. Yet, as alluded to previously, taken in isolation, TQM is not a panacea for the firm struggling against formidable competitors. TQM may have become a rite of entry, a necessary attribute for the firm to compete. The question becomes, what other processes and skills must be incorporated for the firm to be a viable competitor? Undoubtedly, TQM lies at the core of many espoused solutions for corporate transformation. Used in isolation, however, it is not enough. Quality processes, products, and services not based on market realities are fundamentally flawed.

For example, when American Express worked on new quality processes to ensure that phones were answered by the second ring, management initially neglected to ask what happens after the call is answered. To respond quickly and not be prepared to address the customers' questions or concerns is an indication that TQM is merely a partial solution to a more fundamental problem. In short, we can say that (1) quality management processes are essential, but must be defined by the customer and not by the company's internal technical definitions of quality, and (2) quality processes must lie along the value chain and extend backward to suppliers and forward to customers. Despite all the positive press, empirical results have been mixed. Some studies show that there has been no effect on firm performance. However, certain factors appear to affect performance. Quality programs seem to have a positive impact on performance when associated with cross-functional teams, a committed management, and strong customer relationships.[6] In addition, supplier involvement and employee commitment are also important.

Business Reengineering

A second partial solution has been the use of business reengineering, which refers to a process or view that discards all the old rules, resulting in managers looking for new ways to manage the business. Reengineering gurus Michael Hammer and James Champy believe that business reengineering is intended to help the firm manage uncertainty while simultaneously questioning not only how to do things faster, cheaper, and better, but also whether certain functions or processes should be done at all and whether other functions can be done better by others. In some organizations, business reengineering is being used as a code word for downsizing or rightsizing. In other organizations, reengineering exercises have stripped certain functions from the firm and have outsourced other activities. The question often *not* asked is whether such skills are critical to the firm and whether future success depends on the development of certain capabilities.

One problem with business process reengineering is that cost reduction alone is not the goal. Reengineering should entail a fundamental assessment of the firm and its capabilities and an analysis of what skills, human capital, and resources are critical for future success. A second problem is that business reengineering should not be confused with benchmarking. Reengineering acknowledges that being world class at a particular activity is a laudable and worthy pursuit; however, one should not seek such a goal blindly. Instead, we should question the basic underlying activity and fundamental processes, first deciding whether, in fact, they are useful or necessary. However, caution must be exercised in this situation. A third problem is that business reengineering should not be attempted without full recognition of the firm's strategic intent and goals. A fourth problem is that business reengineering cannot be effectively applied unless the firm includes its suppliers and customers in the process. We must calculate the impact of shedding certain activities and determine who is willing and able to assume these tasks.

Mass Customization

A third partial solution in this discussion of current management practices is mass customization, which is linked inextricably to the two previously mentioned programs. The concept of mass customization grows from a failure inherent in the mass-production paradigm espoused by bureaucratic organizations.[7] While low costs are important and are an essential component of the mass-production paradigm, the premise that such a model is built on is no longer valid across a number of industries. Markets are not homogeneous; they are fragmented. Product life cycles are shorter, and cycle time has become a critical element of competitive response. Customers are demanding products and services that are tailored specifically for them. Mass customization demands processes, systems, and structures that are responsive to changes in the marketplace and can be implemented with little change in the cost and structure of the product and service.

Management scholars, Andrew Boynton, Bart Victor, and Joseph Pine caution that one cannot move directly from mass production to mass customization. Interim stages, such as continuous improvement, must precede this evolutionary change. Such changes affect both organizational structure and information technology; these changes are not trivial. Cross-functional teams become central to the process, functional silos must fall, and firms must acknowledge that R&D, manufacturing, procurement, and marketing must be linked if the firm is to treat each customer as a unique segment. Such dynamic processes require a very sizable investment in information technology, which is the central nervous system of these processes. It is not enough to manage inventories and production processes to reduce setup times and production scheduling; one must link customers, suppliers, R&D, production, and logistics in order for the entire process to operate seamlessly across functional and occasionally across organizational boundaries. Clearly, it is not enough for a company to convey that each one of its customers be treated as a unique market segment. You must begin to question where along the value chain customization occurs and how information is shared among all the functions and firms that deliver value to the customer. Flexible manufacturing or service delivery is a small part of the process.

To be able to focus on segments of one requires that a firm have the ability to mass-customize both the message and the delivery of the final product/service. Dell has created customized web pages for its larger business customers, and Amazon creates customized offerings for customers based on their past purchase history. Given the array of products and services from which consumers can choose and the clutter that we are exposed to each day, any attempt to break through the noise and make customers feel that they are listened to and important will have a positive outcome. Again, technology is the enabler and customer relationship management (CRM) becomes a critical tool in our ability to collect, analyze, and act on the massive amounts of data that exists regarding our purchasing behavior and spending patterns.

Alliances and Partnerships

A fourth partial solution is the use of alliances and partnerships. There is no question that these organizational forms (e.g., joint ventures, technology agreements, long-term purchasing arrangements, and horizontal marketing relationships) are on the rise. The numbers of alliances and partners have increased exponentially in recent years. For example, one cannot pick up the *Wall Street Journal* without seeing an announcement of a new alliance or partnership in the biotech, computer, telecommunications, pharmaceutical, or airlines industries. Despite the increase in alliance activity, the results of these activities are not that encouraging. A majority of alliances fail, according to work by Harrigan, Bleeke and Ernst, and others.[8] Failure can be attributed to a number of factors, ranging from how firms conceive of alliances as part of their strategy to the implementation and management of the alliance over time.

Alliances must be seen as strategic in nature and must be tied intimately to the strategic goals of the firm. Managers must be able to articulate how the alliance fits within the larger strategic framework of the firm's objectives.[9] All too often, managers become enamored with the thought of a partnership and fail to develop a comprehensive business case for the alliance to understand why one form of alliance is better than another. It's not unusual to find that managers spend more effort building a case for the internal request for funds than they do for the rationale for an alliance. In addition, firms fail to conduct adequate research in selecting alliance partners. For instance, how do you make sure that the potential partner isn't really a pirate whose sole intent is to expropriate expertise or knowledge? In some industries (most noticeable today is the multimedia industry), firms are caught up in the feeding frenzy, attempting to partner so they are not left without an alliance. In these high-stakes games in which billions of dollars are at risk, fundamental questions are often ignored regarding the alliance health (as opposed to the financial health) of the potential partner. In the heat of the deal, it's easy to ignore the more behavioral, qualitative aspects of the partner. Companies fail to address questions that affect the development of personal relationships that must grow concurrently with the building of the business. Key issues to resolve prior to consummating the partnership agreement include management style, corporate culture, compatibility of goals, and an ability to share decision making.

Problems arise also as the alliance grows and moves forward. Questions of equity (i.e., reward for effort and resources), interdependence, quality of personnel assigned to the alliance, conflict management techniques, and so forth can all affect the tone and health of the alliance. As long as the business prospers you can easily ignore the personal and interpersonal dimensions of the alliance. If the business begins to falter, these alliance management processes and skills become essential to weathering the economic turbulence facing the partners.

We have developed the argument for the virtual corporation and the advantages of virtual integration. To be sure, the Internet has moved us far down that path. Keep in mind that 60 percent of alliances fail. Alliances are not the answer to business success, although they do offer a number of opportunities. If viewed as a singular solution to competitive problems, alliances are bound to fail. There are a number of management challenges to overcome. It is probably better to focus less on the alliance per se, recognizing instead that the effort (and the ultimate reward) lies in the alliance management process itself.

Partial Conclusions about Partial Solutions

Although improvement can be achieved through these efforts, these programs represent incremental improvements when seen against the backdrop of corporations as a whole in the context of the last decade of the twentieth century. Specifically, in areas such as manufacturing, R&D, and product design, these programs have offered sufficient incremental improvements to be deemed justifiable by those responsible for budgeting the monies. From the longer-term viewpoint of the corporation and its critical outside linkages to customers and suppliers, however, these programs have been only partial solutions. They are palliatives that have eased the pain without curing the disease. Unfortunately, the partial successes of these programs have deflected attention from more fundamental questions about the challenges facing leaders. In reality, these programs rarely alter the core assumptions and mind-sets of the companies within which they are introduced; therein rests the problem.

This outcome is not surprising. Short-term, verifiable improvements in competitive positioning can disguise the predictable and ever-present inertia of corporate hierarchies that hold tightly to the mind-sets and operating assumptions that have guided them for the past 25 years. While change to the status quo may be recognized as desirable and even essential, the power and comfort of doing things as they have always been done, defined, and implemented held a quiet stranglehold over most companies, even as the tremendous effort and commitment of resources to reengineering and TQM efforts reassured participants that something significant was happening.

Another way to view these proposed solutions as partial is to go back to Figure 12.1. While each solution proposes some rethinking that could be called "leading from the middle," none goes far enough. Total Quality Management encourages middle managers to lead from the middle of the hierarchy and to lead from commitment, but it is difficult to see how TQM is applicable in the network arena. Similarly, strategic alliances, though they allow leading from the middle of a network, do little to redefine the hierarchy or focus on core commitments or values. Business process reengineering can break up the hierarchy and put companies in control of their key processes, but again, it does not address purpose and commitment.

While the latest fashionable programs represent new and higher standards for operating, these programs have distracted managers from the new paradoxes that represent a more fundamental competitive challenge. Leaders at every level of the organization, particularly at upper levels, must make a leap of vision to see this equally important arena for strategic thinking. This leap of conceptualization takes corporate leaders from their often implicit and unconscious focus on hierarchy to a cognizance of the power and potential of networks. It shifts the lens through which we define leadership responsibility from a preoccupation with things (capital, equipment, budgets, information technology) to a radically different understanding of people. What we need is a new framework, a new mind-set that revitalizes the practice of management.

REINVENTING THE PRACTICE OF MANAGEMENT

Take out an organizational chart and use it to describe your organization. You are quickly able to show the functional units and the formal lines of responsibility. Now try to use it to describe how work really happens. You can't. Add the informal lines of communication that truly govern the day-to-day operations and you have a more accurate picture of what really happens in an organization. Given the rapid and profound changes we have witnessed over the past 30 years, it should be obvious that this formal structure and its lines of authority would crumble under its own weight. We now talk about cycle time and speed to market. We emphasize technology to handle mundane tasks and to provide linkage with other divisions, partners, suppliers, and customers instantaneously on a global basis. Now companies focus on core skills and competencies and rely on others to provide complementary skills to fill the requisite gaps.

Noel Tichy uses the analogy of football versus rugby.[10] In football (U.S. definition), the coach has total control and orchestrates the game from the sidelines. In rugby, the game is more fluid and the coach has little control after the game begins. The coach becomes teacher, motivator, and facilitator. The command-and-control framework is in the process of being displaced by a new managerial mind-set that stands in stark contrast to this mentality. This new mind-set puts the liberalization of markets and people at its very center, causing us to revolutionize our concept of how organizations should work in the

To take this analogy, further, won't certain types of firms (teams) be managed better if done w/ old style?

Reinventing the Practice of Management   **247**

twenty-first century. In what follows, we set forth some of the elements of this new managerial mind-set and show how it turns the concept of leadership on its hierarchical head.

We have called this new mind-set *leading from the middle*.

Leading from the middle may appear to be ambiguous, because it has at least three related meanings. First, leading from the middle signals that the traditional role of the middle manager must be transformed. This is the hierarchical sense of leading from the middle. The fundamental changes that have occurred have made the job of the middle manager superfluous in many instances, replaced by information technologies deployed in flatter organizations with processes that have been reengineered across organizational functions. The middle manager as functional expert is simply no longer needed in a transfunctional world. Therefore, if any middle managers are left (and we know that there are plenty), they must lead rather than manage. They must begin to adapt the mind-set that redefines who they are and what they do. The second view of leading from the middle is the commitment view. In this case, leading from the middle means that one leads from the middle of a set of core values, a core competency or capability, or from a purpose. Jerry Porras and Jim Collins, Peter Drucker, and other management thinkers have reinforced the idea of answering the question "What do you stand for?" as an anchor in times of uncertainty and great change. The changes that have affected business are too fundamental to allow organizations just to drift. Only a core purpose that is well understood and agreed on can serve as a cornerstone to action. James Burke, former CEO at Johnson & Johnson, remarked about the use of such a purpose, called the Credo at J&J, during the Tylenol crisis: "We had lots of people making decisions on the fly, and we made very few mistakes."[11] Burke attributes the successful handling of the crisis to the fact that all of the employees involved were working off the same basic page: the J&J Credo. While credos and values statements are not for everyone, leading from the middle requires that there be a sense of purpose that drives the business. When this purpose includes a shared vision, then managers can lead from the middle of the hierarchy or from the middle of a network.

The third sense of leading from the middle is the network view. In this case, the hierarchy of power and the pyramid of organizational control has been replaced by a network of relationships. Some of these relationships are within the organization, some are outside, and some cross the boundary. Leading from the middle implies leading from the middle of a network of people, products, and relationships. Such a vantage point does not confer positional power, expert power, or even referent power. Rather, it offers an opportunity for creative destruction: the marshaling of resources, people, and ideas to create value that others in the network find worthwhile. The manager becomes the facilitator and the catalyst for action and creative change. Such a networked view of capitalism is increasingly the model for both large and small firms.[12]

Exhibit 12.3 summarizes some of the elements of this new framework. Many authors and business leaders have discussed these ideas in a piecemeal fashion. However, when you compare these two managerial models, the new mind-set stands out in stark contrast to the old.

Owning the Whole Enterprise

The new mind-set requires that every employee feel some ownership of the whole enterprise. To *own* is to feel accountable for, not simply to participate in. To focus on the *whole* rather than the part (or even the sum of the parts) is to challenge employees and managers to think broadly about *outcomes* rather than narrow tasks. This enterprisewide thinking allows the firm to develop new offerings and find opportunities that bring together parts of the firm that previously saw no advantage to combining skills or leveraging complementary capabilities. Such thinking facilitates the formation of communities of interest to examine a common set of problems or to address a new challenge with different views and perspectives. It can also speed the innovation process because barriers that arise due to the not-invented-here syndrome are a nonissue. Moreover, the ability to transfer knowledge is facilitated since everyone appreciates the leverage gained by institutionalizing learning processes.

Boundarylessness

Equally important is the fact that the new mind-set requires managers to think outside of traditional boundaries. Boundarylessness stands for an end to

---

EXHIBIT 12.3   Elements of the new managerial mind-set: leading from the middle.

Owning the whole enterprise
Boundarylessness
Customer orientation
Dynamic engagement
Invention of the future
Role of learning
Integration of the personal with the professional

---

functional stovepipes and an openness to alliances, partnerships, and new ideas without regard to who commands and controls the resulting activity. Outcome orientation demands access to information, expertise (or critical judgment), and tangible resources. The new mind-set eliminates walls around functions and encourages lateral interaction.

When boundarylessness is combined with owning the whole enterprise, managers must see themselves amidst a network of relationships. The boundary between customer, supplier, employee, and traditional stakeholder roles is becoming hopelessly blurred. Throughout the book we have spoken about the Internet and its power to connect people without consideration for time or place. Colleagues can work seamlessly around the world to solve internal problems or to meet customers' needs.

Customer Orientation

Rather than aiming to dominate or exploit markets, the new mind-set encourages firms to delight customers. It is important to note that *customer delight* is different from *customer satisfaction*. Just doing the job for customers and satisfying them is no longer enough in a world of global capital markets. Instead, today's companies have to be distinctive. They want customers to think of them when they think of service. In the airline industry, legends are being created at SAS, Singapore Air, and British Airways as they leave the pack behind. Likewise, everyone is familiar with success stories such as Nordstrom, Wal-Mart, Honda, Sony, Toyota, and upstarts like Saturn.

The difference between the old and new mind-sets is in an attitude of *caring* about the customer and focusing on specific relationships rather than on aggregate demographics. Selling, as a corporate activity, is frequently being replaced by relationship management as the dominant mode of dealing with customers. Information is readily accessible in many markets because markets are global, companies from around the world have raised service standards, and political regimes have gone through a liberalization process. There are increasingly fewer places for companies to hide if they exploit customers or treat them as if they are part of a one-shot negotiation, never to be seen again.

Dynamic Engagement

Desired outcomes and the challenges to achieving them shift constantly. No rigid organizational structure in place today will be appropriate for tomorrow. The new framework aims to construct an organization that reconstitutes itself as the situation requires. The result is an *agile* organization, one in which time and relationships change constantly and yet the level of engagement remains high. We have called that element of the mind-set *dynamic engagement*.[13] This element says that, above all, values are important. People can achieve extraordinary things if they believe their achievements are important and if these achievements resonate with their sense of self and what they want to accomplish in life. In short, these factors point to values. Dynamic engagement means that organizations must be value-driven. This usually requires a sense of urgency. Values are not trifles. They are urgent, to be acted on precisely because they are values.

In a recent book about what distinguishes truly great companies from those that are better than average, Jim Collins and Jerry Porras remarked that being driven by values (their own notion of ideology equals values plus purpose) distinguishes the likes of GE, Motorola, Merck, Hewlett-Packard, and others. These values have been fairly constant over the long histories of these companies. It is no coincidence that Collins and Porras's list of visionary companies includes precisely those in a position to respond to the fundamental changes we have seen. Many have had to dismantle the bureaucracy or literally blow up the command-and-control systems and procedures they have placed on top of the values. However, these cutting-edge companies have been engaged (and still are engaged) in this very task with a sense of urgency that has enabled them to leapfrog their competitors.

Invention of the Future

The fundamental assumption of the leading-from-the-middle mind-set is that the future will vary significantly from the past. This implies that simple extrapolation of the present into the future is doomed to failure. Instead, managers need to develop out-of-the-box skills in thinking, questioning, and learning. Additionally, the current fashionability of business process reengineering is recognized as a remedy for past and present problems rather than as a proactive effort to build for the future. In the world that we see, the future is there to be invented, not predicted and responded to.

Rosabeth Moss Kanter speaks about a culture of innovation, where leaders will spend more of their time creating a culture that supports innovation, knowledge exchange, and collaboration.[14] By leveraging relationships across boundaries, employees are empowered to seek and exchange knowledge for purposes of innovation. Despite the importance of these objectives, there are obstacles to be overcome. Silo thinking, an inability to think long term, corporate incentives that do not encourage new thinking, and a lack of senior management commitment all affect the firm's ability to adapt to this culture of innovation. Different roles and perspectives will drive the process, and effective leaders will view these differences as a positive opportunity to gain from the diverse views and opinions.

Role of Learning

As with dynamic engagement, a *zest for ideas and information* is essential, both at the personal and organizational levels. Learning becomes an end in itself and is recognized as having many dimensions: the acquisition of new information, the mastery of new techniques and technologies, and the growth in expertise and judgment. It is only through learning that the new mind-set becomes sustainable and produces a renewing corporation. Learning is more than job training; it is an *attitude and a value*. Peter Senge has set forth the disciplines of learning: *mental models, shared vision, team learning, personal mastery,* and a fifth discipline, *systems thinking,* which ties the others together. Competitive advantage goes to the organization that can learn the best and that practices these disciplines as a routine matter of course. Whether it is at Motorola University or a skills training class at Johnsonville Sausage Company, leading from the middle requires continuous attention to learning and improving your ability to learn. The role of the manager is to model that learning and to foster others' desires to learn in the workplace.

Integration of the Personal and the Professional

All of the other elements of the mind-set mentioned so far require that people not only show up at work, but show up with their hearts. The new mind-set asks managers and workers to be whole people. In the old mind-set, employees were willing to trade some of their individuality for a promise from the company to take care of them. Such loyalty is the exception in today's new world. Continuous improvement and transformation work only if corporations can embrace the differences of many kinds of employees. Differences provide diverse and rich knowledge. Greater knowledge fosters competitive advantage as well as meaningful work. Employees today must make critical judgments in addition to performing what used to be normal, unthinking jobs. Thinking and doing, separated at birth in the old mind-set, are inextricably joined together in leading from the middle. People are treated as ends in themselves: They have projects and values of their own that they are going to accomplish by working together in the corporation. Differences are respected and celebrated. Companies who are shortsightedly restructuring by slash-and-burn management are destroying any hope of a great future.

Leading from the Middle: Managerial Skills

Michael Hammer remarked that "A successful career will no longer be about promotion. It'll be about mastery."[15] But mastery of what? We offer four essential elements for the tool kit for those who will lead from the middle:

1. *Learning, and learning how to learn.* The competitive environment is currently so fluid and fast-paced that learning set-piece concepts and skills dooms the learner to obsolescence in the short term. You don't go to school to "get fixed" just once; today you must constantly "be getting fixed." We must emphasize three dimensions about learning. First, learning must be *in real time* (i.e., it must be occurring constantly). Second, you must learn *from actual experience.* From this standpoint, mistakes and defeats are hugely important, more so than merely absorbing information from secondary sources. Third, to learn in real time and from actual experience requires a *mastery of the art of reflection.* Donald Schön has studied accomplished professionals in a variety of fields and remarked that the central intellectual attribute in all fields was an ability to reflect and learn.[16] In other words, professional work is a process of reflection. Chris Argyris has warned that "single-loop" kinds of communication such as surveys, focus groups, and management-by-walking-around can block the ability of an organization and middle managers to learn at a more fundamental level.[17] "Double-loop learning," as Argyris calls it, springs from asking why, challenging assumptions, disclosing potentially embarrassing information, and taking personal responsibility. Numerous examples of effective and ineffective learning appear in the history of technological innovation. James Utterback believes the displacement of dominant product designs by newer, more effective designs is usually effected by outsiders to the industry.[18] Utterback speculates that owners of the dominant designs become so invested in their positions that they fail to see (i.e., learn) the threat posed by radical new alternative designs.

2. *Teaching, coaching, acculturating.* The skills of learning and the learning mind-set are virtually useless to a firm if held in isolation. Their powerful impact on the firm increases exponentially to the extent that they spread. Thus, essential skills for the manager include *direct teaching* (conveying lessons to others), *coaching* (motivating and guiding others to learn), and *building the learning culture* (legitimizing, cheerleading, and rewarding learning efforts). The need to acquire and practice these skills has not been obvious to middle managers; until recently, business school curricula and the practitioner press have had virtually nothing to say about them. *Challenging and motivating* the inquisitive natures of employees become

essential foundations of the learning environment. Chris Argyris has remarked that ". . . for companies to change, employees must take an active role not only in describing the faults of others, but also in drawing out the truth about their own behavior and motivation. . . . Leaders and subordinates alike and—those who ask and those who answer—must all begin struggling with a new level of self-awareness, candor, and responsibility."[19]

3. *Developing and involving others in creating local visions.* Active learning without a compelling vision to motivate it is like deploying a weapon without aiming. The emphasis of the new framework is both on the *process* (developing and involving) and *scope* (i.e., local) of the visioning effort. To create the new corporation, middle- and junior-level managers have a responsibility to facilitate the development of *meanings, concepts,* and *insight* about the business or desired outcome at hand. In some sense, developing a vision for the large-scale business is easier than a local vision. Large-scale visions are abstract and not easily linked to the day-to-day lives of employees; local visions are much more immediate and graspable. To develop a local vision requires an ability to manage downward and sideways (rather than upward) and to grapple with fears and aspirations of the people who must try to deliver the vision. Moreover, the visioning process should be ongoing. As Gary Hamel and C. K. Pralahad have stated,

Developing a point of view about the future should be an ongoing project sustained by continuous debate within a company, not a massive one-time effort. Unfortunately, most companies consider the need to regenerate their strategies and reinvent their industries only when restructuring and reengineering fail to halt the process of corporate decline. To get ahead of the industry change curve, to have the chance of conducting a bloodless revolution, top managers must recognize that the real focus for their companies is the opportunity to compete for the future.[20]

4. *Using and inventing technologies to involve others.* Employment of new information technologies can enable and accelerate the foregoing skills. Many middle managers, however, find themselves to be followers rather than leaders in the use of information technology. The realization that their junior (and younger) employees have information system skills that exceed theirs is threatening to many middle managers and at the same time presents a fresh opportunity to improve the manager's engagement with the team or organization on behalf of learning and visioning. Given the relatively nascent status of systems hardware and software, it may be desirable to design or customize systems that meet the needs of the team. The rise of virtual teams illustrates the power of information technology to help achieve crucial new-framework objectives. Boeing designed its new 777

airframe entirely on computer in a networked system that connected engineers and specialists throughout the company as well as customers and suppliers. The virtual design process slashed development costs and shortened cycle time. Similar stories abound throughout the automotive industry. At Kodak, a new, single-use 35mm camera was developed in half the normal time, with a reduction of engineering and tooling costs by 25 percent and 15 percent, respectively.

LEADING FROM THE MIDDLE: SOME CONCLUSIONS

First of all, leading from the middle recasts the role of senior managers. In fact, leading from the middle makes no great distinction between senior and other managers—or even other employees. Leading from the middle is about fluidly marshaling resources to create value and doing it with a sense of purpose and engagement. In place of command and control, corporate executives must substitute a style of "release and guidance." Managers need to be chosen less for their ability to kowtow to the prevailing philosophy in the executive suite and more for their ability to make decisions and to implement proficiency for their businesses and teams. *Letting go* is a radical departure for senior managers whose careers may have been shaped in the old command-and-control crucible. To let go is not merely to release others from their immediate tight control, it also means *blowing up* the hierarchy that imposes its own stultifying force on the forward ranks of the organization.

When asked where leadership comes from, CEOs from 300 companies[21] responded that they thought 40 percent of leaders were born with the trait and that 60 percent developed their abilities through experience (e.g., job-related relationships, coaching, and training). The key is to identify those leaders-in-waiting and to give them the opportunity to develop and grow. To begin, you could ask a series of questions to help find the proper talent pool:

- Do the candidates have conceptual flexibility?
- What is their interpersonal style? How do they influence people?
- Do they think beyond their silo?
- How do they develop talent in their organization?
- How much do they get out of their people with respect to high standards and accountability?
- Are they calculated risk takers?

It has been suggested that all the skills can be boiled down to the three Cs: courage, communication, and caring. *Courage* is the willingness to take on challenges every day and to encourage others to do the same. It is not just about rising to the crisis and taking command. *Communication* is the ability to clearly present your ideas, to motivate and inspire others. It is also the ability to listen. *Caring* engenders a bond of trust that allows people to speak freely and openly.

A final example of developing a culture in which the principles of leading from the middle flourish can be seen in the merger that created Asea Brown Boveri (ABB) in 1988. They became formally engaged in the transformation process using many elements of leading from the middle. This process enabled two small-country firms to unite as a potent global competitor. Like any successful business transformation, the ABB story doesn't have an ending. (Only failed transformations end.) However, like almost all successful transformations, it began with a vision. Percy Barnevik, former CEO of ABB, believes that world-class global competitors need to simultaneously manage three contradictions: being global and local; being small and large; and being decentralized and centralized.

Barnevik's solution for ABB was to organize the merged companies into a federation of 4,500 companies and profit centers, each with its own governing board and bottom line. This allowed at least 4,500 people to lead from the middle. Residing in a cell of ABB's matrix, companies such as ABB Germany and a business area affiliation provide each country with a national locus and a local perspective. Its business area affiliation places the company within a global business as part of a network of firms contributing marketing, production, or technology to achieve worldwide success. Because it is one of thousands of such companies, it is necessarily small and relatively independent. Yet because of ABB's control system, named Abacus, each firm is monitored by ABB's small headquarters staff. Managers at ABB have to lead from the middle, marshaling people, resources, and ideas to create value, while being coached and helped by ABB's senior managers.

Second, according to Bartlett and Ghoshal, senior managers must create an environment in which an *entrepreneurial process* exists: "A bottom-up entrepreneurial process can occur only when frontline management's role is transformed from implementer to initiator, and when senior management's role is to provide a context in which entrepreneurship can happen. At the foundation of an institutionalized entrepreneurial process is a culture that sets great store by the ability of the individual."[22]

Finally, a challenge for senior managers is to *create a learning culture*. Contrary to the assertions of business reengineering consultants, this means more than just investing in job training. A learning culture springs from basic attitudes about intellectual honesty, the virtue of debate and challenge, and a zest for new ideas.

Where this leaves senior management, and indeed all managers, is with a different task and learning challenge. In the leading-from-the-middle mind-set, control (such as it is) is imposed through the second sense of the phrase: articulation of *vision and core values* of the firm. Recruiting and setting compensation remain crucial responsibilities. However, in the new mind-set, these factors are deployed for change rather than for stasis. Attending to high-level relations with suppliers, customers, creditors, stockholders, and governments is a critical task for all who lead from the middle, not just so-called senior management. In the new framework, these relationships are developed not with a view toward dominance and exploitation, but rather toward partnering for mutual benefit. These relationships provide the very foundation for learning that is so vital.

Simple yet profound changes have occurred in the underlying conditions that modern corporations face. Many companies have responded to some of the effects of these changes by restructuring their processes, by involving their people in broader and deeper decision making, and by attempting to change their cultures to become more focused on the external world, especially on shareholders and customers.

However, such restructuring, as difficult as it has been, is not enough. The changes require a dismantling of the hierarchy and a reinvention of what constitutes good practice. Such tasks are not easily accomplished, and we have no pretensions to having done so in this chapter. However, we are convinced that something similar to leading from the middle will have to emerge if Schumpeter's prediction of the demise of capitalism is to be proven wrong. We look at the profound changes that have occurred with a sense of optimism and a sense of drama that those people who see the opportunity to create value in the very turbulence that drives today's world are rewriting the real story of capitalism before our very eyes.[23]

FOR FURTHER READING

Badaracco, Joseph Jr., *Leading Quietly* (Boston: Harvard Business School Press, 2002).

Bennis, Warren, and Patricia Biederman, *Organizing Genius* (Reading, MA: Addison Wesley, 1997).

Heenan, David, and Warren Bennis, *Co-Leaders* (New York: John Wiley & Sons, 1999).

Hesselbein, Frances, *Hesselbein on Leadership* (San Franciso: Jossey-Bass, 2002).

Kouzes, James, and Barry Posner, *Encouraging the Heart* (San Franciso: Jossey-Bass, 1999).

Pfeiffer, Jeffrey, *The Human Equation* (Boston: Harvard Business School Press, 1998).

13 STRATEGIC ALLIANCES

Despite the economic problems facing Latin America, the trade agreements among many of the countries has resulted in a revitalized set of national airlines with flagship carriers in Columbia, Argentina, and Brazil all enjoying an increase in market share of 20 percent. Yet there is also pressure from U.S. carriers, which have added capacity to serve this region. Alliances have been formed throughout Latin America to help the U.S. carriers strengthen their foothold and provide security to the Latin American airlines. These alliances have been formed out of necessity to add stability to the local carriers, to provide them access to much-needed cash, and to combat the global consolidation that has made it difficult for smaller airlines to compete.

There is no doubt that the nature of competition in virtually all global businesses has changed over the past decade. The preceding example could easily have used the telecommunications, aerospace, banking, or automotive industries. The reality of business today is that alliances are on the rise. Firms from every corner of the world and across all sectors of the economy find that global competitive advantage is partially a function of a firm's ability to successfully find and manage a range of alliances. Management's challenge is to develop the skills and competencies that enable their firm to better formulate, nurture, and implement a viable alliance strategy. Alliance-competent firms will have distinct advantages over their less competent rivals, which will be relegated to second-class competitors. Alliances are key to future competitive success, and most companies are ill equipped to develop the skills and capabilities needed to be alliance-savvy.

Take the Global One alliance between Sprint and its two European partners or AT&T's much touted but recently disbanded alliance with British Telecom, Concert, and we immediately see that these and other high-profile alliances of the mid-1990s began to unravel at the start of the new century. Failure here is not a function of a flawed idea or a strategy that could not succeed. These alliances made perfect sense because global customers wanted to have one point of contact and responsibility for their global telecom needs. Failure is attributable, in part, to execution and an inability to translate the alliance plan into action. In addition, these alliances promised far more than they could deliver, and unfulfilled expectations plagued both management and the financial community.

To be sure, despite the rise of alliance activity, the academic data and the anecdotal evidence are less than encouraging because the failure rate associated with alliances is quite high; in some instances, it is estimated to exceed 60 percent. However, if we use as a comparison point the rate of failure associated with the introduction of new products, alliance-related activities share a similar profile. Alliances are often a response to an uncertain world or set of market conditions. As a consequence, alliances inherently have a high degree of risk built into the process. When seen in this light, the failure rate should not be too surprising. Although alliance formations are increasing and growing across a number of business sectors, the rate of alliance failures has not diminished.

For instance, the number of alliances in the banking industry has increased almost tenfold since 1990. While some of this alliance activity can be attributed to the need for reducing backroom expenses by combining operations, the bulk of this activity is linked to new delivery mechanisms such as smart-card technology and PC and Internet banking. A simple explanation for this alliance activity is that banks have formed alliances in response to the threat that these nonfinancial companies pose to the retail banking industry. In addition, firms have used alliances as a way to offer clients a wider set of products and services so that they might increase their share of wallet. Brokerage houses and mutual fund companies have added services to better compete with each other as investors look for greater access and one-stop shopping. In 2000, to combat other online brokerages, including TD Waterhouse, E*Trade, and Ameritrade, Schwab sought alliance partners to offer sophisticated investors the opportunity to place their own trades on whatever exchange or alternative venue offered the best price. Rather than receiving commissions for services, the new business model charges customers for the ability to execute trades over the system.

This chapter investigates the rise of alliances and specifically explores alliance-related behavior—from the formation of alliances to the management of those alliances over time. Alliances and alliance-related thinking are tied to the strategic intent of the firm. Additionally, we examine the role of the alliance manager. Finally, we explore the rise of short-term alliances.

WHAT IS A STRATEGIC ALLIANCE?

Alliances are often formed as a reaction to uncertainties that are either market- or technology-based. A small biotech firm might have developed an expertise in certain immunological research and be looking to partner with Glaxo Wellcome, which can maneuver the FDA requirements and clinical trial process and which has access to the market through its sales force. In this scenario, both companies gain from the alliance because each brings complementary strengths to the partnership. More and more pharmaceutical companies are forming alliances to gain access to new technology, to outsource manufacturing, and to increase sales efforts upon introduction of new drugs. This is accomplished through comarketing agreements and by using independent sales forces. Both the Indian and Chinese governments require that all foreign companies who wish to do business in their countries work with a national joint-venture partner within their respective countries. In some instances, the venture has a finite life. In China, once the Chinese partner gains the requisite skills or expertise, the foreign partner is required to sell its interest in the joint venture. In this example, the alliance becomes the only mechanism for gaining a market presence in China. In other instances, many corporate buyers are finding they can leverage the competence of their partners by single-sourcing with a supplier that provides knowledge and expertise in addition to products and services. Ford Motor Company shares its new-vehicle plans with Johnson Controls, which provides seats and related components that fit Ford's performance requirements. Thus, through this buyer-supplier alliance, Ford provides only performance specifications, and Johnson Controls invests its own resources to ensure that these requirements are met. In the past, Ford would play one supplier against another in search of lower costs, issuing a request for proposal (RFP) containing lengthy design requirements. Lockheed Martin just won a $200+ billion contract for the joint striker fighter through a set of alliance partners that competed against Boeing and its partners for the next-generation fighter. One of the logistical challenges facing Lockheed Martin is that partners are located in 26 states as well as in foreign countries.

From these examples, you can see that the term *strategic alliances* includes a wide array of organizational forms, ranging from long-term purchasing agreements to comarketing and licensing agreements, R&D collaboration teams, and joint ventures. Despite the differences in organizational form, each of the definitions of these alliances converges on several salient themes. Each alliance has goals that are both compatible and directly related to the partners' strategic thrust. Each alliance also has access to the resources as well as the commitment of its partner. Alliances additionally represent an opportunity for organizational learning.[1] A *strategic alliance* is a close, long-term, mutually beneficial agreement between two or more partners whereby resources, knowledge, and capabilities are shared with the objective of enhancing the competitive position of each partner.

THE RATIONALE FOR ALLIANCES

Alliances should be positioned within the strategic efforts and goals of the firm. A sure sign of problems is the inability to succinctly answer the question, "How do your alliances fit into your firm's strategic thinking?" Alliances are driven by both offensive and defensive factors. *Offensive alliances* include focusing on accessing or creating markets, defining or setting industry standards, anticipating and preparing for new political developments, and preempting market access from competition. *Defensive alliances* concentrate on protecting or solidifying an existing market position, sharing the financial risk of an expensive technology, or gaining economies of scale. In some instances, one firm will partner with another to preempt a third competitor from doing so. Defensive alliances are often accomplished by combining processes and production capabilities.

Alliances are formed also to facilitate learning. For example, learning may involve gaining access to innovative new technology or to financial, marketing, and production expertise. One outcome of this approach is to speed time to market or access to technology. One Belgian specialty metals company partners with smaller firms that offer access to complementary coating technology that not only strengthens its position, but could be potential acquisition targets. Learning is, in fact, a very legitimate alliance outcome; yet it is difficult to measure since tacit knowledge is not often easily discernable and develops over time. Imagine a meeting in which senior management is reviewing the progress of a troubled alliance and the entire argument is based on the fact that goals were not accomplished but that a great deal was learned. The firm's tolerance for such a response is an indication of the culture of the firm and its level of alliance competence. If there is no tolerance for failure or recognition that learning is a legitimate alliance outcome, it does not bode well for the firm. Failure is built into the alliance process, and partners do learn from one another (although we all want to learn from our partner, not the other way around).

However, a darker side exists to such learning. Firms might use alliances as a means to expropriate proprietary technology at the expense of a willing, albeit naive, partner. A number of companies have developed a reputation for partnering with the express purpose of expropriating technology and for disengaging their partners once they have learned all they need to know about the business. Potential partners who are aware of the danger might still go forward, but often set up mechanisms to protect themselves, thereby raising the transaction costs associated with the alliance and minimizing the potential gains. Attempts to black-box certain technology or to work in sequence rather than in tandem might be ways to decrease the likelihood of expropriation. Often, licensing enables a firm to share technology and minimize the opportunity for the leakage of unintended information.

to prevent other firms from stealing technology

In other instances, alliances can be formed as a precursor to a merger or an acquisition. Hamilton Standard and Sundstrand had been partners in a number of ventures over the years and knew each other fairly well prior to the purchase of Sundstrand by United Technologies (UTC), a U.S.-based multinational that owns several aerospace companies. The success of the merger is attributed partly to the close ties that had existed prior to the acquisition and partly to the knowledge of each other's businesses and technical capabilities. Recent work by McKinsey examines the pros and cons of progressing from an alliance to a merger.[2] On one level, an alliance allows partners to establish a level of comfort and rapport before engaging in an expensive merger. On another level, these alliances allow firms to proceed slowly, thereby reducing some of the costly mistakes often associated with a rapid acquisition. Time, however, is a two-edged sword: On the one hand, time encourages rapport building; on the other hand, a need for consensus can slow the process, thus allowing resistance to the alliance to build. This was the case with the failed merger between Volvo and Renault in 1993. In the case of Volvo and Renault, the alliance was flawed because mechanisms for dealing with cultural differences were never put into place, and the alliance really never achieved its objectives. The merger would have solved the problems related to slow decision making and the need for equal treatment for both partners. Yet the fundamental problems related to cultural differences were never addressed in the merger. Had the merger gone forward, the illness would have remained even though several of the symptoms would have been cured.

Exhibit 13.1 demonstrates a range of trade-offs that a firm must consider when deciding whether to form an alliance. Questions arise regarding how to manage expectations pertaining to the gains and costs associated with the outcome of the alliance. In a conversation with one senior executive from a company engaging in many alliances and whose alliance management is acknowledged to

EXHIBIT 13.1   Balancing alliance trade-offs.

Acquire Capability	Yield Control
Access to markets	Market overlap
Access to technology	Use of technology
Access to networks of firms	Entanglements
	Loss of some control
Knowledge	Sharing of profits
Risk sharing	Access to proprietary skills/expertise

[handwritten margin note: pros vs cons of forming an alliance]

be a core competence, I was told to "... try to avoid forming alliances if you have a choice—the amount of management energy and attention needed to keep the relationship on track is enormous." Despite this warning, this particular firm had no choice but to form alliances. Because its skills were in basic science and technology, many downstream ventures and opportunities became available to this company only through alliances with market-facing partners.

Interestingly, little is known about which kind of alliance is better for a set of partners and how to evaluate the risk or reward profiles are of one form versus another. For example, if partners wish to share technology, it is difficult to determine whether a joint venture is better than a less complex, technology-sharing agreement. That is, different alliance forms can achieve the same results. However, under conditions of high uncertainty, where the consequences of failure are costly, less structured forms of alliances are apparently preferred. Similarly, when control is important to minimize the loss of proprietary information, highly structured alliances (e.g., joint ventures) are more advantageous. Even within the same industry, different alliance forms often emerge. Some firms will rely on licensing agreements and other will use joint ventures. What works for one firm might not work for another, based on a tolerance for ambiguity, a need for control, and level of trust. Exhibit 13.2 describes a continuum of alliance types and compares them on three critical criteria: cost, control, and flexibility. While the alliance rationale may appear to be the same, different alliance forms can emerge, depending on other organizational demands or constraints.

EXHIBIT 13.2   Different alliance forms.

Networks of firms	Buyer-seller alliances	Horizontal marketing programs	Value-added distribution	Joint ventures
Low cost to implement	←	→		High cost
High flexibility	←	→		Low flexibility
Low control	←	→		High control

EXHIBIT 13.3   Questions to help determine a closer or more distant alliance relationship.

- Do we want the partner to get close to our business?
- Is a major concern the ability to protect skills and information transfer?
- Is the partner bringing something very unique to the relationship?
- How quickly might we want to uncouple the relationship?
- Is trust a driver, or are we just doing business?
- Is transparency an issue?
- Do we have a high need to monitor the relationship regularly?
- Was it very difficult to learn about this partner?
- Do we have some level of discomfort working with this partner?
- Do arm's-length agreements seem to be appropriate in this relationship?
- Do you sense reluctance on the part of the partner to share sensitive data?

When working with clients we find that many times a firm calls a relationship an alliance when, in fact, they really have a contractual relationship. By asking a number of questions, it is possible to understand what kind of relationship management is comfortable. Exhibit 13.3 lists a series of such questions. If the concern is not to let the partner become too close, a form of licensing might be better than an embedded relationship where information flows more freely and partners work in close proximity, thereby enabling greater learning and cross-pollination of ideas. Questions regarding trust and the fear of allowing the partner to become too close might suggest the need for a more formal, contractual agreement that can be more easily monitored and managed. The intent is to more easily circumscribe the scope of the alliance and limit the degree and nature of the information and technology being shared. However, there are downsides as well. These arms length agreements do not allow information to flow easily between partners and limit the amount of learning that can be exchanged.

[handwritten margin note: every relationship is different]

CORE DIMENSIONS OF ALLIANCES

Despite the different structural forms alliances might take, each alliance must share certain key dimensions and elements. Such clarification is important, because the term *strategic alliance* is overused. In addition, companies tend to talk in code, using the term to mean something else. For example, many sellers hear the term *alliance* and become concerned that the buyer is interested only in price concessions, playing one seller against the other in search of these concessions. In other alliance contexts, trust and the fear of opportunism loom large, and these factors detract from any mutual gains the alliance might offer. Moreover, using the term sets expectations for certain kinds of behavior; that is, if you use the term *alliance* it establishes in the mind of your partner a certain set of behaviors.

Certain key dimensions must exist, and the higher the value associated with each dimension, the more stable the alliance. Keep in mind, alliances are naturally fragile and unstable and require an entirely different managerial mind-set. The instability stems from the inherent nature of an alliance: Two or more independent firms come together to accomplish mutually beneficial goals while maintaining their separate identities and autonomy. Given that the default option is self-interest, it should come as no surprise that the term *stability* is used. Alliances are quasi-organizational forms in which hierarchy and command and control are no longer meaningful concepts. Alliances are governed by a loose set of rules and norms that emerge between firms so that they might work together in support of mutual gain. Influence and cooperation replace administrative fiat. Discussion of key dimensions follows.

Goal Compatibility

Both parties have agreed that their goals, while not necessarily similar, are compatible, so that each party can achieve its own objectives as well as the objectives upon which the alliance is built. Part of the dilemma facing the partners is whether their individual goals and independence will be sacrificed for the good of the alliance. The loss of autonomy is often viewed as a potentially serious detriment to the formation of such close ties, and this is held in check when the parties acknowledge that both sets of goals do not need to run counter to each other. Firms might find that because of changes in one partner's business, an alliance no longer makes sense. Although Continental and Northwest joined forces to compete more favorably against the Big Three airlines (United, American, and Delta), Continental decided in 2000 to repurchase the shares it sold to Northwest as part of the initial agreement. Now that both airlines are stronger, Continental is interested in gaining more independence. In addition, a potential source of tension centers on transatlantic service, where the two compete in a very tough market oversaturated with capacity.

Strategic Advantage

The perceived benefit that will be gained from the alliance is often the raison d'être for the relationship. A strategic advantage for the partners includes the pooling of resources, the ability to gain access to markets and technical information, complementary strengths to be leveraged, and the ability to lower the total cost of production. As a screening device, each party must assess what the potential partner brings to the alliance. Furthermore, companies must determine whether a strategic alliance is the most appropriate vehicle for achieving relative competitive advantage. While the data suggests that the ROI of alliances is higher than for mergers and acquisitions, it still remains a complex problem to determine the best vehicle for achieving long-term competitive advantage.[3] In fact, whether to engage in outsourcing alliances often involves decisions about a firm's core values and what a more experienced or capable partner can offer. Many firms, for example, have made the decision to outsource their logistics and information technology functions. However, given the competition and very high costs of innovation and product introduction in the pharmaceutical business, a number of companies rely on many forms of alliances: contract manufacturing, cross-licensing, comarketing agreements, and joint ventures for the development of new drugs.

Interdependence

Broadly speaking, to engage in any exchange relationship is to become dependent on your partner. Part of the purchase decision process entails an evaluation of the benefits and risks involved in becoming dependent on the exchange partner. While interdependence is an antecedent to cooperation, it is also a precursor to conflict and is endemic to any relationship. The key is to manage the relationship in such a way that the cooperative and cohesive aspects of interdependence emerge and the dysfunctional aspects of conflict are minimized. Prior to the announcement that Bell Atlantic would merge with Nynex, the two firms formed a joint venture to combine their cellular operations. Given that both companies together controlled the mid-Atlantic and northeast corridors, a large percentage of cellular phone traffic flowed through their respective territories. Each firm became stronger because of the other, and it would be difficult to untangle the contribution made by one versus the other. To ignore this interdependence places partners at risk since there is a temptation to engage in opportunistic behavior and advance one partner's cause to the detriment of the other. Self-serving behavior is seen as a major cause of alliance conflict and, if unchecked, often leads to dissolution.

Trust and Commitment

As firms begin to share resources and decision making, opportunistic behavior can have a devastating effect on the partnership's survival. Despite the natural tendency for deceit and guile, implicit in all strategic alliances is trust, which serves to counterbalance such threats. Trust is the belief that a party's word or promise is reliable and will fulfill its obligation in the relationship. Without trust there can be no alliance. When trust is strong, roles are better understood, performance outcomes are better, partners rely on the more expert partner to execute on behalf of the alliance, the chemistry between partners is better, and partners understand more about each other's business. The bottom line is that trust builds a more solid relationship from a tentative alliance and helps to weave the safety net that gets partners through the tough times.

Commitment builds from trust and connotes solidarity and cohesion. A challenge for many alliances in the area of distribution is for both the manufacturer and the distributor to show commitment. Since both channel partners tend to have different objective functions and strive for different goals, they will find it difficult to cooperate unless they acknowledge that they can succeed *only* if they cooperate. Competition is not the goal between channel members; better channels is. Procter & Gamble does not compete with its distributors and retailers; competition is between P&G and its channels and Unilever and its channel partners. Manufacturers are reluctant to provide exclusive territories and must look for other ways to demonstrate commitment—for example, by providing product/market education, distributor support programs, lead-generation programs, and cooperative advertising dollars. Distributors often show commitment by agreeing not to carry competing lines or by dedicating personnel to the manufacturer's products. One small software firm thought that a high licensing fee would cause commitment. Sadly, the high fee was a problem. It did not lead to commitment and resulted in compliance such that the letter of the contract was adhered to, not the spirit of the relationship.

Communication and Conflict Resolution

Conflict resolution can take two paths: constructive and destructive. The direction taken by the firms involved depends on whether the relationship is cooperative or competitive. Although partners in an alliance are, by definition, joined in a cooperative venture, some aspects of the exchange are likely to be competitive. Managing the situation in order for cooperation and constructive conflict resolution to prevail becomes the problem. Open and honest communication of relevant information leads to the constructive resolution of conflict. Mohr and Spekman show that open channels of communication not only reduce conflict but also lead to higher levels of satisfaction between alliance members.[4]

Conflicts are likely to be resolved through problem solving and persuasion when there is agreement about goals. Given the contingent and uncertain nature of many alliances, it would be virtually impossible to establish a priori a set of rules for resolving problems and conflicts in the future. A legal contract would not be able to address each and every future exigency. Many successful strategic alliances are based instead on self-regulation, whereby alliance partners establish mechanisms and processes for resolving future conflicts. To the extent that the alliance is perceived as being fair and providing equitable resolution of future conflicts, the alliance will rest on a stronger foundation.

Researchers at the Darden School have developed the concept of the "blameless review," whereby alliance managers attempt to reduce conflict by working together and using facts rather than determining which party is at fault.[5] This is done to better understand how to create mechanisms to gain mutually beneficial resolutions to problems affecting the alliance. The primary goal of the blameless review is for firms to work jointly to address obstacles facing the alliance. If resolution cannot be attained, it is hoped that dissolution will occur, following a spirit of fair dealing. In fact, other data collected by the Darden team suggests that conflict resolution skills are far more important than negotiation skills in improving the performance of an alliance.[6] This is true especially if the negotiations are not framed within a win-win context and one partner attempts to extract the maximum it can from its partner.

Coordination of Work

As mentioned, interdependence is tied closely to the specialization of work. With recognition of interdependence, strategic partners exchange valued resources, and, in many cases, specialization is viewed as an extension of the workflow. Clearly, one advantage of collaboration is that the coordination of activities such as production scheduling, delivery, inventory management, and research and development can be approached at the level of functional integration without the bureaucracy and costs of ownership. Just-in-time (JIT) systems, electronic data interchange, joint marketing programs, shared R&D, and dedicated production facilities are examples of possible strategic alliances where the linkages between two companies must be flawless if the entire system is to run effectively. Programs whereby suppliers provide technical assistance or predesign expertise are often less obviously linked, but are no less important to the value chain and the efficiency of the production process. The important point to consider is not the linkage per se; rather it is the quality of the information exchanged that is key. If the information remains at a workflow level and does not capture higher-level strategic thought and longer-term planning, the relationship might not be considered an alliance, although the partners engage in alliance-like behavior.

Planning

The substance of planning in open market exchanges is limited to the scope of what is being exchanged. To a large degree, planning (probably a misnomer) equates to the form and substance of the contract under negotiation. Strategic alliances are built on a belief that planning the substance of the exchange is secondary to planning the structure and processes of exchange. Parties recognize that the future planning of substantive issues will occur naturally as a function of the structure and processes established at the beginning of the relationship. These processes must also be flexible to accommodate future change. Partners must openly share future plans and take each other's concerns into consideration when planning. By sharing information and being knowledgeable about each other's business, partners are able to set compatible goals that help maintain the relationship over time. Jointly forecasting the impact of technological advances or market developments enhances the alliance's ability to evaluate its joint outcomes. In other cases, the investments required to meet projected changes in technology and markets raise switching costs and exit barriers. To protect a firm's investment in an alliance, it is crucial that planning not be done in isolation.

Alliances Grow from the Strategy of the Firm

In a fall 2001 speech about the importance of alliances to his firm, Robert J. Stevens, COO of Lockheed Martin, said that Lockheed's partnership arrangements themselves are now routinely optimized to address the emerging value premises desired by its global customers. The underlying premise for the alliances/partnerships is the principle that the whole not only can be, but must be, greater than the sum of its parts. Here, alliance thinking is born from the strategic intent of the firm.

First and foremost there must be a strategy that addresses the future vision of the firm. Both partners must be able to articulate how the pending alliance fits into present and future direction of each firm. Without this sense of strategic direction, the alliance is flawed, and this omission could prove fatal. One senior executive in a telecommunications firm woke one morning and pronounced that all his competitors were forming alliances and he wanted some! Partner selection, setting objectives and milestones, and understanding which performance metrics are important all flow from the following question: What is the alliance trying to accomplish, and how does it support the strategic intent of the firm?

If strategic intent attempts to design the future state of the firm, management must ask what should be done to prepare for the future. Implicit in this question are several considerations: (1) What is the value proposition? That is, what customer needs will the company attempt to fill and how will the customer benefit. (2) What skills and capabilities are required to create value and gain a sustainable competitive advantage? (3) Do these skills lie currently within the core capabilities of the firm? If yes, these skills must be nurtured and honed. If no, how does the firm ensure that the skills are available? One option is to develop them internally; the other is to find a world-class partner who already possesses the requisite skill set and, through an alliance, leverage these skills. As part of this analysis, questions of fit should be addressed. Alignment, or fit, ensures that there is compatibility among partners' objectives as well as between the overall alliance goals and each partner's strategy.

It should be apparent that the need for strategic alignment has an immediate and profound effect on partner search and selection. The decisions regarding the right partner are based in part on the complementary skill set needed to bring value to the market and the core competence of the partner that enables the alliance to work smoothly and without conflict. On one hand, there are skills and resources that allow the alliance to potentially achieve a competitive advantage. Partner A brings a set of skills/assets and partner B brings a different, albeit complementary, set. On the other hand, without a certain level of alliance competence, partners will suboptimize although they separately have the requisite ingredients for success. The alignment of strategy and alliance thinking provides a fundamental appreciation for how the alliance dovetails with the future direction of the firm. Alignment is an essential starting point, but it also must be linked to issues of process and implementation. A concern for process adds a temporal dimension that affects how managers negotiate, execute, and modify alliances over time. A focus on process suggests that significant gaps remain when considering the following kinds of questions: How do alliances evolve over time? What are the managerial skills and perspectives required to manage an evolving alliance? What kinds of problems can alliance managers expect to address over the life of an alliance?

A LIFE-CYCLE APPROACH TO STRATEGIC ALLIANCES

Studying an alliance's evolution over its life cycle helps us understand the process view of alliances.[7] Life-cycle analysis is a widely accepted approach in the marketing, management, and organizational literature. It is applied to products and markets, research and development, organizational growth and evolution, production processes, and personal relationships.[8]

Exhibit 13.4 illustrates the different stages of the alliance life cycle. Each stage is built on a changing alliance landscape as the vision becomes reality and

EXHIBIT 13.4 Differences can be found over alliance life-cycle stages.

	Anticipation	Engagement	Valuation	Coordination	Investment	Stabilization	Decision
Characteristics of life cycle stage	Pre-alliance Competitive needs & motivation emerge	High energy Complementarity Congruence Strategic potential	Financial focus Business cases Analysis Internal selling	Operational focus Task orientation Division of labor Parallel activity	Hard choices Committing Resource reallocation Broadening scope	High interdependence Maintenance Assessment of relative worth and contribution	Where now?
Key business activity	Partner search	Partner identification	Valuation Negotiation	Coordination Integration	Expansion Growth	Adjustment	Reevaluation
Key relationship activity	"Dating"	Imagining	Initiating	Interfacing	Committing	Fine-tuning	"Reassessing" "Dialoging"
Role of alliance manager	Visionary	Strategic sponsor	Advocate	Networker	Facilitator	Manager	Mediator

the reality grows into a mature business. *Anticipating* is the preliminary stage whereby an organization envisions the possibilities, ideas, and dreams of an alliance. A firm begins to articulate its strategic intent for the alliance as well as forming the requisite criteria for a potential partner. Prework is performed at this stage to determine why an alliance is the preferred strategic option. Consistent with the previous discussion, it is here that the question of alignment surfaces and a linkage must be made between future direction and the goals of the alliance. This discussion continues through the second stage as well. *Engaging* is the next stage, which is characterized by the partners beginning to sort or shape their mutual expectation for the alliance. Key managers begin to take ownership of the proposed partnership. *Valuing* is that period during which the terms of the business exchange are finalized. It is at this time that the business case is fully and completely made. Previous attempts to make the business case were more pro forma and spoke in more general terms with less precision regarding performance metrics and outcomes. Terms and conditions are negotiated, relative contribution of each firm is assessed, and resultant benefits are determined. *Coordinating* describes the stage where joint work formally begins and more permanent governance structures begin to emerge. Firms at this stage focus on the integration and coordination of complementary business activities so that the alliance partners can leverage the anticipated gains derived from the alliance. *Investing* captures the hard realities of the alliance, at which point partners must invest (i.e., commit to) the future course of the alliance. Now the vision must be translated to an economic reality as key resources are dedicated to the alliance. Finally, *stabilizing* defines the stage in which the alliance has become an ongoing, viable entity. Homeostasis exists, and efforts by each partner are dedicated to managing the alliance with the adjustments and fine-tuning needed to keep it on course.

Beyond the delineation of each of the stages, there is also a dynamic interplay of activities, people, and processes. By examining this interplay, a more robust picture emerges.

From Exhibit 13.4, it is also clear that an alliance is a complex interaction of business and interpersonal activities whose purpose is to achieve mutually beneficial goals. Both of these activities are at work in an alliance's development; both work simultaneously with each other. An examination of the business cycle helps us understand the evolution of the commercial side of the alliance, whereas a study of relationship activities provides insight into the interaction between partner organizations and individuals. The *business life cycle* relates to the economic purpose of the alliance and can be best appreciated from a traditional product-life-cycle perspective. Each phase is characterized by a set of questions and can be recognized by a concern for issues such as business processes, environmental changes, potential or actual competitive responses, financial projections, market access, customer acceptance, and mechanisms for sharing risks and rewards.

Business and relationship activities work together. One cannot focus exclusively on the commercial logic of the deal. Interpersonal relationships are key to working relationships, and they are more important when they occur across organizational hierarchies. The interpersonal relationship provides a cushion of trust that braces the alliance, especially when the business is under stress. It is the safety net that protects the alliance from self-destruction when the business is underperforming or when expectations are not being realized. It would be naive to contend, however, that a strong relationship is sufficient for an alliance to succeed; there must first exist a strong business proposition. A number of alliances evolve initially because senior managers look for reasons to work together; however, a strong business rationale must prevail if the alliance is to succeed. A cushion of trust can prevent partners from acting rashly in an attempt to fix the business quickly and salvage the investment. There is a tendency for partners in the alliance to take a more measured approach to business problems.

Ironically, when the business is strong, partners are very willing to ignore problems facing the interpersonal side of the relationship. It is natural to ignore problems when there are slack resources and goals are being reached. However, if attention is diverted from the interpersonal relationship, a false sense of security can easily develop in the good times. As a result, strength of conviction disappears in the face of adversity. Conversely, a company must also guard against the possibility that the relationship might exhibit greater value than the alliance itself. If the business proposition is truly bankrupt, the strength of interpersonal ties must not cloud sound business judgment.

Alliance management is made even more complex because of a firm's culture. For example, it is not limited to national differences; there are corporate cultures that affect firms' abilities to work together. If partners do not share certain core elements of their culture, the conflict that arises could seriously damage the alliance. Volvo and Renault seemed to differ in their dedication to safety at any cost. In a jointly developed platform for a new car, the P4, the simulated crash tests placed the engine partly in the passenger compartment, and the partners reacted quite differently. To many consumers Volvo equals safety, and Renault was less willing to spend the time and the money to placate Volvo's obsessive concerns. Such a disagreement could be a deal breaker, because a value held sacred by one is not by the other. In other instances, complications arise because objectives can change as the alliance develops and matures. Changes in management, business models, competition, external economic conditions can all call into question the basic goals upon which the alliance was built.

THE ALLIANCE MANAGER

Exhibit 13.4 also highlights the role of the alliance manager. We have previously made reference to the importance of trust and commitment. These dimensions exist at the individual level and are fundamental to the role of alliance managers, who provide coordination and integration between the alliance partners. Yoshino and Rangan state that firms that make the best use of alliances tend to assign responsibility for their management to a specific manager.[9] Simply put, an effective alliance manager is essential to alliance success.

Exhibit 13.3 further suggests that different alliance management roles follow different stages of the alliance life cycle. In the early stages of the alliance, alliance management is concerned with *visioning* and *sponsoring*. Alliance management first requires the formulation of the alliance idea, followed by internal selling, which helps the firm recognize the potential benefits of the alliance. As the alliance begins to take shape, alliance management concentrates on being an advocate for the alliance to important stakeholders and *networking* within and across companies to secure the commitment and participation of key organizational players. As the business solidifies, alliance management becomes concerned with *managing* and overseeing the operation of the ongoing alliance, in addition to *mediating* conflicts between partners, which can occur through the alliance's normal maturity and decline. What is important here is that the management focus shifts in concert with the temporal evolution of the alliance.

With all of the changing priorities and evolving focus in management, it is not surprising that managers are ill prepared to deal with the complexities of managing alliances. This problem raises the following question, which is critical to understanding how successful alliances are built and managed: What makes a good alliance manager at a given stage in an alliance's evolution?

Successful alliance management must operate simultaneously on three levels. These levels are interorganizational, intraorganizational, and interpersonal. On the *interorganizational level*, the alliance manager must balance the needs, resources, and desires of each of the partner companies. On the *intraorganizational level*, alliance managers must manage the needs, resources, and desires of their own company. On the *interpersonal level*, the alliance managers must manage relationships with superiors, peers, and subordinates, not only in their own firm, but also across boundaries of their various partner organizations.

Alliance management poses a unique set of challenges that set it apart from hierarchical management. Alliance management is dependent on terms like *compromise, influence, trust,* and *commitment*. Since partners maintain their autonomy, you cannot make demands, dictate, or issue directives. The partners' agreement must be obtained on mutually achievable goals, and processes must be enacted to achieve these goals. Research on alliances between entrepreneurial firms demonstrates that formal contracts have little effect in maintaining the relationship between trading partners.[10] Informal relationships create the social bonds between alliance managers that play a critical role in alliance development and continuity.

Alliance managers must possess skills and competencies in three areas: functional skill sets, interpersonal skill sets, and alliance mind-sets. *Functional skill sets* can be considered the tools that a manager calls upon to accomplish specific objectives throughout the business cycle. These skill sets are similar to the range of skills learned in an MBA program. *Interpersonal skill sets* can be considered the tools an alliance manager uses to initiate, cultivate, and maintain relationships throughout the relationship cycle. *Alliance mind-sets* are an overarching perspective that frame how a manager approaches alliance problems and creates order from ambiguity and chaos.

In Search of an Ideal Managerial Profile

A host of alliance management challenges interplay regarding relationship ambiguity, a shift in managerial mind-sets, and the complex linkages among strategies, structure, and systems of both the partner firms and the alliance. These factors work in tandem and are best illustrated by the different role requirements of successful alliance managers.[11]

Given the skill sets and mind-set constructs, alliance managers exhibit varying degrees of skill-set capabilities and different mind-sets; the optimal blend of skill sets and mind-set will vary across alliance stages. For example, in the very early stages of an alliance, the ideal alliance manager would be expected to display strong business and interpersonal skill sets, framed in the interpretive perspective of a learning mind-set. This combination would form an optimal fit between the alliance environment and the manager. The strong business skill set takes advantage of the breadth of industry knowledge required to formulate sound strategy. The strong interpersonal skill set addresses the need to rapidly develop and cultivate strong relationships. The learning mind-set draws on a variety of experiences to interpret and manage the uncertainty of the early alliance environment. As this environment becomes more complex, a learning mind-set becomes more critical.

Conversely, in the late stages of an alliance, the ideal manager might display strong functional skill sets and moderate interpersonal skill sets, framed in the interpretive perspective of an incremental mind-set. The strong functional skill set allows the manager to squeeze every bit of remaining value out of the venture. The moderate interpersonal skill set addresses the need to maintain, rather than

grow, the alliance relationship. This incremental mind-set is able to work confi-
dently within the managerial parameters laid down by the alliance partners.

The particular managerial needs of any given alliance will vary in response
to a wide variety of influences. Nevertheless, this framework offers a perspective
for identifying the most appropriate manager for a given set of situational circumstances and an appreciation for the different roles played by the alliance
manager over the various stages of the alliance's life cycle. As stated previously,
in the early stages of the alliance, the alliance manager might be a strategic sponsor and a combination of visionary and emissary. As the alliance grows, the manager takes on the role of networker and facilitator responsible for linking key
people, functions, and business areas in the pursuit of the alliance's goals. In
addition to being a manager who shoulders responsibility for the business of the
alliance, the alliance manager must also be an adept mediator.

Kotter's view of a prototype for a twenty-first-century executive is also similar to our vision of a successful alliance manager.[12] The commitment to learning,
seeking challenges, and reflecting honestly on success and failure is consistent
with our profile. The successful alliance manager is the symbol of the learning
organization. Kotter describes this lifelong learner as someone who is a risk taker
and a careful listener, reflective and open to new ideas. However, a number of
issues can either enable or obstruct the alliance manager's ability to forge the
alliance and reap the intended gains. Even if the manager is alliance-competent,
a number of structural and process considerations can affect the abilities of even
the most competent.

Alliance Competence: The Effects of Organizational Structure and Process

Firms viewed as alliance-competent tend to be highly sought after by other firms
as possible partners. These firms can better leverage the skills of their partners
so that the hoped-for synergies are more likely to result. These firms experience
less conflict and have higher rates of return. To focus on structure and process
forces, attention must be paid to those more subtle characteristics that support
or inhibit alliance-like behavior. A representative list of these characteristics is
reflected in Exhibit 13.5. Successfully managing the four areas of structure and
process will separate those firms that are more likely to flourish from those that
are more likely to squander time and money developing alliances that will underperform because the requisite supportive mechanisms do not exist. Despite the
good intentions of management, mixed signals are often sent. Inconsistent policies and procedures are fundamental structural barriers that will undermine the
firm's alliance efforts.

EXHIBIT 13.5   Organizational structural and process considerations and their impact on alliance formation and success.

Overview	Characteristics	Implications
Stop silo-bound thinking.	• Information flows laterally. • Coordinative and integrative mechanisms exist. • Interdependence is appreciated.	If there is no enterprisewide thinking and information flows are limited to the intended hierarchy, firms cannot engage the informal network that nurtures alliance activities.
Information is a public good.	• Trust that shared information will be used as intended. • Information flows easily across the boundaries of the firms. • Informal communications are as important as the formal	If information is closely held because of the fear of expropriation, and managers are very skeptical of how information is used, alliance partners will spend more effort monitoring each other's actions than hierarchy. working together to create value in marketplace.
Encourage decentralization.	• Decision-making authority flows to the point of contact. • Management empowers and shares responsibility willingly.	Given the rise of information networks, it is important for both information and responsibility for decisions to flow to the point where the decision should be made.
Develop compatible reward systems.	• Long-term thinking is encouraged. • Team and individual reward systems are developed. • Workers are encouraged to share both good and bad news.	Alliances are inherently long term. They require performance metrics, reward systems, and overall perspectives that reflect the long-term view.

Our entire previous discussion assumes that alliances have anticipated lives that span a number of years. In fact, alliance longevity is often used as a surrogate measure of alliance success. Interestingly, these more sustainable alliances are often described through the marriage metaphor, which itself implies that a relationship is expected to last a long time. While many alliances do in fact last decades, managers cannot afford this luxury under conditions of rapidly changing markets and technologies. Therefore, in a number of newly developed industries, we are witnessing a class of alliances whose life expectancies are quite short.

INTERIMISTIC ALLIANCES

Interimistic alliances represent fast-developing, often short-lived alliances where partners combine their skills and resources to address a transient, albeit important, business opportunity. This opportunity may involve market access, technology development, or new product development. Interimistic alliances are typically found in swiftly evolving industries and markets marked by rapid technological change and uncertainty. Examples of these alliances abound, appearing in nascent industries such as biotechnology or electronic commerce. These alliances often are spawned by new technological developments, such as recombinant DNA or the Internet.

These alliances appear to challenge conventional academic wisdom with respect to how partners develop relationship attributes necessary for the creation of alliance value, at what levels these attributes must exist, and the definition of alliance success. As suggested previously, it is natural to take a long-term view of alliance creation. Conventional wisdom suggests that the relationship characteristics (for example, trust and norms) are necessary for effective operation and value creation and are developed over a considerable length of time. In fact, the life-cycle research referred to previously suggests that it could take alliances about three years to work through their start-up problems. Such a time frame can often exceed the entire life of an interimistic alliance, given the rapidly evolving environment in which it operates and the fact that competitive requirements often change in turbulent markets. Because of the need for immediate strategic impact and the fact that their objectives are typically short term in nature, interimistic alliance partners must hit the ground running. The partnership characteristics required for the effective operation of the interimistic alliance have to be either in place or developed in a highly compressed period of time.

In addition, questions arise about such issues as trust, opportunistic behavior, and commitment. Academic literature often uses the analogy of marriage to describe alliances, assuming long-term relations as the norm. Because of the shorter-term nature of interimistic alliances, relationship attributes necessary for a functional alliance, such as commitment and trust, exist—but in modified form. For example, commitment in interimistic alliances appears to be more project-bound than broad-based. Norms tend to be tied more to expectations derived from the industry rather than established through the relationship. Moreover, these relationships tend to be less proprietary in nature and are often nonexclusive. This is particularly true if the goal of the alliance is to set standards or to gain wider acceptance of a singular operating system. In order to jump-start the relationship, the behaviors and expectations of the partners are often a reflection of the industry in which the partners reside. It is almost like a clan in that partners feel a part of a family in which the rules are known. Often, when the partners intermarry, the rules for one may no longer apply for the other since their industry experience is quite different. We see this when large, established firm's partner with smaller start-ups. There is often a lack of trust between large and small companies, but this sense of vigilance is made even more salient when the partners' past experiences have not been the same.

Finally, it appears that interimistic and sustainable alliances have different measures of success. Interimistic alliances appear to be more focused on achieving success that is narrower in scope and not as results-oriented as the strategies pursued by sustainable alliances. Interimistic alliances help firms achieve milestone objectives on the path to greater final measures of success, such as market share or profitability. These alliances accomplish goals that, if not reached, make it very difficult for the final objectives to be attained. Companies involved in sustainable alliances often define success with a metric that more closely monitors the initial business proposition on which the alliance was formed. Conversely, interimistic alliances focus on intermediate measures of success that, it is to be hoped, at some future time will result in financial gain for each partner. For instance, many of these interimistic alliances merely position firms to participate in a future market or to avail themselves of a new technological opportunity. These types of alliances allow firms to hedge their bets and, in effect, purchase options on future market and technological developments. These alliances provide an opportunity for firms to experiment with the future, to learn from that experience, and to continue to move forward wiser and better informed. For example, CyberCash has formed a number of alliances with the intent to promote its encryption protocol as the standard for Internet commerce. If its technology does not emerge as the dominant standard, CyberCash is likely to have difficulty participating as a full player as Internet commerce grows.

With respect to scope, traditional alliances are often broadly defined, encompassing sets of interrelated activities or functions. For example, alliances in the airline industry are often quite complex and far-reaching, involving the need for coordination at the operations level with flight crews, kitchens, and baggage handlers and at the administrative level with joint procurement of fuel, integrated frequent-flyer programs, scheduling, and mechanisms for revenue sharing. Interimistic alliances, on the other hand, are often designed to achieve more narrowly defined objectives such as acquiring know-how, producing a new product, or influencing industry standards.

Differences in the environmental drivers of these alliances account for differences in how relationship variables develop and at what levels these variables are present in both types of alliances. While all alliances are intended to mitigate uncertainty, sustainable alliances are more conducive to an environment of relatively low to moderate market and technology turbulence. These conditions allow for a longer time horizon and the deliberate development of the necessary relationship attributes. Interimistic alliances, however, appear to be motivated during times of very high market and technological instability. Because the market and technology underlying the alliance's value proposition are rapidly changing and speed to market is often critical, partners are forced to proceed to the value-creation stage of relationship development very quickly. Also, rapidly changing competitive requirements, such as changes in product or process technology needed to compete or changes in the marketplace (e.g., when the proprietary online market was replaced by the Web), compel partners' perspectives to be much more transient in nature. The speed of relationship development and the partners' expectations that the alliance will be short-lived force the firms to either find ways to truncate the relationship development process or to modify the form of the relationship attributes achieved. Moreover, success in an interimistic alliance often allows participation in later alliances. This progression is analogous to the new product development process and the use of gates. In a gating system, requirements for an earlier stage must be met before the process can proceed to the next gate.

Imagine situations (for example, Internet commerce, digital cellular, EDI) in which there must first emerge a widely accepted standard before a new market or technology can be developed. If a firm is not involved in the setting of standards, it might be precluded from competing at a later point. Also, given the rapid technological changes and the convergence of different technologies, it is expected that partners work both in tandem and in sequence with partners entering and leaving and possibly reentering the alliance as their capabilities and skills become relevant. Think of the interimistic alliance (all alliances) as fitting the pieces of a puzzle. Here, the pieces are not always known in advance; the puzzle evolves over time, and not each partner has skills that match with each piece, so the number of partners might change as we complete different sections of the puzzle. The pieces of the puzzle are held together by the strength of the business case and the bonds that are formed among the different alliance partners. These bonds are derivatives of the relationship attributes that help establish the roles, norms, and range of acceptable behaviors of the partners.

A Comparison of the Development of Relationship Attributes

Relationship attributes, such as trust and commitment, are dimensions that have been used as predictors of relationship performance, and they are necessary for an alliance to mature to a value-creation stage.[13] The manner in which these attributes evolve and at what level they exist in interimistic alliances is often different from the traditional model of alliance development. These attributes include trust, mutual goals, norms, interdependence, social bonds, commitment, and performance satisfaction. Our conclusions are summarized in Exhibit 13.6.

Trust is a precondition for alliance formation and is not an attribute that emerges over the life of the alliance; there is often insufficient time for this attribute to develop. Two important points arise here: (1) Trust is assumed to exist at a threshold level *before* the alliance partners consummate an interimistic alliance, because there is little time to let trust emerge. The alliance decision becomes binary: There either *is* sufficient trust or there *is not* sufficient trust. Thus, past behavior as a partner becomes the predictor of future expectations about behavior and trustworthiness. (2) Trust is more context-specific and is limited to the scope of the interimistic alliance and the parts of the partners' business affected by it. Since many interimistic alliances tend to be nonexclusive, trust must be framed within that context. In traditional alliances, trust is viewed almost as an emergent core value of the alliance, built through the interactions of the partners.

Similarly, commitment, social bonds, and norms are tied more closely to the context of the alliance and are less embedded in a web of strong social ties between alliance partners. Dependence is linked to the goal of the alliance, and partners are motivated to cooperate as long as each views the other as essential to accomplishing each firm's longer-term goals and the alliance's mutual goal. While seemingly opportunistic, such self-serving behavior is held in check by the fact that partners are likely to meet again in the future, and opportunistic behavior would be self-destructive in the long term. One partner's enlightened self-interest is modified by a set of norms that exist in the industry, which serve to guide interfirm behavior, thereby shaping expectations. This is in contrast to research that shows how social norms emerge over time as part of the alliance partners' continued interaction.[14] Interimistic alliances are driven by the moment, and the mutual goals become part of the "contract." In this sense, goal compatibility is seen as conditional on the changes in environmental events that can drastically alter industry demands. Both partners recognize that influences beyond their control, such as changing technology or a set of unexpected competitors, can make initial motivations for the alliance irrelevant, thereby eliminating goal congruence. At that moment, partners may decide to go their separate ways. Or they might agree to refocus their energy and jointly pursue a new opportunity. Nimbleness clearly is a virtue.

The nature and development of norms in interimistic alliances differ from those of sustainable alliances. When environmental influences dictate otherwise, it is understood that the alliance could end quickly and that the partners might well become competitors. In this context, parties have expectations about potential individualistic or competitive actions by the partners and harbor less of a sense of continuity about the relationship. There is a mutually expressed or tacit

EXHIBIT 13.6 A comparison of sustainable and interimistic alliances.

Relationship Attribute	Sustainable Alliances	Interimistic Alliances
Evolution to value-creation stage	Deliberate and lengthy	Quick and short
Expected life span	Long	Short
Environmental/industry conditions	Stable technological change; reasonably predictable market and technology trajectory; increasing competition forces cost reduction and/or increasing value-added	Rapid technological change; high level of uncertainty regarding market and technology; importance of speed to market
Trust	Evolves over time	Based on previous experience with partner and/or on reputation and/or a pragmatic view of the partners' mutual-hostage position
Mutual goals	Critical, often broad-based	Critical, although it is project- or condition-oriented
Norms	Relational exchange norms, based on the expectation of mutuality of interest; prescribing stewardship behavior; enhance the well-being of the relationship as a whole	Shared, enlightened self-interest; norms based on the mutual understanding that the firms will work together as long as the alliance makes good business sense
Interdependence	High and self-renewing	Recognized but specific to the alliance task at hand
Social bonds	Strong and pervasive	Some level is essential; broad reach is limited by virtue of the narrow scope of project; some preexisting relationship sometimes exists
Commitment	Strong	Strong, but conditional, and/or bounded by scope of project
Performance satisfaction	The usual measures of corporate success: development of long-term cost and/or differentiation advantages and achieving a certain threshold level of profitability/market share	Less tangible measures of success: influencing standard setting, part of achieving a portfolio of technology options, strategically positioning for the future, acquiring know-how, signaling partners/competitors/the market

understanding that the firms will work together as partners as long as the alliance makes good business sense. One key difference between sustainable and inter-imistic alliances is the emphasis placed on competitive considerations. For example, Visa and MasterCard International cooperate in such areas as standards setting, encryption, and basic smart-card technology. However, they knowingly and vigorously compete against each other once agreement has been reached.[15] These companies know that without agreement on fundamental strategic points facing the whole credit-card industry, both will face limited opportunities. In this context, it might be more appropriate to refer to the emerging literature on *co-opetition*, which attempts to combine the best elements from research on cooperation and competition.[16] The notion of complimentors might become salient as parties ally to reap certain mutual gains so that they might both later compete in an expanded marketplace.

Interimistic alliances are partial solutions to business problems that exist in a turbulent environment. Therefore, performance metrics should be pegged to the goals associated with the reason for the alliance. In addition, it is best to view interimistic alliances as providing a set of options for partners to pursue in future, or a series of future, alliances. Failure in an early alliance may preclude access to a later alliance. As such, it is very likely that firms will engage a series of alliance partners as they attempt to achieve competitive advantage.

Performance satisfaction is the degree to which the business transaction meets the business performance expectations of the partners. Defining appropriate measures of success and performance have been debated without resolution in the literature.[17] In interimistic alliances, in addition to social outcomes having a reduced priority, more project-oriented measures of success are used. These might include influencing standards setting, developing a strategic portfolio of technology options for the future, strategically positioning for the future, acquiring know-how, signaling to partners, competitors, and customers, or simply taking the only avenue open to the firm if it wants to be a player in an emerging arena. Success might better be viewed as a staging point or intermediate position on the way to a future competitive gain. Parties might successfully partner now so that each can successfully compete later in what is expected to be a larger market. If this alliance fails, neither partner might have acquired the requisite skills, knowledge, or influence over the market to compete later. Success in the interimistic alliance is necessary, but not sufficient, for the individual firm's future profitability.

Importance of Reputation

Because partners have different temporal expectations about interimistic alliances, these alliances require that partners play by rules that are somewhat different from those applicable to sustainable alliances. While these interimistic alliances might often be as close and collaborative as any sustainable alliance, they tend to exhibit a higher degree of self-interest and bounded commitment. To a greater degree, partners in this type of alliance must adopt a stance of duality tinged with a sense of opportunism: How can the partners manage the existence of such seemingly diametrically opposed postures without jeopardizing the collaborative spirit that must exist between the partners for them to quickly create value? In part, expectations must be shaped to tolerate a certain level of self-interest. However, it seems that a more significant factor affecting the ability of the partners to balance self and alliance interests and quickly bring the alliance up to speed is the pivotal role of each partner's *reputation* in interimistic alliances.

Having a reputation as a fair-dealing and competent alliance partner is critical to shortcutting the relationship development process. This reputation can be based on prior direct experience with the firm or general business community consensus. Without strong positive mutual reputational effects, firms in alliance cannot quickly progress to the value-creation stage, as is often necessary in rapidly evolving markets. A reputation for *fair dealing* is the platform from which partners can take the leap of faith necessary to quickly achieve a state of close collaboration.

The second important reputational component is *competence*. Competence has two dimensions. One dimension deals with a partner's skills, know-how, and core competencies. Partners are desirable by virtue of their technical or market acumen. For example, because of their recognized expertise, both Sun Microsystems and Netscape participate in a number of nonexclusive, nonproprietary, potentially competitive alliances. Corning enjoys a stellar reputation as an alliance partner and works very hard to focus on what is important to their alliances. Ego is not a key concern for Corning. Note that in each of their joint ventures, the Corning name is second, which speaks volumes regarding the values of the company and the acknowledgment that self-serving behavior or any semblance of it can adversely affect the relationship.

The second dimension captures the notion of alliance competence, which is a more nebulous construct. A reputation for alliance competence assures potential partners that the firm is managerially well versed in structuring and implementing alliances. We introduced the notion of competence earlier in this chapter. This makes the firm more attractive to potential partners, because it enhances the ability of the alliance to quickly get up to speed and improves the probability of alliance success. In this case, the partner is an enabler or a facilitator who is able to achieve heightened alliance results by minimizing the nonproductive energy associated with alliance formation and value creation. In addition, firms with high alliance competence have a wider choice of potential partners and have more discretion in selecting the best partners. Better partners are chosen early, while less competent partners have fewer choices available to them.

Perhaps the best way to develop both alliance competence and, simultaneously, a reputation for competence is to develop a deep base of alliance experience. However, learning how to manage successful alliances is an evolutionary process. Firms can truly learn only by doing. For example, not only does Hewlett-Packard spend a considerable amount of money and effort training its managers on the art of alliance management, but it also uses alliances to learn about alliances. A business development manager at Hewlett-Packard commented that "after each alliance is formed, we hold a postmortem with all the involved (HP) parties. We look at the original objectives, the implementation, what went right, what went wrong." This information goes into a written management briefing, which later goes into an alliance database. By building a systematic approach to learning from alliance experiences, HP improves, throughout the corporation, its future alliance management capabilities on a real-time basis. It is no surprise that HP enjoys a positive reputation as an alliance partner. Corning, as well, seems to have as a core strength a positive alliance culture. Managers are tested early in alliance situations and, over time, gain escalating alliance responsibilities. In instances where alliance-like thinking is not institutionalized and made part of the fabric of the firm, we believe that these firms will be relegated to second-class status. The world is too uncertain, the cost of market entry and technological development is too high, and firms do not have the luxury of developing a go-it-alone strategy.

ALLIANCE PERFORMANCE AND BALANCED SCORECARDS

Many companies use a balanced scorecard approach to developing performance metrics. The advantages of this approach have been discussed elsewhere, and we need not elaborate here.[18] Suffice it to say that the methodology helps clarify and translate vision and strategy, and it combines a long-term and short-term perspective in pursuit of the firm's goals. Similarly, this approach is relevant for understanding better alliance performance. As can be seen in Exhibit 13.7, we can map the balanced scorecard perspective with alliance-related thinking. The goal is to reenforce the close linkage between strategy development and alliance formation and to demonstrate that the two are quite compatible and, in fact, feed into each other.

EXHIBIT 13.7   A balanced scorecard (BSC) for alliances.

BSC Perspective	Translation to Alliance Thinking	Alliance Measures	Implications
Financial perspective	Alliance financial objectives	These metrics flow from the business case and could relate to • Cost savings • Revenue targets • Market share	What is the impact of our actions? Given the longer-term focus of alliances, an investment made today might not reap rewards for a longer period of time. Expectations must be set for a longer-term horizon.
Customer perspective	Customer perspective	Above all, alliances must create value in the marketplace. • What is the value proposition? • How does the alliance contribute to a competitive advantage?	Knowing the contribution of each partner to value creation is often tricky and must begin with understanding the role each plays and the skills each brings. Complementarity is key, and each partner must acknowledge the contribution of the other.
Business process perspective	Internal perspective	This perspective captures the internal changes and adaptations that are needed for the alliance to achieve its goals. Very often, processes must be adapted, structural barriers must be removed, and so on. Questions related to expectations, roles, risk profiles, decision-making styles, attitudes around information sharing, and the like are important	If partners do not have a common platform from which to launch their alliance, problems can cause the alliance to underperform. Some of the issues are very subtle and are hard to discern, but nonetheless they must be considered.
Learning and growth	Learning perspective	Alliances are most successful when partners value learning and have mechanisms in place to encourage the transfer of knowledge and information both internally among divisions and externally with partners.	If partners do not tolerate mistakes, do not have a process for institutionalizing alliance learning, and do not invest in their people, their probability of achieving high levels of alliance success is low.

SUMMARY

In this chapter we have described the alliance phenomenon as a major corporate activity. As conglomerates in the 1960s and 1970s, alliances have emerged as an important organizational form in the twenty-first century. It is estimated that by 2004, there will be alliance-related revenue of close to $40 trillion produced, yet

60 percent of these alliances will underperform. We still have a long way to go before we crack the code on how to ensure alliance success.

We have defined what alliances are and have established precise criteria partly in response to the observation that the term *alliance* is overused and little understood. Moreover, alliances and alliance management have been described as a dynamic process that appears to follow a life cycle in which objectives, demands, and managerial processes vary over time. Finally, we have introduced the concept of interimistic alliances, more fast-paced, transient relationships that appear to capture the nature of alliances in more embryonic industries. These shorter-term alliances capture the notion of networks of firms competing with other networks. These alliance forms have been compared to more traditional, stable alliances, which are often described through the use of marriage analogies.

FOR FURTHER READING

Doz, Yves, and Gary Hamel, *Alliance Advantage* (Boston: Harvard Business School Press, 1999).

Dyer, Jeffrey, *Collaborative Advantage* (New York: Oxford University Press, 2000).

Harbison, John, and Peter Pekar, *Smart Alliances* (San Francisco: Jossey-Bass Publishers, 1999).

Lewis Jordan, *Trusted Partners* (New York: Free Press, 1999).

Segil, Larraine, *Fast Alliances* (New York: John Wiley & Sons, 2001).

14 INTERNATIONAL BUSINESS

In a provocative article written in 1990, Robert B. Reich, secretary of labor in the first Clinton term, asked the question, "Who is us?" Reich made the point that identifying companies as American, German, or Japanese because they originated or were headquartered in those countries was a distorted view of business and a poor basis for policymaking. Because of the growing importance of international business, companies have expanded their manufacturing, research and development, and sales activities across borders. Many companies have more foreign employees than domestic ones, greater global sales than local ones, and a higher proportion of profits generated overseas than at home. This being the case, in what sense are such companies designated as a particular nationality? Reich argues that they are not national and that government policies should recognize this, encouraging companies to invest in the human capital of a nation, regardless of the origin of a particular company.

Reich makes an important point, but it tends to obscure an equally important one—namely, the difficulty of conducting international business and balancing the often conflicting cultures and objections of various participants. It brings with it extraordinary opportunities, but also new challenges and risks for corporations and the managers. Some of the challenges are broad: how to organize the firm, how to understand the economics and policies of the host country. Others are narrower but quite crucial: What should the compensation system be, and how do we manage exchange risk?

In this chapter, we are going to focus on four aspects of doing business globally: (1) making the foreign investment decision, (2) managing political risk, (3) understanding foreign exchange, and (4) organizing the transnational firm.

MOTIVES FOR INTERNATIONAL INVESTMENT

Operations in distant and culturally different places are inherently more difficult than domestic operations; domestic companies have a competitive advantage. Consequently, firms must have a variety of positive reasons to invest overseas.

Possible Competitive Advantages of Foreign Firms

There are several possible compensations for incurring the risk and problems of foreign investment. Some industries are characterized by economies of scale. That is, firms with larger market shares globally are able to operate more efficiently, with lower cost structures. A large multinational corporation (MNC) therefore has an advantage over smaller, local firms because of its lower unit costs of production. Moreover, local production might be the only way to capture or maintain market share. Many firms shift from an export orientation to overseas production because trade barriers restrict or threaten their access to current or potential markets. If competitors establish production facilities inside the trade barriers, they might be able to expand their market share, reduce costs, and compete more effectively in all other markets. This is one example of defensive foreign investment—overseas expansion motivated by a desire to protect market position. As regional trading agreements have grown in importance, companies from outside those areas have sought to establish insider positions by investing in a member country. For example, Japanese firms invest in England and Mexico to be inside the European Economic Community and NAFTA.

Another advantage that firms can exploit is superior knowledge or technical expertise. This might be the result of research and development activities or skills related to the marketing of products. Knowledge-intensive industries, such as the chemical, pharmaceutical, and electronics industries, have been major sources of foreign investment activity. So have consumer products industries, where brand identification and promotion skills are important. Both types of knowledge—production and marketing—can be exploited to compensate for the additional difficulties of overseas investment. They might provide reduced operating costs or product differentiation that allow the firm to compete, even though it may have a higher cost structure.

Although the advantages of superior knowledge explain how firms can successfully compete overseas, they do not necessarily explain why. Those advantages can be used to expand export sales, but it is when export sales are threatened by restrictions or competition that overseas production is desirable. Once a foreign firm has established a market for a product or service through exports, domestic competitors enter that market. With protection through quotas or tariffs, the domestic firms are able to compete with and, in some cases totally displace, foreign producers.

In the current economic environment, debt-burdened, less-developed countries are pursuing aggressive trade policies. These policies frequently include import substitution. Encouraging local production causes imports to be reduced and incentives to be created for foreign investment.

Many of the countries are engaging in extensive privatization programs. Formerly state-owned enterprises are being converted to private firms, often with substantial foreign ownership. Within the telecommunications industry, privatization frequently entails a continuation of a protected market in order to attract the foreign investment.

Another primary motive for overseas expansion is directly related to cost reductions. Foreign investment is often necessary in order to secure low-cost raw materials such as petroleum, bauxite, or rubber. Without access to those materials, firms find themselves at a competitive disadvantage in comparison to vertically integrated competitors. Labor can be viewed in this context as a raw material, so establishing foreign operations to take advantage of lower overseas labor costs fits into this category.

Related to cost reductions is the need to establish overseas offices and facilities to serve customers located abroad. Even companies that market primarily through export channels have found that after-purchase relationships with customers require in-country operations. This is true even for service companies such as banks, which have followed the flag as their domestic customers have expanded overseas.

Another motive for overseas investment is to take advantage of subsidies offered by foreign governments. To attract technology, jobs, and foreign exchange, many countries offer foreign firms special tax treatment, tariff protection, or below-market financing. These subsidies frequently represent crucial considerations when a firm is evaluating an overseas location. Without the added inducement, the project would not be justified, but with it, the project is acceptable.

A final motive for direct foreign investment is the desire to diversify one's wealth position. Modern financial theory has shown the advantages of holding a diversified portfolio of assets. Just as there are potential gains from diversification across industries, there are gains from diversification across national borders. Unfortunately, a number of factors make it difficult for individual investors to own securities in other countries.

These factors include the following: (1) Many nations have restrictions on capital flows that disallow portfolio investment; (2) capital markets in less developed countries (and even in many developed nations) often lack depth and breadth; and (3) there are relatively few traded securities and large concentrations of ownership among them, making it almost impossible for investors to acquire assets in those countries even in the absence of formal restrictions.

Foreign investment, even in developed countries, can be difficult to accomplish. Tax rules are different from nation to nation, and information about securities is not as available in other countries as it is in the United States. Consequently, although investors believe that there are benefits to international diversification, they may be unable to diversify their own portfolios.

An alternative to individual diversification is to invest in MNCs. With their legal staffs and industry knowledge, these companies are able to engage in direct investment despite the information barriers that thwart individuals. The logical extension of this argument is that shareholders want management to diversify in order to substitute for individual diversification that is blocked by formal and informal barriers. However, there is no direct evidence that firms are in fact motivated by the diversification issue.

Disadvantages Related to Foreign Operations

As stated previously, firms face added difficulties related to overseas operations. It is worthwhile to keep the following potential difficulties in mind when cash-flow forecasts and risk adjustments are discussed later in the chapter.

- The firm is perceived as being foreign, which causes resentment among consumer groups, domestic competition, and government officials. Often, those interest groups or stakeholders mistrust the foreign parent. They perceive such firms as having a different loyalty. It is that attitude that Reich suggests is inaccurate.

- Foreign operations are physically very far from headquarters. Information is more difficult to gather and disseminate, making managerial control more challenging.

- Cultural differences exist that need to be considered in determining organizational design and personnel policies.

- A new set of tax and legal rules must be learned and incorporated into financial planning and firm policy.

- Transactions occur in a foreign currency, which adds to the uncertainty of cash flows and becomes a significant new element of risk.

- The firm must operate in a different political environment. Failure to understand that environment and its laws could lead to severe penalties. It might also place a firm in conflict with the laws of its home country.

In addition, if the political atmosphere is less stable than in the home country, the firm must deal with a rapidly changing environment. Keeping up with events requires resources expended on information gathering.

Assessment of Foreign Cash Flows

A frequent shortcoming of cash flow forecasts is that they fail to identify all of the potential benefits and problems related to an overseas investment. It is likely that fewer errors will be made if the motivation for the project is kept in mind at the time the cash flows are estimated.

The major difficulty faced by analysts evaluating foreign investment cash flows is the divergence between the cash flows generated by the investment project as a freestanding local project and the cash flows accruing to the parent. Several factors contribute to the differences, some controlled by the investor and others determined by the firm's operating environment, including the government. These are discussed later, but regardless of the source of the discrepancy, it is important for the investor to recognize that cash flows that affect the firm's position are the relevant ones to include. Estimation of those cash flows involves a three-stage process. The first stage is to forecast the total for the freestanding project; the second stage is to estimate the corporate, systemwide benefits and costs; the third stage takes into account all of the tax and exchange rate effects and leads to an estimation of investor cash flows. This three-stage process requires an identification of the factors that cause the two cash flows to diverge and a procedure for converting estimated foreign currency flows into the home currency of the investor.

SOURCES OF DIVERGENCE

A number of factors generate a divergence in the cash flows between the project and the parent company. We analyze the most important here.

Interdependencies

As indicated in the preceding section, overseas investment is often prompted by defensive motives: reaction to trade restrictions or competitive pressures. In those cases, some of the sales generated by the project are cannibalized from export sales formerly made by existing divisions of the firm. Sales that are taken away from other units but that would have been maintained without the overseas expansion should not be included among the project's revenues. At the same time, if those sales would have been lost owing to trade restrictions or competition, they are correctly attributed to the project.

An example can help clarify this point. A firm is contemplating an overseas investment that will have sales of 6,000 units per month at a price of $50 per unit. The firm currently services that market with export sales of 4,000 units at a price of $60 per unit. A major competitor is establishing a facility in the same region to avoid import quotas that will be in place in the next year. If the firm does not follow suit and make the investment, its estimated export sales will be 1,500 units at $50 per unit. If it does make the investment, export sales will fall to 1,000 units. What is the amount of sales revenue that should be credited to the foreign investment?

The correct answer is the amount that is incremental to the project compared with what would be generated if the project were not undertaken. That amount is $275,000 per month, the difference between the $350,000 total sales with the expansion and the $75,000 that would be realized without it. The $275,000 represents the $300,000 in sales that the investment generates less the $25,000 that is cannibalized from existing sales. The remaining decline in export sales ($165,000) is not deducted from the project because those sales would be lost even if the investment were not made. This example is summarized in Exhibit 14.1.

Changes in sales revenues are used in the example to illustrate interdependencies, but they are only one side of the cash flow equation. In a more complete analysis, costs are also considered. If costs were higher at the foreign operation, the increase would have to be taken into account when cash outflows were estimated. It is the net impact on total cash flows that is relevant.

Interdependencies also show up through transfer pricing. Once foreign operations are established, it is likely that intracompany transactions will cross international borders. Firms establish transfer prices at which those transactions clear between the operating entities. Those transfer prices are not always set at market levels because of tax effects and currency restrictions. Transfer pricing might be used to shift earnings from a high-tax jurisdiction to a low-tax

EXHIBIT 14.1 Incremental cash flow analysis.

	Current Export Sales	**Sales with Expansion**		**Sales without Expansion**
Units	4,000	1,000	6,000	1,500
Price	$60	$50	$50	$50
Revenue	$240,000	$50,000	$300,000	$75,000

jurisdiction. An internal effect of that pricing policy is to reduce stated cash flows in the high-tax country and increase them in the lower-tax country. From a corporate viewpoint, the tax reduction increases total cash flows, but without careful analysis, the source of the cash flows might be identified incorrectly. The following problem exemplifies interdependency in transfer pricing.

A firm is considering an overseas assembly plant that will buy components from the parent. The market price of the component is set at $30, at which price the contribution margin for the parent is $8. After assembly, which adds $10 to the cost, the subsidiary will sell the finished product for $50. The effective tax rates in the parent's and subsidiary's countries are 30 percent and 40 percent, respectively. At the existing transfer price, the after-tax cash flows for the corporation are $11.60–$5.60 at the parent level and $6.00 at the subsidiary level. Because of the differences in tax rates, a higher transfer price would lead to higher after-tax cash flows for the corporation as a whole. At a transfer price of $40, the subsidiary's profits are eliminated entirely, whereas the parent's after-tax earnings rise to $12.60. If the $40 transfer price is used in evaluating the overseas project and the subsidiary is not credited with its share of the final cash flows, the investment will be turned down. As an extreme case, suppose all of the sales are dependent on building the assembly plant (because of trade restrictions). The correct cash flows to the project then would be the full $12.60, even though none of these show up on the subsidiary's books. Because of the presence of interdependencies, it is important to identify accurately the amount and source of all relevant cash flows.

Remittance Restrictions

Countries frequently impose limits on the amount of funds that subsidiaries can pay to their overseas parents in the form of dividends. These policies are generally part of a more comprehensive program to reduce a balance-of-payments deficit. Descriptions of restrictions in force and changes in policies can be found in *Exchange Arrangements & Exchange Restrictions,* published annually by the International Monetary Fund. At the time that an investment decision is being made, it is important that current restrictions are understood and that some estimate is made of the probability of continuing restrictions or of restrictions being imposed in the future. The latter necessarily involves an evaluation of the host country's balance-of-payments position.

Restrictions come in a variety of forms, usually allowing only a maximum percentage of annual earnings, retained earnings, or sales to be paid. Whatever their form, they have the effect of deferring the receipt of cash flows and thereby reducing the value of those flows. The amount of the loss is determined by the severity of the restriction, the length of time that receipt of the flows is delayed, and the opportunity available for investing the blocked funds before repatriation. For example, assume that an investment with a 10-year life generates annual net cash flows of $1 million. Restrictions on dividends limit payments to $400,000 each year for the first nine years but allow payment equal to accumulated retained earnings at the end of the tenth year. The appropriate cash flows to consider in this case are then $400,000 per year for the first nine years and $6.4 million in the last year. If the funds can be reinvested during the interim, the additional interest income should be included. If the $400,000 can be invested at 10 percent and those earnings are also available for dividends at the end of the tenth year, the final cash flow will be $6.4 million plus $2,303,600 in interest.

In the example, cash flows and earnings are considered to be the same. That is usually not the case because of the presence of noncash expenses such as depreciation. The disparity between earnings and cash flows creates some ambiguity about which cash flows are available for repatriation. If the dividend restriction establishes a limit on payments that is based on earnings, the positive cash flow related to depreciation will not be available to the firm for repatriation. Unless these funds can be used beneficially elsewhere in the country, it will usually be in the parent corporation's interest to keep depreciation expenses low in order to maximize after-tax income available for foreign dividends. There is no general rule to follow that fits all cases, but it is necessary to understand fully whatever restrictions exist and their implications.

Taxation

Differences in tax rates have already been shown to enter the cash flow calculations. Effective tax rates in different countries vary a great deal. From the standpoint of a U.S. investor, the tax rate that applies is usually the higher of the two effective rates. The United States gives credit for foreign taxes, but only up to the maximum U.S. rate. Therefore, any taxes beyond that rate reduce the return to the investor.

Subsidies

Decisions to invest in particular projects are often influenced by inducements offered by the host country. As indicated in the preceding section on motives for foreign investment, these can take a variety of forms. Given sufficient subsidies, projects that otherwise would not be acceptable become viable investments. For potential investors, a key question is whether the subsidies can be taken away if the host country has a change of policy. The current government may offer a tax benefit that is of substantial value if it stays in effect for the life of the project. It serves as the necessary incentive to attract capital or technological knowledge. Once the investment has been made, the government may alter the tax laws or impose new restrictions that offset the original subsidy.

Potential investors need to evaluate the subsidy and the probability that it will be eliminated. A very conservative approach is to accept only projects that would be viable without the subsidy. A more reasonable method is to adjust the cash flows to account for the risk or probability of losing the subsidy at some future time: Being aware of the importance of the subsidy also allows the investor to take steps to reduce the impact of its loss.

POLITICAL AND OPERATING RISK

Definitions of political risk vary, but some general characteristics and examples may be readily identified. First, however, it is important to distinguish between the closely related concepts of country risk, economic risk, and political risk, and to note their relationship to each other.

Country risk refers to elements of risk inherent in doing business in the economic, social, and political environment of another country. In international lending decisions, for example, bankers typically examine the economic conditions of the country in question, the balance of payments and its management, central bank policies and effectiveness, principal economic sectors (imports and exports, trends and prospects, flow of funds, and financial intermediation), social conditions, international relations, and the impact of world events on the domestic economy.

Generally speaking, *economic risks* are not politically generated and include those resulting from technological changes, the actions of competitors, or shifts in consumer preferences. In many cases, however, there is a close link between political events in a country and economic risk. For example, the disintegration of the market structure in Lebanon during its civil war, the banning of certain Western products by the Khomeini regime after the success of the Iranian revolution, and the uncertainties posed by the breakup of the Soviet Union are clear instances where economic risks were exacerbated by political events.

Similarly, while most labor strikes are limited in scope and economic in origin (e.g., disputes over wages, benefits, or other work-related issues), many general strikes, such as those in Nicaragua in 1978 and Poland in 1980, are clearly political in nature and have wide-ranging economic repercussions. Even events with clear economic purposes, such as price controls designed to control

political + operating risks

country risk   *economic risk*

political risk

inflation, often carry political overtones. Thus, it is sometimes very difficult to distinguish between economic risk and political risk, and few events are purely one or the other.

While definitions of political risk vary, for the purposes of this discussion, *political risk* should be regarded as a subset of country risk, and it may generally be defined as the exposure to a change in the value of an investment or cash position because of government actions or other nonmarket events that are political in nature. Whereas country risk focuses generally on the overall investment environment of a country, political risk arises from the political environment. The following are examples of political risk events that may negatively affect the magnitude and distribution of cash flows from an overseas investment:

- Changes in tax regulations and exchange controls, especially those that are discriminatory or arbitrary
- Host-country stipulations about local production, sourcing, or hiring practices
- Commercial discrimination against foreign-owned businesses
- Restrictions on access to local borrowings
- Governmental interference with privately negotiated contracts
- Expropriation without adequate compensation
- Damage or destruction of facilities or harm to personnel resulting from political riots or civil war

Because the effects of political risk events may be varied, managers should be aware of the full range or types of political risk events that may affect the host country as well as their particular industries, companies, or projects.

Among the most dramatic losses stemming from political risk events are those resulting from revolutionary upheaval and terrorism. For example, in December 1977, GTE signed a telecommunications contract worth more than $500 million with the Iranian government. In accordance with the contract, GTE advanced Iran $94 million in open letters of credit, which are commonly used in the Middle East in lieu of performance bonds. Given its longtime experience and confidence in Iran, the company did not specify the grounds on which Iran could call the letters of credit, and no insurance was taken to cover the risks. After the revolution, work on the project proved impossible, and the company stood to lose over $50 million, not including the letters of credit. If those are included, GTE's potential after-tax losses could have exceeded $60 million, making the firm the biggest potential loser in Iran.

In addition to revolutions, coups, and violent acts of terrorism, political risk can also take the form of legislative or regulatory changes. In Iran, for example,

B.F. Goodrich had built the largest tire plant between Europe and the Far East, with assurances of trade and investment protection from the government. Such protection was prematurely lifted, however, in favor of two competitors in the mid-1970s, forcing the U.S. firm to go from three shifts to a single eight-hour production schedule. Changes in the law or in regulations can also be directed at companies collectively, as when the shah decided to mandate public stock offerings on the part of Iranian-based corporations to increase worker ownership and participation. The action was expensive and very disruptive to foreign businesses.

Changes in government, whether the result of an election, a coup, or a revolution, may be partly determined by economic events and may thus bring about changes in policy toward foreign investors. For example, shifts in political-economic ideology may lead to the expropriation of most, if not all, foreign-owned firms.

While dramatic events such as revolutions or expropriations attract a great deal of attention and might cause a company to shy away from more turbulent parts of the world, a political event in itself does not necessarily constitute a risk to business. In fact, political instability can present opportunities as well as risks. For example, Gulf Oil Corporation in 1975 was able to negotiate a very favorable relationship with the Marxist governing party during the Angolan civil war, and Dow Chemical was able to reenter Chile after the overthrow of Salvador Allende in 1973.

Such dramatic events are the exception rather than the rule, however. Although the Cuban and Iranian revolutions undeniably created major problems for U.S. firms, most politically generated contingencies present macro- rather than microrisk and, increasingly, affect operations rather than ownership. Rather than full or partial expropriation, such changes in government or ideology more typically entail price controls, restrictions on expatriate employment, local content regulation, or other regulatory constraints. For example, when Venezuela ran short of foreign exchange in 1983, it ordered domestic companies to extend payments on their foreign debts for several years. Recognizing that money has time value, many creditors negotiated immediate settlements at steep discounts and suffered heavy losses.

Indeed, political instability and conflict are not necessary or even frequent prerequisites to constraints on foreign firms as a result of changes in the political environment. Price controls and other regulatory constraints may result from the regular functioning of the political process owing to losses or gains in the regime's power or to changes in the character and power of the opposition or of interest groups. The privatization program in the United Kingdom under Prime Minister Thatcher in the 1980s and, in contrast, the nationalization policy pursued by President Mitterand in France during the same years are examples of how different political philosophies are manifested in economic terms, with important financial consequences for managers and investors.

Another example of how the normally functioning political process affects international investment is the European Community (EC) 1992 single-market movement, which carried with it enormous political risks as well as opportunities for global companies. As Europe proceeded with its economic and political unification, companies found themselves shut out of certain markets owing to regulatory changes. For example, countries such as Spain and Portugal, which enjoyed a great deal of foreign investment because of their cheap labor relative to the rest of Europe, became less attractive in the future when they increased wages to comply with the EC 1992 single-market program. Companies that made significant investments in Western Europe based on pre-1992 economics found their investments turning sour in the post-1992 world. The importance of keeping up-to-date with political and regulatory changes can hardly be overstated.

Turning to Eastern Europe, the relatively stable economic and political climate that accompanied the Cold War has become turbulent and unsettled as the former Communist countries attempt the transition to a market economy. A glance at the former Eastern bloc reveals the full panoply of political risk. In the former Yugoslavia, once-prosperous towns and productive factories have been devastated by ethnic fighting and civil war. In Czechoslovakia, the split between the Czechs and Slovaks over the pace of economic reform has led to the breakup of the country, which could have adverse effects for the foreign companies that have invested in the Slovak republic. General Electric's much vaunted $150 million investment in the Tungsram lighting plant in Hungary has lost money because the government has not devalued the forint in line with Hungary's soaring inflation. Chevron, which entered into a joint venture agreement with the former Soviet government, now finds itself in the position of having to negotiate with several independent republics. Moreover, Russia is chronically short of hard currency, and its vacillating monetary policy and price reforms cast a long shadow of uncertainty over any prospective investments.

Russia offers an example of another type of political or country risk. The economic transformation taking place there has moved more quickly than the transformation of the legal system. Investors in Russia have to contend with nonexistent or rapidly changing rules and laws affecting private property. That makes it difficult to protect investments and establish the rights of investors.

The tangled and often contentious U.S./China trade relations offer another interesting example of political risks. American companies have invested billions of dollars in China to gain access to the enormous Chinese market as well as to manufacture for exportation to the United States. A critical requirement of using China as an overseas manufacturing base for products sold in the United States is that China maintain its most-favored-nation status (MFN), which allows Chinese goods to enter the United States at the lowest prevailing tariff. Revocation of MFN would lead to prohibitive tariffs that would offset any cost advantage gained by manufacturing in China.

Continuation of China's MFN status has been questioned on several grounds: China's human rights policy, its sale of nuclear materials, and its failure to uphold trade agreements on copyright protection for intellectual property. Each of those issues has provoked an outcry from human rights organizations, by firms hurt by the pirating of intellectual property, and by members of Congress to revoke China's MFN status. Thus far, those efforts have been rebuffed, but the threat of such action jeopardizes the value of investing in China and must be considered as part of any investment decision.

In 2001, China was granted membership in the World Trade Organization. As a member, China will eventually have to adhere to WTO standards on many of those issues. Companies doing business in China will benefit from greater transparency and standardization of China's policies. At the same time, those that have relied on privileged status within the Chinese market will see many of their advantages disappear.

Another example of political risk and the odd twists that it might take involves the executive of a Canadian firm, Sherritt Inc, whose executives and their families have been banned from the United States because the company operates mining properties in Cuba that were nationalized by the Castro regime. The United States passed the Helm-Burton Act in 1996, establishing sanctions on non-U.S. companies. Sherritt does no business in the United States and has broken no Canadian laws, yet the children of its executives are not allowed to go to Disney World or anyplace else in the United States.

As these examples indicate, the global marketplace is by its very nature uncertain and turbulent. The question of whether particular aspects of this turbulence and uncertainty constitute a risk to business is problematic, and its answer depends on industry, firm, or project characteristics and managerial actions. Thus the elements of political risk will vary widely among different countries and different companies. Even within a country, political risk is usually industry-specific and, in many cases, project-specific as well. Rural insurgency, for example, may pose serious problems to a commercial farming operation, but its impact on a company specializing in financial services or insurance might be minimal. Assessing the political risks of direct foreign investment, therefore, involves the analysis both of elements of aggregate or countrywide risk and of elements of political risk specific to the company or to its project.

Monitoring Developments

Monitoring involves establishing an intelligence network that provides political, social, and economic information with which to understand events in the host country. For large firms with extensive worldwide investments, such as the major petroleum companies, the intelligence-gathering process can be done almost entirely in-house. The same is true for multinational banks with extensive branch systems. Area or divisional personnel can be assigned the primary responsibility for collecting information and forwarding it to headquarters for evaluation.

Many large companies now have staff economists and political scientists who provide country risk assessments. Although these staff people play an important role in the monitoring process, their analyses should be used in conjunction with evaluations of line personnel who are stationed in the country. Relying solely on either staff or line personnel can provide biased analysis. Staff evaluations tend to be more objective, but because they are done at a distance from a country, they often ignore insights that can be gained only by extensive experience living in an area. Line personnel have that experience but are often unwilling to recognize or admit negative aspects of their own nation or the country for which they have managerial responsibility, in part because negative information might adversely affect their own activities. For example, bank-calling officers or branch managers would be the appropriate line personnel to provide country information, but their personal interest is in expanding loans or the sale of other bank services. This basic conflict often introduces a bias into the information-gathering process.

Smaller firms generally do not have the resources to develop their own information networks. Instead, they rely on information purchased from firms organized for that purpose. Even if the company's primary information sources are external, it should still establish an internal monitoring system as a secondary source. Area personnel should file informal country evaluations, and the headquarters' staff should visit the country on a regular basis. Their assessments should be matched against those of the external source to check for consistency and accuracy. A firm should not become too dependent on a single source or too complacent to change to another advisory service if its current one is missing too many trends or changes.

Anticipating Policy

All information should be evaluated with the objective of anticipating policy changes of the government or in the attitudes of other stakeholders in the host country. Some changes affect the general operating environment of the firm, whereas others have a direct impact on the operating or ownership structure of the firm.

Environment changes can be both general and specific. Among the former are macroeconomic policies that attempt to stimulate or restrict economic activity. Countries with accelerating inflation or difficulty servicing external obligations are likely to pursue contractionary monetary or fiscal policies. For a firm with largely domestic sales, this would reduce revenues. Other changes related to macroeconomic policy are the imposition of price and wage controls and currency restrictions. From the earlier discussion of cash flow forecasts, it should be clear how these changes would affect the firm and the value of the investment. If management can anticipate the policies, it can take steps to reduce their impact: Prices might be raised prior to controls being enacted; foreign currency payments might be made before the local currency becomes inconvertible; or arrangements for parallel loans might be made to reduce the amount of local currency blocked in the country.

There are other longer-term policies that a firm might pursue to reduce risk. Labor unrest in the form of strikes varies in severity from country to country. In nations where strikes are frequent, the firm might choose less labor-intensive technology or adopt employment policies that reduce the threat of strikes.

A large U.S. electronics firm with major manufacturing facilities in the United Kingdom has a totally nonunion labor force in a highly unionized country. It has been able to maintain that status by having generous benefits and an open employee-management relationship. These policies entail some added costs, but reduce the risk of labor strife. The company has not lost manufacturing time owing to strikes and has added flexibility in establishing its seniority and compensation system.

More specific policies that arise from concerns about the economic environment can directly affect the operating structure of the firm. Requirements concerning local content in manufacturing and domestic nationals in management positions, pricing to subsidize local consumption, or requirements that firms provide investment in infrastructure are examples. In general, so are regulations that affect transfer pricing or establish restrictions on licensing arrangements and royalty payments.

The final type of political risk comes in the form of government interference with the ownership of the assets or investment. There are many ways in which governments can garner the wealth of foreign investors, ranging from punitive taxes and fees to outright expropriation. In between are requirements for local participation in ownership and nationalization with some form of compensation. Regardless of the form it takes, it is unlikely that any involuntary change in ownership structure will benefit the original investors. If it would, then they would have brought it about without coercion. Generally, increased interference or changes in attitudes toward foreign investment are preceded by significant economic or political events. That is what makes the monitoring and anticipation activities worthwhile: They allow a firm to reduce its exposure while there is still room to maneuver.

Adapting to Conditions

Adjustments and alterations in policies that firms make in response to changes are signs of their adaptability. Doing business overseas requires a willingness and ability to respond to different legal, political, social, and economic environments. Sometimes those adjustments are undesirable on other grounds, but necessary in order to reduce risk related to investing overseas. Entering into a joint venture is an important example.

Joint ventures represent shared ownership and control of operating entities by two or more independent firms or groups of investors. A requirement of local joint ownership is often mandatory for foreign investors. It arises from a sense of nationalism and a desire that some of the returns on capital investment be retained in the host country. At other times, firms voluntarily seek out joint venture relationships because of synergy. For example, one firm may have capital or an established distribution network and its partner may have special technological skills or a brand name.

Despite some major exceptions, survey research has indicated that the majority of U.S. firms are a priori opposed to joint ventures, especially those involving local partners. Most of the grounds for opposition focus on the control aspects. The partner acquires access to technology and pricing information that might make it a formidable competitor at some future date. Differences in objectives might lead to disputes over dividend policies, transfer pricing, financial structure decisions, licensing agreements, and efforts by the foreign partner to rationalize production among its worldwide subsidiaries.

The trade-offs in favor of joint ventures include access to markets that might otherwise be unavailable and a reduction in the probability of government interference directed toward foreign investors. By having local nationals involved in ownership and management, the subsidiary loses some of its foreign character. That helps deflect criticisms related to exploitation, capital flight, and external control. The local partners have a stake in the company, which leads them to lobby on its behalf. Any restrictions imposed by the government might adversely affect local interests.

It is important to be careful in choosing a local partner. Under the best of circumstances, the local partner brings to the enterprise skills or attributes other than a convenient nationality. If nationality is in fact the only contribution, the foreign investor should try to find a partner that is reliable and in the mainstream of local politics. Having a local partner that is in the opposition party might lead to harsher treatment than would otherwise be the case.

A final course that might be followed to reduce risk exposure is the purchase of insurance. A number of developed nations, including the United States, have governmental or quasi-governmental programs for insuring foreign investment against the risk of war, expropriation, or currency inconvertibility. There is also a private insurance market organized through the auspices of Lloyd's. In the United States, the Overseas Private Investment Corporation (OPIC) provides insurance for U.S. private investments in less developed countries as well as project financing. Its fees vary depending on the type of coverage and, to some extent, on the risk related to the investment. OPIC has been very successful at marketing its programs, and the majority of nonpetroleum investments in less developed countries have some form of OPIC coverage.

The decision to buy OPIC insurance must be made along the lines of risk management decisions in general. Firms need to weigh the costs against expected losses and their willingness and ability to bear those losses. Buying OPIC coverage might create a moral hazard situation for firms. Having protection could lead firms to ignore other risk-reduction policies and contribute to a higher incidence of loss. Ultimately, this would show up in higher premiums or a lessened availability of insurance. Since settlements under OPIC are usually the result of a long negotiating process, firms should avoid the attitude of "why worry, we're insured."

As a final caveat, investors should not associate political risk only with less developed countries. Each of the types of risk discussed in this section are or have been present in almost every nation. Certainly, the environmental factors are omnipresent, but even in Western democracies, nationalization and changing attitudes toward foreign investment are prevalent. The investor might have better recourse under the law in those nations, but the interference in business operations and the loss of wealth are real possibilities that must be considered in making investment decisions.

FOREIGN EXCHANGE RATES

A big part of what makes international business different is money. It is not that global firms are any more or less interested in making money but that the value of the money they pay and receive changes constantly. For at least one party to every international transaction, the monetary unit used in the deal is not in its own currency, and that adds an element of uncertainty that does not exist in purely domestic transactions. Companies involved in international business need to understand the factors that influence exchange rates, how much risk there is, and ways to manage or mitigate that risk.

A foreign exchange rate is the price of one currency in terms of another. If the exchange rate between U.S. dollars and British pounds is $1.42, it means every pound someone wants to buy costs $1.42. Sometimes the relationship is expressed as the reciprocal, in which case $1.00 could be bought for £0.7022. The two prices, $1.42 per pound and £0.7022 per dollar, are identical.

Exchange rates are quoted for different delivery dates. If the transaction is to take place immediately (actually one or two days later because of the bank-clearing process) it is referred to as a *spot exchange rate;* for transactions that will take place sometime in the future, the exchange rate is referred to as a *forward rate.*

Forward rates are quoted for a number of delivery dates. In the financial press, they are seldom given for more than 90 or 180 days, but financial institutions might be willing to give a quote for a several-year period. Exhibit 14.2 provides both spot and forward rates for several different maturities and currencies. The relationship between the spot and forward rates is determined by the relative interest rates in the two countries. A country with the higher interest rate will have a currency that will cost less for forward delivery than spot delivery. From the table, the British pound costs $1.424 for spot delivery and only $1.4165 for 90-day forward delivery. The pound is said to be trading at a *forward discount* to the dollar. On the other hand, the yen is at a premium to the dollar. It costs more to buy a yen for delivery in 90 days than it does spot. Interest rates in Japan are lower than in the United States, which are lower than interest rates in Britain.

It is important to understand how a forward contract works. The price or exchange rate is established today, and yet the transaction will not take place until the future delivery date. A buyer of forward pounds agrees to pay $1.4165 in 90 days. At that time, he or she is obligated to take delivery and pay the agreed-upon rate regardless of the prevailing spot rate of the pound. If, in 90

EXHIBIT 14.2   Spot and forward exchange rates.
($ per foreign currency unit)

	Pound	Yen	Euro
Spot	$1.424	$0.007775	$0.8825
30-day	$1.4124	$0.007762	$0.8814
90-day	$1.4165	$0.007789	$0.8794
180-day	$1.4097	$0.007973	$0.8765

Source: March 15, 2002, BMO Nesbitt Burns Capital Markets.

days, the spot pound is at $1.5165, the buyer will then make a profit of $0.10 per pound. A $1.3665 spot rate will lead to a $0.05 per pound loss. Forward contracts can be used to speculate on the value of a currency, but, as will be shown, they are the primary means by which exchange risk is managed or hedged.

Firms that engage in cross-border business generally bear some amount of exchange risk. That risk comes from the variability of exchange rates, and therefore the uncertain value of future cash slows. An American company that imports German machine tools priced in euros (€) cannot be certain of the dollar value of the euro obligation when the payment is due. If the machine tools cost €3 million and payment is due in six months, the dollar value will be determined by the spot exchange rate in six months. If the euro is worth $0.90, the dollar cost will be $2.7 million; if it is $1.00, then the dollar cost will be $3 million. It is not unusual for the exchange rates of developed economies to change by 10 to 15 percent over 6- to 12-month periods, so the amount of uncertainty is significant.

Companies that invest overseas have a continuous challenge in managing exchange risk. Budgets, compensation, the cost of financing, and the value of repatriating profits all vary as exchange rates fluctuate. There is also the added complication of preparing consolidated financial statements when operations are conducted in a variety of currencies. The Financial Accounting Standards Board has issued a series of statements to address a very complex and controversial set of issues around the translation of foreign currency denominated accounts.

Another way that companies are significantly affected by exchange risk is in their ability to compete against foreign competitors. When a currency strengthens, or rises in value, it becomes more expensive to buy goods priced in that currency. A strong dollar works to the disadvantage of American companies trying to export or compete with non-U.S. companies that sell goods in the United States. The competition between Caterpillar and Komatsu provides a notable example, in part because the head-to-head struggle between those two companies has been thoroughly documented in the press and in a series of case studies. In the 1960s, Komatsu launched a long-term plan to first catch up to and then to surpass Caterpillar, then the market leader in heavy machinery. That plan was very successful until Caterpillar began an aggressive effort to overhaul its operations.

> Caterpillar made an intense commitment to improving its U.S. Manufacturing. Rather than join the stampede of American manufacturers that set up low-cost operations in Mexico and around the Pacific Rim, Caterpillar sought to make its domestic plants competitive on a world scale. To do so, it launched its so called Plant with a Future program PWAF for short. The program called for overhauling virtually all the company's U.S. factories, installing fancy new robotics and streamlining assembly systems.

But Caterpillar officials worry that the slumping yen threatens years of work at factories like this one. "How long do you think it takes a company to take 20% out of its cost structure?" asks D. G. Paris, a company economist. (The answer for Caterpillar's PWAF program: seven years.) In recent months, Mr. Paris has frequently telephoned Federal Reserve officials to make this point.[1]

That seven years of painstaking and painful change undertaken at a cost of over $2 billion was more than off set by the 30% depreciation of the yen that took place over a 16 month period in 1989 and 1990.

Hedging Exchange Risk

Exchange-related risk such as that faced by Caterpillar is very difficult to manage. Caterpillar's attempt to make its manufacturing efficient and flexible represents a long-range commitment to inoculate itself against the competitive impact of currency appreciation. Within a moderate range, it is effective, but when currencies change dramatically, such efforts can be overwhelmed.

Other types of exchange risk can be managed more directly and effectively by using forward contracts. Recall the example of the American importer of German machine tools. The importer incurred an obligation to pay €3 million in six months. Because it has a liability (a short position) in euros, it could lock in the dollar cost of the debt by acquiring an equal but offsetting position in the forward market. To do so, the importer would buy a €3 million forward contract at the prevailing rate. Using the rates in Table 14.2, the six-month euro is selling for $0.8765. If the importer buys forward, it will lock in a dollar cost of $2,629,500, regardless of the dollar-to-euro exchange rate in six months. The importer will acquire the necessary euros at the forward rate and use them to pay off the liability. The action of locking in the exchange rate and reducing or eliminating the uncertainty is referred to as *hedging*.

Importers, exporters, investors in financial assets, and multinational companies use forward contracts to hedge. Other methods of hedging include borrowing or depositing money in foreign currency and the use of swaps or options. These alternative hedging techniques have different costs and risk profiles related to them. Managers must decide what level of risk they are able to bear and how much they are willing to pay to eliminate risk.

Purchasing Power Parity

It is very hard to predict future exchange rates. Many forecasting services exist, and there is a vast academic literature discussing various models of exchange rate determination. Some of those models are very simple; other are complex. One of the simplest is to use today's forward rate to predict the future spot rate. Others use sophisticated statistical relationships. Unfortunately, there is little evidence the models work particularly well. However, one empirical relationship does seem to hold over relatively long periods of time, and that is that a country experiencing a higher rate of inflation than another country will see its currency decline relative to the other country's currency. This observation and the theory underlying it have led to the *purchase power parity* (PPP) relationship.

The basis for PPP is the relationship between the prices of goods in two countries. The law of one price states that the same good should sell for the same price regardless of the currency used to denominate the price. Suppose that the price of an automobile is $30,000 in Dallas and that same car sells for €40,000 in Paris. For the cars to have the same price, the dollar must equal €1.33. If the dollar were worth €1.5, then someone could take $26,667, buy €40,000 and get the car cheaper in Paris. This would violate the law of one price.

In fact, we know that the law of one price generally does not hold under all circumstances. Transaction costs such as transportation, tariffs, taxes, and different distribution systems lead to different prices. However, as a tendency, it does seem to be valid. Moreover, as prices in the two countries change, we observe that the exchange rate changes to reflect the different rates of inflation. Returning to the example, if car prices in the United States rose 10 percent, to $33,000, and in France they rose 20 percent, to €48,000, then the value of the euro should decline relative to the dollar. PPP says that the depreciation should result in €1.45 = $1.00.

Although by no means perfect, PPP is a very useful way of determining whether a country's currency is over- or undervalued. If it has not depreciated at a rate roughly consistent with the inflation differential with another country then, it is overvalued.

ORGANIZING THE MULTINATIONAL FIRM

Managing a multinational corporation has many additional challenges. Percy Barnevik, CEO of ABB and one of the most highly regarded international executives, summed them up as the need to reconcile three contradictions:

Be global and local.
Be big and small.
Be centralized and decentralized.

The essence of Barnevik's views is that although business decisions are made at a local level, a company must be willing and able to respond anywhere in the world. To do so requires size and the economies of scale that size makes possible. Customers want the efficiencies that only scale economies can provide. To get those economies, certain functions need to be centralized, and throughout the organization best practices must be identified and put in place. Yet because business is local, it is important that the multinational be responsive and agile. That in turn requires a delegation of authority present only in a decentralized organization.

When Barnevik created ABB from the merger of a Swedish and a Swiss company, he sought to create a company capable of competing globally in the twenty-first century. To manage the contradictions, he established a broad matrix organization along business and geographic lines. Individual managers within the matrix are given a great deal of autonomy. At the same time, they are part of global business segments and regional or country organizations.

The organizational structure that Barnevik created at ABB is often described as being transnational, or multidomestic. Transnational implies that ABB does not just export from a central location—or even operate a number of independent overseas subsidiaries. Rather, the company has business areas that are global and headquartered in a number of different countries. The manager in charge of a business area is responsible for formulating and implementing the global strategy for her business. That person must decide what to produce, where to product it, and where to sell it. A global manager such as the business area head must have a global perspective that transcends national or domestic interests. If a business area head is parochial in outlook, he or she will miss opportunities.

At the same time it is important for a firm like ABB to have a corporate presence in countries in which it does significant business. Those multiple presences make ABB multidomestic. ABB has country managers who are responsible for the operations in that country. A country manager, unlike the business area head, is not a global strategist, but a builder of local operations ultimately responsible for ABB's business in a country. This person finds opportunities for ABB in the country and also ensures that ABB is a good corporate citizen, abiding by local rules and regulations.

Those two different managerial roles, global strategist and country manager, address the global and local contradiction that Barnevik identified, but in today's business environment that might not be enough. Three Insead Business School professors, Yves Doz, Jose Santos, and Peter Williamson, have argued in a recent book that firms must go beyond being transnational to metanational. The impetus for the creation of metanational capabilities, according to the authors, is the growing importance of the knowledge economy. New ideas, markets, and styles are not originated at headquarters or at research and development centers in carefully chosen locations. Knowledge is widely dispersed, and Doz and colleagues believe that to succeed companies must specify actions to sense, mobilize, and operationalize knowledge that is developed anywhere in the organization or outside of it. Global firms cannot rely on existing structures and incentives to accomplish the task. Corporations must think and act differently in order to thrive in the global knowledge economy.

FOR FURTHER READING

Doz, Yves, Jose Santos and Peter Williamson, *From Global to Metanational: How Companies Win in the Knowledge Economy* (Boston: Harvard Business School Press, 2001).

Friedman, Thomas L., *The Lexus and the Olive Tree: Understanding Globalization* (New York: Farrar, Straus, Giroux, 2000).

Soros, George, *George Soros on Globalization* (New York: Public Affairs, 2002).

Stiglitz, Joseph E., *Globalization and Its Discontents* (New York: W. W. Norton & Co., 2002).

15 SOME FINAL THOUGHTS

A former colleague of one of the authors used to say, "All you need to know about business is buy low, sell high; pay late and collect early." He was speaking tongue in cheek, but there is a certain appealing wisdom and historic truth to that advice. Clearly, if you don't sell your goods and services for more than they cost you, it will be impossible to earn a profit and stay in business. Paying late and collecting early captures both the time value of money and the distinction between cash and accrued earnings.

Historically, buying low and selling high was the essence of business enterprise until the Industrial Revolution. Business was about trading, primarily commodities, and businesspeople were merchants who bought commodities at one price, transported them, possibly stored them, and hoped to sell them at a higher price—straightforward, although certainly not easy or risk-free.

Today's successful firms must also buy low and sell high, but the tasks of management are far more complex than just trading successfully. In the various chapters of this book we have tried to introduce the primary themes and techniques that today's MBAs master in their programs of study. Those topics range from a basic discussion of financial statements to describing the steps involved in establishing a strategic alliance. How should we think about the lessons if not in terms of the simple concept of buying low and selling high?

Instead of focusing on profit generation, much of what we have written about is value creation. Managers utilize resources in a manner that creates value for customers. The idea of buying low and selling high has been replaced by the notion of creating value through the transformation of resources. Operations, finance, marketing, and other topics are about the use and allocation of resources to create value for customers. As value is created, some of it is retained by the firm in the form of higher profits, some goes to employees in the form of higher wages, and some to shareholders in the form of greater wealth. Value is created through the efficient use of resources. Companies that invest in technology, engage in successful research and development, manage resources well, and focus on the needs of their customers create value. Competition and the economics of the industry determine how much goes to workers, managers, and owners.

Amidst this complexity, it is easy to forget that fundamentally business is about human beings and their imagination. Before there were markets, there were people who had aspirations. We often get so caught up in the technical analysis of business that we forget this simple yet important fact. Business is built on the creative output of human endeavor, be it the arts or the sciences, sports or philosophy. Profits for the individual and the firm and welfare for the citizens of the world come as much from Robin Williams's jokes and Tiger Woods's drives as they do from great technological inventions and the tearing down of the Berlin Wall. Human aspiration is multifaceted, and the beauty of business is that it can transform these aspirations into goods and services. The very idea of business—both entrepreneurship and traditional management—consists of matching up the products of imagination with aspiration to create markets for goods and services that work much as we have indicated in these chapters.

In a book that examines the characteristics of companies with outstanding records of long-term success, Jim Collins and Jerry Porras make the distinction between clock builders and time tellers.[1] The latter focus on short-term profitability, whereas the former attend to building businesses. Collins and Porras compare the financial performance of their outstanding companies and a set of firms in the same industries. The firms that were oriented toward value creation and not just profit maximization wound up creating more wealth for their shareholders and employees.

Success in creating value does not come from the application of specific rules or formulas. IBM and Apple were both successful in the PC industry but followed very different paths, as did Microsoft and Sun Microsystems. Thinking about *how* value is created is as important as realizing that the managers' task is to create value in the first place. The application of the techniques developed in this book and in MBA programs throughout the world is no guarantee of success. If following a set of rules were a guarantee of success, then the value of managerial excellence and leadership would be low. The techniques of management cannot answer the question of what distinguishes outstanding firms. Rather, in today's complex world, individuals who demonstrate an ability to use their judgment to make decisions and to manage resources to create value have become a more valuable resource.

Good managers strive to create value beyond being preoccupied with a single simplistic goal such as profit maximization. The recent tribulations of Enron, World Com, Tyco, and others speak to the problems inherent in that view. Good managers inject purpose and direction into their businesses. Thinking about the entrepreneurial tasks of managers turns the spotlight on the inherent creativity of human action. By allowing business to be concerned with a plurality of human aspirations, we see how it emerges as the dynamic institution of human flourishing.

Throughout this book, especially in Chapter 12, "Leading from the Middle," we have pointed out the characteristics of successful firms. The quality of the people within a firm and their commitment to excellence and value creation are what distinguish successful firms from others. That leadership must come from throughout the organization, not just from one or two senior executives. Organizations that have managerial and leadership depth are able to be flexible and responsive. They can meet the needs of customers, anticipate new requirements of doing business, adapt to changing conditions, and respond to crises without sacrificing core beliefs.

Flexibility and responsiveness are crucial because decisions are made in an environment of uncertainty. The models, techniques, and theories discussed in this book cannot be followed blindly. They are no substitute for judgment. They enhance judgment. The concepts give us frameworks with which to analyze outcomes, to develop solutions, and to monitor progress as we implement those solutions. The future is never what we predicted, so we need to adapt as we go.

We hope that this book is a guide to those who are making business decisions in an uncertain world. It is one of many steps to navigating successfully through turbulent and often uncharted waters. The book and its lessons do not ensure a safe journey, but they increase the chances of one. For those who strive to lead and those who seek to work with others to create value, improving the odds of success is an important point of departure.

CHAPTER NOTES

CHAPTER 1. WHAT IS BUSINESS?

1. Peter Drucker, *The New Realities* (New York: Harper Business, 1989).
2. Michael Piore and Charles Sabel, *The Second Industrial Divide* (New York: Basic Books, 1984).
3. This term is attributed to James Brian Quinn, *The Intelligent Enterprise* (New York: The Free Press, 1992). The section on the intelligent enterprise is based on this book.
4. This term is taken from James Moore, *The Death of Competition* (New York: Harper Business, 1996).
5. This term is taken from Gary Hamel and C. K. Prahalad, *Competing for the Future* (Boston: Harvard Business School Press, 1984).
6. Clayton Christensen, *The Innovator's Dilemma: When New Technologies Cause Great Firms to Fail* (Boston: Harvard University Press, 1997).
7. This section is based on work by Michael Best, *The New Competition* (Cambridge, MA: Harvard University Press, 1990).
8. See Alfred Chandler Jr., *The Visible Hand* (Cambridge, MA: Harvard University Press, 1977).
9. Peter Drucker, *Post-Capitalist Society* (New York: HarperCollins, 1993).
10. Taken from Kristen Bekk De Tienne and Lisa Ann Jackson, "Knowledge Management: Understanding Theory and Developing Strategy," *Competitiveness Review*, vol. 11 (2001): 1–11.
11. This section is based on James Moore, *The Death of Competition* (New York: Harper Business, 1996).
12. For a more complete discussion, see Faith Keenan and Spencer Ante, "The New Teamwork," *Business Week*, February 18, 2002, EB 12–18.
13. Andrew Grove, *Only the Paranoid Survive* (New York: Currency Doubleday, 1996).

CHAPTER 2. THE FUTURE

1. David Einstein, "Think Tank Helps Prevent Future Shock," *The San Francisco Chronicle,* June 10, 1995.
2. Gary Hamel and C. K. Prahalad, "Seeing the Future First," *Executive Excellence,* November 1995.
3. Ibid.
4. Carol Kennedy, "Future Shock or Future Success?," *Director,* July 1995.
5. Ibid.
6. Barbara Ettore, "2020: What's the World Coming To?" *Management Review,* September 1996.
7. Peter Swartz, *The Art of the Long View* (New York: Doubleday Currency, 1991).

CHAPTER 3. MANAGING PEOPLE

1. There are many good introductions to the history of management. We have relied on the textbook, *Management,* 6th ed., by James F. Stoner, R. Edward Freeman, and Daniel R. Gilbert Jr. (Englewood Cliffs, NJ: Prentice Hall, 1995) especially chapter 2; Peter Drucker, *Concept of the Corporation* (New York: Times Mirror, 1946) especially chapters 1 and 2; *Harvard Business Review, Classic Advice on Aspects of Organizational Life* (New York: Harper, 1985); and James Bowditch and Anthony Buono, *A Primer on Organizational Behavior,* 4th ed. (New York: John Wiley and Sons, 1993).
2. Douglas MacGregor, *The Human Side of Enterprise* (New York: McGraw-Hill, 1960).
3. For a wonderful discussion of the history of Deming's ideas, see Lloyd Dobyns and Clare Crawford-Mason, *Quality or Else: The Revolution in World Business* (Boston: Houghton Mifflin, 1991). Of course, Deming precedes MacGregor historically, but it is only since MacGregor isolated theory X and theory Y that Deming's ideas and those of others regarding theory Y began to have an impact.
4. For a discussion of needs theory, see Richard Steers and Lyman Porter, *Motivation and Work Behavior* (New York: McGraw-Hill, 2d edition, 1979).
5. Ibid., p. 104.
6. Stanley Milgram, *Obedience to Authority* (New York: Harper, 1974).
7. Deborah Tannen, *You Just Don't Understand* (New York: Morrow, 1990); and Tannen, *Talking from 9 to 5* (New York: Morrow, 1994).
8. Tannen, 1990, infranote 6, p. 26.
9. Ibid.
10. Judith B. Rossener, "Ways Women Lead," *Harvard Business Review,* November–December 1990, pp. 119–125.
11. Chris Argyris, *Understanding Organizational Behavior* (Homewood, IL: Dorsey, 1960); see Peter Herriot, "Psychological Contract" in Nigel Nicholson (ed.)

Organizational Behavior, vol. 6, *The Blackwell Encyclopedia of Management* (Oxford: Basil Blackwell, 1997), pp. 455–456.

12. D. Rousseau and R. Anton, "Fairness and Implied Contract Obligations in Job Terminations: The Role of Contributions, Promises, and Performance," *Journal of Organizational Behavior,* vol. 12, 1991, pp. 287–299.

13. Charles Heckscher, *White Color Blues* (New York: Basic Books, 1995).

14. This idea is attributed to Tuckman by Stoner et al., infranote 1, p. 505.

15. Stoner et al., infranote 1, p. 501.

16. See F. E. Emery and E. L. Trist, *Towards a Social Ecology* (London: Plenum Press, 1973) for a statement of Trist's view on participatory management and autonomous work groups. The general ideas in this book are even today, 25 years later, just beginning to be understood by management theorists.

17. This paragraph is based on James L. Heskett and Leonard A. Schlesinger, "Leading the High-Capability Organization: Challenges for the Twenty-first Century," *Human Resource Management,* spring 1997, vol. 36, no. 1, pp. 105–113.

18. John Wisdom, *Philosophy and Psychoanalysis* (Berkeley: University of California Press, 1969).

CHAPTER 4. BUSINESS ETHICS

1. This case has been around the business ethics field for quite some time. Thanks to Michael Josephson, Thomas Donaldson, and Joan Dubinsky for pointing it out to us. We have no idea who originally designed it, but it has been validated as real by hundreds of executives.

2. For a more complete view of relativism and its problems, see R. Edward Freeman and Daniel R. Gilbert Jr., *Corporate Strategy and the Search for Ethics* (Englewood Cliffs, NJ: Prentice Hall, 1987).

3. For a more careful statement of "the separation thesis," see R. Edward Freeman "The Politics of Stakeholder Theory," *Business Ethics Quarterly,* vol. 4, no. 4, 1994.

4. For a clear statement of Smith's view, see Patricia H. Werhane, *Adam Smith's Legacy for Modern Capitalism* (New York: Oxford University Press, 1991).

5. These paragraphs are based on R. Edward Freeman, "A Note on Ethics and Business," The Darden School, Charlottesville, VA, UVA-E-0071. Also see William C. Frederick, "Corporate Social Responsibility and Business Ethics," in S. Prakash Sethi and Cecilia M. Falbe, *Business and Society* (Lexington, MA: Lexington Books, 1987), pp. 142–161.

6. The quote from George Merck is from "Merck & Co., Inc. (A)," The Business Enterprise Trust, Stanford, California, 1991.

7. We are glossing over the philosophical point that values are about "the good" and rights are about "the right." Any introductory textbook on ethics can provide more details for those interested.

8. We make no distinction between rules and principles here. Some see principles as

higher-order rules—indeed, as the justification for rules. For more, see Tom Beauchamp and James Childress, *Principles of Biomedical Ethics,* 3d ed. (New York: Oxford University Press, 1989).

9. Stephen Covey, *The Seven Habits of Highly Successful People: Restoring the Character Ethic* (New York: Simon and Schuster, 1989).

10. See Norman Bowie and Stephanie Lenway, "H.B. Fuller in Honduras" in T. Donaldson and P. Werhane (eds.) *Ethical Issues in Business,* 5th ed. (Englewood Cliffs, NJ: Prentice Hall, 1996) pp. 78–90.

11. This section is based on R. Edward Freeman, "Understanding Stakeholder Capitalism," *The Financial Times,* 19 July 1996, and R. Edward Freeman and Jeanne M. Liedtka, "Stakeholder Capitalism and the Value Chain," *European Journal of Management,* vol. 16, no. 3, in press, June 1997. The authors of the present volume are grateful to the editors of both publications for permission to reprint selected paragraphs. Defining *stakeholder capitalism* is an ongoing project. For some preliminary statements see R. Edward Freeman, "Managing for Stakeholders," in N. Bowie and T. Beauchamp, *Ethical Theory and Business,* 5th ed. (Englewood Cliffs: Prentice Hall, 1997) and R. Edward Freeman, "The Politics of Stakeholder Theory," *Business Ethics Quarterly,* vol. 4, no. 4, 1994, pp. 409–422.

12. For a more careful history see R. Edward Freeman, *Strategic Management: A Stakeholder Approach* (Boston: Pitman Inc., 1984), and Thomas Donaldson and Lee Preston, "The Stakeholder Theory of the Corporation: Concepts, Evidence, and Implications," *Academy of Management Review,* vol. 20, 1995, pp. 65–91, and more recently still, Ronald K. Mitchell, Bradley R. Agle, and Donna J. Wood, "Toward a Theory of Stakeholder Identification: Defining the Principle of Who and What Really Counts," University of Victoria, Faculty of Business, manuscript.

13. Thomas Donaldson, *The Ethics of International Business* (New York: Oxford University Press, 1989).

CHAPTER 6. MARKETING MANAGEMENT: LEVERAGING CUSTOMER VALUE

1. This discussion draws from P. Kotler, *Marketing Management,* 9th ed. (Upper Saddle River, NJ: Prentice Hall, 1996).

2. This position is consistent with discussions in Frederick F. Reichheld, *The Loyalty Effect,* (Cambridge, MA: Harvard Business Press, 1996).

3. See, Peter Drucker, *The Practice of Management* (New York: Harper & Row, 1954).

4. The notion of cult-like cultures is developed in James Collins and Jerry Porras, *Built to Last* (New York: Harper Business, 1994).

5. Eric Berggren and Thomas Nacher, "Introducing New Products Can Be Hazardous to Your Company," *The Academy of Management Executive,* Briarcliff Manor, August 2001, pp. 92–101.

6. See Gary Hamel and C. K. Prahalad, *Competing for the Future* (Boston: Harvard Business School Press, 1994).

7. See Fareena Sultan and Hussain Mooraj, "Designing a Trust-Based E-business Strategy," *Marketing Management,* November/December 2001.

8. This term is borrowed from Nicholas Imparato and Oren Harari, *Jumping the Curve* (San Francisco: Jossey Bass, 1994).

9. George Day, "Define Your Business," *Executive Excellence,* vol. 18, February 2001, pp. 12–17.

10. See A. Kohli and B. Jaworski, "Marketing Orientation: The Construct, Research Propositions, and Managerial Implications," *Journal of Marketing,* vol. 54, April 1990, pp. 1–18; John Narver and Stan Slater, "The Effects of Market Orientation on Business Profitability," *Journal of Marketing,* vol. 54, April 1990, pp. 20–35.

11. Adrian Slywotzky and David Morrison, *The Profit Zone* (New York: Times Business, 1997).

12. R. Buzzell and B. Gale, *The PIMS Principle* (New York: Free Press, 1987). (PIMS stands for Profit Impact of Market Strategy.)

13. For a complete presentation of antitrust issues in marketing, see L. W. Stern and T. Evaldi, *Legal Aspects of Marketing Strategy* (Upper Saddle River, NJ: Prentice Hall, 1984).

14. For a complete discussion of mass customization, see Joseph Pine, *Mass Customization* (Cambridge, MA: Harvard Business School Press, 1993).

15. Booz, Allen & Hamilton, "New Product Development for the 1980s," in-house report, 1982; Eric von Hipple, "New Ideas from Lead Users," *Research-Technology Management,* May/June 1989, pp. 82–96.

16. See M. Leenders and D. Blenkhorn, *Reverse Marketing* (New York: Free Press, 1988).

17. Parts of this discussion are based on Reichheld, op cit.

18. See F. Webster, *Market-Driven Management* (New York: Wiley, 1994).

19. See chapter 1, Keenan and Ante, February 18, 2002.

CHAPTER 7. OPERATIONS MANAGEMENT: IMPLEMENTING AND ENABLING STRATEGY

1. Clayton Christensen, "Raychem Corporation Interconnection Systems Division," Harvard Business School Case #9-694-063, 1994.

2. Robert H. Hayes, and Gary P. Pisano, "Beyond World-Class: The New Manufacturing Strategy," *Harvard Business Review,* January–February 1994, pp. 77–86.

3. Leschke and Weiss, "Plastique, Inc.," Darden Graduate Business School Case #UVA-OM-0794, 1995.

4. George Stalk, Philip Evans, and Lawrence E. Shulman, "Competing on Capabilities: The New Rules of Corporate Strategy," *Harvard Business Review,* March–April 1992.

5. Mark Halper, "Campbell Soups Up Inventory," *Computerworld Electronic Commerce Journal,* April 29, 1996 pp. 11–12; Linda Wilson, "Brand Aid," *Information Week,* CMP Publications, Inc., #447, pp. 44–45, October 18, 1993.

6. David N. Burt, "Managing Suppliers Up to Speed," *Harvard Business Review,* July–August 1989.
7. Edward Feitzinger and Hau L. Lee, "Mass Customization at Hewlett-Packard: The Power of Postponement," *Harvard Business Review,* January–February 1997.
8. Marshall Fisher, "National Bicycle Industrial Co.," The Wharton School Business Case, University of Pennsylvania, 1994.

CHAPTER 8. ENTREPRENEURSHIP: CREATING SOMETHING NEW AND ENDURING WITH VERY LIMITED RESOURCES

1. Entrepreneurship can occur within existing firms or individuals can create new firms to pursue their business ideas.
2. B. R. Barber, *Jihad vs. the McWorld* (New York: Ballantine Books, 1995). Presents compelling arguments of how business practices can influence political and social realities.
3. S. Venkataraman, "Stakeholder Value Equilibration and the Entrepreneurial Process," *Special Issue of the Society for Business Ethics,* Ruffin Series no. 3, pp. 45–57. Indeed, of all the forces that give rise to change, including wars, epidemics, and revolutions, the economist, Joseph Schumpeter isolated the unfailing power of innovation in goods and services to bring about changes in social and political landscape. And the agent of this innovation, he argued, is the entrepreneur. The "fundamental impulse that sets and keeps" in motion such systemic change "comes from the new consumer goods, the new methods of production or transportation, the new markets, and the new forms of industrial organization" (1976). "The history of business is littered with such entrepreneurially introduced innovations. Each succeeding innovation has altered the economic, political and social landscape" (Venkataraman 2002).
4. P. Drucker, *Innovation and Entrepreneurship* (New York: Harper and Row, 1985).
5. N. Wiener, *Invention: The Care and Feeding of Ideas* (Cambridge, MA: MIT Press, 1993), p. 7.
6. S. Venkataraman, and S. Sarasvathy, "Strategy and Entrepreneurship: Outlines of an Untold Story." In the *Handbook of Strategic Management,* Michael Hitt, R. Edward Freeman and Jeff Harrison (eds.) (New York: Blackwell Publishing, 2000), p. 652.
7. F. A. Hayek, "The Use of Knowledge in Society," *American Economic Review,* 35(4), pp. 519–530; Shane, S., "Prior Knowledge and the Discovery of Entrepreneurial Opportunities," *Organization Science* 11(4), pp. 448–469.
8. S. Sarasvathy, "What makes Entrepreneurs Entrepreneurial?" University of Washington working paper series, 2001.
9. K. J. Arrow, "Limited Knowledge and Economic Analysis," *American Economic Review,* 64(1), 1974, pp. 1–10.
10. G. A. Akerlof, "The Market for 'Lemons': Quality Uncertainty and the Market Mechanism," *Quarterly Journal of Economics,* 84, pp. 488–500. Economists refer to

this as the adverse selection problem (Akerlof 1970). Overcoming this problem imposes extra costs for revealing credible information, writing in all kinds of contingencies in contracts and, at an extreme, driving better quality entrepreneurs and resource suppliers from the market (as in the case of newly emerging market economies such as Russia) unless some other mechanism exists to reduce such costs.

11. O. E. Williamson, *Markets and Hierarchies: Analysis and Antitrust Implications* (New York: Basic Books, 1975).

12. —— *The Economic Institutions of Capitalism* (New York: MacMillan, 1985). Economists call this the holdup problem.

13. K. J. Arrow, *Essays in the Theory of Risk Bearing* (Chicago: Markham, 1971). Economists refer to this unobservability problem and the incentive to use others opportunistically as the moral hazard problem. Overcoming the moral hazard problem also introduces significant post-contract costs, unless some other mechanism exists to reduce such costs.

14. Amar Bhide, "Bootstrap Finance: The Art of Start-Ups," *Harvard Business Review,* November–December 1992. A nice summary of the bootstrapping process.

15. Donald Hambrick and Ian MacMillan, "Asset Parsimony: Managing Assets to Manage Profitability," *Sloan Management Review,* 25, 1984, pp. 67–74; Rita McGrath and Ian MacMillan, *The Entrepreneurial Mindset* (Boston: HBS Press, 1984); J. Starr and I. C. MacMillan, "Resource Cooptation via Social Contracting: Resource Acquisition Strategies for New Ventures," *Strategic Management Journal,* 11 (summer 2000), pp. 79–92.

16. Zenas Block and Ian MacMillan, *Corporate Venturing: Creating New Business within the Firm* (Boston: Harvard University Press, 1993). This is a significant elaboration of the principles first put forward by Block and MacMillan, 1993.

17. Rita McGrath and Ian MacMillan, *The Entrepreneurial Mindset* (Boston: HBS Press, 2000), p. 245.

18. Starr and MacMillan, 1990, survey an extensive literature in sociology to come up with their typology. They have captured the essence of the diverse nature of social capital with this typology.

19. H. Aldrich and E. Auster, "Even Dwarfs Started Small: Liabilities of Age and Size and Their Strategic Implications." In L. Cummings and B. Staw (eds.), *Research in Organizational Behavior,* vol. 8, pp. 165–198. JAI Press: Greenwich, CT: JAI Press, 1986). An outstanding review of these ideas.

20. Scott Shane and S. Venkataraman, "The Promise of Entrepreneurship as a Field of Research," *Academy of Management Review,* 25(1), pp. 217–226, 2000.

CHAPTER 9. ACCOUNTING

1. Quoted in E. Richard Brownlee, II, "Communicating Corporate Value in a Global Economy," presented at Conference on Finding Reality in Reported Earnings, Association for Investment Management and Research, December 4, 1996, p. 3.

2. CPA stands for Certified Public Accountant, a credential awarded after successful completion of a challenging examination and fulfilling other professional requirements.

3. Auditors are very careful not to promise absolute truth and precision in their work. Disney's auditors, PricewaterhouseCoopers, wrote in their report on the 2001 financial statements: "We conducted our audits of these statements in accordance with auditing standards *generally accepted* in the United States of America, which require that we plan and perform the audit to obtain *reasonable* assurance about whether the financial statements are free of *material* misstatement. . . . We believe that our audits provide a *reasonable* basis for our opinion." (Italics are the author's.)

4. Brownlee, ibid, pp. 9 and 10.

5. The Walt Disney Company Form 10-K and 2001 Annual Report, p. 79.

6. The "going concern" assumption holds that the firm will operate for the foreseeable future, and that its assets will not be liquidated hastily in a fire sale. For instance, hasty liquidation of inventory ordinarily realizes lower values than will the regular conduct of business.

7. Media Networks includes, among others, the ABC Television Network and ABC Radio Networks, primary cable programming services such as ESPN and the Disney Channel, and some Internet Web sites. Consumer Products covers activities associated with licensing and marketing Disney-themed merchandise.

8. In the balance sheets of many companies headquartered outside the United States, the order of priority differs greatly. Don't let the differences confuse you. Just remember that Assets = Liabilities plus Equity.

9. Exchangeable bonds may be exchanged at the firm's option into another type of security, like preferred stock. Subordinated bonds rank behind senior bonds in payment if the firm is liquidated. Exchangeable subordinated bonds were issued by Revco Drug Stores in 1986 in its leveraged buyout. Revco went bankrupt 19 months later. The issuance of these bonds was both creative and imprudent.

10. Days in receivables is also called *days' sales outstanding* and is calculated as the ratio of accounts receivable divided by annual sales multiplied times 365 days.

11. *Financial leverage* generally refers to the use of debt financing. A highly levered firm has a high proportion of debt in its capital structure. There are numerous ratios that measure leverage, but one of the most graphic is the ratio of assets to equity. High leverage would be associated with a high ratio.

CHAPTER 10. FINANCE

1. Warren Buffett is one of the most successful investors in history. Growth in book value per share of Berkshire Hathaway, Buffett's public holding company, has averaged 23.6 percent annually from 1965 to 2000, handily beating the 11.8 percent annual change in the value of the S&P 500 index (including dividends) over the same time period. (Source: *Berkshire Hathaway 2000 Annual Report.*)

Peter Lynch was the legendary manager of the Fidelity Magellan Fund. During his 13 years of fund management (from 1977 to 1990) the average annual return on the Magellan Fund significantly beat the average market returns. "Around Fidelity, Peter Lynch was God," remarked one observer.

2. Berkshire Hathaway Inc. *Annual Report,* 1994, p. 2.

3. Berkshire Hathaway Inc. *Annual Report,* 1992, p. 14.

4. Berkshire Hathaway Inc. *Annual Report,* 1994, p. 7.

5. Peter Lynch *One Upon Wall Street* (New York: Simon & Schuster, 1989) p. 242.

6. Quoted in *Forbes* Oct. 19, 1993 and republished in Andrew Kilpatrick, *Of Permanent Value: The Story of Warren Buffet* (Birmingham: AKPE, 1994).

7. Walter B. Wriston, *Risk and Other Four-Letter Words* (New York: Harper & Row, 1986), pp. 222–223. Walter Wriston was the CEO of Citicorp, one of the premier banks and financial services institutions in the United States, during its era of rapid expansion in the 1970s and early 1980s.

8. Berkshire Hathaway Inc. *Annual Report* 1994, p. 2.

9. Originally published in Berkshire Hathaway's *Annual Report,* 1987. This quotation was paraphrased from James Grant, *Minding Mr. Market* (New York: Times Books, 1993) p. xxi.

10. Quoted in *Forbes* October 19, 1993, and republished in Andrew Kilpatrick, *Of Permanent Value: The Story of Warren Buffett* (Birmingham: AKPE, 1994) p. 574.

11. "Owner-Related Business Principles" in Berkshire Hathaway *Annual Report* 1994, p. 3.

12. The injunction to "sell securities" applies most readily to corporations. But it is equally applicable to individuals. For instance, any homeowner who has borrowed to finance the purchase of a house has "sold" a mortgage.

13. Bonds are rated for their likelihood of default by independent rating agencies. The bond ratings can run from high quality (AAA) to low quality (B). See Exhibit 10.3 for a listing of rating definitions.

14. Traditionally, a coupon was a chit that the investor literally snipped off the bond certificate and sent in to the company to receive interest payment. In common business parlance, the *coupon* of a bond is the annual interest payment of the bond, usually expressed as a percentage rate of return. With the advent of an e-business economy, actual paper coupons have become a rarity.

CHAPTER 11. STRATEGY: DEFINING AND DEVELOPING COMPETITIVE ADVANTAGE

1. This chapter has benefited enormously from the eight years I spent working with and teaching with Michael E. Porter at the Harvard Business School. I also want to thank Michael Rukstad for helpful comments and Katarina Paddack for her assistance.

2. For more on profitability and competitive positioning, see Michael E. Porter, *Competitive Advantage* (New York: The Free Press, 1985). For more on core competencies, see C. K. Prahalad and G. Hamel, "The Core Competence of the Corporation," *Harvard Business Review,* May–June 1990. For more on capabilities, see George Stalk, Philip Evans, and Lawrence E. Shulman, "Competing on Capabilities: The New Rules of Corporate Strategy," *Harvard Business Review,* March–April 1992.

For more on strategic intent, see G. Hamel and C. K. Prahalad, "Strategic Intent," *Harvard Business Review,* May 1989. For more on future scenarios, see Elizabeth Teisberg, "Strategic Response to Uncertainty," Harvard Business School Note #9-391-192, 1991.

3. Michael E. Porter developed the five forces framework for analyzing industry attractiveness in his book, *Competitive Strategy* (New York: The Free Press, 1980).

4. See the related discussion of supply chain management in Chapter 7.

5. Pankaj Ghemawatt, *Commitment: The Dynamic of Strategy* (New York: The Free Press, 1991).

6. For detailed discussion of these challenges, see Michael E. Porter, "The Competitive Advantage of Nations," *Harvard Business Review,* March–April 1990.

CHAPTER 12. LEADING FROM THE MIDDLE: A NEW LEADERSHIP PARADIGM

1. The literature on business transformation grows daily. For a sample, see N. Imparato and O. Harain, *Jumping the Curve* (San Francisco: Jossey-Bass, 1995); F. Gouillant and J. Kelly, *Transforming the Organization* (New York: McGraw-Hill, 1995).

2. Compare Patricia H. Werhane, *Adam Smith and the Legacy of Modern Capitalism* (New York: Oxford University Press, 1992).

3. G. Hamel and C. K. Prahalad, *Competing for the Future* (Cambridge, MA: Harvard Business School Press, 1994).

4. As Mark Twain wrote in *A Connecticut Yankee in King Arthur's Court,* "The best swordsman in the world doesn't need to fear the second best swordsman in the world; no, the person for him to be afraid of is some ignorant antagonist who has never had a sword in his hand before, he doesn't do the thing he ought to do, and so the expert isn't prepared for him; he simply does the thing he ought not to do; and it often catches the expert out and ends him on the spot."

5. For more on the idea of how mental models work and the difficulty of changing them, see Peter Senge's *The Fifth Discipline.*

6. See S. Curkovic, S. Vickery, and C. Droge, "Quality Related Action Programs," *Decision Sciences,* vol. 31, pp. 885–905, 2000.

7. See J. Pine, *Mass Customization* (Cambridge, MA: Harvard Business School Press, 1993).

8. Kathryn Harrigan, *Managing for Joint Ventures Success* (Boston: Lexington Books, 1986); Joel Bleake and David Ernst, *Collaborating to Compete* (New York: John Wiley & Sons, 1993).

9. R. Spekman, L. Isabella, T. MacAvoy, and T. Forbes, "Creating Strategic Alliances That Endure," *Long Range Planning,* vol. 29, 1996, pp. 346–357.

10. See Ray Suutari, "Organizing for the New Economy," *CMA Management,* vol. 75, pp. 12–13, April 2001.

11. *James Burke: A Career in American Business,* Harvard Business School videotape.

12. A. Larson, "Dyads in Entrepreneurial Settings: A Study of the Governance of Exchange Relationships," *Administrative Sciences Quarterly,* March 1992.

13. See J. Stoner, R. E. Freeman, and D. Gilbert Jr., *Management,* 6th ed. (Englewood Cliffs, NJ: Prentice Hall, Inc., 1995).

14. Rosabeth Moss Kanter, "A Culture of Innovation, Executive Excellence," vol. 8, 2000, pp. 10–11.

15. Quoted in Hal Lancaster, "Managers Beware: You're Not Ready for Tomorrow's Jobs," *The Wall Street Journal,* January 24, 1995, p. B1.

16. See Donald Schön, *The Reflective Practitioner: How Professionals Think in Action* (New York: Basic Books, 1983).

17. Chris Argyris, "Good Communication That Blocks Learning," *Harvard Business Review,* July–August 1994, p. 77.

18. James Utterback, *Managing the R&D Innovation Process* (Cambridge, MA: Harvard Business Press, 1994).

19. Chris Argyris, "Good Communication That Blocks Learning," *Harvard Business Review,* July–August, 1994, p. 85.

20. Gary Hamel and C. K. Pralahad, "Competing for the Future," *Harvard Business Review,* July–August, 1994, p. 128.

21. This study was reported in Dal Buss, "When Managing Isn't Enough," *Workforce,* vol. 80, December 2001, pp. 44–48.

22. Sumantra Ghoshal and Christopher A. Bartlett, "Changing the Role of Top Management: Beyond Structure to Processes," *Harvard Business Review,* January–February 1995, p. 89.

23. The authors acknowledge the contribution made by their colleague, Professor Andrea Larson.

CHAPTER 13. STRATEGIC ALLIANCES

1. J. D. Lewis, *Partnerships for Profit: Structuring and Managing Strategic Alliances* (New York: The Free Press, 1990). Yves Doz, "The Role of Partnerships and Alliances in the European Industrial Restructuring," in K. Cool, D. Neven, and I. Walter, eds., *European Industrial Restructuring in the 1990s* (London: MacMillan, 1992), pp. 294–327.

2. Joel Bleeke and David Ernst, *Collaborate to Compete* (New York: John Wiley & Sons, 1995).

3. Ibid.

4. Jakki Mohr and Robert E. Spekman, "Characteristics of Partner Success," *Strategic Management,* vol. 5, 1994, pp. 135–152.

5. Robert E. Spekman, Lynn Isabella, Thomas MacAvoy, Theodore Forbes III, *Alliance and Partnership Strategies,* monograph published by the International Consortium for Executive Development Research, 1997.

6. Robert Spekman, Lynn Isabella, and Thomas C. MacAvoy, *Alliance Competence: Maximizing the Value of Your Partnerships* (New York: John Wiley & Sons, 2000).

7. Much of this discussion is taken from R. Spekman, I. Isabella, T. MacAvoy and T. Forbes, "Creating Strategic Alliances That Endure," *Long Range Planning*, vol. 29, no. 3, 1996, pp. 340–357.

8. See, for example, P. Kotler, *Marketing Management: Analysis, Planning, Implementation, Control,* 7th ed. (Englewood Cliffs, NJ: Prentice Hall, 1991).

9. M. Yoshino and U.S. Rangan, *Strategic Alliances* (Cambridge, MA: Harvard Business School Press, 1995).

10. A. Larson, "Network Dyads in Entrepreneurial Settings: A Study of the Governance of Exchange Relationships," *Administrative Science Quarterly*, vol. 37, no. 1, March 1992, pp. 76–104.

11. This section is derived from a series of case studies (BA-USAir (A) & (B), UVA-OB-0584 & 0585; Shell Italia (A) & (B), UVA-OB-0586 & 0587, Christie-Reid, Inc., UVA-OB-0597, Renault-Volvo Strategic Alliance (A), (B), (C), & (D), UVA-G-0480, 0481, 0482, 0483) based on very extensive field research of existing alliances in different stages of their development.

12. J. P. Kotter, *Leading Change, Cambridge* (Cambridge, MA: Harvard Business Press, 1996).

13. D. T. Wilson, "An Integrated Model of Buyer-Seller Relationships," *Journal of the Academy of Marketing Sciences*, vol. 23, no. 4, 1995, pp. 335–345.

14. Robert E. Spekman, Deborah J. Salmond, and C. Jay Lambe, "Consensus and Collaboration: Norm-Regulated Behavior in Industrial Marketing Relationships," *European Journal of Marketing,* vol. 31, no. 11-12, 1997, pp. 832–856.

15. Although Visa and MasterCard share many of the same bank members (e.g., Citibank, Chase), the example is still quite valid.

16. Adam M. Brandenburger and Barry J. Nalebuff, *Co-opetition* (New York, New York: Doubleday, 1996).

17. Jakki Mohr and Robert Spekman, "Characteristics of Partnership Success: Partnership Attributes, Communication Behavior and Conflict Resolution Techniques," *Strategic Management Journal,* vol. 15, 1994, pp. 135–152.

18. Robert S. Kaplan and David P. Norton, *The Balanced Scorecard* (Boston: Harvard University Press, 1996).

CHAPTER 14. INTERNATIONAL BUSINESS

1. Robert L. Rod, "Currency Squeeze: Caterpillar Sees Gains in Efficiency Impeded by Strength of Dollar," *The Wall Street Journal*, April 6, 1990.

CHAPTER 15. SOME FINAL THOUGHTS

1. James Collins and Jerry Porras, *Built to Last* (New York: Harper Business, 1994).

INDEX

ABOUT THE AUTHORS

Robert F. Bruner is Distinguished Professor of Business Administration and Executive Director of the Batten Institute at the Darden Graduate School of Business Administration, University of Virginia, where he has served on the faculty since 1982. His research in finance has been published in numerous journals. Currently his research addresses issues in mergers and acquisitions, corporate finance, and valuation of assets in emerging markets. He is founding coeditor of two journals. Since 2000, he has directed the Batten Institute, which sponsors applied research and knowledge transfer programs in the areas of innovation and business change. He has received numerous awards for teaching and for his teaching materials, including the highest teaching awards from the University of Virginia and the State of Virginia. *Business Week* magazine cited him as one of the "masters of the MBA classroom." He is the author of over 400 items of teaching material and of a casebook in finance. Industrial corporations, financial institutions, and government agencies have retained him for counsel and training. He holds a B.A. from Yale University and an M.B.A. and a D.B.A. from Harvard University. His web site is http://faculty.darden.edu/brunerb/.

Mark R. Eaker is a Professor of Business Administration at the Darden Graduate School of Business at the University of Virginia. Mr. Eaker has a B.S. from Washington and Lee University and A.M., M.B.A., and Ph.D. degrees from Stanford University. Prior to joining the faculty at Darden, he taught at Duke, SMU, and the University of North Carolina. He has been an adjunct Professor at Institute Theseus in France.

Mr. Eaker has coauthored four books in the areas of macroeconomics, international finance, and international business. He has numerous publications with an emphasis on international finance, foreign exchange, and risk management. He has consulted extensively and taught corporate seminars throughout the world.

Mr. Eaker is also a founding partner of Sire Management Corporation, an investment management firm in New York City.

R. Edward Freeman is the Elis and Signe Olsson Professor of Business Administration, and heads Darden's Olsson Center for Applied Ethics, one of the world's leading academic centers for the study of ethics. Freeman has written or edited 10 books on business ethics, environmental management, and strategic management. His latest book, *Environmentalism and the New Logic of Business, How Firms Can be Profitable and Leave Our Children a Living Planet,* helps executives meet the challenge of being profitable while being environmentally responsible. He has also authored more than 40 Darden case studies. Freeman serves on the advisory board of University of Virginia Institute for Practical Ethics.

Before joining The Darden School in 1986, Freeman taught at the University of Minnesota and The Wharton School. He has received teaching awards at all three schools.

Robert E. Spekman is the Tayloe Murphy Professor of Business Administration at The Darden School. He was formerly Professor of Marketing and Associate Director of the Center for Telecommunications at the University of Southern California. He is an internationally recognized authority on business-to-business marketing and strategic alliances. His consulting experiences range from marketing research and competitive analysis, to strategic market planning, supply chain management, strategic procurement planning, and strategic partnering. Professor Spekman has taught in a number of executive programs in the U.S., Canada, Asia, and Europe. He has edited seven books and has authored (or coauthored) over 80 articles and papers. Professor Spekman also serves as a reviewer for several marketing and management journals as well as for the National Science Foundation. Prior to joining the faculty at USC, Professor Spekman taught in the College of Business at the University of Maryland, College Park. During his tenure at Maryland, he was granted the Most Distinguished Faculty Award by the MBA students on three separate occasions.

Elizabeth Olmsted Teisberg, Associate Professor of Business Administration, The Darden School, University of Virginia, is an economist with expertise in management of innovation, real option valuation, and strategy in the face of uncertainty. Much of her research and consulting focuses on the value of innovation and analysis of strategic opportunities in high-technology and health care industries. She is the author of numerous articles in professional publications such as the *Harvard Business Review, Rand Journal of Economics, Management Science,* the *Energy Journal, Research-Technology Management,* and *Science.* Prior to joining Darden, she was an Associate Professor at the Harvard Business School. She holds an A.B., summa cum laude, from Washington University in St. Louis; M.Eng. from University of Virginia; and an M.S. and Ph.D. from Stanford University.

Sankaran Venkataraman ("Venkat") is Samuel L. Slover Research Professor of Business Administration at Darden. He is also Director of Research of the Batten Institute. Before coming to Darden, he taught at the Wharton School and at Rensselaer Polytechnic Institute. His teaching interests include entrepreneurship and competitive strategy, and he has published widely on these topics in leading journals. Venkat has taught in numerous executive education programs around the world. He has earned the Outstanding Faculty Award at Darden and the Most Popular Professor at *Business Week Online* based on a poll of the Darden class of 2000. As a corporate planning executive in a major Indian firm, he was a part of a founding team that created and developed a highly successful new business venture. He has served as consultant to Fortune 500 firms as well as entrepreneurial firms. He is on the advisory boards of several start-up companies and academic centers. Venkat holds degrees in economics, business, and management from the Birla Institute of Technology and Science, the Indian Institute of Management (Calcutta), and the University of Minnesota, respectively.